Collaborative Research in Economics

Michael Szenberg • Lall B. Ramrattan
Editors

Collaborative Research in Economics

The Wisdom of Working Together

palgrave
macmillan

Editors
Michael Szenberg
Touro College
Brooklyn, NY, USA

Lall B. Ramrattan
University of California Berkeley
Extension, Berkeley, California, USA

ISBN 978-3-319-52799-4 ISBN 978-3-319-52800-7 (eBook)
DOI 10.1007/978-3-319-52800-7

Library of Congress Control Number: 2017934521

Printed on acid-free paper

This Palgrave Macmillan imprint is published by Springer Nature
The registered company is Springer International Publishing AG
The registered company address is: Gewerbestrasse 11, 6330 Cham, Switzerland

B"H

To the memory of my sister, Esther, for bringing me to these shores;
to the memory of my parents, Henoch for his wisdom and my mother, Sara, for giving birth to me—twice;
to my children, Avi and Tova,
and Marc and Naomi;
to my grandchildren,
Chaim and Elki Herzog, Moshe and Batya Shain, Nachum and Devorah Wolmark, Chanoch, Ephraim, Ayala, and Yaakov Nosson,
and to my great-grandchildren,
Chanoch, Faigala, Moshe, Avigail, and Chaim Boruch
And to my wife, Miriam;
And to the righteous German-Austrian officer who took my immediate family to a hiding place just days before the last transport to Auschwitz, where most of my family perished.

—M.S.

To my late mother and father-in-law, Sundermonie and Munisamy Munian from Bath Settlement, West Coast Berbice, Guyana. I thank them for their love, enthusiastic encouragement and generous support in words and deeds in my search for knowledge. I wish their souls eternal peace and happiness.

To my wife Noreena, my children Devi, Shanti and Raj, Hari, Rani and Jonathan, and my grandchildren Brian, Sabrina, and Aditi.

—L.R.

Foreword

The great figures in economics from Adam Smith to Leon Walras to John Maynard Keynes were lone thinkers, contributors and writers. All of us who were in graduate school in the middle of the last century emerged thoroughly imbued with that role model of scholarship whatever our particular research and education interests.

The authors of this incisive volume have assembled a candid assessment and testimonials by leading modern economists of where and how that role model has been modified in the intellectual development of twentieth-century professional economics. The main theme is that co-authorship is pleasurable, and for some of us, it was essential to the work we did.

In spite of the rhetoric and sincerity of intentions expressed in the image of science as a commitment to hypothesis testing, and the advancement of knowledge based on evidence, the reality is that science is the product of a conversation in the science community. Go to a conference paper presentation at a professional association attended by specialists in the topic presented. The questions afterward probe what could be wrong with the experiment; how the data might mis-measure what is needed; where the interpretation of the model or the data might invalidate the whole procedure and so on. In a mature science, all the action is in that conversation. And that conversation begins early in collaborations, teams and dreams.

Every science has a host of bases to be covered—methodological, cross-disciplinary, techniques of execution and person-machine systems, hence, the many-authored reports, articles and books. Collaboration enables conversation before the theory is ready, the hypotheses derived, the experiment designed and the data generated, and sometimes resets the path where things have gone awry.

None of these developments, however, has eliminated single-author entries.

Reflective compositions by single authors are not obsolete and in fact command even more interest and attention. Significantly, although this book is appropriately co-authored, almost none of its contributed papers are. Most of the case for collaboration is articulated in gratitude by a key beneficiary of her collaborations, one who can reflect from the inside on the insights and inspiration that grew out of the collaboration.

I enjoyed and learned from this collection and so, I believe, will you.

Vernon L. Smith
Argyros School of Business and Economics and School of Law
Chapman University
Orange, CA, USA

Preface and Acknowledgments

Observers of the scientific enterprise note that joint authorship is increasing. This is what I had to say about the collaboration at a seminar held at the Centre Detudes Interdisciplinaires Walras-Pareto, the University of Lausanne:

Einstein used to say, "I am a horse for a single harness." I touch upon two examples. The first involves the intellectual partnership of Samuelson and Solow that is considered among the most fruitful of such relationships in the history of economics. As the story goes, Solow was appointed Assistant Professor of Statistics in 1950. His room was located between that of Harold Freeman, Professor of Statistics and that of Paul Samuelson, Professor of Economics. Under Samuelson's influence, his interest, however, began to shift to economics. In 1954 he was promoted to Associate Professor of Statistics, in 1958 to Professor of Economics and in 1973, Institute Professor.

Perusal of their bibliographies and the volumes of collected papers reveal only four articles and one book with a third co-author. This is intriguing. Clearly, even though each provided a testing ground for the ideas of the other, from the creative standpoint, there is a need for further research regarding the collaborators' division of labor on and, more importantly, off the publication stage. Moreover, the scholars' conversations that encompass the thought sequences of their co-authored research projects are almost never recorded and thus our understanding of the creative process by which new knowledge is gained is impaired. The economics discipline is no different from other professions in focusing solely on the results, not the processes. It was James Watson who first indicated how most of the steps toward DNA's structure discovery were communicated informally among the team of research members. E.R. Weintraub went one step further. He published his conversations with co-author, D.A. Graham, which were held prior to reaching their conclusions that first appeared in the Review of Economic Studies. The second example of comradeship centers around Arrow who co-authored books and articles with 50 different individuals.

In *Candide*, Voltaire expressed the wise words, "*Il faut cultivar notre jardin*—We must cultivate our garden." Our interest in learning and analyzing the various paths the contributors have taken is to discover the wellspring of creative impulses in order to cultivate our own garden. When the Danish architect Arne Jacobson designed St. Catherine's College in Oxford in the 1960s, he also designed the school's chairs, the dishes and cups used in its cafeterias and even the gardens. When questioned about this, he responded "God is in the details." The contributors to this volume provide a wide variety of details about collaborative research and the wisdom of working together. To paraphrase Dylan Thomas, the pieces sing their own song and, we hope, will evoke applause.

In the several years that have elapsed between the conception of this book and its publication, we have amassed an enormous volume of debt. My first vote of thanks must go to Vernon L. Smith, who, despite being ferociously engaged in writing and speaking projects, agreed to pen the foreword.

We are deeply indebted to Sarah Lawrence and Allison Neuburger, our editors from Palgrave Macmillan, for shepherding the volume through the anonymous referees.

We would like to acknowledge the cooperativeness of the contributors to this volume. We thank them deeply for their congenial partnership. Deep gratitude and thanks are owed to the members of the Executive Board of Omicron Delta Epsilon, the Honor Society in Economics, for being a source of support: Alan Grant, Stacey Jones, Ihsuan Li, Ali H.M. Zadeh, Subarna Samanta and Farhang Niroomand. A special thanks to the Editor-in-Chief of *The American Economist*, Paul Grimes for his constant support. We are profoundly grateful to Mary Ellen Benedict, Chair and Distinguished Teaching Professor Emeritus at Bowling Green State University, for her impeccable wisdom, big heart and wit. Thank you to Evan Dennis for his warmth, attention to detail and friendship and to Professor Edna Davis for her continuous support.

Our heartfelt gratitude goes out to our Editorial Assistant Stephanie Miodus for her exceptional overall skills, cheerful disposition, meticulous attention to detail, hard work ethic, deep insight and most importantly her warmth and friendship. We could not have done it without her assistance. She assisted the publication of the book to see the light of day. She stepped in and finished the job—"Make Bepatish Av Lakol Gomrei Mlacha."

I owe an awesome debt of gratitude to Iuliana Ismailescu and Oscar Camargo for their goodness of heart, enduring support, positive attitude, gracious good cheer and deep friendship. In the same category, I would like to include Anna Geller, who is an outstanding marketing professor. They are a constant source of affection. I also want to recognize Elki and Chaim Herzog; Batya and Moshe Shain; Chanoch and Ephraim Kunin; Devorah and Nachum Wolmark; and Ayala Szenberg. They work with diligence, character, good humor, exactitude and patience. They have all lightened many a task. Their assistance was incalculable and I am grateful to them.

My heart still warms with gratitude toward Ester Budek, Lisa Ferraro, Laura Garcia, Yelena Glantz, Janet Lieben-Ulman, Jennifer Loftus, Sadia Nabi, Andrea Pascarelli, Sandra Shpilberg, Marina Slavina, Janet Ulman, Aleena Wee and Lisa Youel—my past talented and devoted graduate research assistants who have helped directly and indirectly in more ways than I can list. They all lead successful, productive lives. Their input lives on in these pages.

In addition, a number of former students deserve thanks for their invaluable input and assistance—Tamar Gomez, Lorene Hiris, Richard LaRocca, Esther Levy, Luba Sagui, Cathyann Tully and Alan Zimmerman.

Once more, thanks to my wife, Miriam, and to Naomi, my daughter, an ophthalmologist, and to my son, Avi, a lawyer, and their spouses, Marc and Tova, as well. They are my fortitude; I can always count on them when I need someone to lean on.

Touro's library is a superbly run unit by the Director of Libraries, Mrs. Bashe Simon, where efficiency and kindness dwell together. Special thanks to Touro's Vice Presidents Stanley Boylan and Robert Goldschmidt and Deans Henry M. Abramson, Barry Bressler, Sandra Brock, Moshe Sokol and Marian Stoltz-Loike—for their ongoing support and commitment to scholarly endeavors and helping me navigate Touro's waters. And to Dr. Mark Hasten, the chairman of Touro College's Board of Trustees and Board of Overseers, for his friendship and support.

My deepest gratitude goes to Dr. Alan Kadish, President of Touro College and University System, for his extraordinary leadership, dedication to excellence, kindness, cheerfulness and inspiration. He holds the wheel and steers Touro's ship in the right direction.

Thanks also to my most important champion, hero and mentor, Dr. Victor R. Fuchs, Past President of the American Economic Association and Henry J. Kaiser, Jr. Professor Emeritus at Stanford University. I know that my life would have been less without him.

Contents

List of Contributors

Walter Adams Emeritus, Michigan State University.

William A. Barnett Oswald Distinguished Professor of Macroeconomics, Department of Economics, The University of Kansas and Director of Center for Financial Stability, New York City.

William J. Baumol Harold Price Professor of Entrepreneurship and Academic Director of the Berkley Center for Entrepreneurship and Innovation in the Stern School of Business at New York University; Professor Emeritus, Princeton University.

Mary Ellen Benedict Professor Emeritus of Economics, Bowling Green State University.

James W. Brock Moeckel Professor, Department of Economics, Miami University.

***Graciela* Chichilnisky** Professor of Economics, Columbia University.

David Colander Christian A. Johnson Distinguished Professor of Economics at Middlebury College.

Ronald G. Ehrenberg Irving M. Ives Professor of Industrial and Labor Relations and Economics at Cornell University and a Stephen H. Weiss Presidential Fellow.

Stanley Engerman Department of Economics, University of Rochester.

Daniel S. Hamermesh Professor in Economics, Royal Holloway University of London and Sue Killam Professor Emeritus in the Foundation of Economics at the University of Texas at Austin.

Geoffrey Harcourt UNSW Australia and Emeritus, Cambridge University.

Charles F. Manski Professor of Economics, Northwestern University.

Rachel McCulloch Emerita, Rosen Family Professor of International Finance, Brandeis University.

Susan Rose-Ackerman Henry R. Luce Professor of Jurisprudence and is co-director of the Center for Law, Economics, and Public Policy at Yale Law School.

Paul Samuelson Emeritus, MIT.

Vernon L. Smith Professor of Economics at Chapman University's Argyros School of Business and Economics and School of Law.

L.G. Telser Professor Emeritus in Economics at the University of Chicago.

W. Kip Viscusi University Distinguished Professor, Vanderbilt University Law School.

Richard Zeckhauser Frank P. Ramsey Professor of Political Economy at the Kennedy School of Government at Harvard University.

List of Figures

List of Tables

CHAPTER 1

Introduction

Lall B. Ramrattan and Michael Szenberg

The study of economics embraces a number of terms that are used in the sense of collaboration. When two or more people work together on a publication, we refer to them as joint authors, coauthors, cooperators, or collaborators. The word "collaboration" can also be used in a broader sense. Auguste Comte, the father of positivism, used three guiding principles for collaboration ("Love, Order, Progress") as a way to "generalize our scientific conceptions, and to systematize the art of social life" (Comte, 1848, 3–5). For Thomas Kuhn, people collaborate within a paradigm where they need not contact each other, but solve problems as if they are in an invisible college (Kuhn, 1962). For Imre Lakatos, people collaborate on research programs in the sense that they share hard-core beliefs and create a protective belt around those beliefs in order to make their program progressive (Lakatos & Musgrave, 1970).

Philosophers have examined relationships between a collaborator on the one hand, and the idea, form or universal concept of collaboration on the other hand. Plato posited that a collaborator merely expresses opinions

L.B. Ramrattan (✉)
University of California, Berkeley Extension, Berkeley, California, USA

M. Szenberg
Touro College, Brooklyn, NY, USA

M. Szenberg, L.B. Ramrattan (eds.), *Collaborative Research in Economics*, DOI 10.1007/978-3-319-52800-7_1

about a true thing called collaboration. We find this view in Plato's dialog "The Parmenides." The philosopher Parmenides expresses skepticism over whether a particular thing, such as a chair, exists because it is under a point or under the whole of the universal concept of a collective name say "chair-ness." The collaborator is ego-centric, while collaboration is an objective, real truth in which the collaborator participates.

Collaboration with coauthors was not popular among the big-name orthodox economists such as Francois Quesnay, Adam Smith, David Ricardo, Thomas Malthus, and John M. Keynes. Joseph Schumpeter wrote that among the Physiocrats, "Mirabeau … may have been … in collaboration or consultation with Quesnay" (Schumpeter, 1954, p. 217). The orthodox writer Adam Smith, the equilibrating paradigm of the Physiocratic school, and the self-interest ideas of the Scottish Enlightenment philosopher David Hume formed the bed-rock research program for the classical economists. The unorthodox writer Karl Marx shared the class paradigm of the Physiocratic school and the dialectic idea of the philosopher G. Hegel, which manifested themselves in a strong collaboration between Karl Marx and Friedrich Engels, and a fundamental research program for Vladimir Lenin and others Marxists. John M. Keynes shared the aggregate demand paradigm with Thomas Malthus to rescue the capitalist system in crisis. While collaboration tends to proceed nomologically or step by step under orthodox paradigm or research programs in economics, it tends to proceed chaotically with spurts and jumps under Marxian dialectic method and under modern wage-setting or price-setting views.

The concept of combination for gain is associated with the idea that under capitalism, the combination of firms in vertical, horizontal, and conglomerate mergers leads to increased concentration in industries for higher profits. As Adam Smith put it, "People of the same trade seldom meet together, even for merriment and diversion, but the conservation ends in a conspiracy against the public, or in some contrivance to raise price" (Smith, 1976, V.1, p. 145). Smith made similar statements to the effect that masters tend to make constant and uniform combinations to keep wages at or below their actual level (ibid., p. 84). In general, economists are divided as to whether the purpose of such combinations is productivity or profits in light of modern performances in the global economy where profits are high but productivity is falling. The imperialist position is that such combination "levels out the fluctuations of trade and therefore assures to the combined enterprises a more stable rate of profit

... it has the effect of rendering possible technical improvements, and, consequently, the acquisition of superprofits" (Hilferding, 1912; cited in Lenin, 1917, p.15). This idea is still modern in that it underscores the point that there is gain from collaboration. Of course, profits can dissipate for a lack of coordination. As the economist E.A.G. Robinson puts it, "A platoon may drill very well as a platoon, but it may not always cover itself with equal glory in a battalion drill" (Robinson, 1953, p. 45). The loss may be due to the "cost of the necessary co-ordination, or, as more often happens, the loss of efficiency" (ibid.).

Both capitalism and socialism are concerned with individual cooperation. On the one hand, the Communist motto expects full cooperation according to each person's ability in production. On the other hand, Professor Hayek described capitalism as "the extended order of human cooperation" (Hayek, 1988, p. 6). He thought that a "somewhat more satisfactory name for the extended economic order of collaboration is the term 'market economy'" (ibid., p. 111). Such an order requires the rule of law to guarantee freedom (ibid., p. 35). But Hayek allowed that "overlapping sub-orders within which old instinctual responses, such as solidarity and altruism" also have a role to play (ibid., p. 18). Paul Samuelson considered a mixed capitalist system where cooperation occurs between the private sector and government. This system rests on the cooperation of neoclassical and Keynesian economics, emphasizing "how the entire gross national product is determined and how wages and prices and the rate of unemployment are determined with it" (Samuelson, 1986, Collected Papers, V. 5, p. 280).

In the physical sciences, individual collaboration is sometimes made analogous to collaboration. In chemistry, for instance, atoms pair their electrons, and the term co-valence applies. Wilfred Bion, a renowned psychotherapist, has adapted the term valency from Sigmund Freud to explain group dynamics. He uses it to mean "the capacity of the individual for instantaneous combination with other individuals in an established pattern of behavior" (Bion, 1961, p. 175). On matters of collaboration, the collaborators tend to be rational, honest, and open. But on matters of conflict, they may exhibit fear and anxiety and may resort to basic assumptive cultures, which are categorized as fight-flight, dependency, and pairing.

In Bion's psychoanalytic paradigm, "the individual is, and always has been, a member of a group" (Bion, 1961, p. 168). Collaboration allows some observations of individual characteristics that cannot be known otherwise (ibid., p. 340). Economic knowledge can be enhanced by studying these observations. The following are some observations we have made, with thoughts on how they can enhance economic knowledge through collaboration:

1. *Factors that prevent a group from working productively.* This is based on the idea that some groups "work" and some do not. The work-group is concerned with reality. In work-group function, people are constrained by time and must translate thought to action. Time is not a binding constraint for basic assumptive activities, in that people may make a "to-do list" and not act on it. But the two are not clearly demarcated to say that the work-group is good, and basic assumption group is bad—but only that there might be tension between these two mentalities at play in collaboration (French and Simpson, 2010, p. 1862–1866). These observations are important inputs for the study of hidden information problems—adverse selection and moral hazard problems that are now the frontier of economics research.
2. *Members tend to free-ride.* A collaborator might believe, "I do not need to talk, because I know that I only have to come here long enough and all my questions will be answered without having to do anything" (Bion, 1961, p. 147). An example from economist and philosopher David Hume is instructive in this regard: Two neighbors may agree to drain a meadow, which they possess in common; because 'tis easy for them to know each other's mind; and each must perceive, that the immediate consequence of his failing on his part, is the abandoning the whole project. But 'tis very difficult, and indeed impossible, that a thousand persons shou'd agree in any such action; it being difficult for them to concert so complicated a design, and still more difficult for them to execute it; while each seeks a pretext to free himself of the trouble and expense, and wou'd lay the whole burden on others (Hume, 1896, p. 275).
3. *Dependence on the group leader for all the answers.* Some collaborators may want to fulfill emotional needs and avoid feared relationships. Imitation problems in economics that follow the old motto of "What is good for GM is good for the country" still have a stronghold in economic modeling.
4. *Unions can handle unsettled questions.* Unifying minds may bring a certain power, which is called group rationality in game theory. It has its own decisive logic apart from individual rationality.

1.1 Theories of Collaboration

One can imagine a space for collaboration, S, defined by the characteristics of the collaborator, C_{n-1}, and an index of their performance, C_n. Such a product in Cartesian space may be represented by the expression:

$$S = C_1 \times C_2 \times \cdots C_n = \prod_{i=1}^{i=n} C_i \tag{1}$$

We find such models as Eq. (1) in the Case-Based literature (Gilboa and Schmeidler, 2001, p. 153). This can be extended into a Collaboration-Based model (Sampaio et al., 2014). Operationally we expect the collaborators to set an objective or aspiration, such as getting a joint product done; to act on it by each providing some or different tasks over time; and to realize a payoff such as finishing a project or publishing a work. The reward can be in the form of utility or money.

Theories of collaboration implicit in Eq. (1) can manifest themselves in a variety of forms. The economic literature witnesses them in the form of collusion, partnership, teamwork, and joint production. It should not be forgotten that economists collaborate in project accomplishment where a joint paper is not the goal. For example, dear to economists is the allocation of resources to different tasks, where methods of networking, dynamic programming, or other Operational Research are used to achieve the optimal allocation.

Through reason, we recognize that division of labor is more productive than working alone. In society, cooperation arises because of "feelings of sympathy and friendship and a sense of belonging together" (ibid.). Collaboration may come easily to friends and relatives, who are themselves, as Ludwig Von Mises puts it, "fruits of social cooperation" (Mises, 1996, p. 144). He explains that "the human family is an outcome of thinking, planning, and acting" (ibid., p. 168). The TV program 60 Minutes produced a show (aired on June 5, 2015) documenting how families can now use DNA technology to plan the health of their offspring and eliminate a battery of hereditary diseases. The unorthodox view is that "a society cannot exist unless its members have common feelings about what is the proper way of conducting its affairs, and these common feelings are expressed in ideology" (Robinson, 1964, p. 4). When individuals have conflicting interests, they are likely to seek methods on how to cooperate.

Some natural areas of conflict of interest that are possible in this collection of collaborators might be: who shall be the first author; how gains should be divided; should each collaborator complete part of the work, or should they approach all parts of the work uniformly in collaboration.

History provides some outstanding examples of collaboration among friends and families. We have already noted the strong bond of friendship between Karl Marx and Friedrich Engels, resulting in joint outputs such as the *Communist Manifesto*, and the collaboration on some volume of *Das Capital*. This is a collaboration in which the distribution of gains is posited in theories of value and distribution which depend on the social relationship and uncertainties. For an example of family collaboration, we note that Samuelson sourced collaborative statistical work on the law of large number to the St. Petersburg paradox founded by the Bournoulli family from James to Daniel Bournoulli (Samuelson, 1986, V5., p. 146).

John Maynard Keynes, who did not coauthor, nevertheless had a circle of trusted economic colleagues which included Richard Kahn, Joan Robinson, and Piero Sraffa. We may ascribe the term "project collaboration" to his case. We find that Kahn's writing on the multiplier had a significant role in Keynes' *General Theory* (Keynes, 1936, V.VII, Ch. 10). Keynes encouraged Robinson to write *Introduction to the Theory of Employment* (Robinson, 1969), referred to as a "told-to-the-children" version of the *General Theory* (Keynes, 1973, V. XIV, p. 148). In 1930 Pierro Sraffa formed the "Circus" in order to discuss Keynes' *A Treatise on Money* (Keynes 1971, V. V–VI). Members included Joan Robinson and Richard Kahn. While Keynes did not attend the Circus, Kahn acted as a messenger between him and the Circus (Keynes 1973, V. XIII, pp. 338–339).

Two's company and three is a crowd: collaboration becomes more complex when three or more authors are involved. One can analyze these complexities by looking for causal connection. David Hume, a proponent of causal analysis, divides human perception into impressions and ideas. He explains that these can be surmised as simple or complex, and proposes to study them through the lenses of cause and effect (Hume, 1896, p. 7–8). This mode of study can be applied to family relationships as well, for "all the relations of blood depend upon cause and effect, and are esteemed near or remote, according to the number of connecting causes interpos'd betwixt the persons" (ibid., p. 13). In modern times, game theory helps us to uncover the causal relationship for collaboration. We will look to game theory to explain how collaborators come together, how they work (inputs) and how gains (output) are divided, and why collaborations succeed or fail.

1.1.1 Game Theory and Collaboration

In the non-cooperative form of game theory, a type of cooperation can be reached in repeated games. For example, General Motors (GM) may wish to follow a cooperate strategy with Ford Motor Company (FD) for advertising expenditures. To get around the Antitrust Laws, GM may play a signal game by not increasing its advertising budget one year and waiting to see if FD will do the same in the next period. If FD gets the message, it may cooperate by not increasing its own advertising budget. But if FD ignores GM's signal, then GM can come back with an advertising budget that will punish FD.

A separate cooperative form of game theory is built on axioms about the outcome. A game is cooperative if players are allowed to communicate and make binding agreements about their strategy before they play (Aumann 2000, V. 2, p. 31). Such axioms may include the following.

1. *Feasibility:* That a solution point is available to the players. Usually this means that the paper will be acceptable for publication in a standard journal. The journal is likely to be one that shares the paradigm upon which the paper's topic is based. It is possible in some situations for one person, a teacher, to threaten a student, that if he does not cooperate, then he may not graduate. In some cases this might be looked as a side payment as well: if the teacher promises to see the student through, then they will graduate and get good recommendation.

   In addition to side payments, a game may also feature transfer of utility. One collaborator may pay the other monetary compensation. Utility is transferable if there is no diminishing return to the increment of money transferred. We run into this problem when a rich person values an additional $1 less than a poor person. Threat and side payment might be at issue with colleagues in an institution as well in regard to tenure, research funding, or other benefits.
2. *Individual and Group Rationality:* A player expects more from cooperation than he can achieve by working alone. A collaborator may be too busy to finish the task in time, or may lack complementary skills. One reason why gains accrue to group rationality is because members share knowledge with one another.

3. *Pareto Optimal Point:* Neither player can increase his utility without decreasing that of the other player. Each one may read or observe the other's input and have some reasoning why the finished choice will enhance their joint utility.
4. *Fairness:* Equal credit for equal effort. For example, when two workers are carrying a sack, they appear to be doing equal work; a 50:50 split of monetary reward may be considered a reward equal to their marginal product of labor (MPL). This approach is what economists take to be the equilibrium solution. A 50:50 split is an efficient way to distribute the gains. The philosopher John Rawls proposed a concept of justice as fairness. In his model, fairness requires that one first find the minimum he can get, and then try to maximize that minimum. John Nash proposed an alternative solution that maximizes the product of each individual utility function.

Results in experimental games find that a 50:50 split has nothing to do with fairness or altruism. Some authors consider a win if their name appears first on a publication. If it is possible to measure each person's effort, then the credits can be set equal to the marginal effort.

5. *Independence of Irrelevant Alternative [IIA]:* The introduction of a third alternative should not change the preference of the first two alternatives. As there are bilateral and multilateral trades, some authors may exclude the others to begin with and have no IIA problem. They may agree not to work with the other unless they are both credited.

6. *Invariance under Linear Transformation of Utility:* If one were to scale up or down the benefits of the collaborators, then ranking of their benefits will not change. This is usually done by multiplying or adding the utility function by a constant. Because those activities make up a line, the transformation is called Linear Transformation.

7. *Monotonicity:* This is best explained by an example. If one is inside a production possibility curve, one needs to be assured that further action will move one toward the curve that shows the maximum benefit. A monotonically increased move from the interior to the surface guarantees that an improvement is made.

One kind of solution we find in game theory is where the authors share the credit equally. For a simple intuitive illustration, suppose $100 is to be divided by two persons. The Pareto Optimal points will lie on a line: $y = 100 - x$. Following the method of John Nash, we want to maximize: $xy = 100 - x^2$. Setting the derivative $100 - 2x = 0$, yields x share to be \$50. So, a 50:50 split is the Nash point for the game.

More generally, potential collaborators can have (1) A maximum payoff function, $u(u_1,u_2)$, (2) Nothing, if they fail to agree, (0, 0), or (3) Some disagreement point, (d_1,d_2). By subtracting 2 from 1, we get the possible utilities that can be gained if the players obtain maximum payoff. John Nash proposed that the players should Maximize $(u_1 - 0)(u_2 - 0)$.

One can imagine that some collaborations are ultimatum games. This can be true for, say, a teacher and student collaboration. The teacher makes an offer to the student to write about a particular topic, and the student can accept or reject the offer. Also, collaborations are founded on morals bases such as fairness, justice, equal treatment, and characteristics such as efficiency.

1.1.2 Edgeworth Box and Collaboration

The Edgeworth box is sometimes considered as a precursor to collaboration in game theory. It can illustrate two persons as well as n-persons collaboration. One can postulate a production function for two collaborators based on their capital and labor as inputs. In an Edgeworth box with labor and capital on the axes, we can create a contract curve that joins the points at which the players' isoquant curves are tangent. Then one can find core points based on the players endowment, $C(e)$, that are Pareto Optimal, and proceed to find Walrasian like equilibria points, $W(e)$ in the core, that is, $W(e) \subset C(e)$. For more than two persons, one can classify persons into types, and study convergence to equilibrium in the core as the economy enlarges.

It might be worthwhile to characterize the situation in game theory where the two collaborators' share should be equal. Say the two authors are Samuelson and Modigliani. They share the value of their article on the Dual Pasinetti Theorem. Let that be v. Each collaborator has a utility function defined in the domain of $[0, v]$, which is usually characterized as strictly increasing and concave. Since Samuelson said he did not do much of the work, he will be willing to accept a share that is less than $d_s = 0.5$. Similarly, Modigliani will be willing to accept a share $d_a > 0.5$. Now, if the sum of each contributor's share equals less than the total value, that is, $\theta_S + \theta_M < 1$, then positive gains, $v - d_s - d_m$, will be available for further sharing. The maximum can therefore be found for their utilities.

1.1.3 Team Collaboration

People working in teams have been an old concern for economists. Collaboration of teams may imply free-riders. If two people are carrying a sack, their marginal product of the task may not be known. Basically what we observe is that "The output is yielded by a team, by definition, and it is not a sum of separable outputs of each of its members" (Alchian & Demsetz, 1972, p. 779). Free-riding can be avoided if the specific skills contributed by each collaborator are known, or because they help each other (Brickley et al., 1997, p. 463). In general, if the expected team output exceeds the sum of the expected individual output from working alone, then teamwork is profitable.

We have settled on the term "collaboration" to describe the work of the collaborators whose chapters appear in this volume. The term "cooperation" does not seem fitting for this collection, since in game theory it is done in order to increase profit over the non-cooperative level. Economists use the term "joint production" to provide another shade of meaning, namely a double output that seems inevitable: from a sheep, we get both wool and mutton. We have therefore chosen "collaboration" for the economists whose work appears here, and use other synonyms only if the contributors do so.

1.2 Hypothesis on Collaboration

In this section, we drill down from general terms to examine some popular hypotheses on collaboration. Moving toward hypothesis allows us to do some arithmetic with the general, particular, and theoretical views we have expressed above. In some cases we have added, in other cases we have expanded, and for others we have repeated some ideas more formally. Without any attempt to be exhaustive, we present some of the most frequent hypotheses that appear in the literature on collaboration. Collaboration can embrace a single or multiple of these hypotheses.

John Maynard Keynes, the founder of macroeconomics, held that even the explanation of simple ideas in economics may require collaboration. He took a time and experience perspective of collaboration. These concepts are inherent in his statement that "If the simple basic ideas can become familiar and acceptable, time and experience and the collaboration of a number of minds will discover the best way of expressing them" (Keynes, 1937, p. 212). High-tech media help to facilitate such collaboration. Wikipedia is the obvious exemplar in this regard, a platform where many collaborative minds converge on a topic. Yet, one may require laws or the discovery of new laws to explain how something comes to be the case (Moore, 1962, p.16). Explanation and prediction sometimes form one domain where collective minds meet.

The term explanation is used synonymously with prediction, and thus forms the backbone of positive economics that is buffered from normative judgments by artistic elements.

The virtues of collaborative efforts cannot be over-stated. For Keynes, it is a metaphor for light over darkness. "The writer of a book … is extremely dependent on criticism and conversation if he is to avoid an undue proportion of mistakes. It is astonishing what foolish things one can temporarily believe if one thinks too long alone, particularly in economics" (Keynes, 1936, Preface, p. xxiii). Keynes was acknowledging the inputs of persons like R.F. Khan, Joan Robinson, R.G. Hawtrey, and R.F. Harrod, who all made significant inputs in his book. Summing up, it is fair to say that Keynes' hypothesis about collaborative work touches upon two aspects of economics:

Hypothesis I [Keynes]: *Collaboration of a number of minds helps to best explain simple ideas and illumine darkness.*

This was a significant foresight of Keynes, considering that prior to the 1930s, collaboration was not prevalent in the major economics journals. Collaboration increased significantly after the early 1950s, and by the 1990s, "over 50 percent of the featured articles published in the *A.E.R.*, *J.P.E.*, and *Q.J.E* … were coauthored, a more than fivefold increase over a roughly 40-year period" (Laband & Tollison, 2000, p. 636). One cannot ascribe this result to the complexity of the subject matter of economics alone, as many economics texts are still being published by single authors.

Keynesian hypothesis is of a particular vintage in collaboration, dealing with collaboration from the general help point of view. Another exemplar of this type of collaboration is the invention of linear programming.

Experience and collaboration have close ties. As George Bernard Dantzig, the father of linear programming, puts it: "Man has always had to turn to a leader whose 'experience' and 'mature judgment' would guide the way" (Dantzig, 1990, p. 70). Dantzig goes on to describe how he consulted with John von Neumann "to see what he could suggest in the way of solution techniques" (ibid., p. 75). He seems to be on the verge of suggesting a theorem for collaboration when he utters the words: "I guess everyone has a finite capacity"—which we take as our next hypothesis.

Hypothesis II [Dantzig]: "Everyone has a finite capacity." (ibid., p. 76)

Experience and time have taught us that benefits accrue from collaboration. In game theory we use the term cooperation, synonymous with collaboration. From the works of the Nobel laureate Robert Aumann, we surmise that the ultimate goal of competition is collusion.

The time and details involved in large projects foster collaboration. Wassily Leontief, the founder of input–output analysis, wrote: "Because of its scope the research program will have to be carried out over a number of years and by many hands. … A four-year grant from the Rockefeller foundation made possible the formation of a research organization which could push the research in this field further and more effectively than I had previously been able to do with very limited research assistance" (Leontief, 1953, vi–vii). In this scenario, some authors completed works individually while other worked jointly. In Paul Samuelson's contribution for this volume, he has underscored this dual method of collaboration. The hypothesis suggested can be stated as follows:

Hypothesis III [Leontief]: *Large-scale collaborative work requires both individual and group rationality.*

Other seismic collaborative works in economics can be listed in line with the Leontief hypothesis. Certainly Oskar Morgenstern and John Von Neumann on game theory fall within that category. Milton Friedman and Anna Schwartz on the history of money in the United States is another such collaboration. In Finance theory, we pick two: Black–Scholes' model in financial portfolio theory and Modigliani–Miller's hypothesis that meets such requirements. On the radical side, Marx and Engels' joint works fit the bill.

In modern parlance, collaboration may manifest itself through the Kuhnian's "invisible college," perhaps the broadest platform for the promulgation of scientific work. This problem–solution-based paradigm does not require practitioners to meet; they can share their ideas by publishing their results. In this regard, Joan Robinson and Edward Chamberlain were collaborating on the same problem–solution when they independently published papers on imperfect or monopolistic competition. A more celebrated collaboration in this sense is the independent work of Leon Walras, Stanley Jevons, and Carl Menger, the three who created the marginal revolution in economics around 1870. The underlying hypothesis here seems to be the Kuhnian one:

Hypothesis IV [Kuhn]: *Collaboration pools practitioners into an invisible college which uses publication as an outlet for their shared beliefs.*
Corollary I [Kuhn]: *The pool of collaborators complement and supplement each other's work.*
Corollary II [Kuhn]: *New frontiers often require team effort to conquer.*

Because more than one specialty is often involved in a piece, people of different specialties are necessary to complement the thought processes. These are among four points based on economic reasoning: (1) division of labor over time increases complexity, (2) opportunity-cost-of-time, (3) maintenance of a desired level of quality, and (4) random factors not under the control of authors (Piette & Ross, 1992). Researchers, many of whom need publications either for tenure or for promotion, may find themselves subject to a variable review process. As a result, authors may collaborate for the sake of market saturation.

Complementary and substitution forces may go on simultaneously. While researchers were trying to find a way to price options, Black was able to finish the task when Myron Sholes complemented his approach with his knowledge of the partial differential equation. Another pair of complemental researchers were von Neumann and Morgenstern: the former's math skills complemented the latter's economic skills in game theory.

Practitioners of a paradigm are allowed to disagree in their shared commitments. F.A. Hayek (1899–1992) and Ludwig von Mises (1881–1973) exemplify this point. Hayek explained in a video (Axel Leijonhufvud, November 1978) that he was not able to make von Mises see his main point, namely that the analysis of individual planning is an *a priori* system of logic, which fits in with Mises' idea of "*a priorism*—his views about mathematical economics in general and the measurement of economic phenomena in particular" (Hayek, 1979, *The Counter-revolution of Science*, p. 52). Empirical concerns come in for Hayek only when individuals learn what other persons do. But Hayek was not able to persuade von Mises to give up his stance that the market mechanism was wholly *a priori*. They both are credited with the introduction of dynamics to the early static economics of the school: von Mises with his Human Action element, and Hayek with individual and economic order.

But in the case of Marx and Engels, a shared paradigm united their collaborative efforts. Their collaboration resulted not only in three books—*The Holy Family, The German Ideology,* and *The Communist Manifesto—but also in their ideas, so much so that, as in a good marriage, their names cannot be separate (see* Hypothesis VII *below). Some say that reality in a state of conflict is their shared paradigm. Engels continued his faith in Marx by publishing Volumes 2 and 3 of Marx's Capital after his death. Joseph Schumpeter, however, would have us believe that their collaboration was one of a lord-servant relationship (see* Hypothesis VI *below). He wrote:* "Throughout he (Engels) aspired only to be the faithful henchman and mouthpiece of the Lord Marx … he was not Marx's intellectual equal and, while fairly up to the latter's philosophy and sociology, he was particularly deficient in technical economics" (Schumpeter, 1954, p. 365).

Columbus needed the king and queen of Spain to achieve his dream. The US space program requires NASA to pave the way for new accomplishments. Newton said he was standing on the shoulders of giants. In teamwork, the value of output can be greater than the sum of the value of each individual worker. The reason comes from the interdependence of the members and their assets. For instance, the team can combine their assets uniquely, and select a particular division of labor and communication medium.

Hypothesis V [Lakatos' Research Program]: *People who collaborate share some core values in a research program, not subject to change, but fenced in with elements of a protective belt with elements they are willing to change.*

This is true of collaborators who mainly associate with a school, for instance Keynesian, Monetarist, Marxist, or Classical. They may choose broader categories such as orthodox and non-orthodox, or more particular concepts such as Post-Keynesians, New Classical, New Keynesians. Or they may choose to associate with a discipline such as psychology, physics, mathematics, or sociology. Kahneman and Tversky chose to mix economics and psychology. Gary Becker collaborated mainly on work involving sociological research. Arrow and Debreu collaborated in general equilibrium economics. In this piece, Graciella Chichilnisky's contribution has built on some of those works. Milton Friedman sometimes collaborated with statisticians, and Paul Samuelson was partial to bringing mathematical physics to economics.

A number of researchers have argued that among other causes, the increased complexity of research has made collaboration common and necessary. The reasons are "increasing specialization across disciplines and fields; the complexity of research problems; the rising costs of technological apparatus; the development of new information and communication technologies" (Duque et al., 2005, p. 756). Since high technology is still budding, it will continue to drive collaboration in the future.

Hypothesis VI [Leader-Follower]: *Collaboration is formed from the desire to follow or imitate the leader.*

The 2004 Nobel Prize in economics was awarded to Edward Prescott and Finn Kydland for their contributions to dynamic macroeconomics: the time consistency of economic policy and the driving forces behind business cycles. Kydland was initially a graduate student of Prescott's at Carnegie Mellon University. In his Nobel Lecture, Kydland noted: "I've had the fortune to work with the greatest economist in the world, Ed Prescott" (Finn E. Kydland, *Prize Lecture*, December 8, 2004).

This type of collaboration, in which one partner wishes to emulate the other, is most notable in teacher–student relationships such has jointly published dissertations. But it can also be extended to the governance point of view that now permeates the literature consequent to the Great Recession. Leadership positions can be taken from exclusive or joint ownership points of view, where "the ownership relationship starts without a formal arrangement between both partners, whereas under joint ownership accrues some stakes in the venture from the beginning" (Lülfesmann, 2004, p. 254).

Herbert Robbins and Richard Courant's well-known mathematical work *What is Mathematics?: an elementary approach to ideas and methods* exemplifies a teacher–student relationship. Robbins explained that he did all the writing and that Courant did all the review. But when the work was first published, Robbins did not receive full billing for his work. The matter was contested with the publisher and corrected in subsequent editions. This is a case where recontracting, in the Edgeworth sense, worked. But what seems wanting is a certain function to measure each collaborator's sacrifice (Edgeworth, 1881, p. 17).

This type of collaboration may take on a methodological basis as well. The mathematic discipline provides such an example in regard to the

Moore method. The leader, Robert Lee Moore, is said to have had the most rigorous method for discovering new theories. He taught his students to prove theorems for themselves, with only basic assumptions given to them (see Burton, 1977).

The leader in this type of collaboration may be obligated or may choose to credit followers. One monumental example of this is the John Keynes–Richard Khan relationship. Keynes wrote in his *General Theory* that "The concept of the multiplier was first introduced into economic theory by Mr. R. F. Khan" (Keynes, 1936, p.113). Today, it is hard to separate the multiplier concept from the Keynesian economic model.

Hypothesis VII [Favoritism, Nepotism, and Discrimination] *Collaboration may be done from a point of view of up-showing one's friend or family member, or discriminating against the other.*

This may include coauthorship with family members, such as in the case of Milton and Rose Friedman. We have witnessed such efforts by Janet Yellen and George Akerlof, Graciela Chichilnisky and Geoffrey Heal, and Charles and Mary Beard. Relationships may also be implicit in the sense that "articles authored by those with editorial connections, particularly serving on the publishing journal's editorial board, are both statistically and numerically of higher quality" (Medoff, 2003, p. 434).

Mary Ellen Benedict's chapter in this volume illustrates how her own trajectory of collaboration began in a doctoral program and blossomed in an academic environment. For Benedict, collaboration encompassed a wide spectrum of associations: colleagues, students, friends, and her husband. She makes the point that criticism among closely related collaborators, while often reserved, can be successful.

Nobel laureate Franco Modigliani wrote with his granddaughter Leah Modigliani. They collaborated on the stock risk rating system used by Morgan Stanley worldwide, which is now known as Modigliani–Modigliani or M-squared (Szenberg & Ramrattan, 2008, p. 129).

The Nobel laureate Gary Becker has pointed out that using a discrimination coefficient does not pay. The alternative cost would be the better choice that is foregone, which may have improved the quality of the project. But there can be a positive discrimination coefficient as well—for example, Kip Viscusi and his wife Joni Hersch, founders and co-directors of the Ph.D. Program in Law and Economics at Vanderbilt Law School, first met when they worked as coauthors on a project.

Hypothesis VIII [Paul Halmos]: *Collaboration bears affinity to the principle of marriage.*

The marriage principle of collaboration is "the principle is that a collaboration once joined together shall not be put asunder" (Halmos, 1985, p. 98). This model predicts that that once collaboration is effected, then what product it converges to is accepted as the collaborative result. What is meant is that one should not ask what each partner contributed—"the count must not be made. Perhaps one partner contributed the insight and the other the technique, perhaps one partner asks the question and the other knows the literature well enough ... or, possibly, one is active and the other is the foil needed to keep up his morale and inspiration" (ibid.). One can also read into the marriage principle, complementary activities described in Hypothesis IV above.

The twentieth century was blessed by the collaboration of John von Neumann and Oskar Morgenstern, who wrote *Theory of Games and Economic Behavior* (1944). The pair "had complementary properties that led to a fruitful co-operative product" (Samuelson, 2011, V6, p. 209). Von Neumann published his mathematical proof of the saddle-point solution in 1928, and Morgenstern published a book on forecasting in the same year, using the terms "games" and "strategies." Morgenstern wrote that a mathematician named Eduard Cech informed him at one of his presentations that von Neumann dealt with the problems he posed in his game theory paper (Morgenstern, 1976, pp. 806–807). However, they first spoke of game theory about a decade later, in 1939, when they met at Princeton University. Subsequently, Morgenstern began to write a paper on game theory, which von Neumann decided to read. On reading it, von Neumann was the one to suggest that they both collaborate on it (ibid., p. 808). That effort eventually led to their 1944 book. "We wrote virtually everything together and in the manuscript there are sometimes long passages written by one or the other and also passages in which the handwriting changes two or three times on the same page" (ibid., p. 812). They have steered economics from being a tool of physics to a tool of mathematics, most notably with point set theory and topology. It is said, "He darted briefly into our domain and it has never been the same since" (Samuelson, 2011, V. 6, p. 215).

Hypothesis IX [Unity of Mental and Physical Forces]: *Collaboration is more of a need to unite mental forces that have physical symptoms.*

Unlike the need to exchange vital forces that draws one into a marriage, mental collaborators are drawn toward a mental force which may operate consciously or subconsciously. In the latter, we find that some people are driven by a psychic desire to collaborate without making any demands. Samuelson explained how he and Modigliani began collaborating on the *Dual Pasinetti Theorem*. Modigliani gave a memorial speech at MIT's Sloan School of Management, which his colleague Paul Samuelson saw as a display of a deep and focused thought process. Samuelson's wish to collaborate with Modigliani came to fruition on a tennis court. "One day, between serves, he asked me what I thought of a new theory," Samuelson said. "I admitted I hadn't heard of it. He explained it. We kept playing. I responded. Our collaboration was born right there."

In a collaborative effort, sacrifices are made by each participant, and the principle of distribution of the benefits seems wanting. Perhaps this can be settled by a contract, where the benefits accruing on a 50:50 basis may be deemed fair. The case of mathematicians Courant and Robbins underscores this point.

Hypothesis X [Change in Economic Demographics Group]: ***Structural change in the group of economic demography favors more collaboration.***

Charles Manski argued that the demographic breakdown of economics groups has shifted over time, slowly moving away from its extreme dominance by single males. The recent period sees more female coauthors than previously. Perhaps structural changes in the economy itself, including the shift from manufacturing to professional services in the 1960s and 1970s, had some instrumental effect on this change.

Hypothesis XI [Time Intensiveness]: Both theoretical and empirical work can be time intensive and require collaboration.

Perhaps the best illustration of this is the collaboration of Pierro Sraffa and Maurice Dobb in editing the works of David Ricardo. According to Paul Samuelson, this collaboration can be one of complementarity. Some reported that the writing was stalled because of Sraffa lagging in his ability of composition. Who wrote the introduction to Volume I is in question (Samuelson, 2011, V6, p. 10–11). Although the ten-volume work of Ricardo can be time extensive, it was all piled up in Sraffa's mind because he had a hard time to put pen to paper.

Hypothesis XII [Necessity of Parallel Research Work]: *Some industries require parallel research work that requires many teams.*

Research in the pharmaceutical industry exemplifies this work. Because a new chemical entity may take a dozen of years of research to complete, and the necessity of obtaining Food and Drug Administration (FDA) approval creates further delays in its development, limiting research to one project at a time can be devastating to the company's finances if it is not successful. Therefore, it is the practice in this industry to diversify research over many parallel research projects to hedge the risk.

Hypothesis XIII [Short term vs. Long term]: *Collaboration can endure or be still born.*

Just as there are one-short or continuous games, there are also such types of collaborations. A joint effort can peak the career of a collaborator. Black and Sholes collaborated on one major work in option theory. Arrow collaborated on one work in general equilibrium analysis with Debreu, and one with Hahn. Collaborators may part because of disagreement, such as in the case of Courant and Robbins in mathematics. Certainly, the collaborations of John von Neumann with Oskar Morgenstern in game theory and Bertrand Russell with Whitehead in Principia Mathematica were peak experiences. Samuelson seems to play the one-shot collaboration game a lot, for instance with Dorfman and Solow in *Linear Programming*, with Modigliani in the *Dual Pasinetti Theorem*, and with Stolper in *Protection and Real Wage Rates.* In his chapter for this volume, Kip Viscusi explains that "specific projects or narrowly framed research questions" led him to collaborate with 45 people only once.

A deeply shared paradigm can make for long-term collaboration. Perhaps no collaboration in economics is more time enduring than the case of Karl Marx and Freidrich Engels. Their collaboration went beyond their shared paradigm of dialectical materialism: each was deeply concerned with the other's welfare.

A more modern deeply shared paradigm is Arthur F. Burns and Westley C. Mitchell's collaboration in Business Cycle theory. Their books *Statistical Indicators of Cyclical Revivals* (1938) and *Measuring Business Cycles* (1946) have led to a research program that continues today at the *National Bureau of Economic Research.* The economic profession owes them thanks for publishing the first set of leading economic indicators.

Long-term collaboration seems to favor complex over simple ideas. An operational definition of a simple idea is one that cannot be analyzed into constituent parts. Such are the ideas of Plato's theory and form or Aristotle's ideas of the soul (*de Anima*). It also underscores the ancient Greek ideas of first principles, such as air, water, wind, and fire. As the literature demonstrates, these philosophers can hold only contradictory or contrary views, but not collaborative ones. The human brain is a complex machine that has been tied to economics. Friedrich Hayek, in his book "The Sensory Order," argues that the information economists need for decision-making resides in these brain cells. This makes any collaboration such as a planning body incapable of accessing the information. We have to fall back on each individual who possesses such unique information to make better decisions, and only the market mechanism can coordinate such information in the aggregate.

It seems that modern general equilibrium analysis requires long-term collaboration. Arrow (1951) and Debreu (1951) wrote separately at first, and then jointly (Arrow & Debreu, 1954). One collaborator may see elements unseen by another, and they are drawn together because their ideas belong to the same set. While they were working independently on the classical welfare propositions, Kenneth Arrow and Gerard Debreu both used convex analysis in general equilibrium. But "Debreu requires convex preferences without satiation, whereas Arrow allows satiation but assumes strongly convex preference" (Debreu, 1989, p. 12). To a mathematician, this may be a difference of assumptions between continuity rather than derivative, but to an economist it is about behavior which is a long-term phenomenon.

Sometimes it is hard to determine whether an idea is simple or complex. In physics, gravity or space-time curvature orders the universe. For Newton, these are absolutes. Space and time are nothing in and of themselves, according to Einstein's Theory of Relativity. But space contains bodies and energies, and time contains events happening. Complex ideas are conducive to collaborative effort if only because they are a set of elements.

In social relationships, collaborators can have explicit (formal) and tacit (informal) knowledge. At the formal level, collaboration is easily understood. But a communicator may not know that it has tacit knowledge to communicate. He or she must first reflect on it and then communicate. Reflection is one way to bring up that knowledge. Another may be for potential collaborators to interact informally for some time, and then try to collaborate. In economics, we have incidents of collaborative efforts from people working together in an "invisible college." The great example is in monopolistic market structure pioneered independently by Edward H. Chamberlin (1899–1967) and Joan Robinson (1903–1983). Samuelson argued that both of them were reacting to the "cost controversy" of that time (Samuelson, 1972, V3, p. 18).

1.3 Chapter Summaries

Chapter 2: Paul A. Samuelson—On Collaboration in General Economics

This collection of chapters on collaboration was initiated two decades ago, when Michael Szenberg solicited an essay by Nobel laureate Paul Samuelson on the subject and published it in the Fall 1996 issue of *The American Economist*. By all customs and traditions, Samuelson must be considered a master collaborator. A cursory look at the tables of contents of his seven volumes of Collected Scientific Papers (CPS) will reveal the quantity and quality of his collaborative pieces. Samuelson also cooperated on classical books such as *Linear Programming and Economic Analysis*, for which Sir John Hicks coined "a single name for this composite author": DOSSO, for Dorfman, Samuelson, and Solow (Hicks, 1983, p. 247).

In spite of this, the always modest Samuelson writes that "Mostly, I have been a loner" (1976, p. 16). By his count, he defined "loner" by the fact that only 5 percent of the 500 articles in his CPS at that time were collaborative. Samuelson was referring to Volumes 1–5 and not 6–7, which were published posthumously. In retrospect, he appears to put more weight on the quality of his collaborations, saying: "Well, in a second Monte Carlo run of history, I'd write more joint papers. More with Bob Solow. And if the gods were kind a second classic with Wolfgang Stolper."

Samuelson will be concerned with Paul Halmos' thought that one should not be concerned with who contributes what. He was concerned about free-riding, and referred to his own contribution to the classic Stolper article as "kitbit." In retrospect, he is willing to say that his famous multiplier and accelerator piece was "all Hansen's exact model, prettied up, generalized, and mathematically explicated" (1996, p. 17).

Samuelson addressed how cooperation comes to be. It is complementary particularly if the ideas are complex: "Von Neumann and Morgenstern represent the pairing of one who knows mathematics with one who knows economics" (p. 18). He theorized that "Just as scholars divide up into soloists and duet singers, diverse patterns of collaboration abound." Here, division of labor becomes the mother of collaboration.

Samuelson was aware that a cooperator or collaborator was looked down upon, an idea that became stark in his Harvard days when he collaborated with a student. He considered it one of the reasons for his move from Harvard to MIT. This issue is even more present in the present day setting. Samuelson's chapter is a gold mine for cooperative effort in other fields as well, though unintentionally.

Chapter 3: Walter Adams and James W. Brock—Reflections on Our Collaborations in Industry Studies

Adams and Brock credit their success to "congruence of values … cemented by personal compatibility and congeniality." They stay away from large projects and abstract theories. On regulatory matters, they look at functional aspects of firms, industries, and markets. They source problems involving power to the domain of political economy. They emphasize values over value-free methodology. Adams and Brock share a taste for the absurd and adore the Socratic dialog approach in teaching.

Chapter 4: W. Kip Viscusi—The Productivity Impact of Collaborative Research in Industrial Economics

Viscusi subscribes to the technical complementary aspect of collaboration. Viscusi relates to the hypothesis, both theoretical and empirical work can be time intensive and require collaboration, regarding time-intensive survey work and data analysis in empirical research and also address the hypothesis that some industries require parallel research work that requires many teams. Viscusi notes that 62 of his coauthors were former doctoral students.

Chapter 5: Daniel S. Hamermesh—Age, Cohort, and Coauthorship: The Statistics of Collaboration

The contributions of the authors in this section focus on the statistical side of their collaborations, with empirical implications for collaboration in general. Hamermesh argues that age, below and above 51, does not make a difference in collaboration based on his regression analysis. From a sample of 79 labor economics collaborators, he reveals that a search cost is necessary to find scholarly collaborators. Nevertheless, the number of coauthors seems to trend upward with time.

Chapter 6: Charles F. Manski—Collaborative Choices in Econometrics

For Manski, collaborations in economics grew as rapidly as those in mathematics. Technological progress, particularly the advent of word processing and the Internet, has enabled this growth, making it easy for collaborators to exchange and revise their inputs and work with increasingly large and complex data sets. Manski points out that norms have expanded to accept collaborations more readily, and that the demographics of economists have undergone changes that make collaboration more enticing.

Chapter 7: William J. Baumol—On the Pleasures and Gains of Collaboration in Microeconomics

Baumol classifies his coauthors as either "profound" or "fleeting," and suggests that it's a "crime" to hold up the former over the latter (Baumol, 1997, p. 15). Collaboration was a medium to spread his knowledge into other areas such as the performing arts, and in sub-disciplines of economics such as mathematics and industrial organization.

In working out the idea of contestable markets in industrialization, Baumol suggested something like a relay race method in collaboration where "each of us can claim our individual contributions, usually then taken up by the others and carried forward far beyond the relatively primitive original idea. For example, John and Bobby provided a set of necessary conditions for subadditivity of the cost function, while I arrived at a set of sufficient conditions" (p. 19). Perhaps this method can be taken as a linear progression in collaborative efforts.

Baumol extolled the 50:50 rule of financial credits for coauthors because he believed that "any other arrangement must threaten to remove much of the pleasure a collaboration can offer" (p. 18). This does not mean that coauthors should not disagree, for he had shouting bouts with one of his coauthors, and in regard to his introductory text with Alan Blinder, Baumol was forced to change some of his ideas. He wrote, "When Alan offered a criticism of something I had done, it was almost invariably right. I never could think of a good counter-argument" (p. 18). In his chapter, Baumol suggests that one should select collaborators who are simpatico: likable, patient, and easy to get along with.

Chapter 8: David Colander—A Serial Collaborator

Colander's body of work includes 80 collaborative pieces. He started with a big push, collaborating with his teacher Abba Lerner. Colander's original dissertation, which focused on mathematics, had backfired. He was rescued by two stalwarts, Ned Phelps and William Vickrey, who put him on a new path. Colander's new idea came during the double-digit price inflation of the 1970s, which underscored the need for "market in rights to change prices," which could have solved the inflation problem.

Colander points out that his original meeting with Abba Lerner at an American Economic Association meeting was also related to collaborative ventures. This falls into one of his categorical reasons for collaboration, namely institutionally fostered collaboration. The other reasons for collaboration include some combination of the following: (1) gains from trade, (2) collective enjoyment, (3) desire to help someone or to be helped, and (4) strategic collaboration. He also highlights that "collaboration comes naturally."

Chapter 9: William A. Barnett—Collaboration with and without Coauthorship: Rocket Science versus Economic Science

Barnett came to macroeconomics from an engineering perspective. His early collaboration was on group work, which was secretive, and therefore his coauthorships were put on hold until he became an economist. Barnett coauthored pieces at the FED, an experience that was subject to much screening. Essentially, he finds the academic environment more conducive to coauthorship, and he collaborated extensively with students and colleagues in an academic setting.

Chapter 10: Graciela Chichilnisky—Why We Collaborate in Mathematical Ways

Graciela broached collaboration in terms of social acceptability rather than in terms of naked competition based on division of labor. The social paradigm is more adaptable to the modern information economy where information stored in brain cells is accessible from social interactions. She built on the learning-by-doing model, individually and in collaborative efforts. She enlisted a task-trial model of experimental psychology that shows regime shifting from convex to concave shape as trial increases. An implication of her model is that collaboration is superior to division of labor at higher levels of output.

Chapter 11: Richard Zeckhauser—Collaborative Is Superadditive in Political Economics

Zeckhauser examined the shift from single-author works to mostly multiple-author works, a shift in modern trends. He zeroed in on the target population comprising of Nobel laureates and the younger population of winners of the John Bates Clark Award. Collaboration was absent among the first ten Nobel Prize winners on their single most cited work. Similar findings were found for the John Bates Clark Award. Besides the increasing needs for specialization, collaboration is lauded for its superadditiveness, where the contribution of two specialists amounts to a value greater than the sum of values of their individual contribution.

Chapter 12: Geoffrey Harcourt—"Heinz" Harcourt's collaborations: Over 57 varieties in Post-Keynesian Economics

Harcourt's experience with 57 collaborators has been both happenstance and deterministic. His record contains an impressive list of interactions that include two types of collaborators: present or past graduate students, and internal or external colleagues. Harcourt's adventures in collaboration have involved personalities in the post-Keynesian world including Joan Robinson, Pierro Sraffa, Paolo Sylos-Labini, John Hicks, Maurice Dobb, and Luigi Pasinetti.

Chapter 13: Ronald G. Ehrenberg—Coauthors and Collaborations in Labor Economics

Ehrenberg analyzes his contributions through a logit model, revealing that econometric studies are more likely to attract collaboration over policy-related and thought pieces.

Chapter 14: Mary Ellen Benedict—Two Heads are Better than One, and Three is a Magic Number in Labor Economics

Her chapter in this volume illustrates how her own trajectory of collaboration began in a doctoral program and blossomed in an academic environment. For Benedict, collaboration encompassed a wide spectrum of associations: colleagues, students, friends, and her husband. She makes the point that criticism among closely related collaborators, while often reserved, can be successful.

Chapter 15: Rachel McCulloch—Why Collaborate in International Finance?

Rachel McCulloch thinks collaboration is an inveterate, established habit, and therefore not easily changed. Surveying her fellow scholars' collaborations, she sources the reason for collaboration to circumstances and tastes, and the nature of research itself. She suggests that the cost of collaboration can block entry. The tradeoff is between benefits from collaboration and two types of costs relating to "coordination and credit for completed work, with emphasis on the latter." Short- and long-term partnerships may be a function of circumstances. McCulloch's many collaborations with Janet Yellen tapered off as "Janet's published research in her own major area of interest, macroeconomics, started to take off only after she left Harvard, and especially after she began to collaborate with her husband, George Akerlof [Nobel Prize 2001]."

Chapter 16: L.G. Telser—My Collaborations in Game Theory

Telser detailed his collaborative experience mainly of the type that requires joint work with one or more associates. He considers dissertations and similar work to be a sort of leader–follower type.

Chapter 17: Stanley Engerman—Coauthors in History

Engerman focuses on substitutes and complements nature of collaboration. The former explains why some coauthors prefer to be theoretical and some empirical. The latter explains why some prefer to pool their skills, which can result in substantial economies of scale. While some coauthors may prefer division of labor, others might just want to duplicate scholarly inputs.

Chapter 18: Susan Rose-Ackerman—Collaboration: Making Eclecticism Possible in Economic Law and Politics

She puts herself in the category of loner; her collaborations have been diverse and mostly one-shot. She has collaborated with her spouse, senior and junior colleagues including her students, and people with unique knowledge such as about Russia. She finds fields such as comparative law to be tailor-made for collaborative efforts.

Chapter 19: Vernon L. Smith—Collaboration and the Development of Experimental Economics: A personal perspective

Traditionally the economics profession has long been identified with the sole proprietor model of research, publication, and education. The history of economic thought shows that economics was written by lone contributors from classical to neoclassical, and into twentieth-century, economics. Graduate students of Smith have read vintage articles and books by individual scholars, as did our predecessors. With minor exceptions he followed that tradition for the first two decades of his career. The great change came in the years 1975–1985, his first decade at the University of Arizona. He had followed a similar seminar teaching model at Purdue, from 1963 to 1967, then imported that model into Caltech in 1974, but with little in the form of joint collaborative research exercises.

1.4 Conclusion

This collection of essays dispels the myth that no two economists can ever agree. Collaboration itself implies some form of agreement, even if it is about items in the protective belt and not necessarily one's cherished beliefs. People of varied backgrounds and relationships collaborate for one of the many hypotheses we enumerated.

We also get a sense that the maxim that collaborators can be free-riders is downplayed or not a serious problem. Everyone claims to carry a share of the burden. While Samuelson came close to the claim that Maurice Dobb had free-ride on the editing of David Ricardo's work by Pierro

Sraffa, he admits that the matter is still unsettled (Samuelson, 2011, CSP, V. 6., pp. 58–59). Samuelson is subject to similar skeptical claims, for he relied overwhelmingly on Franco Modigliani in regard to the *Dual Pasinetti Theorem* and on Stolper for the *Stolper Samuelson Theorem*. But, as Paul Halmos hypothesized, we can follow the norm that no contributor's input should be questioned, for the output is a joint product.

Game theory offers the only objective solution of how the gains in collaboration are to be shared. Under an invisible hand mechanism, a 50:50 split in gains appears likely. In more complex cooperatives, the number of collaborations that will be formed and the division of the gains seem to suffer the same solution as, say, how to share a birthday cake evenly. The proof of that is still outstanding.

We find that some people such as Samuelson, who would classify himself as a loner, still find it necessary to cooperate at times.

One can surmise the logic of collaboration. If collaboration is not possible, then important pieces will not come to fruition. The rationale for collaboration seems to be complementary, supplemental, need for additional knowledge, or one among the many hypotheses we surmised in this introduction.

Collaboration is like a torch that makes the existence of a product visible. This is true especially for students where collaboration can give one a big push and an early start in their career. In the parlance of statistics, we have here only a sample of collaboration bounded in space-time. From some of the general ideas we touched on, collaboration comes out as a genuine route that truth-seekers can take. For nearly 20 years, the coeditors of this book have been collaborating on over a dozen book and approximately 50 articles and can attest that the hypotheses and reasons given for collaborating in this book are on firm foundation. This book has started a journey of laying bare the rationale behind collaborations as well as the joys of it, and will hopefully stimulate future masterpieces in economics.

References

Alchian, A. A., & Demsetz, H. (1972). Production, information costs, and economic organization. *The American Economic Review, 62*(5), 777–795.

Arrow, K. (1951). An extension of the basic theorems of classical welfare economics. In J. Neyman (Ed.), *Proceedings of the Second Berkeley Symposium on Mathematical Statistics and Probability* (pp. 507–532). Berkeley, CA: University of California Press.

Arrow, K. J., & Debreu, G. (1954). Existence of an equilibrium for a competitive economy. *Econometrica, 22*, 265–290.
Aumann, R. J. (2000). *Collected paper volume II*. Cambridge, MA: MIT Press.
Bion, W. (1961). *Experiences in groups*. New York: Basic Books.
Burton, J. F. (1977). The Moore method. *American Mathematical Monthly, 8*, 273–277.
Lülfesmann, C. (2004). Collaborations with sequential investments. *Economica, New Series, 71*(282), 241–259.
Comte, A.. (1848). *A General View of Positivism*. Trans. J. H. Bridges, M.B. Stanford, CA: Academic Reprints.
Dantzig, G. B. (1990). Interview. In D. J. Albers, G. L. Alexanderson, & C. Reid (Eds.), *More mathematical people*. New York: Harcourt Brace Jovanovich.
Debreu, G. (1989). *Mathematical economics: Twenty papers of Gerard Debreu*. New York: Cambridge University Press.
Debreu, G. (1951). The coefficient of resource utilization. *Econometrica, 19*, 273–292.
Duque, R. B., Ynalvez, M., Sooryamoorthy, R., Mbatia, P., Dzorgbo, D.-B. S., & Shrum, W. (2005). Collaboration paradox: Scientific productivity, the Internet, and problems of research in developing. *Social Studies of Science, 35*(5), 755–785.
Edgeworth, F. Y. (1881). *Mathematical psychics: An essay on the application of mathematics to the moral science*. London: C. Kegan Paul & Co.
French, R. B., & Simpson, P. (2010). The 'work group': Redressing the balance in Bion's *Experiences in Groups*. *Human Relations, 63*(12), 1859–1878.
Gilboa, I. & Schmeidler, D. (2001). *A theory of case-based decisions*. Cambridge: Cambridge University Press.
Hayek, F. A. (1988). *The collected works of Friedrich August Hayek, Volume I: The fatal conceit*. London: Routledge.
Hayek, F. A. (1979). *The counter-revolution of science: Studies on the abuse of reason*. Liberty Fund: Indianapolis, IN.
Halmos, P. R. (1985). *I want to be a mathematician: An automathography*. New York: Springer-Verlag.
Hicks, J. R. (1983). *Classics and moderns: Collected essays on economic theory, volume III*. Cambridge, MA: Harvard University Press.
Hilferding, R. (1912). *Finance capital*. Moscow: Russian Edition.
Hume, D.. (1896[1739]). *A treatise of human nature*. Ed. L. A. Selby-Bigge, M. A. Oxford: Clarendon.
Keynes, J. M. (1971). *The collected writings of John Maynard Keynes, Volumes V and VI, A Treatise on Money, 2 vols*. London: Macmillan.
Keynes, J. M. (1973). *The collected writings of John Maynard Keynes, Volume XIV, the general theory and after, Part II: Defence and development*. Cambridge University Press.

Keynes, J. M. (1937). The general theory of employment. *The Quarterly Journal of Economics, 51*(2), 209–223.

Keynes, J. M. (1936). *The collected writings of John Maynard Keynes, Volume VII, the general theory of employment, interest and money.* Cambridge University Press.

Laband, D. N., & Tollison, R. D. (June 2000). Intellectual collaboration. *Journal of Political Economy, 108*(3), 632–662.

Lakatos, I., & Musgrave, A. (Eds.). (1970). *Criticism and growth of knowledge.* Cambridge: Cambridge University Press.

Leijonhufvud, A.. (1978, November). Interview with F. A. Hayek. San Jose, CA. http://www.youtube.com/watch?v=cDNLKMYYArc

Leontief, W. (1953). *Studies in the structure of the american economy: Theoretical and empirical explorations in input-output analysis.* New York: Oxford University Press.

Lenin, V. I. (1973). *imperialism: the highest stage of capitalism.* Beijing, China: Foreign Language Press.

Medoff, M. H. (2003). Editorial favoritism in economics? *Southern Economic Journal, 70*(2), 425–434.

von Mises, L. (1996). *Human Action* (4th ed.). San Francisco, CA: Fox and Wilkes.

Moore, G. E. (1962). *The commonplace book of G. E. Moore 1919–1953.* Ed. Casimir Lewy. New York: Macmillan.

Morgenstern, O. (1976). The collaboration between Oskar Morgenstern and John von Neumann on the theory of games. *Journal of Economic Literature, 14*(3), 805–816.

Piette, M. J., & Ross, K. L. (1992). An analysis of the determinants of co-authorship in economics. *The Journal of Economic Education, 23*(3), 277–283.

Robinson, E. A. G. (1953). *The structure of competitive industry.* Cambridge: Cambridge University Press.

Robinson, J. (1964). *Economic philosophy.* New York: Anchor Books.

Robinson, Joan. (1969). *Introduction to the theory of employment.* 2nd ed. London: Macmillan.

Sampaio, L. N., de AR Tedesco, P. C., Monteiro, J. A. S., & Cunha, P. R. F. (2014). A knowledge and collaboration-based CBR process to improve network performance-related support activities. *Expert Systems with Applications, 41*, 5466–5482.

Samuelson, P. A. (1986). *The Collected Scientific Papers of Paul A. Samuelson*, edited by Kate Crowley. Vol. 5. Cambridge, MA: MIT Press.

Samuelson, P. A. (2011). *The Collected Scientific Papers of Paul A. Samuelson*, edited by Janice Murray. Vol. 6. Cambridge, MA: The MIT Press.

Schumpeter, J. A. (1954). *History of economics analysis.* London: Allen & Unwin, Ltd..

Smith, A. (1976 [1776]). *An inquiry into the nature and causes of the wealth of nations*. Ed. R. H. Campbell, A. S. Skinner, and W. B. Todd, Volume I. Oxford: Clarendon Press.

Szenberg, M., & Ramrattan, L. (2008). *Franco Modigliani*. Palgrave Macmillan.

Von Neumann, J., & Morgenstern, O. (1944). *Theory of games and economic behavior*. Princeton University Press.

CHAPTER 2

On Collaboration in General Economics

Paul Samuelson

Asking me to write about joint authorship is rather like going to a vegetarian for a treatise on the proper cooking of steak. Mostly I have been a loner: out of half a thousand papers in my collected volumes, perhaps 5 percent have been jointly authored. Still that leaves more than a score of collaborations. Toward the end of his life, Maynard Keynes was asked: If you had to do it over, what would you do differently? He is supposed to have answered: "I'd have drunk more champagne." Well, in a second Monte Carlo run of history, I'd write more joint papers. More with Bob Solow. And if the gods were kind, a second classic with Wolfgang Stolper.

Many say they find scholarship a lonely business. It's you and your pencil in a closed room. (I know one busy professor who was beset by teaching and administrative duties. Finally after years of this, he carved out a sabbatical year at the Stanford, Behavioral Science Center: nice stipend, serene office, great secretarial backup. The anticlimax was writer's block!)

P. Samuelson (✉)
MIT, Cambridge, MA, USA

M. Szenberg, L.B. Ramrattan (eds.), *Collaborative Research in Economics*, DOI 10.1007/978-3-319-52800-7_2

Collaboration with a congenial mind may well then be a prescription for enjoyable research achievement.

I am against the Carlyle–Schumpeter Great Person theory of history. Science is knowledge—public knowledge. We each add our bit: the result is the sum, and the product, of its parts.

R.A. Fisher was a great statistician, even though he was a cantankerous individualist and a capricious genius. Neyman and Pearson—one word, like Gilbert and Sullivan or Rodgers and Hart—were also great statisticians. Their cooperation was carried on by slow mail between prewar Poland and England with turnaround time measured in months and not in today's e-mail nanoseconds.

It is nonsense to say that nothing wonderful was ever created by a committee. The maligned camel is a magnificent adaptation of form and function. The King James Version of the Bible is a Beethoven symphony. Never ask about *Principia Mathematica:* How much was Bertie (Russell)? How much Alfred (Whitehead)?

G.H. Hardy, dean of British mathematicians in World War I era, said: "Mine has been a good life; I have collaborated with Littlewood (and Ramanajuan!) on not too uneven terms." Stealing Hardy's line, I can boast that Solow and I have made good music together.

As they say, cut out the cackle and get down to the facts. By chance, it was writing a 1940 joint article with Russ Nixon, a fellow graduate student in the prewar Harvard graduate barnyard that got me my lifetime job at MIT. Let me explain. Harold Freeman, a non-Rotarian statistician (more Peer Gynt than Baron Munchhausen), started a one-man crusade to move me from Harvard to MIT. Harvard, it developed, was no great obstacle. But the MIT Department Head (Ralph Freeman, later a dear friend and no relation to Harold) resisted. "Yes," he said, "I know Samuelson is a promising economist, but is he a cooperator?" "A cooperator?" Harold replied, "Why, he even writes joint articles." Clio the Muse of History has a sense of humor. It was my *first* joint article; and in a decade, it was the only one. Besides, as a theorist I was not destined to be a prolific writer on empirical statistical matters like the pre-1939 measurement of total US unemployment. I came to write on that subject only because I learned that a third-party go-getter was elbowing Nixon out of a joint venture: it was none of my business but I have had some weakness for the underdog. (No good deed goes entirely unpunished. The late Russell Nixon, who had been John F. Kennedy's instructor in EcA, pursued an active career in CIO and leftist labor unionism. I am sure J. Edgar Hoover has my name in his FBI files as a collaborator with Nixon, but I have not had the curiosity to use the Freedom of Information Act to learn the details. There were no untoward consequences in the McCarthy Witchhunt days, but it is not a laughing matter that careers of useful folk were destroyed for less.)

I move on to less accidental collaboration. One of the most cited articles in trade theory is the 1941 Stolper–Samuelson paper on "Protectionism and Real Wages." Fifty years after its publication, the University of Michigan called a two-day conference to commemorate its content and extend its scope. Note that Samuelson beats out Stolper in alphabetical order, but the name of Stolper comes first on the paper. This is only as it should be. Wolfgang Stolper had been a pupil of Schumpeter at Bonn and followed him to Harvard. The newly married Samuelsons and Stolpers lived on the same Ware Street two blocks from the Harvard Yard. (In those days I needed no watch: every quarter hour the Memorial Hall bells told me the time; being absent-minded I was not equally sure of the date but mostly I did have a good guess as to the month.) One day Wolfi mentioned to me: Ohlin's factor-price equalization theorem must imply that an American tariff ought legitimately to raise US wage rates. Obvious. Yes, *today* obvious. But then in the shadow of Frank Taussig, Gottfried Haberler, and Jacob Viner, this was heresy. I replied: "By George, you're right. Work it out." And that he began to do. But there were snags and surprises, which he would discuss with Midwife Paul A. Samuelson. Kibitzers do not deserve to have their names on a paper; a footnote acknowledgment is adequate. But Stolper is a person of excessive conscience. He declared that he could not publish the paper without my name as joint author. Not wishing to be an aborter, I gave in.

The rest is history. We were turned down by the best editors of the best journals. (This is written up somewhere.) Also, we have here a prime example of Robert K. Merton's Matthew Effect in the history of science. TO HIM WHO HATH SHALL BE GIVEN.

Broadly I have been given too much credit and Stolper too little-except by experts who know better. If A and B make the same discovery at the same time, and B is the more prolific name, then A will fail to get the deserved 50 of the credit. (Whitehead and Russell display the same effect: Bertrand Russell's fame as a logician exceeds Whitehead's, so that the *Principia* began to be called Russell's *Principia;* Russell had to scold Keynes in print for this provocation.)

I am not digressing when I mention here "Samuelson's" classic 1939 article on the "Interactions Between the Multiplier Analysis and the

Principle of Acceleration." It is published as the work of one author only. Written in an afternoon, it brought that young economist instant international fame. Yet, as I later explained in print, Samuelson was only correcting a subtle mathematical mistake in the writings of his beloved mentor Alvin Hansen ("the American Keynes"). It was all Hansen's exact model, prettied up, generalized, and mathematically explicated. In a world where it is so often the case that an older scholar gets his name on a manuscript largely done by an assistant, and gets his name first on it, this counterexample of generosity deserves special notice. (In organic chemistry, a star publishes as many as half a hundred papers a year, probably with a score of junior authors. I asked MIT's late chemist John Sheehan—the synthesizer of penicillin—how his authors' name were listed. He replied: "I used to put my name last, but that didn't fool anybody and it did make bibliographical referencing more confused. So now it reads Sheehan and Smith, Sheehan and Jones, Sheehan and Tom, Dick, and Harry." "Do you think that's fair?" I asked. Prior to Jack Kennedy, he replied: "Is life fair? Besides I have an unrealistic hope that it all evens up in the end. When you're young you get too little credit, when you're old too much." But what about premature dying and also the inevitable narrowing down that leaves fewer on top than began at the bottom?)

Unlike R.G.D. Allen and J.R. Hicks who teamed up from the beginning to write their classic 1934 "Reconsideration of the Theory of Value," it is apparent that often my few joint efforts came when my midwife role grew too large for the conscience of some friend. Thus, in my first 1953 collaboration with Solow, uncharacteristically I contributed to the proof of his original conjectured theorem. (I happened to remember a similar case in A.J. Lotka's mathematical demography.) A footnote would have sufficed but he insisted on joint authorship. The shoes were on the other feet in our second 1956 collaboration: he saved me from a wrong conjecture. My name did not appear on a different article denying the possibility of double reswitching in a Sraffa input/output model; but since its author wrote as an MIT student of mine, it was proper that I be given much blame for what was an inexplicable stupidity.

I could go on spinning anecdotes about Merton and Me, Hansen and Me, Modigliani and Me. But space is short and more representative matters need mention.

Let me therefore report only on working with Franco, a unique and grueling experience. We all envied the legendary cooperations of Modigliani and Gruenberg, Modigliani and Brumberg, Modigliani and

Ando, Modigliani and Dreze, Modigliani and Miller, Modigliani and I used to say facetiously, "Franco, when I am dead you will regret never having heard the sound of my voice." So even in my Walter Mitty dreams of Napoleonic glory, I never dared hope for Franco and Paul. But fate destined me to be the man who had everything.

Like a French revolution, it all began on the tennis court. (*The New Yorker* carried under the heading "Things We Doubt Ever Happened" a news bite describing this; but it was the literal truth.) Franco, not wishing to waste time between his first and second serve, had said to me: "Do you believe Luigi Pasinetti's new theory?" "Tell me what it is and I'll let you know." "Pasinetti claims that a rise in workers' saving rate can't affect long-run capital stock or interest rate." "Impossible," I said after Franco had double faulted. "Only begin with Harrod's model and now increase workers' saving propensity above *rentiers'*. That does raise K/L and does lower longrun profit rate." Thus, the dual anti-Pasinetti equilibrium regimen was conceived; but the child was not delivered into print without painful travail. Every line had to be argued out at length. It was like going over Niagara Falls in a barrel. I wouldn't have missed the experience for a million dollars but I wouldn't give two cents for a second helping. (I jest. My sky high opinion of Modigliani went up. I knew it was a deep well but had not realized its unbounded dimension.)

Just as scholars divide up into soloists and duet singers, diverse patterns of collaboration abound. Even the same composer Richard Rodgers worked differently with the undisciplined Lorenz Hart and the on-schedule Oscar Hammerstein III. With Hart, Rodgers wrote the music first and then tried to trap Hart into an afternoon of inspiration. Oscar's autonomous lyrics, by Granger causality (an inside econometrician's joke), evoked Rodgers' beautiful music.

Dale Jorgenson and Franco Modigliani are similar and different. Dale's is the chemists' pattern (recall John Sheehan) in which workshop participants join with the Master and themselves later become Masters. Complex data call for such group efforts. Von Neumann and Morgenstern represent the pairing of one who knows mathematics with one who knows economics: it was a fertile marriage even though each brought out some of the foibles of the other. (When asked what was Morgenstern's role in the game theory book, von Neumann gave the waggish answer: "Without Oskar I could never have written the book." Humor, as George Stigler has instructed us, can often be cruel. Truth should never be told so as to be interesting. It is enough that it be true.) In the development of linear programming, the economist W.W. Cooper and the mathematician A. Charnes, formed a synergestic team. Dick Zeckhauser's restless mind has identified many new problems for him and one or another statistician to put to rest. Milton Friedman's innovative boldness and Jimmie Savage's mathematical power conspired to forge the classic 1948 "The Utility Analysis of the Choices Involving Risk." Savage told me Friedman's virtuosity educated him on how research should be formulated: the wood Milton chopped warmed science twice.

Some authors almost always work with others. In modern physics, it seems ludicrous when 100 names are on a paper. But that kind of research may involve giant machines that need numerous attenders. When Segre and Chamberlain got the Nobel Prize in Physics, Owen Chamberlain was a visiting professor at Harvard from Berkeley. He told the press: "A committee at Berkeley gave me that prize, by happening to pick me for early use of the new cyclotron." A surgeon friend of mine was one of many co-authors of a paper relating cancer and coffee consumption. He told me laughingly, "I provided some of their patients, that's all I did." When the paper's initial result didn't pan out under replication, my friend was very little put out. As Mark Twain said, "Most men will defend their home but few will go to the stake to save a boarding house."

One young Harvard M.D. in a hurry wrote 50 papers a year with names on their masthead of all his mentors. When his jealous peer group caught him creating on the computer before their eyes 24 hours of data, the fat was in the fire. Under microscopic examination, the skein of wool completely unraveled. Like Typhoid Mary this crook had contaminated dozens of teachers, who revealed how little was their knowledge of what bore their names. I hasten to point out that my casual investigations over the years into outright plagiarism among economists reveals that our field is better refereed and audited than seems to be the case in the harder sciences where there is much dependence on "soft money" for research, and where pressure for publication fabricates most papers that go widely unread. In economics, plagiarism is a rare phenomenon in which fourth rate people with high time preference steal from third-rate people and where what is pilfered has not much value in the market place. On a cost/benefit basis crime does not pay: even with a 99 percent chance of not getting caught the penalty to permanent reputation is too great to make it a rational gamble. (Mining data and selective stopping rules are more serious blemishes in scholarly Machiavellism, and are harder to spot early. Still, facts are remorseless and over time it all tends to come out in the wash.)

Ours is not a field of Saints and Sir Galahads only. Just as some brokers "front run" and "back run" to capture rents on their knowledge of others' intentions, certain scholars earn repute for joining band wagons early; give them a paper to referee and they are off to the races; it is even worse when an editor is too quick off the mark just after the post brings a new batch of manuscripts. These are not felonies nor even indictable misdemeanors, but they are lapses of taste that do not escape notice. (In the eyes of paranoids everyone is a predatory enemy.)

A more difficult normative problem arises for fast-thinking scholars. Mention to them your lemma and they know your theorem before you do. It is fair that the race should go to the swift—if it is a footrace against time. But what is golden about an Invisible Hand that makes a speculator rich just because she digests new news a minute before her slower brother-in-law? Would science be much hurt if West, Malthus, and Ricardo had stumbled over the Law of Diminishing Returns in 1816 rather than 1815? Yet the coin we poor scholars work for is priority in discovery. The perversity of Prisoners' Dilemma applies widely in real life. Alas.

One pattern that recurs occasionally is the monogamous Damon and Pythias syndrome: two scholars, Brothers Grimm so to speak, who *always* write together. When asked to evaluate one of them for a university chair, that can become problematic. Also, there have been cases where longtime partners came to a parting of the ways. After all, marriage itself is a cause for divorce. Sir Arthur Sullivan thought himself too good for the vulgar W.S. Gilbert.

When a team publishes always under, say, the names Aaron and Zeiss, that alphabetical ordering does less injustice to Zeiss. But the repeated trademark of Zeiss–Aaron, if it is a truly symmetric cooperation, would be an unfair syndrome. Better surely to use A–Z on Monday–Wednesday–Fridays and Z–A on Tuesday–Thursday–Saturdays. The injustice seems even worse when by historic chance, a long series of researchers got first published under say the heading Thompson–Dickson–Harrison—maybe for no better reason than that Thompson was a full professor first and carried most initial weight in fundraising. Twenty years later, and n publications on, it is hard cheese if citation indexes concentrate on Thompson et al. only. I would not like to have to explain to St. Peter that I was legitimately in the Et al category. A sensitive Harrison would insist, in early times, on the doctrine "Each of equals is more equal than the others" and drive home this point by a scrupulous permutation of names.

Does all this seem like making heavy weather about a tempest in a teapot? It is not. Dorfman, Samuelson, Solow was the meticulous alphabetical ordering on the spine of a 1958 treatise. Merton's *Sociology of Science* demonstrates that proper credit is all important to scholars. Who steals my legitimate claim for innovation steals all. Indeed it is only natural that junior assistants should if anything exaggerate their unique contribution to a research enterprise, while those who wear medals all over their chests can be expected often to be insensitive to the legitimate inputs of their rotating coworkers. It is tempting to hope that in advance all these imputations and acknowledgments be agreed upon and codified by contract. But experience teaches that in real dynamic life imputation and property rights cannot be unambiguously quantified. (Gossips said that one professor got a Nobel Prize historically for making an observation that his female assistant had to call repeatedly to his notice! Another got the Prize for curing a disease today not believed ever to have existed: maybe his lab slave let him down?—an unlikely alibi.)

Success has a thousand fathers. Failure is an orphan. John F. Kennedy—or Theodore Sorenson—said that: but before them this was noted in the wartime diary of Count Cianno, Mussolini's son-in-law. Quarrels can arise when time comes to cash in on the wages of fame. James Watson's *Double Helix* is the greatest account ever written about a scientific breakthrough told by a breakerthrough. It is not a pretty story; but if a chap will write it, it should get published (as written). The Harvard Press and the lawyers of the Harvard Corporation decided otherwise. It was feared that Sir Lawrence Bragg, head of the Cambridge Cavendish Lab, might sue. Defenders of women's rights regarded Rosalind Franklin (whose crystallography data pointed Crick Watson toward the helix hypothesis) as the one most cruelly libeled. When I read the manuscript, it was Crick who seemed most harmed: if he was a full 50–50 partner and one less ruthlessly ambitious, to my mind he would have a grievance. In any case it took some years for a complete reconciliation between the young comrades at arms.

Hard cases make bad law. In my overall experience, scholars and scientists have been no better or worse as persons than judges or ditchdiggers. Maybe I've been lucky, but in another run of the game I'd settle for the same crew that have been my teachers, colleagues, and students.

2.1 Conclusion

Collaboration is wrongly measured—for anyone and especially for me—by relative number of researches jointly authored. I can genuinely say "Adam and I" about the Smith who wrote in 1776. And can say "Black-Scholes and I" about the pair who discovered the options-price formula that I never quite arrived at. I revealed a preference to learn more (of what there was to learn) from Sir John Hicks than he cared to learn from me: who said life is symmetric? I advanced Keynes' football beyond the yard line where he left it. Why should I expect any record of mine to stand throughout time eternal?

I cannot help but feel sorry for libertarians. It is a personal failing for which I should reproach myself. Whenever I feel myself feeling too egotistical, I try to reread the following 1922 words of L.T. Hobhouse:

The organizer of industry (the achieving scholar) who thinks that he has "made" himself has found a whole social system ready to his hand in skilled workers, machinery, a market, peace, and order (a corpus of past knowledge and contemporary researchers)—a vast apparatus and a pervasive atmosphere, the joint creation of millions of humans and scores of generations. Take away the whole social factor and we have not Robinson Crusoe, with his salvage from the wreck and his acquired knowledge, but the naked savage living on roots, berries, and vermin.

References

Allen, R. G. D., & Hicks, J. R. (1934). A reconsideration of the theory of value, Parts I–II. *Economica N.S., 1*(February–May), 52–67; 196–219.

Dorfman, R., Samuelson, P. A., & Solow, R. M. (*1958*). *Linear programming and economic analysis.* New York: McGraw-Hill.

Friedman, M., & Savage, L. J. (1948). The utility analysis of choices involving risk. *Journal of Political Economy, 56*(August), 279–304.

Hicks, J. R. (1983). *Classics and moderns: Collected essays on economic theory, volume III.* Cambridge, MA: Harvard University Press.

Hobhouse, L. T. (1922). *The elements of social justice* (pp. 162–163). New York: Holt.

Merton, R. K. (1973). *The sociology of science.* Chicago: The University of Chicago Press.

Nixon, R. A., & Samuelson, P. A. (1940). Estimates of unemployment in the United States. *Review of Economic Statistics, 22*(August), 101–111.

Samuelson, P. A. (1939). Interactions between the multiplier analysis and the principle of acceleration. *Review of Economic Statistics, 21*(May), 75–78. Reproduced as Chapter 82 in *The Collected Scientific Papers of Paul A. Samuelson*, Vol. 2. Cambridge, MA: The MIT Press. 1966.

Samuelson, P. A., & Modigliani, F. (1966). The pasinetti paradox in neoclassical and more general models. *Review of Economic Studies, 32*(October), 269–301. Reproduced as Chapter 146 in *The Collected Papers of Paul A. Samuelson*, Vol. 3. Cambridge, MA: The MIT Press, 1972.

Samuelson, P. A., & Solow, R. M. (1956). A complete Capital Model Involving Heterogeneous Capital Goods. *Quarterly Journal of Economics, 70*(November), 537–562. Reproduced as Chapter 25 in *The Collected Scientific Papers of Paul A. Samuelson*, Vol. 1. Cambridge, MA: The MIT Press, 1966.

Samuelson, P. A., & Solow, R. M. 1960. Analytical aspects of anti-inflation policy. *American Economic Review*, 2(May), 177–194. Reproduced as Chapter 102 in *The Collected Scientific Papers of Paul A. Samuelson*, Vol. 2. Cambridge, MA: The MIT Press, 1966.

Solow, R. M., & Samuelson, P. A. (1953). Balanced growth under constant returns to scale. *Econometrica*, 21(July), 4 I 2–24. Reproduced as Chapter 24 in *The Collected Scientific Papers of Paul* A *Samuelson*, Vol. 1. Cambridge, Mass.: The MIT Press, 1966.

Stolper, W. F., & Samuelson, P. A. (1941). Protectionism and real wages. *Review of Economic Studies*, 9(November), 58–73. Reproduced as Chapter 66 in *The Collected Scientific Papers of Paul A. Samuelson*, Vol. 2. Cambridge, MA: The MIT Press, 1966.

Watson, J. D. (1968). *The Double Helix: A personal account of the discovery of the structure of DNA*. New York: Atheneum.

CHAPTER 3

Reflections on Our Collaboration in Industry Studies

Walter Adams and James W. Brock

The commonality in values is cited by two economists as the basis for the success in their collaborative writings. They both prefer to work independently and not to participate in research projects funded by private or government organizations. In their analysis of economic problems, they recognize the influence of power which is neglected by mainstream economists. Denying the claim that economics is a "value-free science," they also reveal their views as being libertarians and their advocacy for a decentralized power structure.

"How has it been possible for you—over the relatively short period of a decade—to have produced five books,[1] ten book chapters, some twenty-four articles in professional economics and law journals, as well as a plethora of popular pieces in newspapers and magazines?" "Given the differences in your age, background, and education," we are asked, "what made you decide to embark on these joint ventures?" "How do you

W. Adams (✉)
Michigan State University, East Lansing, MI, USA

J.W. Brock
Department of Economics, Miami University, Oxford, OH, USA

M. Szenberg, L.B. Ramrattan (eds.), *Collaborative Research in Economics*, DOI 10.1007/978-3-319-52800-7_3

work together?" "Who does what?" "How do you stay on the same wavelength?" "How do you reconcile differences?" Most frequently, "what is the secret of your successful collaboration?"

Without dabbling in psycho-autobiography, we think the explanation is quite simple: a congruence of values—a common Weltanschauung, cemented by personal compatibility and congeniality.

First, we share a temperamental allergy to large-scale, mission-oriented research projects, financed by government or private interest groups. Participation in such research, we believe, deprives scholars of their independence. It demands an undue degree of conformity, adherence to rules and authority, respect for the status quo, and a not insignificant measure of human homogeneity. We prefer to function in an atmosphere where we feel free to reject accepted routine and convention, to rebel against orthodox modes of thought, to repudiate the "tried and true" and "expert authority," to go where "angels fear to tread"—in short, to feel free to be incorrigible non-conformists.

Some years ago, Hans Morgenthau warned that universities, through the very dynamics of their undertakings, have transformed themselves "into gigantic and indispensible service stations for the powers-that-be, both private and public. They serve society but they do not sit in judgement on it." Much of what they present "as truth is either not true at all or truth only by accident, arrived at because it furnishes the powers-that-be with ideological rationalizations and justifications for the status quo."[2] This judgment may be too harsh, but we have always taken it as a warning against the temptation to become spokesmen for the dominant power groups of our time.

Second, we are deeply suspicious of abstract theorizing that produces general theorems, reached with clearness, consistency and by sophisticated logic, but based on assumptions inappropriate to the facts. Such theorems are particularly dangerous when used by powerful groups and their political representatives to subvert the public interest.

A case in point is the application of price theory to the enforcement of Section 7 of the Clayton Act, which prohibits corporate mergers "where the effect may be to substantially lessen competition or tend to create a monopoly." According to the apostles of the Chicago School, "There is no body of knowledge other than conventional price theory that can serve as a guide to the effects of business behavior upon consumer welfare." "Basic economic theory," they say "is an intensely logical subject and much of it consists of a drawing out of the implications of a few empirically supported postulates. … In many cases the theory is so well grounded that we can be certain, or virtually so, of its reliability." Once its "basic premises are accepted, the rest follows like a proof in geometry. The system is entirely circular, which is its strength because circular logic is not rebuttable."[3] Having said that, the Chicago theorists conclude (without empirical investigation) that mergers are efficiency-enhancing and conducive to maximizing consumer welfare. Trends toward greater concentration in an industry, they claim, indicate that there are emerging efficiencies or economies of scale and therefore constitute "prima facie evidence that greater concentration … is socially desirable."[4] Vertical and conglomerate mergers should be totally immune from the law, because they do not involve a combination of direct competitors; indeed, attacking such mergers would obstruct the "creation of efficiency."

Such theorizing, of course, begs the crucial questions. For example, in analyzing the impact of a merger which is neither de minimis nor of monopolistic proportions, economic theory can only be the beginning of the analysis—only the first approximation in deciding whether the merger may substantially lessen competition or tend to create a monopoly. It can provide no simple algebraic equation or sophisticated geometric diagram that can help us make that prediction. To make the assessment required by statute, it is necessary to painstakingly examine the case in the functional context of the firms, industries, and markets involved. As Chief Justice Earl Warren noted, it is necessary to examine whether the consolidation was to take place in an industry that was fragmented rather than concentrated, that had seen a recent trend toward domination by a few leaders or had remained fairly consistent in its distribution of market shares among participating companies, that had experienced easy access to markets by suppliers and easy access to suppliers by buyers or had witnessed foreclosure of business, that had witnessed the ready entry of new competition or the erection of barriers to prospective entrants, all are aspects, varying in importance with the merger under consideration, which would properly be taken into account.[5]

Obviously, these are fact- and case-specific questions that no amount of abstract speculation or crude ideology (cloaked as "science") can resolve.

It is these kinds of questions which, because of their importance in adjudicating antitrust disputes and fashioning antitrust policies, have been a constant source of fascination to us and occupied much of our research efforts.

Third, unlike our mainstream colleagues, we believe that any meaningful analysis of economic problems must be undertaken in the context of political economy, rather than artificially constrained within the narrow confines of economic "science." We must take cognizance of the fact that power exists, and that it may appear in many guises—economic or political, personal or organizational, private or public. Such power comprises more than the ability to influence price in a particular market. It involves the broad discretion to influence how society's resources shall be used, the rules by which the economic game shall be played, and the kind of society in which we shall live. If we are to understand how the economy functions, we cannot finesse the existence of power. If we are to be relevant as political economists, we cannot avoid asking some crucial questions: What is the distribution of power? Is it concentrated or decentralized? Is its exercise subject to external restraints, either by the invisible hand of the market or the heavy hand of government? Is power responsible and accountable, and if so to whom? What are the safeguards against its abuse? Are its abuses readily correctable? If so, by what mechanism(s)? In short, if we are to understand the anatomy and the physiology of an economy, we must inquire who makes what decisions, on whose behalf, for whose benefit, and at what cost.

The neglect of the power problem by modern mainstream economists is, we believe, attributable in large part to an almost obsessive addiction to a mathematical-econometric methodology, which represents a formidable misallocation of intellectual resources. Economists have tended to ask themselves questions that can be analyzed with their new techniques, rather than finding techniques to deal with the questions they ought to ask. They play games they find amusing, rather than contemplate issues that are crucial and pressing. They quantify what appears to be quantifiable, even though it may not be important, and pass over what should be analyzed even though it may not be decisive. No wonder that Wassily Leontief, Nobel laureate and past president of the American Economics Association, criticizes the profession for having constructed such elaborate theoretical structures on so narrow and shallow a factual foundation.[6]

Fourth, again unlike so many of our mainstream colleagues, we refuse to deceive ourselves into believing that economics is a "value-free science" like physics or astronomy. Quite the contrary. As Joseph Schumpeter observed, "analytic work begins with the material provided by our vision of things, and this vision is ideological almost by definition."[7] In other words, the conclusions derived from a theory depend on underlying assumptions which, in turn, depend in large part on the theorist's metaphysical core, his ideological predilections, his cosmological outlook—on "what he thinks before he starts thinking."[8]

If, for example, an economist builds a theoretical model on the assumptions that (1) a market economy is subject to natural laws which make it inherently self-stabilizing; (2) economic behavior is based solely on rational utility- and profit-maximizing conduct; (3) markets are freely accessible to newcomers; (4) industry concentration is based solely on "superior skill, foresight and industry"; (5) monopoly and oligopoly power is constantly vulnerable to erosion whenever it fails to serve consumer welfare; and (6) government intervention in the economy generally does more harm than good—then the conclusions are predetermined from the start, and can be used to justify an extremist, neo-Darwinist policy of untrammeled laissez-faire. Obviously, theories built on different assumptions, based on a different view of the world, will lead to quite different conclusions and point to contrary public policies.[9]

In assessing the scientific claims of economic theory—especially when it is to be used as a guide to public policy—we believe it prudent to follow the time-tested maxim of caveat emptor. It is important to know as the Italian proverb suggests, "da che pulpito viene questa predica?"

Fifth, in our discussions of public policies, we do not claim to be "value-free" scientists. We readily confess that our cosmological outlook is profoundly influenced by the insights of the Federalist Papers and Adam Smith's system of liberty. But we are libertarians who believe that individual freedom can be meaningful only within a pattern of freedoms—within a free economic system—which in turn makes some types of government intervention indispensible. It is not enough, as some of our Chicago colleagues are wont to do, to shout "laissez-faire" and oppose all government intervention. As Jeremy Bentham pointed out, "To say that a law is contrary to natural liberty is simply to say that it is a law: for every law is established at the expense of liberty—the liberty of Peter at the expense of the liberty of Paul."[10] The maintenance of a free economic system requires an irreducible element of governmental force, coercion, and intervention so as to preserve the framework in which alone freedom can flourish. The crucial task, as Lord Robbins suggests, is to distinguish between government interventions that destroy the need for intervention and those that tend to perpetuate it.[11]

As Henry Simons has so ably articulated it, the cardinal principle of libertarianism holds that "no one may be trusted with much power—no leader, no faction, no party, no 'class,' no majority, no government, no church, no corporation, no trade association, no labor union, no grange, no professional association, no university, no large organization of any kind."[12] True libertarians must forever repeat with Lord Acton: "Power corrupts"—and not merely those who exercise it but those subject to it and the whole society.

As we see it, the paramount structural challenge to an advanced industrial society, intent on preserving both economic freedom and democratic institutions, is this: How to prevent private concentrations of power, organized into potent political pressure groups, from achieving dominance over the economy and, eventually, over the state; and, at the same time, how to do so without creating an omnipotent government, strong enough not only to control private oligarchies but also to become an instrument of oppression beyond public control. To this challenge, of course, there are no simple answers.

Sixth, mindful of the foregoing concerns, we have consistently advocated a decentralized power structure. On the political front, we are Jeffersonians. With the Sage of Monticello, we believe that the structure of the political system is more important than the integrity of the individuals who exercise power under it—that the "time to guard against corruption and tyranny is before they shall have gotten hold of us. It is better to keep the wolf out of the fold than to trust to drawing his teeth and talons after he shall have entered."[13] On the economic policy front, we are unreconstructed antitrust traditionalists. With Justice Douglas, we believe that power that controls the economy should not be in the hands of an industrial oligarchy. Since all power tends to develop into a government in itself, industrial power should be decentralized. It should be scattered into many hands so that the fortunes of the people will not be dependent on the whims and caprice, the political prejudices, and the emotional stability of a few self-appointed men. The fact that they are not vicious men but respectable and social-minded is irrelevant. That is the philosophy of the antitrust laws. It is founded on a theory of hostility to private power concentrations so great that even a government of the people can be trusted with it only in exceptional circumstances. [14]

Needless to say, these views do not conform to the currently prevailing orthodoxy, nor are they likely to enshrine their protagonists in the pantheons of conventional wisdom. But not to worry. The practitioners of our "value-free" science may be finely attuned to the fashions of the day, but the "truths" they dispense are transient and effervescent. During the heyday of the conglomerate merger wave of the 1960s, for example, venerable "experts" advised Congressional committees, as well as Fortune 500 corporations, that conglomerates were the wave of the future. They rationalized conglomerate bigness by appealing to "synergy" (2 + 2 = 5), by pointing to what they portrayed as a "revolution in management science," and by citing the alleged scarcity of "super-managers" whose wizardry could enhance economy-wide efficiency if more and more control were concentrated in their hands. Synergy, they assured us, translates into a lowering of costs and real social gains.[15] Today, alas, the fashion has changed. Now, respectable experts bemoan the reverse synergy of collapsed conglomerate empires. Their advice? "It's best to divest!"[16] A similar fate befell the highly-leveraged corporate deal-mania of the 1980s and its "scientific" defenders.

In our collaborative efforts, we have always felt that being fashionable exacts too high a price. Nevertheless, we recognize that there is a cost to being prematurely right.

Finally, a note on our career as playwrights—a source of curiosity and amusement among our colleagues. Looking back, we suppose that this choice of genre is primarily attributable to pedagogical philosophy, and secondarily to our literary tastes. In the classroom, we prefer the Socratic dialog to the magisterial lecture system. Believing as we do that learning is not a spectator sport, and that students must therefore be directly involved in the learning process, we prefer to use the discussion method in analyzing and elucidating economic problems. This method has the further advantage of demonstrating to students the complexity of economic issues, and tends to inspire in them an appropriate sense of humility.

As for our literary tastes, we are both aficionados of the Theater of the Absurd. Adams has long been a student of Samuel Becket, Arthur Adamov, Eugene Ionesco, and Jean Anouilh. Brock has avidly devoured the writings of Czech dissident Vaclav Havel, now president of the Czech Republic. This genre, we feel, provides a felicitous mechanism and a useful touch of irony for understanding contemporary debates of public policy. The nature of those debates is abundantly familiar: There is an absence of communication—a terrifying diversity of utterances, with the actors on the stage listening only to snatches and fragments of the dialogue, and responding as if they had not listened at all, At times, the dialogue consists of statements that are in and of themselves perfectly lucid and logically constructed but lacking in context and relevance. At other times, absurd ideas are proclaimed as if they were eternal truths. In this dialogue of the deaf, the actors are animated by the certitude and unshakable nature of their assumptions—one side relying on the wisdom of past experience, the other prepared to sweep away the beliefs that have been tested and found wanting—beliefs they consider illusions and self-deceptions.

Our decision to embrace this genre evolved quite naturally. Back in 1989, having spent a frustrating stint at the Bibliotheque Nationale in Paris, and after participating in the bicentennial celebration of the French Revolution, we decided to relax for a while at the charming little Val Majour in Fontvieille. There, in the peaceful ambience of a pastel countryside, idly reflecting on some of the absurdities of current economic policy quarrels, while lazily sipping our Rose de Provence, the idea struck us to try our hand at a "play." And so the initial plans were laid for Antitrust Economics on Trial: A Dialogue on the New Laissez-Faire. Our purpose was to put in perspective the polemical books and pretentiously "scientific" articles that have done little to resolve the antitrust debate; to lay bare the states of mind and images that constitute the hidden assumptions in the debate—to provide an intersection between what is visible and what is under the surface, to expose the latent content that forms the essence of the controversy; to expose the disguised meaning of the words used by the protagonists in the debate. Our dialog, as we planned it, would find absurdity not in the depths of the irrational, but what on the surface would appear as rational. It would demonstrate (in the words of Milan Kundera) that a "false vocabulary systematically places the debate on false ground and makes it practically impossible to analyze concrete reality."[17]

According to our publisher, Princeton University Press, the experiment was a success both in the classroom and among non-academic readers. We were asked to write a sequel—this time selecting as our subject the debate over the use of "shock therapy" in engineering the transition from communism to capitalism in Eastern Europe. It was published by Princeton under the title Adam Smith Goes to Moscow in 1993. A Russian translation appeared two years later.

Economics is a dismal science. Its practitioners tend to be endowed with dour personalities and a foreboding outlook on life. They find it difficult to laugh—especially at themselves. Aware of this congenital defect, we try our best to overcome it: We un-puritanically tolerate each other's penchant for nicotine delivery systems; we exploit our age difference, sometimes with guile; we endure the fortunes of a physiological fate (as at the American Economics Association meetings a few years ago, when back pain prevented one of us from sitting and the other from standing);

and we each attribute to the other sole responsibility for whatever value our writings may have. Above all, we enjoy the team effort that unites us.

Vernon F. Taylor Distinguished Professor of Economics, Trinity University (TX) and past president of Michigan State University; and Moeckel Professor, Miami University (Ohio), respectively.

Notes

1. The Bigness Complex (New York: Pantheon, 1986); Dangerous Pursuits: Mergers and Acquisitions in the Age of Wall Street (New York: Pantheon, 1989); Antitrust Economics on Trial: A Dialogue on the New Laissez-Faire (Princeton, NJ: Princeton University Press, 1991); Adam Smith Goes to Moscow: A Dialogue on Radical Reform (Princeton, NJ: Princeton University Press, 1993); The Structure of American Industry, 9th ed. (Englewood Cliffs, NJ: Prentice Hall, 1995).
2. Hans J. Morgenthau, Truth and Power (New York: Praeger, 1970), p. 434.
3. Robert H. Bork, The Antitrust Paradox (New York: Basic Books, 1978), p. 117; Idem, "Judicial Precedent and the New Economics," in Eleanor M. Fox and James T. Halverson eds., Antitrust Policy in Transition (Chicago: American Bar Association, 1984), p. 16.
4. Bork, Antitrust Paradox, pp. 205–06.
5. Brown Shoe Co. v. United States, 370 U.S. 294 (1962).
6. Wassily Leontief, "Theoretical Assumptions and Nonobserved Facts," American Economic Review, vol. 61, March 1971, pp. 1–7.
7. Joseph A. Schumpeter, History of Economic Analysis (New York: Oxford University Press, 1954), p. 42.
8. Axel Leijonhufvud, "Ideology and Analysis in Macroeconomics," in Peter Koslowski ed., Economics and Philosophy (Tubingen: J.C.B. Mohr, 1985), pp. 182, 189.
9. For a fuller analysis of this point, see Walter Adams and James W. Brock, "Antitrust, Ideology, and the Arabesques of Economic Theory," University of Colorado Law Review, vol. 66, (1995), pp. 257–327.
10. J. Bowring ed., The Works of Jeremy Benham (Edinburgh: W. Tait, 1843), vol. 3, p. 185.
11. Lord Robbins, Politics and Economics (London: Macmillan & Co., 1963), pp. 50–51.

12. Henry C. Simons, Economic Policy for a Free Society (Chicago: University of Chicago Press, 1948), p. 23.
13. Notes on the State of Virginia, reprinted in Thomas Jefferson: Writings (New York: Library of America, 1984), p. 246.
14. United States v. Columbia Steel Corp., 334 U.S. 495 (1948).
15. See, for example, Henry Manne, "Mergers and the Market for Corporate Control," Journal of Political Economy, April 1965; Neil H. Jacoby, "The Conglomerate Corporation," Center Magazine, July 1969; Business Week, "Special Report: Conglomerates—The Corporations that Make Things Jump," Nov. 30, 1968, pp. 74–80; U.S. Congress, Senate, Subcommittee on Antitrust and Monopoly, Hearings: Economic Concentration, Part 8, 91st Cong., 2d Sess., 1970, pp. 4736–37 (testimony of Professor J. Fred Weston); U.S. Congress, House, Antitrust Subcommittee, Hearings: Investigation of Conglomerate Corporations, 91st Cong., Part 3, pp. 247–48 (testimony of Harold Geneen, Chairman, ITT Corp.); and Oliver E. Williamson, Markets and Hierarchies (New York: Free Press, 1975), pp. 158–62.
16. Adams and Brock, Dangerous Pursuits, pp. 97–99.
17. Kundera, "Candide Had to Be Destroyed," in Jan Vladislav ed., Vaclav Havel, or Living in Truth (London: Faber and Faber, 1986), p. 261.

CHAPTER 4

The Productivity Impact of Collaborative Research in the Economics of Risk and Uncertainty

W. Kip Viscusi

4.1 Introduction

Most collaborative research efforts involve some type of coauthorship of the research product in recognition of the fundamental contribution that the collaborative effort made to the research. Historically, extensive collaboration was not the dominant research approach among economists, who tended to be solo authors to a greater extent than researchers in the hard sciences. Adam Smith (1776) did not coauthor *The Wealth of Nations*, Kenneth J. Arrow (1951) wrote *Social Choice and Individual Values*, and Paul A. Samuelson (1996) coauthored only about 5% of his articles. The dominance of singly authored work has changed over time in economics, as coauthorship has become increasingly prevalent. As a result, my publication history and that of many other economists involve a coauthorship trajectory over the academic life cycle that reflects in part the rising role of coauthorship in economics generally as well as individual life-cycle effects.

W.K. Viscusi (✉)
Vanderbilt University Law School,
131 21st Avenue South, Nashville, TN 37203, USA

M. Szenberg, L.B. Ramrattan (eds.), *Collaborative Research in Economics*, DOI 10.1007/978-3-319-52800-7_4

In this singly authored chapter, I provide some background on the impetus for collaboration, various statistical analyses of my coauthorship experiences, and a sampling of case studies of the nature of the collaborative ventures. My selection of topics and coauthored works that I discuss is intended to be suggestive of some of the rationales for coauthorship and the dividends yielded by such collaborations rather than a comprehensive review of all the collaborations that have been important in my career. Much collaboration, particularly those that involved only single papers, will receive less attention in the discussion below. My failure to include them in my discussion is not meant to suggest that they are less consequential than the other contributions.

4.2 The Impetus for Collaboration

Collaborative efforts emerge for a variety of reasons, such as a difference in the areas of expertise needed to carry out the project. In some cases, the skill sets of the potential collaborators may be similar, but time constraints and pending deadlines may dictate that a project enlist more than a lone researcher. Empirical projects involving time-intensive survey work and data analysis often meet this test. Such collaborations may entail more than matters of convenience, as there are often components of the project that require the acquisition of specialized skills. To carry out the project successfully, there is often not a need for all the coauthors to make an investment in the project-specific skills. My first article coauthorship experience was of this type. When I was a Harvard economics graduate student working for Richard Zeckhauser, he suggested that I devote some time to learning Markov decision model techniques—a methodology we subsequently used in an article on environmental policy choices under uncertainty (Viscusi and Zeckhauser 1976).

More typically, there is a genuine division of labor among the authors based on quite different skills and interests. A notable example of this phenomenon is my textbook with John Vernon and Joseph Harrington, Jr., *Economics of Regulation and Antitrust*, which is now in its fourth edition (Viscusi et al. 2005). The desired coverage of this book included antitrust, economic regulation, and social regulation. These are distinct but related areas of economics, and there are very few economists who are well versed in all these fields. The initial edition of the book split the book's topics among the three coauthors. While there were substantial efforts to maintain a consistent tone and approach throughout the book, there are identifiable, distinct contributions of each of the authors. Because the intent of the book was to serve as a textbook rather than to break new ground, to the extent that the coauthors ventured onto the turf in the other topic areas, the intersections tended to focus on pedagogical and expositional issues. This example is unrepresentative of my typical coauthorships in that there was more separability of the components than is typically the case.

Parallel research efforts can, however, lead to productive interactions that transform and improve the academic content of the research product. After the Exxon Valdez oil spill litigation, a series of researchers whose primary expertise was in psychology and behavioral economics (Reid Hastie, Daniel Kahneman, John Payne, David Schkade, Cass Sunstein, and myself) undertook a series of experimental studies of how juries assessed punitive damages. The studies, which were undertaken independently, generally involved large samples of mock jurors who considered alternative legal cases. I augmented the mock juror approach by administering the survey to samples of state judges as well. The research appeared in separate articles, and ultimately there was a distillation of much of this work on punitive damages in a book by Sunstein et al. (2002). Although the research studies were undertaken in parallel without much coordination, the research themes echoed across the different studies. For example, after one of the studies documented the importance of hindsight bias on jurors' assessment of punitive damages, I ran a similar survey on judges to assess whether they were subject to this same class of cognitive biases. Subsequently, in research with Reid Hastie, who had coauthored the hindsight bias juror studies, we were able to compare the behavior of the judges in my sample with the results of his jury samples to document the widespread prevalence of hindsight bias influences. This experience represents the somewhat unusual collaborative situation in which a series of independent parallel research projects interact and ultimately lead to research outcomes that extend beyond the findings of any particular study.

4.3 Assembling a Large Collaborative Team: The Hazardous Waste Policy Project

Easily my most ambitious single project from an operational standpoint was my study with James T. Hamilton of the US Environmental Protection Agency's (EPA) hazardous waste cleanup effort policy known as the Superfund. Our project for the agency sought to assess the risks, benefits, and overall desirability of hazardous waste cleanup efforts. The research led to our coauthored book (Hamilton and Viscusi 1999) as well as ten coauthored articles. Two economics graduate students who worked on components of the project, P. Christen Dockins and Ted Gayer, also developed dissertations based on this work.

In the 1990s hazardous waste cleanup was the most prominent environmental policy issue, stimulated by the public's concerns with contaminated landfills and companies' concerns with cleanup costs. Although EPA had some summary data on the hazardous waste sites at the agency headquarters in Washington, D.C., there was no central repository or computerized version of all the key information needed to form a judgment on the desirability of the current policy. This informational gap made it infeasible for even well-intentioned government officials to undertake cost-effective policies. Which sites merit cleanup, and to what extent? The starting point of the project was to address the absence of the most fundamental information needed to structure a sound policy. Our army of 14 research assistants visited all the EPA regional offices and obtained thousands of pages of hard copy and microfilm that we used to construct the data base. Our sample of 267 sites included an enormous body of data for each site that enabled us to undertake a fully independent assessment of the merits of alternative cleanup efforts.

Our starting point was to assess the risk levels, building up from scratch the entire analysis of the costs and benefits of the cleanup of each site. Based on the chemical concentrations at the site and the implications of these chemicals for human exposure, what risks did the sites pose? EPA utilized conservative upper bound values for a series of parameters that entered multiplicatively in the cancer risk calculation. Doing so led to a compounding of the conservatism biases, greatly overstating the actual risks and creating different degrees of bias for different sites because of differences in upper bound measures. Using mean values for various parameters based on our review of the pertinent literature, we developed risk estimates that dramatically reduced the estimated risks. Moreover, unlike the EPA risk assessments, we used a consistent methodology across all sites so that the risk estimates for the different sites were comparable. The first major result was that the current risk assessment practices greatly inflated the risks, but it was possible to construct unbiased risk assessments for each site.

Although EPA was concerned only with cancer risk probabilities, the more fundamental benefit issue for economists is the effect of these cancer risk probabilities on health. In particular, what is the value of the expected number of cancer cases that will be reduced? Thus, the extent to which these cancer risks actually generate risks to which people are exposed should be considered. Somewhat surprisingly, EPA never was concerned with whether there were any populations exposed to the risk or if there were large numbers of people exposed. Governed by the agency's precautionary approach, real and hypothetical risks counted equally. Hypothetical future risks at vacant land with no current or prospective exposed populations received the same weight as risks to large currently exposed populations. By matching the risks to exposed populations by block group in one of the first large-scale uses of Geographic Information Systems methods in economics, we demonstrated that this misguided agency practice led to the disproportionate emphasis on sites with no exposed populations. This emphasis in turn had the overall counterproductive effect that sites with large exposed populations received lower priority for cleanup. Because sites with these large populations often tended to have high minority representation, inattention to the role of exposed populations had the unanticipated effect of disadvantaging minority groups, such as Hispanics exposed in the western USA. The result is that the biases in EPA policy targeting that were justified on precautionary grounds were principal contributors to the environmental equity problems that the agency was tasked to address by President Clinton's executive order.

The hazardous waste cleanup efforts not surprisingly failed the usual economic efficiency tests. At over two-thirds of the sites, the cleanup costs far exceeded $100 million per expected cancer case prevented. The agency's targeting of the site cleanups reflected a combination of political factors, such as counties' voting percentage, and cognitive biases, such as the availability heuristic. The analysis of the role of political factors in site cleanups drew on James T. Hamilton's particular expertise, as much of his research has been on the political science/economics border. One of the more surprising findings is that the trade-off rates between cost and risk reflected in the housing price decisions by the public were less alarmist than the cost-risk trade-offs embodied in decisions by the regulatory agency. The housing price effect estimates for the risks of cancer led to estimates of the value of a statistical life comparable to those found in the literature, whereas the costs per case of cancer averted by the EPA cleanups were often several orders of magnitude greater.

4.4 The Coauthor Roster

My group of coauthors has included many repeat players, with most of the continuity arising from involvement in long-term research projects. At the top of the list in Table 4.1 are Joni Hersch, Joel Huber, and Richard

Table 4.1 W. Kip Viscusi coauthors by number of publications[a]

Number of publications	*Coauthor*
20	Joni Hersch, Joel Huber
19	Richard Zeckhauser
18	
17	
16	
15	Wesley A. Magat, Michael J. Moore
14	
13	
12	Patricia Born
11	
10	Jason Bell, James T. Hamilton
9	
8	
7	William N. Evans, Ted Gayer, Jahn K. Hakes
6	Joseph E. Aldy, Thomas J. Kniesner
5	
4	Harrell Chesson, James P. Ziliak
3	Fernando Antoñanzas, Roy Boyd, Irineu Carvalho, Kerry Krutilla, Joan Rovira, Robert L. Scharff
2	Francisco J. Braña, Alan Carlin, Gerald Cavallo, Alison Del Rossi, Mark K. Dreyfus, Reid Hastie, Jeffrey O'Connell, Fabiola Portillo
1	James Albright, R. Michael Allen, Jay Austin, Tom Baker, Donald A. Berry, Glenn Blackmon, Carl Bruch, Caroline Cecot, Mariam Coaster, Mark Cohen, Christopher J. Conover, Joan Costa, P. Christopher Dockins, Howard L. Dorfman, Hristos Doucouliagos, David L. Durbin, Scott Farrow, Anne Forrest, Anil Gaba, William M. Gentry, John C. Gore, Wendy L. Gramm, Henry Grabowski, Warren Hart, Joseph M. Johnson, Owen D. Jones, Chulho Jung, Paul W. Kolp, Stephan Kroll, Randall Lutter, Benjamin J. McMichael, Kristen Merkle, Bruce D. Meyer, John F. Morrall, Charles O'Connor, Mary O'Keefe, Owen R. Phillips, Baxter P. Rogers, Steven R. Rowland, Frank A. Sloan, T.D. Stanley, Charles J. Walsh, Kathryn Whetten-Goldstein, Christopher Woock, David H. Zald

[a]This list includes all articles published through 2014

Zeckhauser. Each of these individuals has collaborated with me on an enormous and quite varied body of work extending over many years.

The longest-term coauthor of this group is Richard Zeckhauser. I prepared my undergraduate thesis under his direction at Harvard, and he served on my doctoral dissertation committee as well. During graduate school I worked for him as a research assistant. In that capacity, I had the opportunity to collaborate with him on two of my first articles. We have continued to coauthor articles, as two of our articles will be published in 2015, which will make him my most frequent coauthor. In addition to his original mentorship role, a principal reason for the coauthorship efforts is a commonality in research interests, particularly with respect to societal regulation of health and safety risks. The principal continuing approach in our joint work has been the application of benefit-cost analysis principles to health, safety, and environmental regulations. Our joint research has also involved an increased exploration of the role of behavioral factors as they relate to anti-terrorism policies, climate change policies, and federal drug regulation.

Notwithstanding the commonality of many of our interests, there is a difference in our skill set with respect to relative emphasis on economic theory and empirical research. The dividends of this coauthorship experience extend far beyond the article count and the impact of the particular articles. This collaboration early in my career helped to shape my subsequent research efforts and to deal with the strategic aspects of the publication process. I attribute much of my early ability to publish articles from my dissertation to the experience I acquired in working with him.

Joni Hersch is my wife, and we met as coauthors. The genesis of our first article, "Cigarette Smoking, Seatbelt Use, and Wage-Risk Tradeoffs," which appeared in the *Journal of Human Resources* in 1990, was as follows. When she came to the Northwestern economics department as a visiting professor, she had an original employment data set based on a survey that she designed and administered in Oregon. The survey made it possible to estimate compensating differentials for job risks and to link these choices to personal risk-taking behaviors based on other questions in the survey, principally cigarette smoking and use of seatbelts. These potential linkages were of tremendous interest to me given the primary focus of my research on health and safety risks.

Much of our subsequent research also focused on determinants of wage-risk trade-offs. Perhaps our most prominent collaboration is with respect to estimation of compensating differentials for risk in which we found that there is labor market segmentation as different labor market groups face different market offer curves for job risk. Our conceptualization of the market opportunities facing workers differed from that of standard hedonic labor market models, which assume that workers are picking off different points on identical labor market offer curves, that is, the maximum wage rate workers can receive for different levels of health and safety risk. Contrary to the standard theory, we found that different labor market groups faced quite distinct labor market offer curves with starkly different rates of trade-off between wages and risks. In particular, the wage gradient that workers receive for increases in the risk on the job is often quite different. These differences in labor market offer curves account for the lower premiums for job risks received by smokers and by Mexican immigrants (Viscusi and Hersch 2001; Hersch and Viscusi 2010). In the case of Mexican immigrants who are not fluent in English, the workers incur much greater fatality risks on the job than do other comparable workers, but they receive much lower total compensating differentials for these risks. Contrary to the usual predictions of the theory, these workers do not receive more additional wage compensation for the greater marginal risks that they incur. We have continued to collaborate on related topics that often reflect the intersection of law and economics with the regulation of health and safety, such as the proper use of value of statistical life estimates in setting punitive damages amounts in litigation contexts.

The third of my most frequent coauthors is Joel Huber, who is a marketing professor at Duke University. Our long-term collaboration has emerged out of a series of survey projects, many of which were undertaken with the late economist, Wesley A. Magat. Huber's expertise in the design, administration, and analysis of survey data has been of continuing importance on a broad range of topics. The first set of studies involved an exploration of the role of hazard warnings for chemical and pesticide products. The surveys involved the development of alternative labels and mock consumer products and the administration of the survey to ascertain the impact of alternative labels using an experimental design. The research documented the potentially constructive effect of different warnings on risk beliefs and precautionary behavior, thus providing an economic foundation for many of the recent policy recommendations advocated by those in favor of regulations that rely on "nudge" approaches rather than on command and control regulations.

The survey studies have also examined a wide range of issues that cannot be readily resolved using available market data. These studies have illuminated the role of ambiguity aversion in the presence of conflicting risk studies, the asymmetry between willingness-to-pay and willingness-to-accept values for changes in product risks, the determinants of household recycling behavior, and stated preference valuations for environmental benefit effects such as reductions in the risks of chronic bronchitis, cancer, and gastrointestinal illness. Many researchers in the field of marketing were more receptive than were economists to alternatives to the standard expected utility model so that this collaboration often adopted a behavioral economics perspective that served to provide a good check on the validity of more traditional economic frameworks.

At the other extreme from these regular coauthors are 45 individuals who have coauthored only a single article with me. These collaborations often arose because of specific projects or narrowly framed research questions. And, in a few instances, the people are listed because I was collaborating with a scientist who works in a field where there is often a large roster of coauthors including some people who were not directly involved in the research.

Since my publication efforts were jump-started by my collaboration with Richard Zeckhauser, who was my advisor as both an undergraduate and graduate student, I have attempted to carry on the tradition. A total of 62 of my coauthorships listed in Table 4.1 are with former doctoral students or graduate student research assistants. The most frequent collaborator in this group is Patricia Born, who developed expertise in working with detailed firm level insurance data that we used in our collaborations while she was a graduate student at Duke University. All of our coauthorship projects since then have involved similar insurance data analyses. Jason Bell has served as the computer programmer and frequent coauthor of my survey-based research with Joel Huber. William N. Evans, Ted Gayer, Jahn K. Hakes, Joseph E. Aldy, Harrell Chesson, Robert L. Scharff, and Mark K. Dreyfus have all collaborated with me on risk-related projects, almost all of which involved some aspect of the estimation of the value of a statistical life.

Notwithstanding the prominence of Joni Hersch and Patricia Born among my most frequent coauthors, there is a pronounced gender disparity in my list of coauthors. Only 19% of my collaborations in Table 4.1 are with female coauthors. This gap may be due in part to the greater representation of men in the economics profession generally or perhaps due to the nature of the research topics. The differential is not driven by the most frequent coauthors, as female coauthors constitute a very similar 17% of the one-time coauthors.

4.5 Summary Statistics of Publications

Although economists tend to focus primarily on writing articles, my research output has consisted of both articles and books. In each case, half of my research output has been coauthored. I have written or edited 24 books. Of this group, 19 are authored rather than edited volumes. Nine of the authored books were coauthored. The five edited volumes show a similar emphasis, with two of the five edited books being coedited. The division for academic articles is similar with half of my articles being singly authored, as 167 out of 331 articles are singly authored.

The average article statistics across my career shows a similar pattern. For purposes of these calculations of annual output, I use the 1976 date of my doctoral dissertation as the starting point, thus excluding one previously published article drawn from my undergraduate thesis. As indicated in Table 4.2, the mean number of articles per year is 8.4, of which 4.2 are coauthored. Almost identical annual article publication values of 8 for total articles and 4 for coauthored articles are reflected in the medians. The distributions for the first quartile and the upper quartile indicate that the high coauthorship years are also associated with higher total article output.

4.6 Publications Over the Life Cycle

Figure 4.1 provides a graphical summary by age of the total number of articles and the number of coauthored articles. The starting point at age 23 is an article from my undergraduate thesis, and age 27 was the year I obtained my Ph.D. Apart from my two collaborations with Zeckhauser,

Table 4.2 Distribution of annual number of articles and coauthored articles

			Percentile		
	Mean	*Std. Dev.*	*25th*	*50th*	*75th*
Total articles	8.4	4.3	5	8	11
Coauthored articles	4.2	3.0	2	4	7

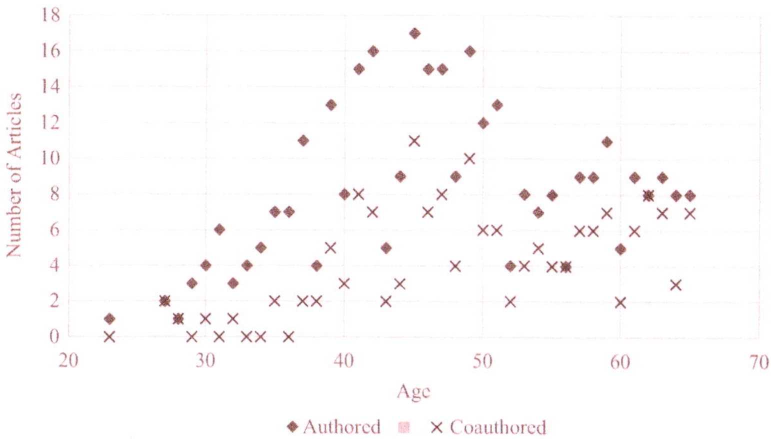

Fig. 4.1 Annual number of authored and coauthored articles

most of my articles through my late 30s were singly authored. Most of these articles were based on topics first addressed in my doctoral dissertation on job safety, which was subsequently published as a book (Viscusi 1979) and led to a series of related explorations. The reliance on singly authored work regarding the value of a statistical life has continued throughout my career, including an article just published in early 2015. However, I have also collaborated with other researchers on important facets of the topic. Among my most notable collaborations not already discussed above are estimations of age variations in both the value of a statistical life and the value of a life year with Joseph E. Aldy, explorations of the role of discounting years of life with Michael J. Moore, and analyses of compensating differentials using panel data with Thomas J. Kniesner and James P. Ziliak.

The last year in which I had no coauthored articles on any topic was at age 36 in 1985. The number of coauthored articles jumped to five at age 39 in 1988, which marked the development of two ongoing collaborations with colleagues at Duke University. The lines of research were separate as I undertook studies of job risks with Michael J. Moore and a series of studies funded by the EPA with Joel Huber and Wesley A. Magat. Nevertheless, the singly authored article total for that year was eight, which exceeded the number for collaborative efforts.

As the trends in Fig. 4.1 indicate, the collaborations continued at an increasing level through my 40s. The peak both in terms of total articles published in that year and total coauthored articles was at age 45 with a 17 article total, of which 11 were coauthored. However, the tally of ten coauthored articles out of 16 total articles in 1998 is not far behind. This publication surge is attributable in large part to a series of ongoing EPA-funded research projects on several different topics.

The decreased role of EPA-funded research in the past few years has stabilized my productivity over the past decade to about eight total articles per year, most of which have been coauthored. All eight of the articles at age 62 were coauthored, marking only the fourth year in which all of my published articles were coauthored.

The increased rate of coauthorship has also tracked the changes in my institutional affiliations. My coauthorship rate was 22% at Northwestern, 43% at Duke, 57% at Harvard, and 69% at Vanderbilt. This upward trend seems largely attributable to the temporal trend of coauthorship in economics and life-cycle effects rather than institutional influences. Most of my collaborations while at Vanderbilt have been with long-time coauthors, with my principal Vanderbilt colleague coauthor being Joni Hersch, who moved to Vanderbilt with me.

4.7 Conclusion

Certainly the major payoff of coauthorship has been with respect to providing insights and developing methodological approaches that would not otherwise have been possible. All of my coauthors have made genuine contributions to the research, and hopefully my contributions have been valuable as well. The result is that I have been able to pursue a much broader range of economic issues using much more diverse methodologies than would have been possible working alone. In some cases, the research would not have been feasible at all working as a solo researcher. While it is quite feasible for theorists to work alone in their offices and develop path-breaking theorems, much empirical and policy research necessarily requires a larger-scale enterprise. It is not entirely surprising that the optimal production functions for economic research often require more than one worker.

Another contributor to the value of collaboration is drawing on researchers in different disciplines. My coauthors have principally been economists. But they have also included psychologists, lawyers, mathematicians, marketing professors, neuroscience professors, and an occasional political scientist or industry official. Drawing on insights from different fields often generates substantial rewards. For example, the emergence of law and economics as a field of inquiry and the rise of behavioral economics each are due in large part to the collaboration of economists and researchers with quite different disciplinary backgrounds.

Working with coauthors has also been a very entertaining and enjoyable experience wholly apart from the productivity effects. I hope my coauthors have enjoyed the collaborations as much as I have.

References

Arrow, K. J. (1951). *Social choice and individual values.* New Haven: Yale University Press.

Hamilton, J. T., & Viscusi, W. K. (1999). *Calculating risks? The spatial and political dimensions of hazardous waste policy.* Cambridge: MIT Press.

Hersch, J., & Viscusi, W. K. (1990). Cigarette smoking, seatbelt use, and differences in wage-risk tradeoffs. *Journal of Human Resources, 25*(2), 202–227.

Hersch, J., & Viscusi, W. K. (2010). Immigrant status and the value of statistical life. *Journal of Human Resources, 45*(3), 749–771.

Samuelson, P. A. (1996). On collaboration. *The American Economist, 40*(2), 16–21.

Smith, A. (1776). *The wealth of nations.* New York: Modern Library (1937).

Sunstein, C. R., Hastie, R., Payne, J. W., Schkade, D. A., & Viscusi, W. K. (2002). *Punitive damages: How juries decide.* Chicago: University of Chicago Press.

Viscusi, W. K., Vernon, J. M., & Harrington, J. E., Jr. (2005). *Economics of regulation and antitrust.* 4th ed. Cambridge: MIT Press.

Viscusi, W. K. (1979). *Employment hazards: An investigation of market performance.* Cambridge: Harvard University Press.

Viscusi, W. K., & Hersch, J. (2001). Cigarette smokers as job risk takers. *Review of Economics and Statistics, 83*(2), 269–280.

Viscusi, W. K., & Zeckhauser, R. (1976). Environmental policy choice under uncertainty. *Journal of Environmental Economics and Management, 3*(2), 97–112.

CHAPTER 5

Age, Cohort and Co-authorship: The Statistics of Collaboration

Daniel S. Hamermesh

The previously documented trend toward more co- and multi-authored research in economics is partly (perhaps 20 percent) due to different research styles of scholars in different birth cohorts (of different ages). Most of the trend reflects on profession-wide changes in research style. Older scholars show greater variation in their research styles than younger ones, who use similar numbers of co-authors in each published paper; but there are no differences across cohorts in scholars' willingness to work with different co-authors. There are only small gender differences in the impacts of age on numbers of co-authors, but substantial differences on choice of co-authors. I offer advice to aging economists on aiding their junior co-authors.

5.1 Background

In medicine and the natural sciences it has long been *de rigueur* for scientific articles to list numerous co-authors (Zuckerman 1977). In economics co- and multi-authorship are increasingly the norm, as shown through the

D.S. Hamermesh (✉)
Royal Holloway University of London, Egham, UK

M. Szenberg, L.B. Ramrattan (eds.), *Collaborative Research in Economics*, DOI 10.1007/978-3-319-52800-7_5

Table 5.1 Distribution of full-length refereed articles by co-authorship status, *AER*, *JPE* and *QJE*, 1963–2011*

Year	*Number of articles*	*Distribution of number of authors*			
		Pr{2+}	*Pr{3|2+}*	*Pr{4|3+}*	*Pr{5|4+}*
1963	86	0.163	0.000	0.000	0.000
1973	119	0.286	0.029	0.000	0.000
1983	125	0.456	0.140	0.000	0.000
1993	136	0.551	0.280	0.095	0.000
2003	135	0.741	0.280	0.214	0.000
2011	147	0.796	0.385	0.222	0.200

*Includes all full-length original articles, except Nobel and Presidential addresses. Calculated from Table 2 of Hamermesh (2013)

1970s by McDowell and Melvin (1983) and through the early 1990s by Hudson (1996) and Laband and Tollison (2000). Especially noteworthy is the acceleration of co-authorship in economics since then. Consider the evidence in Table 5.1 (reproduced from Hamermesh 2013), showing patterns of co-authorship in the three leading general journals in economics—the *American Economic Review*, the *Journal of Political Economy* and the *Quarterly Journal of Economics*. In the 1960s a jointly authored paper was a rarity; today in these leading outlets it is standard. Moreover, these summary statistics show that the distribution of the number of authors of a paper in these journals has shifted monotonically rightward, so that today having four or more authors on a paper in these top journals is quite common.

Along with this growth in the number of authors on published papers in economics has come a surprising shift in the age distribution of those authors. From the 1960s through the early 1990s top-flight publishing in economics appeared to be a young person's "game." As Table 5.2 shows, beginning in the 1990s there was a sharp increase in the fraction of articles that included older co-authors. While the nearly 20 percent of co-authors ages 51 and over is still below the fraction of academic economists in that age range (Hamermesh 2013), the distribution of ages of those publishing in these journals is much closer to their representation in the relevant population today than it was in the last half of the twentieth century.

This striking change in the age patterns of publishing and the increasing presence of older authors make a positive examination of the relationship

Table 5.2 Percent distributions of age of authors, top three general economics journals, 1963–2011*

Year	*Age Distribution of Authors*		
	≤35	*36–50*	*51+*
1963	50.5	45.3	4.2
1973	61.5	32.6	5.9
1983	48.5	47.2	4.3
1993	49.8	43.1	7.1
2003	36.8	50.4	12.8
2011	33.0	48.1	18.9

*Includes all full-length original articles, except Nobel and Presidential addresses. Age could not be found for three authors in 1963, one author in 1973. The distributions are weighted by the inverse of the number of authors in the publication. Calculated from Table 1 of Hamermesh (2013)

between aging and co-authoring interesting. Also, my personal interest in aging and co-authorship (as a 71-year-old still trying to publish in refereed outlets) makes this topic personally attractive. So too, perhaps comments based on my experience in co-authoring may be useful to other older economists—and to their juniors who may co-author with them.

In this chapter, I therefore examine several sets of data that I have assembled on patterns of co-authoring to discover some new facts about the relationship between co-authoring and age among economists. I focus on the determinants of the trend in co-authorship in relation to age and on the interactions among co-authors—the differences in age among them and the persistence of co-authoring relationships as careers progress. Based on my personal experiences, I finish by offering some advice to older economists that might help them advance the careers of the younger scholars with whom they work and have the additional benefit of offering a self-control mechanism that might enable them to avoid being viewed as senescent limelight-hogs by their colleagues.

5.2 Age, Cohort or Time?

Is the growth of co-authorship in economics publishing specific to the times? Does it result from the predominance among those currently publishing of scholars who came of age in the 2000s? Or does it stem from the effect of aging on scholars' behavior? This last possibility seems unlikely from the cross-section evidence above, since regression estimates in Hamermesh (2013) showed that scholars ages 51+ are no more likely than much younger scholars to publish co-authored works in the very top journals in the field. But that comparison does not allow us to examine this possibility seriously. To distinguish cohort effects from time effects, we need to obtain longitudinal data describing individuals' careers from their beginning until, where possible, advanced age (as pointed out by Borjas 1985, in the analogous case of the time paths of immigrants' earnings relative to natives').

As a start to examining this issue I provide an anecdote—my own publishing history. By my count I have published 118 journal articles in my career, beginning in 1966 and going through 2013, of which 54 (46 percent) were co-authored (with 52 different individuals). During the first half of my career thus far (24 years, 1966–1989), 12 of the 40 papers published (30 percent) were co-authored; during the second half (1990–2013) 42 out of the 78 published papers (54 percent) were co-authored. These longitudinal data ($N = 1$, $T = 48$) are obviously not drawn from a random sample. If, however, one makes the giant leap to assuming that one economist's professional life is a random sample from the population of all economists, a test of the difference in publishing behavior over these two halves of my career rejects the hypothesis that these two fractions are equal ($t = 3.79$).[1]

As Zvi Griliches once remarked to me, "The plural of anecdote is data." To go beyond anecdote and examine these issues seriously, I have collected the publication records of all the economists ages 80 or under who were alive on January 1, 2014, and who are or were either: (1) Fellows of the Society of Labor Economists; and/or (2) Winners of the Institute for the Study of Labor (IZA) Prize in Labor Economics or its Young Labor Economist Award. This population of awardees—this sample of labor economists—consists of 83 scholars, of whom I excluded four because I could not obtain *curricula vitae* that were less than four years old. The remaining sample members were born between 1933 and 1980.

The analysis is based on a highly selected sample of 79 people from the population of all scholars who might be classified as labor economists. It includes three Nobel Prize winners, five Past Presidents of the American Economic Association or the Royal Economic Society, six winners of the John Bates Clark Medal or its European equivalent (the Yrjö Jahnsson Award) and 37 who are also Fellows of the Econometric Society (and who include all members of the first three groups as subsets).

The data set contains information on 3968 articles published in journals by these 79 people up through early 2014. In constructing the data set I included both refereed and non-refereed publications, although the overwhelming majority of papers apparently consist of refereed papers. Notes, comments, Presidential/Nobel lectures and so on are all included, so long as they were published in a journal outlet. For each paper we collected the names of all authors listed on the paper, right-truncating (in two cases) at seven authors. The 79 authors' names are listed in the Appendix.

Unlike the samples underlying Tables 5.1 and 5.2, which include all authors regardless of their distinction who published in the most prestigious outlets in the economics profession in several particular years, this sample contains all the journal publications by a distinguished sample of authors. Thus as a first check on this new sample I examine whether the pattern of increasing co-authorship over time that was shown in Table 5.1 also prevailed here. Data describing the numbers and frequency distributions of journal articles published by these scholars in each of the same six decades as in Table 5.1 are presented in the upper panel of Table 5.3.

These data show very similar patterns of co-authorship to those in Table 5.1. The fraction of co-authored papers rose from around two-fifths in the 1960s and 1970s to five-sixths in the 2010s. These fractions are slightly above those in the first column of Table 5.1, but the rise in

Table 5.3 Distribution of Journal Articles by Co-authorship Status, 79 Labor Economists, 1964–2014, and Descriptive Statistics—Means, Standard Deviations and Ranges

Year	*Number of articles*	*Distribution of number of authors*			
		Pr{2+}	*Pr{3+|2+}*	*Pr{4+|3+}*	*Pr{5+|4+}*
1960s	33	0.424	0.000	0.000	0.000
1970s	338	0.328	0.129	0.067	0.000
1980s	741	0.587	0.195	0.165	0.357
1990s	1081	0.717	0.289	0.156	0.143
2000s	1273	0.739	0.451	0.267	0.265
2010s	502	0.833	0.660	0.308	0.412

Birth year	*Ph.D. year*	*Age when published*	*Number of articles*	*Age at Ph.D.*
1956	1984	45.2	50.3	27.9
(12.9)	(13.8)	(10.9)	(35.7)	(2.2)
[1933, 1980]	[1962, 2012]	[21, 79]	[3, 184]	[24, 35]

co-authorship is of similar size. The differences in levels may arise from the nature of research in what is predominantly an empirical sub-specialty and from the broad range of quality of the journals in which these scholars' articles are published.

Even beyond matching the secular change in the pattern of co-authorship, these data replicate the increasing fraction of multi-authored (3+ authors) papers conditional on any co-authorship. While the incidence of co-authorship rose sharply after the 1970s, the incidence of multi-authorship increased monotonically across the decades in this sample, so that in the 2010s a majority of these authors' publications were part of at least three-author collaborations. Indeed, in the current decade over one-sixth of their publications contain four or more authors.

The criteria for inclusion in the sample are based partly on career distinction, so that unsurprisingly the mean age of the sample members in 2014 is quite high—58. As the lower half of Table 5.3 shows, however, the mean age when the articles in the sample were published was only 45. The 58-year range in authors' ages at time of publication ensures that we have enough sampling variation to examine the relationship among the incidence of co-authorship, trends and aging. The average age when these authors obtained their Ph.D. degree was 28, but here too there is substantial variation: The age ranges from 24 to 35.[2]

The average number of journal articles published up through early 2014 in this sample was 50. Of course, the more senior members of the sample had published more articles, but even within age groups there are large differences in rates of publishing activity. Thus the 39 authors ages 60+ in 2014 had published an average of 65 papers, with a range of 20–184 journal articles, while those under age 50 in 2014 (21 of the authors) had published an average of 19 papers, with a range of 3–101. In short, there is substantial sampling variation among these authors, even within the same age cohort, and even at the same calendar time.

Having shown that co-authorship and multi-authorship have risen in this sample, as in articles published in the top journals, we can use these data covering entire careers to examine whether their incidence has risen with age over these authors' careers. As a first step consider the results in Figs. 5.1 and 5.2, showing the relationship between authorship and birth year. They make it completely clear that co- and multi-authorship are more prevalent among scholars in more recent birth cohorts.[3]

That there has been an increase over time in the fraction of co-authored and multi-authored articles is well known and clear from both of the data

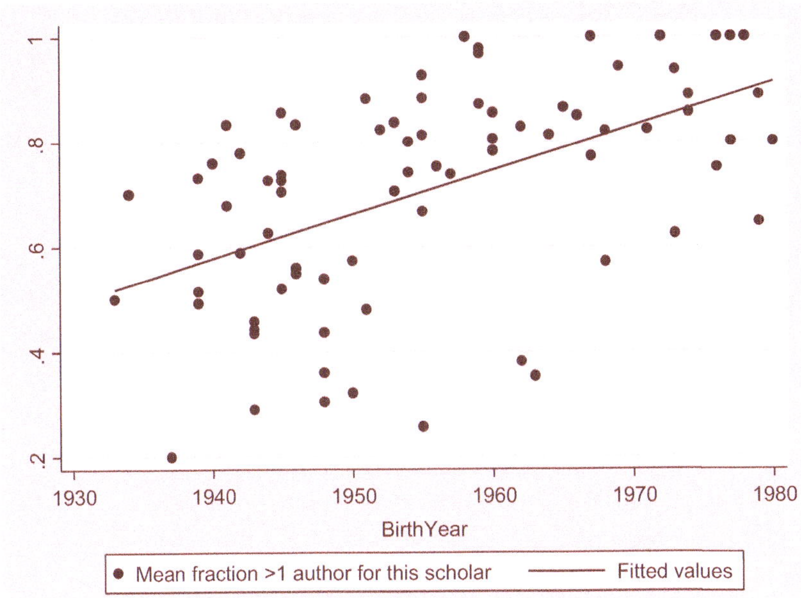

Fig. 5.1 Relation between birth year and co-authorship, $N = 79$

sets used in this study. Is this a general trend? Is it due to the increased fraction of older authors among publishers (since, as Table 5.2 showed, there has been a sharp increase in the fraction of older economists among authors of articles in leading journals), and authors have tended to do more co-authoring as they have aged. Or is it a cohort effect, with authors in more recent cohorts being more likely to co-author at the same age as authors from earlier cohorts?

Let C_{iat} be an indicator of a publication having been co-authored, where i is a publication, a is an indicator for the author (from among the 79 in this sample), and t represents the year. (A similar equation could be written for the number of authors on a paper.) Let AGE_{at} be author a's age in year t, and $BIRTHYEAR_a$ be author a's birth year. Then we can estimate any of the following three equations:[4]

$$C_{iat} = \alpha_0 + \alpha_1 t + \alpha_2 AGE_{at} + \varepsilon_{iat} \quad (1a)$$

$$C_{iat} = \beta_0 + \beta_1 t + \beta_2 \text{ BIRTHYEAR}_a + \xi_{iat} \quad (1b)$$

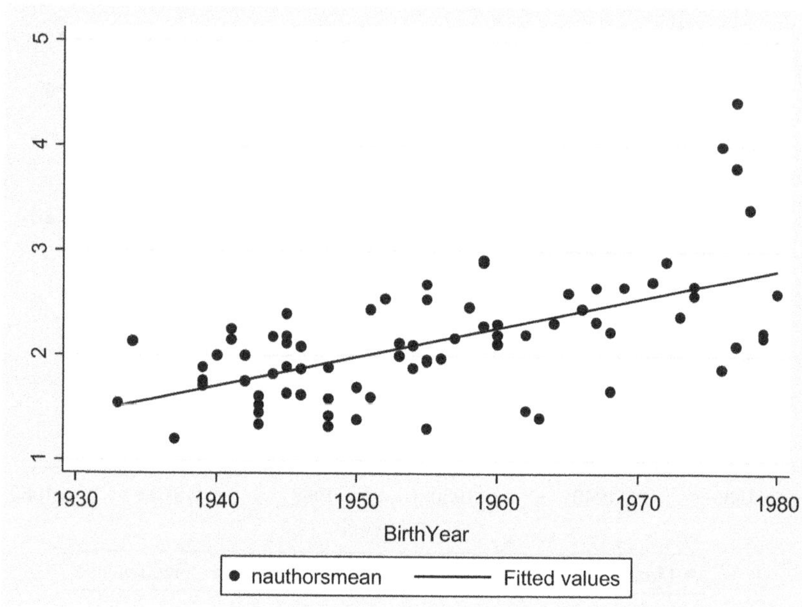

Fig. 5.2 Relation between birth year and average number of authors, $N = 79$

or

$$C_{iat} = \gamma_0 + \gamma_1 \text{ BIRTHYEAR}_a + \gamma_2 AGE_{at} + \nu_{iat}, \quad (1c)$$

where, the α, β and γ are parameters, and the ε, ξ and ν are random error terms. Because of the identity:

$$t \equiv AGE_{at} + \text{BIRTHYEAR}_a, \quad (2)$$

we cannot identify time, age and cohort effects separately; but we can identify the parameters in any of the three pairs implied by the variables included in equations (1). Since the literature has stressed the secular rise in co-authorship, I estimate only (1a) and (1b), implicitly assuming that there is a trend effect and trying to examine how much of the effect that is measured when α_2 or β_2 is set equal to 0 is due to differential behavior across cohorts or with age.

Before estimating (1a) and (1b), much of what might be inferred from the estimates of (1b) is discernable from the statistics in Table 5.4. The first three columns describe the publishing activities of the 34 authors in the earliest cohort (Ph.D. received before 1980) in each of three time periods: 1962–1979, 1980–1999 and 2000–2014. Within this cohort, the propensity to co-author increased over time, as did the propensity to be involved in multi-authorships. The same increase is visible in columns (4) and (5) for the 29 scholars in the 1980–1999 Ph.D. cohort. Comparing columns (2) and (4), or columns (3) and (5), the table also shows that during the same time period scholars from the earliest cohort were less likely than scholars from the middle cohort to co-author or be one of multiple authors. The point is demonstrated even more strongly by adding the statistics in column (6) to this comparison: The 16 members of the most recent cohort (Ph.D. received between 2000 and 2012) are even more likely than scholars in either of the two earlier cohorts to have published co-authored articles, and even more likely to have multiple authors listed on their papers, between 2000 and 2014.

The comparisons suggested by Table 5.4 are borne out by the results of probits and ordered probits describing the propensity for co- and multi-authorship that are presented in Table 5.5. Throughout I present the probit derivatives describing co-authorship and cluster standard errors on the authors.[5] The equations also include indicators for the decade in which the article was published, thus expanding α_1 and β_1 into vectors of parameters and taking into account what Table 5.3 suggested were discrete increases

Table 5.4 Descriptive statistics of articles, 79 labor economists, 3968 articles, by date published and author's Ph.D. Cohort

Authors	*Author Ph.D. Year*			*Year Published**		
	1962–1979	*1980–1999*	*2000–2014*	*1962–1979*	*1980–1999*	*2000–2014*
1	62.2	39.6	34.4	22.9	16.2	15.1
2	33.8	46.3	34.9	55.2	39.8	33.6
3	3.7	12.0	21.6	18.3	31.8	37.1
4	0.3	1.5	6.6	3.2	7.9	9.3
5+	0	0.6	2.5	0.5	4.3	4.9
No. of articles	370	1168	717	652	853	205
No. of authors	34	34	34	29	29	16

*Three of the 3968 articles in the sample are excluded here. One was published in 1979 by a scholar who received the Ph.D. in 1983, and two were published in 1999 by a scholar who received the degree in 2000

Table 5.5 Estimates of the determinants of the number of authors of Journal Articles, 79 labor economists, 3968 articles, 1964–2014*

	Co-authored			*No. of Authors*		
	Probit derivatives			*Ordered probit coefficients*		
Equation	*(1a)*	*(1b)*		*(1a)*	*(1b)*	
Ind. Var.						
Age	–	−0.0051	–	–	−0.0090	–
		(0.0018)			(0.0045)	
Birth year	–	0.0062	−0.0322	–	0.0128	−0.0580
		(0.0019)	(0.0107)		(0.0047)	(0.0262)
Ph.D. year	–	–	0.0375	–	–	0.0684
			(0.0103)			(0.0250)
	0.059	0.062	0.076	0.053	0.055	0.060

*All equations include a vector of indicators of the decade in which the article was published, with the 1960s as the excluded decade. Standard errors are clustered on the authors

in the propensity for co- and multi-authorships in the 1980s, the 1990s and the 2010s.[6] The estimates of (1a) indicate that in a given decade older economists were less likely to write co- or multi-authored articles, while the estimates of (1b) show that scholars in the earlier cohorts were also less likely than their younger colleagues to publish such work.[7]

Adding author fixed effects to the estimates in columns (1) and (4) and including a quadratic in age does not change these conclusions. Indeed, over a 47-year interval of a scholar's journal publications (the longest that is observed in these data—for two authors in the sample) the expected incidence of co-authorship would have risen by 25 percentage points. The quadratic terms are important—the rate of increase of co-authorship slows with age, as does the rate of growth in the number of authors listed on these scholars' articles. But even with the deceleration in these phenomena as the scholars age, the incidence of co-authorship in the sample only stops increasing after age 62, while the estimated number of authors never decreases with age within the sample range of ages.

Assuming that there is some trend in co-authorship, the identity in (2) prevents us from extricating cohort from aging effects in this trend. We can, however, infer how much of the gross upward trends in co- and multi-authorship are due to aging and/or cohort effects in this sample by comparing the estimate of β_1 with and without β_2 constrained to equal zero. Concentrating on the propensity for co-authorship, and estimating

(1b) with only a time trend, the estimated probit derivative $\beta_1 = 0.0102$. With β_2 unconstrained, the estimate of β_1 falls to 0.0079. A reasonable conclusion is that age/cohort effects account for perhaps around 20 percent of the gross trend increase in the propensity to co-author.[8]

While we cannot break the identity in (2), we can take advantage of the fact that authors in the same birth cohort (and thus of the same age in a year when they both published journal articles) earned their Ph.D. degrees in different years. The correlation between birth year and Ph.D. year is, of course, very high (+0.98), but it is not one. I thus re-estimate (1b), expanding the specification to include Ph.D. year. The results when both birth year and Ph.D. year are included in the specification are shown in columns (3) and (6) of Table 5.5. Not surprisingly, the coefficients nearly sum to the estimates of β_2 presented in columns (2) and (5), and their individual significance levels are substantially reduced from those of the earlier estimates. Nonetheless, they do suggest that, given the year when they published and the year when they were born, those scholars who received their Ph.D. degree later in life (who can be viewed as having entered the profession later in life) were more likely to publish co- and multi-authored papers.[9] This finding suggests that the trends in co- and multi-authorship have something to do with the research styles that one learns from what the profession is doing during one's Ph.D. program or very early in one's publishing career.

A number of other variables might be expected to alter the relationships described in (1).

For example, respondents who have positions in the best economics departments might have more and better Ph.D. students with whom to co-author. Adding an indicator for the top ten economics departments in North America and the top two in the United Kingdom, which describes almost half the 79 respondents, to the estimates in Table 5.5 of Equations (1a) and (1b) never changes the first significant digit of the estimate of the crucial parameter; and the indicator itself, although it enters positively, has t-statistics well below one. Another possibility is that co-authoring practices are different between North America and the rest of the world, and that this difference is correlated with age/cohort. Scholars at North American institutions, who account for five-sixths of the sample, are (nearly significantly) less likely to co-author, and have fewer co-authors when they do, than scholars of the same age at the same time on other continents. Nonetheless, the estimated effects of age or birth year hardly change in size or statistical significance from what is shown in Table 5.5.

Until fairly recently tabulations of citations only recorded the name of the first author of an article; and even now the custom in the text of a published paper is to list no more than two authors, relegating additional authors to inclusion in "et al." Not wishing to be known as "Al," and in a discipline where alphabetical order is customary (see Engers et al. 1999), scholars with surnames late in the alphabet may strategically avoid or limit their co-authoring. To examine this possibility I created a variable ranging from 1 for "A" to 23 for "W" in this sample, indicating the numerical position of the first letter of the scholar's surname, and added it to the estimates of (1a) and (1b). Its inclusion changed the estimated impact of age (birth year) by less than two in the second significant digit, and its own coefficients were unexpectedly positive, although with t-statistics less than one.

Overall the results suggest that cohort effects are important in explaining the observed upward trends in co- and multi-authorship in economics. The dominant component of those trends, however, is general and cannot be attributed to differences in behavior among scholars of different cohorts, or to changes in co- and multi-authorship patterns with age. While the causes of these (about which I speculated in Hamermesh 2013, and which Jones 2009, modeled) are unclear, they are not the result of inherent differences in people's behavior resulting from aging or from differences among people educated at different times.

5.3 Prior Co-authoring and Productivity

Does having relied more on co-authors in the past alter the relationship between age and publishing productivity? It is difficult to infer causation—to distinguish heterogeneity from state dependence in co-authoring—but we can infer whether those who are more prolific publishers with age have had more previous co-authors. Also, this examination has implications for people's responses to the incentives to publish.

In the sample of 79 labor economists I measure the years since the most recent prior publication for all but each author's first published article. Not surprisingly given the distinction of the scholars in this sample, 57 percent of papers appear in years when the author publishes two or more papers; and another 34 percent appear in print the year after another published paper. Nonetheless, 6 percent of the published papers in the sample appeared after a two-year hiatus, 2 percent after a three-year hiatus, and 1 percent after four years, so that there is scope for examining how the length of time between publications relates to the author's prior co-authoring practice.[10]

Estimates of Poisson regressions describing the hiatus between publications are presented in Table 5.6, which gives results that are qualitatively the same as those of estimates of Poisson regressions describing the numbers of publications in a given year.[11] In each equation, I include the same vector of indicators of the decade of publication as was included in the estimates shown in Table 5.5. The results in the first column show that there is a negative, but statistically insignificant relationship between time since publication and the author's age. Most important, the estimates in the second and third columns show that having previously published more co-authored or multi-authored papers is associated with a shorter hiatus between publications. The estimates in both columns approach statistical significance.[12]

The positive effect of prior co- and multi-authorship on the frequency of publication might be related to heterogeneity in the sample. For example, it may be that authors from the earlier cohorts in the sample, since I selected them based on substantial lifetime achievement, might have published more frequently at the same age than authors from later cohorts. One way to examine this possibility is to include both age and patterns of prior co- and multi-authorship in the equations. Estimates of these expanded equations are shown in the fourth and fifth columns of Table 5.6. They make it clear that this sort of heterogeneity does not matter: The parameter estimates change only slightly from those in columns (2) and (3), and their statistical significance increases.

The authors in this sample are heterogeneous along a variety of unknowable dimensions. To account for this fact I re-estimate the

Table 5.6 Poisson estimates of the determinants of elapsed time between publications, 1966–2014 ($N = 3889$)*

Ind. Var.					
Age	−0.0072	–	–	−0.0099	−0.0100
	(0.0066)			(0.0068)	(0.0070)
Prior average	–	−0.3670	–	−0.4494	–
Co-authored		(0.2161)		(0.2210)	
Prior Average	–	–	−0.1745	–	−0.2344
No. of authors			(0.1287)		(0.1297)
Pseudo-R^2	0.0044	0.0052	0.0045	0.0071	0.0064

*All equations include a vector of indicators of the decade in which the article was published, with the 1960s as the excluded decade. Standard errors are clustered on the authors

equations in columns (2) and (3) including fixed effects for each author, which generates only small changes in the parameter estimates. Overall, the results suggest that having had more co-authors is associated with more frequent subsequent publication. Indeed, given the estimates that are produced when author fixed effects are included, one might even infer that this relationship is causal—that co-authoring makes one more productive (when one defines productivity as a count of the *number* of publications). For a given individual, having had more co-authors up to a particular age leads the scholar to publish more quickly subsequently.

5.4 Age and the Choice of Co-authors

The choice of co-authors reflects the outcome of a matching process. One chooses co-authors based on such factors as complementarities in production, but perhaps also on one's personal preferences—how comfortable one feels working with different individuals. While we cannot examine complementarities in production here, in this and the next section we examine how preferences for people "like oneself"—particularly age and gender—are exhibited.[13]

5.4.1 The Relation Between Age and Co-authors' Ages

The data underlying Tables 5.1 and 5.2 can provide an initial look at how the choice of co-authors differs by the age of authors. Consider the statistics in the first row of Table 5.7, showing the mean absolute age differences between co-authors of two-authored articles in these journals by age of author, where each article is counted as one observation.[14] Young authors (ages 35 and below) and mid-career authors (ages 36–50) have remarkably similar patterns in the ages of those with whom they publish: The average co-author of scholars in these age groups is pretty much the scholar's contemporary. That is not true for the (relatively small and elite) group of older co-authors (those ages 51+). Their co-authors tend to be much different in age—averaging nearly 15 years different. Nearly all the older authors in the sample co-authored with people in the other two age groups, not with their contemporaries. Thus while we observe partnerships among contemporaries until the latter part of a career, partnerships late in a career are disproportionately with younger people. Their co-authors are not, however, likely to be their very recent Ph.D. students:

Table 5.7 Absolute average age difference between authors of two-authored articles, top three general Economics Journals, 1963–2011, means, standard deviations and number of articles*

	Age of Co-author		
Period	*≤35*	*36–50*	*51+*
All 6 years	6.1	6.1	14.6
	(0.69)	(0.45)	(1.42)
	[119]	[139]	[35]
Subperiods			
1963, 1973, 1983	5.6	5.8	20.4
	(8.66)	(4.20)	(5.81)
	[45]	[46]	[5]
1993, 2003, 2011	6.4	6.3	13.6
	(5.29)	(5.85)	(8.45)
	[74]	[93]	[30]

*Includes all full-length original articles, except Nobel and Presidential addresses. Age could not be found for three authors in 1963, one author in 1973

With an average age of these older scholars of 58, a mean absolute difference of 15 years suggests that they are typically co-authoring with their mid-career colleagues.

Why might the difference in the age structure of co-authoring relationships change with age? One likely explanation is suggested by the relative, albeit decreasing rarity of older authors' appearances in this group of elite publishers. With the majority of older economists having ceased publishing, or even trying to publish, the set of potential co-authors with whom a productive older scholar can choose to work necessarily consists mostly of younger scholars. The results in Table 5.7 are explicable by propinquity of interest and energy.[15]

Some direct evidence on this explanation is obtainable by dividing the sample into articles published before and after 1990, taking advantage of the rise in the prevalence of older authors. The statistics are shown in the bottom rows of Table 5.7. While the age differences between co-authors ages 35 or less, or 36–50, did not change significantly over time, older co-authors worked with others who were significantly closer to their age in the latter period than before 1990. This change is consistent with the increasing availability of publishing older authors, providing their peers with an easier search for co-authors who were contemporaries.

5.4.2 *The Stability of Co-authoring Patterns over the Life Cycle*

A related issue is how scholars vary their co-authoring patterns with age, and the extent to which the choice of individuals with whom to co-author persists over time. To examine the first question I use the data on the 79 distinguished labor economists that underlay the analyses in Sections 5.2 and 5.3. For each publication after an author's first I form the coefficient of variation of the number of authors up to and including that publication. To the extent that the number of authors exhibits some randomness across publications, the coefficient of variation will decrease over an author's career (as the author ages). Thus in the analysis here I exclude the first ten (alternatively the first 40) publications by each author. The mean coefficient of variation of the number of authors on their 41st and later articles is 0.40.

Table 5.8 shows estimates of regression equations describing the coefficient of variation of the number of co-authors on all articles beyond the tenth (40th). To account for possible changes in co-authoring behavior beyond those shown in Section 5.2, the estimates hold constant the indicators of the decade when the article was published. The results are remarkably insensitive to the choice of sample: Those in later birth cohorts (younger authors) are significantly less likely to vary the number of scholars with whom they co-author than are scholars who are born earlier (older authors).[16] These two outcomes are quite strongly associated: Moving from birth year 1934–1967, the extremes in the sample of articles

Table 5.8 Regression estimates of relation of birth cohort to lifetime variation in co-authoring patterns (dep. var. is the coefficient of variation)*

Articles no.	*11+*		*41+*	
	All years	*≥2000*	*All years*	*≥2000*
Ind. Var.				
Birth year	−0.0035	−0.0033	−0.0033	−0.0029
	(0.0009)	(0.0009)	(0.0014)	(0.0013)
No. of articles	3202	1604	1507	1081
No. of Authors	70	69	43	42
Adjusted R^2	0.158	0.198	0.152	0.156

*The equations in columns (1) and (3) include a vector of indicators of the decade in which the article was published, with the 1960s and 1970s as the excluded decades. The equations in columns (2) and (4) include an indicator for the 2010s. Standard errors are clustered on the authors

that are at least the 41st in an author's career, decreases the coefficient of variation by 1.8 standard deviations.

The co-authoring behavior of scholars from earlier cohorts is less stable than that of scholars born later, independent of any confounding factors such as the dates when they published. The difference is not due to greater experience (since I held the number of their publications constant), but perhaps arises from their learned ability to pick out co-authors when that is appropriate and to author alone when it is not, or perhaps to differences in preferences across birth cohorts.

5.4.3 *Age and the Identity of Co-authors*

While authors from older cohorts exhibit less stable co-authoring behavior, that fact says nothing about the identity of the scholars with whom they co-author. Their behavior could be less stable, but they could be choosing the same individual or set of scholars when they co-author. To examine their stability defined in terms of their choices of individuals rather than their number, I calculate for each article the cumulative number of different co-authors with whom the scholar has published and the cumulative total number of co-authors, and then define their ratio as the "novelty index" of co-authorship. The novelty index ranges from 0.21 to 1.00 over all the 2701 co-authored articles in the sample. Figure 5.3 presents a scatter of this index and birth year for the most recent publication by each of the 79 authors. There is absolutely no relationship between the two measures: The most recent article published by someone in a more recent cohort is no less likely to reflect repeated matches with particular co-authors than is one by a scholar born earlier.

Estimates of the relationship between the novelty index and the author's birth year are presented in column (1) of Table 5.9 using all 2701 observations; but unlike in the equation fitted to the scatter in Fig. 5.3, here I include a vector of indicators of the decade when the article was published. The results demonstrate that, once we use the cumulative history of all the co-authored articles in the sample, we observe that those in more recent cohorts are more likely to exhibit novelty in their choice of co-authors. The difficulty with this conclusion is that scholars from more recent cohorts (younger authors) have typically written fewer articles, and even fewer co-authored articles, than their senior colleagues. They can be viewed as being engaged in the early stages of a search process for co-authors. One's first co-authored paper is *ipso facto* written with new co-author(s), and to

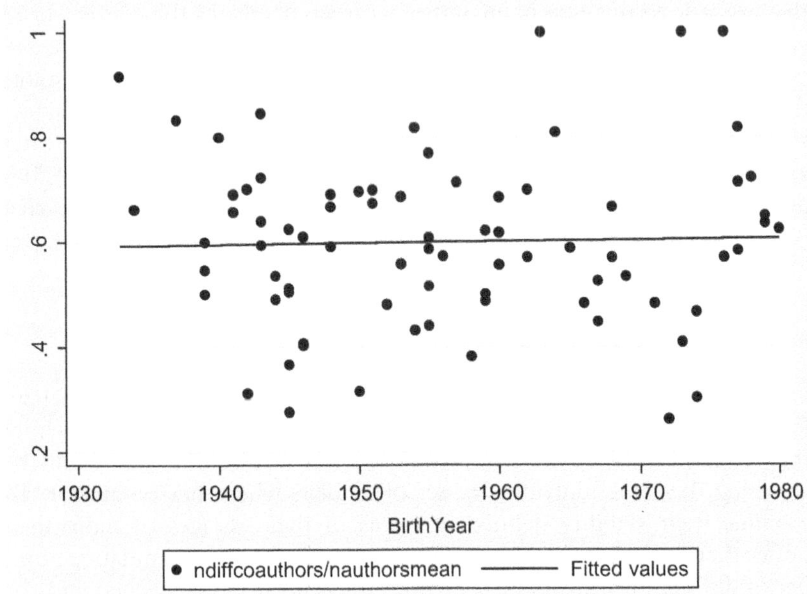

Fig. 5.3 Novelty of co-authors by birth year of author, $N = 79$

Table 5.9 Determinants of the novelty index of co-authors (2701 co-authored articles)*

Ind. Var.			
Birth year	0.0031 (0.0015)	–	−0.0008 (0.0014)
Article number	–	−0.0019 (0.0005)	−0.0020 (0.0005)
Adjusted R^2	0.234	0.295	0.296

*All specifications include a vector of indicators of the decade when the article was published, with the 1960s as the excluded decade. Standard errors are clustered on the authors

the extent that there is some randomness in the choice of co-authors, the next few are more likely to be written with new faces than are subsequent ones. Indeed, the estimates in column (2) of Table 5.9 suggest exactly this—each additional co-authored article reduces the share of an author's new co-authors. Accounting for this fact in column (3), we see that there is absolutely no relationship between birth year (age) and the novelty of co-authors once the authors' differential writing experience is accounted for (holding constant the date when the paper was published).

As an additional step in examining this issue, we can consider whether co-authoring partnerships are stable over a career. Restricting the sample to the 39 authors ages 60+ in 2014 (to allow sufficient time to observe repeated matches), only 36 of the 274 unique co-authorship matches into which these authors entered before age 41 were repeated after age 50.[17] Matching with co-authors does not appear very persistent in this sample—most economists do not "mate" for (their professional) life. Rather, co-authoring in this elite group seems driven by the desire to find the best person or people to work with on specific research questions.

5.5 Aging Female Co-authors

Are women different from men in their co-authoring behavior, in terms of the likelihood of co-authoring as they age and in the relationship between age and the number of co-authors? Previous evidence (McDowell et al. 2006) suggests that gender differences in the propensity to co-author in economics do exist, and Abrevaya and Hamermesh (2012) demonstrate the existence of gender-matching among co-authors. Re-estimates of the models in Section 5.2, however, suggest no difference between men and women in the relationship among age, cohort and time trends in this elite sample (although the paucity of women, 12 of 79 authors, and of their articles, 412 of 3968, sharply reduces the precision of the estimated impact of age for women compared to that for men). We cannot reject the hypothesis that pooled results presented in Table 5.5 describe men's and women's behavior equally well. Female authors are no different from their male counterparts of the same age (cohort) in reflecting the trend toward co-authorship that has characterized published research in economics.

Although the number of authors by age and time period appears independent of gender, perhaps female scholars, whose search for co-authoring partners may differ from that of male scholars, choose their co-authors differently as they age. One possibility is that limitations on search may lead them to "settle down" more than men once they have found co-authors to work with. To examine this possibility, the left-hand side of Table 5.10 presents descriptive statistics on co-authoring behavior by gender, including the number of co-authors and the number of different co-authors. Given the increase in women's participation in the profession, it is unsurprising that the women in the sample are younger, have published fewer papers and have fewer co-authors. What is remarkable is that the novelty index is nearly identical for men and women (0.55 and 0.56).[18] Despite the differences in age of men and women in the sample, novelty in co-authorship is the same for both.

Generalizing from these results may be difficult because five of the twelve women in the sample repeatedly co-author with their spouse/partner, who in some cases is also in the sample. Less important, given the large number of men in the sample, five of the men repeatedly co-author with their spouse/partner. To remove the possible "contamination" of inferences about the search for co-authoring partners by the (previously successful) search for life partners, I delete these ten individuals from the sample. The right hand side of Table 5.10 presents the descriptive statistics for this reduced sample. The remaining women are younger than those who have been deleted (and have published less and have fewer co-authors); but the results on search for co-authors remain essentially unchanged, with the novelty index rising very slightly to 0.56 and 0.58 for men and women, respectively.

The sample of articles published each decade in the top three general journals that underlay Tables 5.1 and 5.2 allows examining whether the general result in Section IV.A., that people choose co-authors of similar ages, differs by gender among authors age 50 or less. (None of the co-authored articles in that sample includes women over age 50, so that I

Table 5.10 Co-author search and gender, descriptive statistics (means and standard deviations)

	All		*Non-partnered*	
	Males	*Females*	*Males*	*Females*
Birth year	1955	1960	1955	1964
	(13.99)	(10.56)	(13.48)	(9.48)
No. of articles	53.13	25.43	34.33	52.98
Total	(37.16)	(20.28)	(37.94)	(11.67)
No. of co-authors	54.34	37.17	54.05	27.29
	(43.98)	(26.38)	(44.68)	(16.49)
No. of different co-authors	29.69	20.92	30.02	15.71
	(21.56)	(17.96)	(21.08)	(8.42)
No. of authors	67	12	62	7
No. of co-authored articles	2399	302	2208	125

cannot examine this issue for scholars over age 50.) The scarcity of even middle-aged female authors might suggest that they are forced to seek out much younger scholars if they wish to collaborate. Comparing authors who are age 35 or less to those who are age 36–50, the average age difference between male authors in the younger group is six years, while that between female authors is five years. The difference between male authors in the older age group is also six years, while female authors age 36–50 write with people who differ in age from them by seven years. The double-difference of two years in age of co-authors by gender is consistent with the need for (the relatively few) middle-aged female co-authors to spread their nets more widely as they age (although the relatively small number of female authors means that the double-difference is not statistically significant).

5.6 Older and Younger Co-authors: Comparisons and Etiquette

5.6.1 Comparing Achievements across Cohorts

Do authors in different cohorts differ in productivity? The difficulty in answering that question is, of course, how one defines productivity. Here I answer this question only very partially, defining productivity as the number of full-time-equivalent journal articles written over a career. Implicitly I am dividing a paper's quality by N, where N is the number of co-authors listed on the paper. I am also ignoring differences in quality, as measured by scholarly impact, that may be related to the joint variation of number of authors and cohort.

Taking this admittedly partial approach, we can at least examine how trends in co-authorship and differences in behavior by cohort affect intercohort comparisons of output (defined here only by quantity). To minimize differences in input quality, I use the sample of labor economists, and I restrict the sample still further to those members who are also Fellows of the Econometric Society and are thus the more successful scholars in this already highly selective sample.

The first two columns of Table 5.11 describe the publishing behavior before age 60 of Fellows in the birth cohorts after 1954 and before 1955. The variables described in the first two rows are obvious and show that the Fellows in the earlier cohort were elected at later ages on average. The number of articles written is almost identical across the two cohorts, but members of the more recent cohort have had more co-authors. The table

Table 5.11 Publication counts and "full-time" equivalent publications, econometric society fellows—means, standard deviations and ranges

	Publications before age			
	60		50	
Sample:	All fellows		Became fellow before age 50	
Birth year:	>1954	<1955	>1964	<1965
Age when elected	39.50	44.78	40.33	40.33
	(5.53)	(7.49)	(5.01)	(5.65)
	[33, 53]	[33, 60]	[33, 47]	[30, 49]
Age when published	40.27	44.15	37.53	38.92
	(7.51)	(8.94)	(5.71)	(6.29)
	[21, 57]	[23, 59]	[26, 49]	[21, 49]
Average article no.	34.02	35.67	33.03	26.00
	(23.39)	(25.77)	(26.70)	(17.40)
FTE/Article	0.490	0.651	0.487	0.628
	(0.106)	(0.136)	(0.114)	(0.157)
No. of authors	14	23	6	24
No. of articles	780	1323	264	1050

then shows the ratio of FTE to total articles, calculated as the number of articles divided by the number of authors. Unsurprisingly given the results in Section II, this ratio is higher among members of the earlier cohort.

If the overall quality of research completed by members of these cohorts of very successful economists has not changed across cohorts (or at least not changed relative to research in the profession as a whole); and if one viewed the appropriate divisor by which to apportion credit for co-authored articles as D^*_{early} when the earlier cohort was being considered for promotion/appointment, then the appropriate divisor for assigning credit among authors in more recent cohorts should be higher. With the same inherent quality, today's top scholars are publishing more papers per year than their top predecessors. Indeed, given the change in FTE/article shown in Table 5.11, one might conjecture that the appropriate divisor today is $D^*_{recent} = 1.33 \cdot D^*_{early}$ (i.e., 1.33 = 0.651/0.490), thus accounting for the increasing propensity to co-author over time. Whatever divisor one uses to assign credit at a point in time, this evidence suggests that one should use a larger divisor when comparing publication lists of scholars in more recent cohorts to those of scholars in older cohorts.

One might argue, based on differences in the first two rows of the left-hand columns in Table 5.11, that the authors in these two birth cohorts in this sub-sample are not comparable in terms of ability. To account for

Table 5.12 Authors in the labor economists sample

Abowd, J	Katz, L	Welch, F
Abeler, J	Kennan, J	Wibral, M
Abraham, K	Krueger, A	Willis, R
Acemoglu, D	Kube, S	
Altmann, S	Lang, K	
Altonji, J	Lange, F	
Angrist, J	Layard, R	
Ashenfelter, O	Lazear, E	
Autor, D	Lemieux, T	
Bailey, M	Lundberg, S	
Bandiera, O	MacLeod, W.B	
Barankay, I	Mas, A	
Bertrand, M	Meghir, C	
Blank, R	Michael, R	
Blau, F	Miller, A	
Blundell, R	Moffitt, R	
Borjas, G	Moretti, E	
Brown, C	Mortensen, D	
Burdett, K	Murnane, R	
Cain, G	Murphy, K.M	
Card, D	Neal, D	
Carrell, S	Neumark, D	
Chetty, R	Nickell, S	
Chiappori, P-A	Pencavel, J	
Chiswick, B	Pissarides, C	
Currie, J	Pollak, R	
Ehrenberg, R	Prendergast, C	
Farber, H	Rasul, I	
Freeman, R	Rosenzweig, M	
Goldin, C	Shaw, K	
Gronau, R	Shimer, R	
Hall, R	Smith, James	
Haltiwanger, J	Solon, G	
Hamermesh, D	Stafford, F	
Heckman, J	Taber, C	
Hershbein, B	Todd, P	
Hoekstra, M	Van Reenen, J	
Kahn, L	Weiss, Y	

this possibility, I further restrict the sample to authors who were elected Fellows before age 50 and consider only publications before that age in both cohorts.[19] The right-hand columns of Table 5.11 show the results for this even more restricted sub-sample. Members of these cohorts look remarkably similar in terms of the ages at which they were elected Fellows and the ages at which their average publication in print before age 50 was produced. Scholars in the more recent cohort published many more articles before this age, but they also worked with more co-authors. The FTE/article is much lower than that of the earlier cohort. Indeed, the numbers of FTE articles are almost identical for the two cohorts, 15.5 in the more recent cohort and 15.4 in the earlier cohort. The ratios hardly change from their values in the first two columns, suggesting that this further attempt to compare scholars of identical ability does not alter the conclusion that today's divisor should be well above what it had been.

5.6.2 *Co-authoring Etiquette for Older Economists*

In economics publishing, the implicit assumption is that authors' names will be listed in alphabetical order (Engers et al. 1999), although there are a few exceptions loosely related to stature and contribution (van Praag and van Praag 2008). In the sciences, with nearly all published papers stemming from research grants to a principal investigator, that person is customarily listed as the last author (see, e.g., Nagaoka and Owan 2014). The difficulty in economics is that very junior authors, especially current or recent Ph.D. students who co-author with an established scholar, are assumed by many or even most readers to have either been glorified research assistants or to have executed a project on which the original idea was suggested by the senior author. As such, even if they contributed equally or more than equally, they typically receive less credit than the senior author in the eyes of neutral observers.

What can be done about this difficulty, one which is of growing importance as the profession allows more joint work, even with a doctoral supervisor, to be part of a Ph.D. dissertation? One solution might be for junior people to avoid co-authorship with their seniors, at least beyond the Ph.D. dissertation. This policy, however, restricts scholarly inquiry and will in the end reduce the overall quality of research.

Given the evidence above that older economists still tend to co-author with scholars who are very much their juniors, their choices about the ordering of names on such papers are important. A recent negative example arose when a Ph.D. student (W) asked me to read a draft paper on which the authors were listed in the order M-B-W, where M is a very senior economist. I told him that this ordering of authors' names guaranteed that readers will assume that B, also a junior person, and he were M's assistants, and that he will receive very little credit from the profession for this work. Of course, M may write letters to W's potential employers delineating W's tremendous contributions to the project, but those letters will wrongly or rightly be viewed as cheap talk.

An alternative policy is to place the senior author's name last regardless of the relative contributions of the authors. My policy in the past decade has been to do that on the first paper I write with much more junior people, then to rotate the ordering alphabetically on subsequent papers. Thus my first paper with K and L was L-K-H, the next K-L-H and the most recent is H-K-L. I do not know if this solves the potential excess attribution to the senior co-author, but it may go partway toward a solution. Beyond that, it is not clear what can be done to signal that each co-author made a substantial original contribution to the project.

In economics, unlike in some of the physical sciences, there are no formal guidelines about who should be included as a co-author. Of course, if the profession gives full credit to each co-author, there is no reputational cost to including another person among the co-authors. Even if credit is divided by the number of co-authors, however, there is little cost to a very senior author of adding another co-author, since the reputational and monetary gains that any credit for the research will generate for the senior author are minimal or even zero.

Twice in the past decade an additional junior co-author whose contribution I would rate as below 5 percent of the project has been included on papers I have published. While the cost seemed small or zero to me at the time, in retrospect I view having included these co-authors as a mistake. First, and less important, in both cases there were other co-authors, each very junior. If credit is assigned by dividing by any number greater than one, including this nearly superfluous co-author harmed the productive junior co-author(s). Second, the nearly superfluous co-author whose reputation may be enhanced by inclusion in the list of authors will eventually demonstrate his/her lack of research expertise and be exposed as having done very little on the project. (Of course, with a sufficiently high rate of time preference, this consideration may be irrelevant for that junior person.) Third, and most important, including this person as a co-author is just wrong.

5.7 Implications and Summing Up

The economics profession is aging. Using a large data set on lifetimes of publishing a number of distinguished scholars, I have shown that this fact and differences in research habits across cohorts of scholars can explain only a small part of the simultaneous trend toward more co- and multi-authorships of scholarly articles in the field. While scholars' choices of research methods as they age appear to become more eclectic—they exhibit more variation in the number of, if any, co-authors—they are no more likely than their younger peers to choose to work with different sets of co-authors on successive publications.

Working with other scholars is basically a search process—involving both personal preferences and potential production complementarities. Nearly all the findings here are consistent with the implications of search theory. In particular, the increasing positive assortative matching of older co-authors over time, and the changing interaction of gender and age in co-authoring behavior, are explicable by the increasing percentages of older scholars and women among those publishing articles in economics.

All the empirical results in this study are based on elite samples, in one case of individual scholars who have achieved substantial distinction over their careers, in the other of articles published in the three leading general journals in the field. Obviously these are not random samples of journals or scholars; but these authors and published works are the leaders in the field, reflecting the research that generally receives the most attention from other scholars. Moreover, given the general decline in publication rates with age, which is especially sharp for those who are relatively less productive early in their careers (Oster and Hamermesh 1998), if anything our results understate the effect of age on co-authorship and productivity. For those reasons, while not necessarily representative of the co-authoring behavior of all economists or of the content of all economic research, the results here indicate what is occurring at what is arguably the forefront of the economics literature.

As today's earlier birth cohorts are replaced by scholars from later cohorts who have developed somewhat different research habits, the results suggest that the trend toward increasing co- and multi-authorship will continue. To the extent that these collaborations enhance scholarly productivity, the disappearance of more senior scholars whose habits do not lead them toward collaboration can be viewed as beneficial. The central question for considering the structure of scholarly inquiry, however, is whether the marginal scholarly collaboration is truly productivity enhancing, or, if instead of collaborating, the same scholars would contribute more by working on their own.

Notes

1. Restricting the "sample" to refereed papers hardly changes the conclusion.
2. Three of the sample members (all English, and all currently over age 60) do not have a doctorate. To retain them in all the empirical work, I imputed their Ph.D. age as 28, the mean in the rest of the sample.
3. Among those ages 60+ in the sample, the average fraction of sole-authored papers was 0.41, while the average number of authors was 1.83. But the ranges were 0.12 to 0.83, and 1.17 to 2.55. Similar heterogeneity exists among authors in the later cohorts, although that is partly due to the much smaller samples of articles for which they have been responsible. This generates the heteroscedasticity shown in the figures.
4. I also use "calendar age" rather than "Ph.D. age" because of the three previously mentioned imputations of the latter and because 2 percent of the articles in the sample were published when or before the degree was received. None of the results discussed here changes qualitatively if we make this substitution.
5. If we do not cluster, the estimated standard errors in these equations are typically around 40 percent of those shown in the table. If we exclude the author who, with 184 articles, is a very extreme outlier (the second-most published author has 125 publications), the absolute values of the parameters shown here increase slightly.
6. The coefficients on the decadal indicators mirror the differences in co-authorship rates by decade shown in Table 4. The vector as a whole is statistically significant and remains so even if we add a time trend to the specification.
7. Excluding the 4 percent of articles published when a scholar was over age 65 (and thus probably excluding disproportionately articles that were not refereed), the impact of age in the probit in (1a) falls to −0.0050 (s.e. = 0.0020). Going further and excluding the 11 percent of articles published after the authors were age 60 reduces the estimated impact to −0.0043 (s.e. = 0.0020). Similar

small decreases in the estimated impact of Birth Year occur in re-estimates of (1b) and in the impacts in the ordered probits on the number of authors. The changes in all cases are thus minor and do not alter the general conclusions.
8. The estimates of the coefficients in the ordered probits describing the number of authors show a qualitatively similar set of results. The analogous estimates of the ordered probit coefficients are 0.0372 and 0.0324.
9. The results and comparisons are nearly identical if we exclude the three authors whose Ph.D. year was assigned and their 269 published articles from the sample.
10. Only 0.4 percent of the articles appeared after a five-year or longer hiatus. None of the results discussed in this section is at all sensitive to the inclusion of these few observations in the estimation.
11. The equations were all re-estimated using a negative binomial estimator. While the dependent variable is significantly over-dispersed, so that this estimator is more appropriate than the Poisson estimator, the coefficient estimates are hardly affected. I thus present the more easily interpreted Poisson estimates.
12. If we exclude the six authors whose most recent publication appeared before 2010, which deletes 258 articles from the sample, the results shown in the table hardly change.
13. Freeman and Huang (2014) examine another demographic characteristic—ethnicity—in the process of matching of co-authors.
14. There are too few multi-authored articles involving older authors to make any statistical analysis worthwhile.
15. They seem consistent with the results of Fafchamps et al. (2010) showing the role of nearness within a social network on the choice of co-authors.
16. This result is not due to the fact that older authors who publish in a given year have published more papers up to that date: In an expanded specification that includes the number of articles each author has produced to date, the estimated absolute impact of birth year on the coefficient of variation of the number of authors declines but it remains significantly negative.
17. As an aside on this comparison, of the 2237 unique co-author matches in the sample, only 10 percent represent matches that persisted for more than five years (i.e., the authors have published papers with each other that are at least five years apart). Only

1 percent of co-author pairs published together over a 20+ year period, with the maximum interval in the sample being 28 years.

18. Regressions that hold constant the author's birth year, the article number and the date of publication of the article suggest that the absence of gender differences is not due to correlations with other covariates.
19. This restriction retains all the sample members who had achieved the additional distinctions mentioned in Section II.

References

Abrevaya, J., & Hamermesh, D. (2012). Charity and favoritism in the field: Are female economists nicer (to each other)? *Review of Economics and Statistics, 94*, 202–207.

Borjas, G. (1985). Assimilation, changes in cohort quality, and the earnings of immigrants. *Journal of Labor Economics, 3*, 463–489.

Engers, M., Gans, J., & Grant, S. (1999). First-author conditions. *Journal of Political Economy, 107*, 859–883.

Fafchamps, M., van der Leij, M., & Goyal, S. (2010). Matching and network effects. *Journal of the European Economic Association, 8*, 203–231.

Freeman, R., & Huang, W. (2014). Collaborating with people like me: Ethnic co-authorship within the U.S. NBER Working Paper No. 19905.

Hamermesh, D. (2013). Six decades of top economics publishing: Who and how? *Journal of Economic Literature, 51*, 162–172.

Hudson, J. (1996). Trends in multi-authored papers in economics. *Journal of Economic Perspectives, 10*, 153–158.

Jones, B. (2009). The burden of knowledge and the 'death of the renaissance man': Is innovation getting harder? *Review of Economic Studies, 76*, 283–317.

Laband, D., & Tollison, R. (2000). Intellectual collaboration. *Journal of Political Economy, 108*, 632–662.

McDowell, J., & Melvin, M. (Feb. 1983). The determinants of co-authorship: An analysis of the economics literature. *Review of Economics and Statistics, 65*, 155–160.

McDowell, J., Singell, L., & Stater, M. (2006). Two to tango? Gender differences in the decisions to publish and coauthor. *Economic Inquiry, 44*, 153–168.

Nagaoka, S. and Owan, H.. (2014). Author ordering in scientific research: Evidence from the U.S. and Japan. Unpublished paper, University of Tokyo.

Oster, S., & Hamermesh, D. (1998). Aging and Productivity among Economists. *Review of Economics and Statistics, 80*, 154–156.

van Praag, M., & van Praag, B. (Nov. 2008). The benefits of being economics professor A (rather than Z). *Economica, 75*, 782–796.

Zuckerman, H. (1977). *Scientific elite: Nobel Laureates in the United States.* New York: Free Press.

CHAPTER 6

Collaborative Choices in Econometrics

Charles F. Manski

This chapter makes some broad observations on intellectual collaboration in economics and reflects on my own experiences. Being interested in choice behavior, I find it natural to view collaboration as a sequence of decision problems. Individual researchers decide to initiate collaborations or, contrariwise, to go it alone. Having initiated joint research, collaborators jointly decide how to perform and write up the work.

To bound the subject, I will focus on collaborations that yield jointly authored articles or books. Researchers also collaborate in other important ways. They offer face-to-face comments in seminars and cafes. They anonymously review papers submitted for publication. They build on past literature as they perform new work.

C.F. Manski (✉)
Northwestern University, Evanston, IL, USA

M. Szenberg, L.B. Ramrattan (eds.), *Collaborative Research in Economics*, DOI 10.1007/978-3-319-52800-7_6

6.1 Some Statistics on the Prevalence of Completed Collaborations

I will begin with some statistics on the prevalence of completed collaborations in different disciplines and time periods. By "completed collaborations," I mean ones that result in published products. I would like to be able to also give statistics on the prevalence of uncompleted collaborations (ones that aimed to but did not yield publications) but do not have the data.

Starting at a distance from economics, I find it intriguing to consider composition of classical music. Over hundreds of years, collaboration in classical composition appears rare. I have not studied the subject in depth, having consulted only one readily accessible source, an article in Wikipedia (2014a) titled "Classical Music Written in Collaboration." Nevertheless, I find the article informative.

The Wikipedia article names 18 operas, 6 ballets, 10 orchestral compositions, and 9 chamber pieces that have been composed collaboratively from the 1600s on. The article names not even one collaborative symphony. Although my expertise in classical music does not go beyond that of an avid listener, I think it is accurate to say that the collaborative products listed in the Wikipedia article are mainly obscure pieces that are rarely if ever heard in public.

Whereas classical composers have rarely worked in collaboration, they often build on one another's work sequentially, orchestrating chamber pieces and writing variations on earlier music. For example, Ravel's orchestration of the Mussorgsky solo piano piece *Pictures at an Exposition* became part of the standard repertoire. In the late nineteenth and early twentieth centuries Busoni produced edited versions of Bach keyboard pieces originally composed in the first half of the eighteenth century.

Collaborative fiction appears somewhat more common than collaborative classical music, but it is not typical. A Wikipedia (2014b) article on "Collaborative Fiction" describes collaborative fiction mainly as an experimental activity and remarks "in the humanities collaborative authorship has been frowned upon in favor of the individual author."

Turning to economics, a remarkable fact is that collaboration has grown dramatically over the past 50 years. Table 6.1 shows the prevalence of co-authorship in *Econometrica*, in 1963, 1973, 1983, 1993, 2003, and 2013. The fractions of articles with multiple authors in these years were 0.16, 0.23, 0.47, 0.55, 0.70, and 0.75, respectively.[1] Thus, sole authorship was

Table 6.1 Authorship of articles in *Econometrica*

Volume, year	*Number of articles*				
	1 Author	*2 Authors*	*3 Authors*	*4+ Authors*	*Total*
Vol. 31, 1963	43	7	1	0	51
Vol. 41, 1973	67	16	3	1	87
Vol. 51, 1983	52	39	8	0	99
Vol. 61, 1993	24	25	4	0	53
Vol. 71, 2003	18	33	8	2	61
Vol. 81, 2013	17	31	15	4	67

dominant 50 years ago but has gradually diminished to the point that co-authorship now prevails.

I have also examined the authorship of articles published in other leading journals and found broadly similar growth in collaboration with time. For example, in the *Review of Economic Studies*, the fractions of articles with multiple authors were 0.07 (2 of 30 articles) in 1963 and 0.71 (37 of 52) in 2013. I have not attempted to quantify the temporal change in collaboration in particular subfields of economics but, scanning the titles of articles, I have the impression that collaboration has increased in both theoretical and empirical research.

Beyond the prevalence of collaboration per se, Table 6.1 shows the frequencies with which co-authored articles in *Econometrica* have had two, three, or four or more authors. The primary message is that, throughout the 50 years spanning 1963–2013, research teams have tended to be small, mainly with two authors and rarely with four or more. The fraction of teams with two authors remained above 0.80 throughout the period 1963 through 1993. It has declined since then, being 0.76 in 2003 and 0.62 in 2013, but two-author teams are still the norm. Thus, collaborative research remains predominately a small-group activity.

Economics has not become an enterprise such as medicine. Research articles in medicine rarely have fewer than five co-authors and often have more than ten. Our norms are even more different from the "big-science" model of high-energy physics, where articles may have over 100 authors.

The prevalence of collaboration in economics seems broadly similar to mathematics. Data on the authorship of all research articles included in *Mathematical Reviews* from the 1940s through the 1990s shows that the fraction of articles with multiple authors grew each decade: 0.09 in the

1940s, 0.13 in the 1950s, 0.19 in the 1960s, 0.27 in the 1970s, 0.34 in the 1980s, and 0.46 in the 1990s (see Erdos Number Project 2004). As in economics, the research teams producing mathematics articles mainly had two authors, occasionally three, and rarely four or more.

An idiosyncratic feature of collaboration in mathematics is the towering twentieth-century presence of Paul Erdös. His prodigious record of collaboration has inspired the calculation and widespread dissemination of Erdös Numbers that measure the number of degrees of separation of any mathematician from direct collaboration with Erdös. While economists may draw inspiration or reflected glory from co-authorship with famous figures, no economist holds a collaborative position in the profession similar to that of Erdös in mathematics.

6.2 Conjectures on the Growth in Collaborative Economics

The statistics cited above on collaborative research in economics and mathematics aggregate the compounded consequences of thousands of decentralized decisions by researchers to initiate projects, perform the work, write papers, and submit them for publication, followed by the decisions of journal editors to accept or reject the submissions. This short chapter is not the place for extended study of the sequence of decisions that collectively yield published research. I will, however, offer some conjectures on the forces driving the dramatic growth in collaborative economics and then speculate on what lies ahead.

Technological progress enabling increasingly easy communication among researchers who do not work at the same university or live in the same city has almost surely contributed. Advances in communication enlarge the networks of researchers who may potentially collaborate with one another. Considering present-day communication, it is natural to attribute part of the growth in collaboration to the initiation of the Internet in the 1980s and the subsequent multiple leaps in the sophistication and ease of use of Internet protocols. However, the Internet cannot explain all. Presumably also important were earlier advances in electronic communication by voice telephone and fax. Moreover, the expansion of air transportation throughout the twentieth century gradually enlarged the possibilities for face-to-face collaboration by researchers who live apart.

Another important aspect of technological progress has been the development of word processors for personal computers from the early 1980s onward. Word processing is a form of electronic communication, so I could have mentioned it in the paragraph above. However, it warrants separate attention because it eases the production of sole-authored research papers as well as ones written in collaboration. The development of word processing may perhaps have contributed to the growth in collaboration by making it easier for multiple authors to jointly write and revise papers. It may, however, also have been a force that encourages sole authorship by lightening the burden of writing on individual authors.

Considering the relationship between technological advances and the prevalence of collaborative research, it is credible to suppose that the causal direction is entirely from the former to the latter. With less certitude about the direction of causality, I will conjecture that three developments internal to economics may have contributed as well to the growth in collaboration.

First, the subjects of economic research have evolved in directions that make collaboration increasingly useful. As empirical research increasingly studies large and complex data sets, it becomes increasingly productive for economists with substantive empirical concerns to team with econometricians or computational economists with expertise in data analysis. As empirical researchers increasingly generate their own data through surveys, field experiments, and laboratory experiments, it becomes increasingly productive for economists with substantive empirical concerns to team with researchers with expertise in sample design and questionnaire construction. As theoretical research attempts to address increasingly complex mathematical problems, collaboration becomes increasingly useful to decompose projects into solvable sub-problems. Thus, economics has moved in directions that encourage collaboration to effectively divide the labor of research.

Second, I have the impression that the norms in evaluating academic economists have evolved over time to give increasing weight to co-authored publications. I have no hard data to offer on this matter. However, my imperfect recall from 40 years of participation in faculty meetings evaluating candidates for positions is that a compelling record of sole authorship was once a prerequisite for a favorable outcome, with good co-authorships helping mainly on the margin. More recently, on the other hand, I have participated regularly in faculty meetings that have reacted positively to candidates whose research output is almost entirely co-authored.

Suppose that my impression of the evolution of evaluative norms is accurate. Nevertheless, I must caution that inference on causality is not straightforward. Do researchers increasingly co-author because it has become acceptable to do so? Or does the profession increasingly accept co-authorship because it has become increasingly prevalent? Perhaps both forces coexist and have, in conjunction with technological advances, generated a transition from an early equilibrium with low co-authorship to a modern one with high co-authorship.

A third development internal to economics is that the demographic composition of economists has changed over time. Fifty years ago, the economists publishing research in the leading journals were predominately American and Western European males. Today, they hail from around the world and include a substantial fraction of females. At the risk of engaging in pop sociology, there may perhaps be some truth to the view that individualism varies by culture and gender, with American males being particularly individualistic. If so, the growth in collaboration by economists may partly stem from a change in the composition of economists toward demographic groups with stronger preferences for collaboration.

Turning from conjecture about the past to speculation about the future, I find myself wondering whether collaboration in economics will continue to be mainly a small-group activity. The *Econometrica* statistics in Table 6.1 suggest a recent reduction in the longstanding dominance of two-author teams in favor of three-author groups. Will collaboration in economics continue to move in the direction of larger groups? Perhaps, but I think that two forces will continue to favor two-author teams.

First, writing a paper with a single co-author tends to be a highly personal experience in which both authors take full responsibility for the paper even though they may contribute in different ways to the work. Each author usually understands the entire paper well enough to present it in a seminar. Each values the paper more or less as he would a sole-authored paper. The intensity of the experience of co-authoring lessens when writing with multiple co-authors. Division of labor tends to be more explicit and, as a consequence, authors may limit their responsibility for and attachment to the final product.

Second, the confluence of two editorial practices favors two-author teams relative to larger groups. Economists have long maintained a convention of ordering the names of co-authors alphabetically, exceptions occurring only when all authors agree that a strong asymmetry in contribution warrants non-alphabetical ordering. Alphabetical ordering encourages all co-authors to value their papers highly and, hence, promotes collaboration.

The collaboration-enhancing value of alphabetical ordering lessens when articles have multiple co-authors. This is so because the standard text citation practice when mentioning a paper with three or more (sometimes four or more) authors is to cite the authorship of the article as "first author *et al.*" This practice, enforced by publishers in their writing style guidelines, associates an article with its first-named author and hides the contributions of other authors. Thus, the standard citation practice inhibits collaboration among more than two authors.

6.3 My Collaborative Experiences

My collaborative experiences are not sufficiently noteworthy as to warrant special attention, but discussing them provides microdata that may enrich the surface description of collaboration given above. I will begin with some statistics.

Examining my curriculum vitae, I found that through the end of 2013, I had written 144 research articles that were published in journals or edited volumes.[2] Of these, 74 were sole-authored and 70 co-authored—52 with two authors, 14 with three authors, and 4 with four or more authors. I have moreover written seven published books, of which six were sole-authored and one co-authored. Thus, my collaborative experiences have been expressed almost entirely through research articles rather than books.

I will say something about book writing before focusing more closely on my articles. Relatively few economists write even a single book during their careers. (I do not include production of edited volumes as book writing, as the activity is quite different.) Although book writing requires considerable patience and stamina, I have found that I enjoy the process greatly—indeed, I find it liberating. When writing articles for journals, authors often are subjected mercilessly to the substantive prejudices and editorial whims of referees and editors. The rules of the game in book writing are more relaxed. There are quality standards for sure, but I have found that book publishers encourage personal expression and give authors enough space to express their ideas adequately.

Reflecting on why I have almost always written books on my own rather than in collaboration, perhaps the simplest reason is that, few economists showing interest in writing books, opportunities for book collaboration rarely arise. A deeper reason is that I find book writing a more personal enterprise than writing journal articles. I value being able to develop book themes and organize content on my own, without having to negotiate with anyone else. Perhaps composers of symphonies and authors of novels have felt the same way.

Returning now to articles, I was curious to learn whether my frequency of collaboration has grown with time, paralleling the overall growth in collaboration by economists. Examining my CV, I learned this is not so. My first published article appeared in 1975. Decomposing the 40-year period 1974–2013 into four publication decades, I found these fractions and frequencies of co-authored articles: 0.67 (18 of 27 articles) in 1974–1983, 0.31 (11 of 36) in 1984–1993, 0.58 (21 of 36) in 1994–2003, and 0.44 (20 of 45) in 2004–2013. Thus, my rate of collaboration has fluctuated over the years but has not risen with time.

A crude but accessible way to measure the influence of my sole-authored and collaborative work is to consider the citation counts in the Web of Science and Google Scholar. Whereas the former source provides an overly narrow view, covering only journal articles, the latter gives an overly broad one, covering almost everything searchable online. Examining these sources in December 2014 yielded similar findings: my most cited works have mainly been sole-authored. On the Web of Science, four of my five most cited articles and seven of the top ten are sole-authored. On Google Scholar, again four of the five most cited and seven of the top ten are sole-authored.[3]

The above suggests that I could have built a productive career based on sole-authored research alone, in the absence of opportunities for collaboration. Nevertheless, collaborative research has been an essential part of my professional life. Indeed, almost my entire opus of empirical research has been collaborative rather than sole-authored.

6.3.1 My Empirical Research

I have throughout my career engaged in empirical studies of choice behavior. In the 1970s and early 1980s I studied college-going decisions, first with Meir Kohn and David Mundel and later with Winship Fuller and David Wise. During this period I also analyzed automobile ownership decisions, first with Len Sherman and then with Ephraim Goldin. I have subsequently performed empirical research on travel decisions with Ilan

Salomon and then with Mark Manuszak and Sanghamitra Das. I have studied fertility decisions with Joram Mayshar and behavior in experimental games with Claudia Neri. Over the entire past 40 years I have written only one sole-authored article on choice behavior, this being a study of the decision to become a teacher undertaken in the mid-1980s.

Beginning in the early 1990s, I have been engaged in a large program of empirical research measuring subjective expectations probabilistically. For a considerable period, this program developed entirely in collaboration with Jeff Dominitz. I have more recently co-authored with Asher Blass and Shaul Lach, Adeline Delavande, Joseph Engelberg and Jared Williams, Francesca Molinari, and John Straub. My only sole-authored article measuring expectations has been a small exploratory study of probabilistic polling performed in 2000.

Also beginning in the early 1990s I have performed various empirical studies of treatment response in settings with partial identification. Considering educational outcomes, I investigated the effect of family structure on high school graduation with Gary Sandefur, Sara McLanahan, and Daniel Powers. I later examined the effect of an elementary school classroom intervention with Daniel Scharfstein and James Anthony. Considering criminal justice policy, I analyzed the effect of criminal sentencing on recidivism with Daniel Nagin and the effect of the death penalty on murder with John Pepper. With Joel Horowitz I examined the health effects of alternative drug treatments for hypertension. I have performed no sole-authored empirical research using partial identification analysis to study treatment response.

Finally, I will mention the review essay on *The Bell Curve* that I co-authored with Art Goldberger. This article did not perform original empirical research, but it critiqued the empirical work of other authors.

6.3.2 My Theoretical Research

A curious consequence of writing this chapter is that it has sensitized me to the composition of my research. Until composing the above paragraphs, I was not consciously aware that my empirical research has been almost entirely collaborative. Nor, symmetrically, was I sensitive to the fact that my sole-authored work has been almost entirely theoretical. Considering the different theoretical subjects that I have studied, I now see that the prevalence of collaboration has varied considerably from one to another.

In the 1970s and 1980s, my econometric research on the estimation of parametric discrete-choice models from choice-based samples was entirely collaborative, first with Steven Lerman, next with Dan McFadden, then through an article with McFadden and David Hsieh, and yet another with Yu Xie. Also collaborative was my work with Lerman on simulated maximum likelihood estimation of parametric choice models.

On the other hand, most of my early research on semiparametric analysis of discrete choice was sole-authored. This program of research began with my first published article, on maximum score estimation in 1975, and continued through a series of articles in the mid- and late 1980s. All of my articles on this theme were sole-authored except for two written with Scott Thompson and one with Hungtaik Ahn. Other sole-authored contributions to econometric theory included my article on closest-empirical-distribution estimation and monograph on analog estimation methods.

Moving on, my earliest theoretical articles on partial identification with missing data, published in the period 1989–1994, were all sole-authored. A considerable part of my more recent work has also been sole-authored, including my articles on monotone treatment response and the mixing problem. Moreover, I have written several sole-authored books on partial identification.

Nevertheless, some important aspects of my work on partial identification have been collaborative. These include a series of articles with Joel Horowitz on identification of regressions with missing or contaminated data and two with John Pepper on monotone instrumental variables. They include an article with Elie Tamer on regression with interval data, one with Philip Cross on "regression, short and long," one with Guido Imbens on confidence intervals for partially identified parameters, and one with Francesca Molinari on the consequences of skip sequencing in surveys.

Considering other major themes of my theoretical research over the past 20 years, the program of work on econometric and economic analysis of social interactions that I initiated in the early 1990s has been almost entirely sole-authored. The only exception is the theoretical work included within my article on fertility decisions co-authored with Joram Mayshar. Similarly, the program of work on social planning under ambiguity that I initiated in the late 1990s has mainly been sole-authored. Here the collaborative exceptions have been an article with Alexsey Tetenov on statistical decision theory and one with William (Buz) Brock that studied the operation of markets for lending under ambiguity.

6.4 Collaborations as Social Interactions

I have listed about 40 co-authors above and there are others as well. Listing authors conveys nothing about the experience of collaboration as a social interaction. The experiences have been diverse, reflecting variation in the manner that joint projects arose and heterogeneity in the persons involved. In some cases, I can recall precisely how a joint article came into existence.

One was when the *Bell Curve* appeared in print and Art Goldberger, my close colleague and friend at Wisconsin, persuaded me to co-author a critique with him. I agreed with Art that the *Bell Curve* was bad social science and ethically suspect as well. However, I wished that the book would just go away. Rather than taking a large personal effort, along with many others, to debunk the *Bell Curve*, I would have preferred to write new papers and make positive contributions. Nevertheless, Art persuaded me that the challenge must be met. So we both worked for several months to hone our arguments and write our piece for the *Journal of Economic Literature*. In retrospect, I am proud of the result and happy to have co-authored with Art on a subject that he cared about deeply.

A specific question of public policy motivated my collaboration with Joram Mayshar. Joram and I had been graduate students together at MIT and had long been close friends when the idea of co-authoring arose around 2000. While we often visited each other and had intense discussions about economics, it had not occurred to either of us to collaborate. Our fields of research differed considerably, Joram mainly doing theoretical work in public economics and finance.

The question that brought us together was our mutual desire to understand the impact on Israeli fertility of the country's generous family-allowance policy. We both conjectured that this policy, in conjunction with social interactions across families, had produced a bifurcated society in which secular Israelis tended to have small families and religious ones to have large families. Our article presented extensive data documenting the variation of fertility across religious groups and over time. Developing a formal dynamic model of fertility with social interactions, we demonstrated theoretically that a nonlinear allowance policy can in principle generate multiple fertility equilibria, as we had conjectured. We attempted to perform a structural econometric analysis intended to estimate parameters of the model and then use the estimated model to perform policy analyses. However, we found the estimation problem to be too subtle and were unable to report findings that we could defend as credible. This outcome was not a surprise to me, but I think it was to Joram who, as a theorist, had not regularly come face to face with the frequent fragility of econometric analysis.

My article with Guido Imbens on confidence intervals for partially identified parameters began with a conversation at an NBER Summer Institute meeting. Talking over drinks, Guido conjectured that two conceptually distinct forms of interval would turn out to be technically distinct as well. I was initially skeptical, but I encouraged him to try to prove his conjecture. A sequence of email messages followed up over the next months, with loose thinking giving way to theorems and proofs. Guido mainly took the lead and I reacted to his ideas, occasionally contributing original thoughts of my own. Eventually a nice, I think important, short article emerged. The ordering of names on the article was alphabetical but, had our names been in the reverse alphabetical order, I would have suggested to Guido that his name should appear first.

Beyond the specific research contribution of the article, I think that it was valuable more generally for Guido and me to collaborate. We had known one another for a considerable period and had had a complex professional and personal relationship, viewing some matters similarly but sharply disagreeing in other respects. Working together enabled us to understand each other better and to build some trust. The collaboration did not resolve all of our professional differences—it remains true today that Guido and I have partially overlapping and partially conflicting worldviews. However, co-authoring achieved a certain degree of personal bonding that has subsequently helped us to deal with one another frankly and respectfully.

A fourth case in which collaboration had a precise genesis occurred when Joseph Engelberg and Jared Williams, both second-year students in the Kellogg Finance Ph.D. program, came to my office to discuss the course paper that they had jointly written for my elective course in applied econometrics. I had focused the course on the subject of measuring expectations, and these two students had written an interesting paper analyzing data on the expectations of professional macroeconomic forecasters. In the office conversation, Joey and Jared told me that they would like to continue the analysis that begun in their course paper and then asked if I would join them in a collaborative effort.

Their proposal took me by surprise. I had to suppress an initial thought that it was nervy for second-year students whom I barely knew to propose co-authorship on a subject that they had only recently learned from me. I did suppress that thought in favor of some positive ones: (1) what they wanted to do was a good idea and was consistent with my research interests, (2) they had demonstrated considerable initiative in writing the course paper, and (3) my collaboration on the paper would likely improve it and be helpful to them. I decided to accept their offer, we proceeded, and the collaboration worked out well, yielding two published articles. I came to value both of them sufficiently that I would have agreed to supervise either of their dissertations had they asked. However, each chose to focus on questions in finance remote from my expertise or interest.

Whereas I can recall well how the above and some other co-authored articles began, I find it harder to describe how my longer-term collaborations took shape. From the mid-1970s through the early 1980s, I wrote multiple papers with Steven Lerman. From the mid-1970s through the mid-1980s, I did likewise with Dan McFadden and, separately, with David Wise. From the mid-1990s through the mid-2000s, I co-authored frequently with Joel Horowitz and, separately, with Jeff Dominitz. From the late 1990s on, I have co-authored multiple times with John Pepper, a collaboration that continues today. In each case, I have a hazy recollection of collaboration evolving from multiple conversations over time, but I cannot pinpoint particular formative events.

It is easier for me to remark on how each of these collaborations (Pepper aside) eventually ran its course than on how each began. The one with Lerman ended when Steve made a career change, leaving behind travel demand forecasting and econometrics for academic administration. Those with Dan McFadden and David Wise ended when my research program moved away from econometric analysis of discrete choice toward subjects of less mutual interest. My collaborative period with Joel Horowitz came to a close when the center of Joel's research moved toward local asymptotic statistical inference, a subject which has since occupied Joel intensely but which has not appealed to me. My period of intense collaboration with Jeff Dominitz ended when Jeff decided to leave academic research and fulfill his passion for sports econometrics, becoming the Chief Statistician of the Philadelphia Eagles football team. Thus, each of my longer-term collaborations has run its course in its own way. A common feature is that they all ended amicably.

A common feature of all of my collaborations has been that I benefitted from them and have no regrets about undertaking them. I hope that my co-authors feel likewise.

Notes

1. These statistics were compiled from the Web of Science indexing of *Econometrica* and include articles published as "Notes." Notes in *Econometrica* are almost always original research contributions, not comments on previously published articles.
2. See http://faculty.wcas.northwestern.edu/~cfm754/charles_manski_vita.pdf.
3. For these citation counts, see http://wokinfo.com/citationconnection/ and http://scholar.google.com/citations?user=wAwboAcAAAAJ&hl=en. While the two sets of counts turned out to be identical, the cited items are not all the same. Some of the top ten on *Google Scholar* are books and articles in edited volumes, which are not included in the Web of Science.

References

Erdos Number Project. (2004). http://www.oakland.edu/?id=9574&sid=243. Accessed December 22, 2014.

Wikipedia. (2014a). http://en.wikipedia.org/wiki/Classical_music_written_in_collaboration. Accessed December 20, 2014.

Wikipedia. (2014b). http://en.wikipedia.org/wiki/Collaborative_fiction. Accessed December 21, 2014.

CHAPTER 7

On the Pleasures and Gains of Collaboration in Microeconomics

William J. Baumol

I was very grateful for the invitation to write this piece about those with whom I have collaborated over the years, because it gives me the opportunity to go beyond the usual meager introductory footnote or the brief book preface to express my appreciation and my deep and abiding affection for my coauthors. Yet the writing of this piece is also frustrating because it requires me, almost arbitrarily, to focus upon only a small selection of my partners in crime. Lack of space forces me to refer only briefly to other collaborators who have a profound place in my career and affections, and to omit altogether others of my nearly 60 coauthors with whom my association was fleeting for my coauthors have ranged from some as close as my wife and very dear friends to others with whom I communicated only by telephone or by e-mail and never actually met. I have even had one coauthor that is no longer alive.

W.J. Baumol (✉)
Stern School of Business, New York University, New York, NY, USA

M. Szenberg, L.B. Ramrattan (eds.), *Collaborative Research in Economics*, DOI 10.1007/978-3-319-52800-7_7

It must be admitted at once that the attitudes reported here are unlikely to be typical of joint ventures in writing and research. A dispassionate observer may well consider my experience to be somewhat outré, if not a bit pathological. The telltale symptom is the fact that, in more than 40 years of collaboration, harsh words were spoken on only one occasion. But even then matters were not quite as they might have been expected. Lester Chandler, with whom I had several weeks earlier finished the hard work of writing a rather thick volume, was discussing with me some economics issue quite unrelated to the book, when suddenly we found ourselves shouting. This lasted perhaps a minute or two, when suddenly we realized what we were doing, and both of us burst into laughter. Of course, we remained good friends until his death.

7.1 My Coauthor—A Quick Survey

Before turning to a few of my collaborations in greater detail, let me first indicate who my coauthors were. Twenty of them have been colleagues in my departments at the LSE, Princeton, and NYU. Sixteen were students, two of them undergraduates at the time. Of those 16, 14 went on to become professors, 2 became Presidents of Princeton University (Bill Bowen and Harold Shapiro), 1 was awarded the Nobel Prize (Gary Becker), and 1 is today a member of the House of Lords (Maurice Peston). There have been eight women with whom I served as coauthor, five fellow consultants and three mathematicians.

Let me first discuss collaborations that grew out of dire need rather than convenience or happenstance. It is well known to some that I have a propensity to flit from field to field, often entering arenas in which ignorance was my prime qualification (indeed, I embarked on my years of study of productivity growth when the president of the Committee for Economic Development suggested that they wanted me to conduct such a study for them primarily because my mind was not preconditioned by knowledge of the subject). Consequently, I have often had to rely with some degree of desperation on others who were working in the area, and who actually knew what they were talking about.

This was emphatically true of my work on industrial organization, for which I had to lean heavily on Elizabeth Bailey, Gerald Faulhaber, Janusz Ordover, John Panzar, and Robert Willig. I will speak of my collaboration with this group later in somewhat detail. Similarly, when econometric analysis was required, it was necessary to turn that part of the task over to others, and my colleagues Richard Quandt, Stephen Goldfeld and, now, Edward Wolff, have enriched my working life and acted as ideal partners over the years. I have been a coauthor with a number of mathematicians. First, though not a coauthor, there was Solomon Lefschetz, then the grand old man of differential equation theory, who spurred me on to write a piece on nonlinear difference equations. Also in the background was Albert Tucker who was instrumental in arranging partnerships with a number of others, including Michel Balinsky, Ralph Gomory (about whom more anon), Harold Kuhn, and Philip Wolf. This was a period of intense research on mathematical programming, and as new developments emerged I served as coauthor on several articles discussing the economic implications of such things as the nonlinear dual, decomposition and integer programming. My good friend Tibor Fabian, then president of our consulting firm, MATHEMATICA, also participated in this collaboration. There were other fields in which I have had to rely on others to protect me from my ignorance. The one that most needs mentioning is corporate finance, in which Burton Malkiel has been my dependable rescuer (as well as my partner in the consumption of quantities of most delicious, cholesterol-laden cuisine, offset by excellent red wine).

I want very much to single out several of the women with whom I have been a coauthor. Proceeding alphabetically, with one exception that will be obvious, I mention my former student and very dear friend Elizabeth Bailey, whose subsequent distinguished career is widely known. She participated in the discussions and research leading to the theory of contestable markets, about which more will presently be said, and in the process exercised her genius in stimulating the creative efforts of others. Sue Anne Batey Blackman has been my research associate and occasional coauthor for more than 20 years, and has contributed to all of my writings throughout that period. Her ingenuity in digging up information and in extracting unpublished data is extraordinary. The accuracy of her work underlies anecdotes that should be told if space permitted. Most important, of course, are the ideas she has contributed to the work we have done together and on which I am counting for work we have projected. Peggy Heim (now Nelson) is another coauthor whom I became a close friend. We labored happily together for about a decade at the Association of American University Professors, carrying out a national survey of faculty salaries, both for the sake of research and as a bargaining instrument on behalf of faculty in negotiations with college and university administrations. We also carried out two studies of academics' contracts with publishers, in the second of which we were joined by another enduring friend, Martin Shubik. Our long collaboration produced an extraordinary understanding of the ways in which one can study remuneration of academics and contributed to the quality of our product. Helen Makower worked with me when I was a junior faculty member at the LSE and she was very senior. I frankly do not remember any details of our work together, aside from recalling it as another pleasant experience. Mary Oates provides another example of a coauthor who contributed indispensable knowledge from another field (as well as a good deal more). We had a marvelous time writing on the economics of the Renaissance theater in London, she being a specialist in English literature, and I having recently completed a similar effort on the theater of ancient Athens. My most enduring collaboration with a member of other sex is, of course, with my wife of 53 years, with whom I first began to work on the economics of the performing arts some three decades ago. That, too, is a tale to which I will return, but I must mention here that over the years she has contributed in a number of ways: with ideas when I was stuck, by editing and carrying out substantial research and, above all, by continuing to tolerate the partnership.

Let me end this survey with a few words on several of others with whom the partnership was particularly close, though lack of space prevents more extended accounts. I have already mentioned Gary Becker, who was one of my two undergraduate coauthors. He, as a matter of fact, was a senior author of our piece on monetary theory, I having merely contributed the portion on doctrinal history that, though clearly needed in the article, was a secondary issue. The other undergraduate coauthor was Ralph Turvey, who wrote a chapter on the Swedish contribution for my *Economic Dynamics*, though he continues to insist that he took greater pride in correcting my misspellings. He recently cooked a magnificent dinner for my wife and me and Frank and Dorthy Hahn on the occasion of Ralph's 60th birthday. I must not omit Jess Benhabib, with whom I wrote an introductory paper on chaos theory, he supplying the knowledge while I attempted to write up the material so clearly that even I could understand it. I have also profited over the years in a number of collaborations with David Bradford who was able to take suggested ideas that I understood only dimly, showing in each case that there was much more to the matter than I had seen. Alvin Klevorick and I spent several years completing a paper on the Averch-Johnson thesis, one that seems to have brought the discussion to an end. The reason it took so long to complete was the constant flood of ideas pouring out of New Haven, he just having joined the Yale faculty after completing his graduate studies at Princeton. Last, I must not forget Wallace Oates, with whom I wrote two books on environmental economics. Gentle, kind, reliable and hardworking, the task of completing a book with him was a constant pleasure.

7.2 Bill Bowen and Arts Economics—Birth of a Small Industry

Our entry into the performing arts arena in about 1962 was almost happenstance. John D. Rockfeller the third and August Heckshire, then president of the Twentieth Century Fund, had decided that the propitious moment had arrived for an assault on congress and the Administration on behalf of funding of the performing arts, and had decided to sponsor a study to investigate appropriate measures. Various economists had been consulted, and someone had mentioned to the group to which the task of organizing the endeavor had been assigned that there was an economist at Princeton who was heavily involved in artistic activity. I was invited to appear before the group, and explained to them that my activities in sculpture and painting offered me little insight into the economics of the performing arts. However, I pointed out that my consulting experience had taught me ways of approaching the study of industries about which one initially knew nothing, and that a useful study of the subject in which they were interested would be most effective if the arts were treated dispassionately, as a product like beer or breakfast cereal, in which observation was not clouded by sentiment. Something I said that day must have struck a spark, because the next day I received a telephone call saying they had decided to offer me the project. I declined politely because of other pressing obligations. This seemed only to enhance their desire to have the study carried out in the manner I had described, and I finally agreed to do it if I could induce a young colleague—Bill Bowen, then an assistant professor—to join me in a partnership. Our fate the next four years was sealed.

The undertaking turned out to be larger than we had imagined. We recruited colleagues. Our wives joined the enterprise. Undergraduates fanned out throughout the country to survey audiences. A fine subsidiary study was carried out in England by Muriel Nissel. All of this was organized and overseen by Bill with dedication and panache. He tolerated no malingering by anyone, though always with diplomacy. Every day, without fail, we would receive a telephone call at 8 AM. Every day it had a different subject, but the real purpose was clear. It was to our duties.

Bill took charge of the data planning, collection and analysis, while I focused on the more theoretical side of the subject. He would constantly come up with surprising and illuminating observations and conclusions. As an example, I remember the excitement when he found a near perfect inverse correlation between the size of an orchestra's annual budget and the proportion of women among its musicians. In most collaborative work, I usually end up doing most of the writing on the basis of outlines supplied by my colleagues. This case was no exception, but Bill's outlines were extraordinary-logically organized, optimally detailed, full of insights, with clear signposts at every point where there was any likelihood that might go wrong. His outlines were models of planning for the production of the book, and I have many times regretted their disappearance, because I have so often wanted to show them to others.

Careful planning by August Heckshire, with his journalistic experience, yielded publicity that I have never obtained before or since. We made the front page of *The New York Times*, The Washington Post, *The London Times*, and *Pravda*. *Pravda* recounted that in our book two respected Princeton economists had documented conclusively how capitalism destroys the arts.

Bill went on to apply our analytic approach to higher education, while I used it to discuss municipal services, health care and other activities which we said to be infected with what we called the "cost disease." Meanwhile, other talented investigators that have gone further into the economics, of the arts, have formed an association devoted to the subject and published a fine journal in the arena. At the 30th anniversary of the publication of our book, the association held meetings in celebration, for which we are deeply grateful.

7.3 Alan Blinder and the Principles Textbook

Alan Blinder was another of the brilliant Princeton undergraduates who had majored in economics—the group included Gary Becker, Otto Eckstein and Richard Quandt. Thus he, too, had been one of my students and, like the others in this group, had taken my graduate microeconomics course while still an undergraduate. He had gone to MIT for his formal graduate work and returned to Princeton as a junior faculty member.

At the time he returned I had accepted a nominal consulting position with Harcourt Brace Jovanovich as an advisor on its economics list. The head of the enterprise, a very pleasant person (Robert Styron), had dreamed of creating an economics principles text, and had put together a team of three of the nation's most noted economists (no names will be mentioned) who had agreed to produce the volume, but who seemed unwilling to get started. I was induced to join the group but, still, nothing happened. It soon became clear to all of us that nothing was likely to occur, and I assumed, perhaps somewhat relieved, that the project was dead. Then Styron's successor, he himself having retired, called me and announced that he had looked into the project and decided it was too promising to abandon. My reaction was that this was a view to be expected from a publisher, until he told me that he had spoken to a young colleague of mine who had agreed to undertake the task provided I would participate. Knowing Alan's ability in writing and his extreme reliability (very similar to that of Bill Bowen), an undertaking that has so far produced seven editions had been launched.

Since, in textbook publishing, financial issues are more than a little pertinent, it should be noted that, except in a few special cases, the compensation arrangements with my coauthors have always been equal sharing. I believe any other arrangement must threaten to remove much of the pleasure collaboration can offer.

Like Bill, Alan would stand for no nonsense from me. More than once I have hinted that a chapter was good enough and needed no further work, to be informed, gently but firmly, that it required drastic revision. While each of us took responsibility for half the chapters, I was expected to go over those assigned to Alan without reservation or mercy, and the favor was reciprocated. My trouble was that when Alan offered a criticism of something I had done, it was almost invariably right. I never could think of a good counterargument. While there was for each of us a core of chapters that were never shifted, an interchange of a number of chapters would occur from one edition to the next to reduce the chance that we or the book would become stuck in a rut.

There are few incidents to report here. After all, the care and feeding of a text is no laughing matter. We have had many pleasant evenings with Alan's delightful wife, Madeline, an indispensable member of the group, and we have worked together on such profound literary efforts as the faculty skits for the departmental Christmas party. We have had the occasion to collaborate during his period on the Council of Economics

Advisers, but work on the text remains so serious an undertaking that we begin work on the next edition with some foreboding. Incidentally, Alan's recent position as Vice Chairman of the Federal Reserve Board imposed another responsibility upon me. More than once I received a call from a reporter that finally got to the question, "How will Dr. Blinder vote on interest rates next week?" The answer has been easy: "don't know, and if I did, I wouldn't tell anyone!"

7.4 The Birth of Contestability Theory

Among my collaborative efforts, I must describe the design of contestability theory. It all started when I was asked by persons at the National Science Foundation to sum up the case for governmental intervention in support of technical publications. I expected to provide a routine discussion of the role of externalities, imperfect competition and the other usual suspects, but my exposition unexpectedly bogged down when writing about a multiproduct firm such as the publisher of a number of journals. There did not seem to be a readily available story on what constituted a natural monopoly in that case—scale economies just did not seem to do the trick. Other related matters also proved to be less cut-and-dried that I had suspected. Elizabeth Baily, then head of the economic research group at Bell Laboratories, was also teaching part-time at New York University, where I, too, had also recently joined the faculty. She being an ex-student of mine, we had grown close, and I was delighted when shortage of space made it convenient for her to share my office on her weekly visit. We began to discuss the issues avidly, and elements of the solution to the puzzles that had baffled me, concepts such as trans-ray convexity in output space began to emerge. It then transpired that two of her colleagues at Bell Laboratories, John Panzar and Robert Willig, had been struggling with related issues. It also soon emerged that significant contributions had been made some three years earlier by Gerald Faulhaber, then a graduate student at Princeton on leave from Bell Laboratories. It is ironic that I had been Faulhaber's thesis supervisor, and though I remembered his work, its pertinence to what our group was doing at first escaped me.

Elizabeth then assumed a double role. She and I worked together in exchanges, sometimes heated, on the evolving theory. At the same time, she became our communication link, regularly reporting our latest results to John and Bobby, and transmitting their discoveries in the other direction. The race to be the first to solve the current week's conundrum became a cross between collaboration and friendly but avid competition. Each of us can claim our individual contributions, usually then taken up by the others and carried forward far beyond the relatively primitive original idea. For example, John and Bobby provided a set of necessary conditions for subadditivity of the cost function, while I arrived at a set of sufficient conditions. On the same day, independently, John and Bobby produced a workable criterion of incumbent prices sustainable against entry while Betsy and I came up with essentially the same concept.

There is one event that does not entail collaboration, but is sufficiently bizarre to be worth recalling. My wife and I were attending a performance at La Mama, an off-off-Broadway experimental theater that we frequented. That night was a benefit for a transvestite group, starring the most glamorous individuals in that realm, and we were waiting in line surrounded by bespangled and costumed individuals whose sex was not entirely obvious. Suddenly my wife looked concerned as I went silent and then looked at her with astonishment. I reported that out of nowhere there had flashed before me a theorem, complete with outline of the proof, indicating that for a monopoly with a subadditive cost function Ramsey prices must be sustainable against entry. After that, whenever we were stuck on some analytic point, my coauthors would direct me to attend a La Mama performance.

Months later Bobby and I, along with perhaps a dozen others, were asked to represent the National Science Foundation at a meeting in Leningrad with a counterpart Soviet organization. In the airplane we sat up all night and talked, and out of the talk the concept of a contestable market arose. Several years were to pass, and persons such as Dietrich Fischer and Thijs Ten Raa were to contribute to the effort before the book finally emerged. There are tales to be told about the writing process, but I have already devoted an appropriate amount of space to the collaboration that resulted in the contestable market analysis.

7.5 Productivity Growth and the Surprising US Performance

It was probably in 1981 that Robert Holland, the president of the Committee for Economic Development, invited me to serve as the director of its project on productivity policy. I took on the assignment with enthusiasm, and proceeded along the usual CED track, conducting research to a considerable extent by means of discussion among a group of experienced and knowledgeable persons. All of us were convinced of the correctness of the common wisdom at that time: that the United States was already beset by forces that had undermined its productivity growth and threatened its position as economic leader of the world. The evidence we examined seemed to support this position, and the only dispute that emerged among the members of the subcommittee engaged in the production of the CED statement on productivity was about the appropriate means to affect a rescue.

The limited time allotted to the project having passed. I had time to go into the issues more deeply, with Kenneth McLennan (then vice president of CED) joining me in the initial follow-up steps. First, if seemed appropriate to delve into the long-term productivity record, Jacob Viner having long ago drilled into me the importance of considering the long period along with the short. My colleague, Ed Wolff, suggested some data sources to me and identified some of the most important contributions in the literature. Sue Anne Batey Blackman began to follow up. However, at first I did most of the analytic work by myself, and came up with statistical evidence based on Angus Maddison's 1982 sample of countries, indicating that over the past century there had been marked convergence among the industrial countries in terms of productivity growth and per capital incomes. Obviously there had been earlier writers, notably Veblen, Gerschenkron and Abramovitz, who had pursued the convergence hypothesis. So far as I know, however, only Mathews, Feinstein and Odling-Smee had (very briefly) previously studied the statistical evidence directly. My subsequent article on the subject attracted considerable attention, elicited much follow-up work that still continues and, predictably, was met with some deserved criticism. In particular, Bradford de Long pointed out cogently that I had worked with a sample of countries that had proved, in retrospect, to have grown successfully. This, he argued persuasively, biased the result toward a finding that convergence had occurred.

At this point I turned to Ed Wolff for help, and we began to explore the subject more systematically and with the degree of econometric sophistication that he but not I could contribute. Our study spread to related issues, and we gradually and reluctantly were forced by the growing accumulation of evidence to conclude that reports of the demise of US economic leadership were a bit premature. We found, for example, that this country had suffered a drastic decline in productivity growth by the early 1970s, but that declines had occurred in the other industrial countries at about the same time, with Japan's growth rate falling by about the same percentage as ours. We found also that while the USA was indeed moving toward a service economy, so was every other industrial economy, most of them at a pace considerably faster than ours. And the evidence of convergence confirmed that other countries were indeed outpacing the USA in terms of productivity growth rate, but that this was a necessary condition for their emergence out of relative poverty, with no evidence indicating that they were doing more that approaching our productivity level asymptotically.

Our study also indicated that in the course of a century productivity growth had made contributions to living standards so enormous (increasing them, perhaps, eightfold) that the change eluded intuitive comprehension. Ms. Blackman independently carried out a study of the concrete manifestations of the change in living standards that had occurred over a century and succeeded far beyond what might have been hoped in giving to nineteenth century living standards a local habitation and a name. The result was our book that showed how much productivity matters in the long run and documented how wrong I and my associates had been in accepting at face value the despairing view of the US productivity record.

7.6 Ralph Gomory and the Orderly Region of the Scale-Economies Trade Equilibria

One day in about 1958, when I had been a member of the Princeton faculty for nearly a decade, Albert Tucker, the chairman of the Math Department at Princeton (and codiscoverer of the Kuhn-Tucker theorem), came by and suggested that there was a young man whom I ought to meet. "He has solved the integer-programming problem," Tucker told me (revealing to me for the first time that the problem had up until then evaded solution). The young man was Ralph Gomory, then assistant professor on the Math Department.

We did meet and he explained to me how one went about solving a maximization or minimization problem subject to the constraint, among others, that some or all of the variables be integer. As the discussion proceeded, it offered hints of the properties of the dual of the original program, and its interpretation as the values of the constraining parameters—the incremental values in terms of superior achievement in the objective of a loosening of the constraint parameters. An example is the addition to a firm's maximum profits that is made possible by an addition to its warehouse space. In an integer-programming case the usual interpretation requires obvious modification, because of packages to be stored come in a minimum size of, say, one cubic foot, then the addition of a cubic inch of space to that offered by the warehouse clearly is zero, meaning that the first derivative of profit with respect to the constraining warehouse space is also apt to be zero, even if more warehouse space is needed urgently. In that paper we also indicated that integer programming held some promise as a means to approach optimization in the presence of scale economies, where the usual facilitating concavity-convexity conditions are violated—an indication of things to come three decades later.

We both enjoyed our collaboration, and then Ralph left the academic world to rise to the position of the Director of Research and Senior Vice President at IBM. A few years ago I heard that he had left IBM and had joined the Sloan Foundation as its president. I thought no more about it until a bit later when I received a telephone call from Ralph inviting me to join him in a project on the borderline between economics and mathematics. Despite my weak grounding in the field—international trade theory (but when had that stopped me before?)—I leaped at the invitation. The work was fascinating, and I could not resist renewing the pleasures of our previous work together. Aside from its trade orientation, it was a first for me in another respect, for it is the first time, as far as I can recall, in which I had entered a partnership with the other person already having made the breakthrough as well as the intellectual investment. Nevertheless, I flattered myself that before it was over I would be able to make a contribution sufficient to qualify as a legitimate junior partner.

The topic was equilibrium in the presence of scale economies or substantial startup costs. The subject had previously been explored by very capable economists who had, particularly in recent years, made profound contributions to the subject, on a number of which we were to build. For example, the underlying scenario, in which scale economies are external to the film but internal to the industry within a nation, had already been used widely. Earlier studies showed that under scale economies equilibrium is not unique. Moreover, it was already known that in the theoretical case of universal scale economies, equilibria generally entail perfect specialization, with no product produced in more than one country. Ralph had been able to carry this reasoning several steps further. He had shown that in this model each and every perfectly specialized assignment among countries is an equilibrium, and one, moreover, that is stable locally. In addition, he showed that as the number of traded commodities grows, the number of equilibria grows astronomically, in the case of two countries and n goods, on the order of [2.sup.n], that is, the number of different ways of dividing up the specialized production of goods between two countries. Most exciting of all, he devised a workable calculation method which permitted representation of each equilibrium by a point in a graph, and showed that the region of equilibrium points is well defined and that it always takes the same general shape, a shape with a very illuminating economic interpretation, notably that many of the equilibria are far from ideal and that they constitute a newly recognized source of rivalry among trading countries.

Later, we were to show that part of the explanation is the fact that scale economies undermine the role of comparative advantage. We have just recently proved that in this case many equilibria violate comparative advantage, that an equilibrium that violates comparative advantages may nevertheless be efficient, and that many equilibria may be inefficient. We have described some of this work on the 1994 Lionel Robbins Lectures at the London School of Economics and are now engaged in writing various articles reporting the details of the analysis. Two books are currently expected to emerge from the work.

7.7 Concluding Comment

What is to be said by way of peroration? Only that collaboration can be fun and profitable intellectually, provided that one selects only coauthors that are simpatico and very patient.

CHAPTER 8

A Serial Collaborator

David Colander

I am a serial collaborator. I have collaborated on over 80 articles and books with a wide variety of coauthors, and I am currently collaborating on another dozen or so, some of which will lead to fruition and some not. So collaboration for me comes naturally.

8.1 Collaboration with Abba Lerner

Probably my best known collaborative work, at least among older economists, is that done with Abba Lerner. Many ask whether I was Abba's student; I wasn't. In fact, I only met him late in his life. Telling how my collaboration with him came about may shed some light on why I am so positive about collaboration. I was a young assistant professor who had just finished an unorthodox dissertation exploring a plan to create property rights in prices, so anyone who wanted to change their value-added quantity-weighted price had to buy the right from another who wanted to change his or her value-added quantity-weighted price in the opposite direction.

D. Colander (✉)
Middlebury College, Middlebury, VT, USA

M. Szenberg, L.B. Ramrattan (eds.), *Collaborative Research in Economics*, DOI 10.1007/978-3-319-52800-7_8

The dissertation was highly unconventional, to say the least, and I probably would not have done it had my advisors not essentially signed off on it before I started. Here's what happened. I was working on a more standard dissertation—three essays on optimal taxation—under Ned Phelps and Bill Vickrey. It was a pedestrian dissertation, filled with equations that showed my technical prowess, but little imagination or insights of importance. In short, it was your standard economics dissertation. I had two essays tentatively approved and was finishing a third essay on optimal income taxation with multiple-skill dimensionality.

It was the 1970s and inflation was a big topic, and one day, I was daydreaming about economic ideas—something I often do. I was thinking about what would happen in a general equilibrium system if there was a market in rights to change prices. In such a system there could be no inflation, and the price of changing price would be a measure of the inflationary pressure in the economy. If there were no inflationary pressures, the price would be zero. If there were inflationary pressures this "market in price changes" would control those pressures. The idea intrigued me and I kept playing with it in my mind. I put my optimal income taxation paper aside.

I wrote up a short piece on my idea of a market in price changes, and sent it to Vickrey. He wrote me back telling me it was brilliant. He had said nothing of the sort about my other work. Given his enthusiasm, I asked him if I switched my dissertation to exploring the idea, whether I could complete it in a year. He said yes, and encouraged me to do it. I then went to Phelps, telling him what Vickrey had said and asking him whether I could complete it in a year. He agreed I could. So I switched, and about a year thereafter, I defended my thesis, which was full of ideas, but was far from a true thesis. But they let me through, and I was a Ph.D. economist.

Vickrey had also told me that the work would be highly publishable, so I sent it off to a top journal. I received a harsh rejection; the reviewers saw the idea as stupid and me as incompetent. So I sent it to another top journal: same result. At that point I figured I was in trouble and started thinking about other careers. I could return to writing publishable, but not especially insightful, technical papers, but that was not especially appealing to me. My other option, which I probably would have followed, was to turn to consulting, which paid much better than economics, and would be more likely to encourage creativity.

Then I came upon a paper by Abba Lerner which was exploring a wage inflation plan that had a lot of similarities to my plan. I thought about the unfairness of academic life; his plan was being discussed, and I couldn't get published. I went to a crowded AEA session with hundreds of people in the audience in which Abba was presenting a paper on the topic, and was recognized by the chair to ask a question. I addressed my remarks to Lerner. I told him that while I found his plan interesting, it has some problems which I listed. He didn't respond; time was short, and the session quickly moved on to other questions.

I was presenting in the last session of the last day at the same AEA conference. Instead of hundreds, there were three people in the audience—all of them friends of the presenters. But then right after the session began, in walked Abba Lerner. He listened intently as I spoke, and came up to me afterward and said that he was thinking of the problems I listed, and that I might be right; we should discuss them. I said, yes definitely, asking when? He said "How about now?" So we canceled our reservations home (I was in Oxford at the time), and for the next three days we holed up in a Chicago hotel discussing how such a plan might work and what its implications were. At the end, he invited me to collaborate on some articles (Lerner and Colander 1979, 1980a, 1982) and a book (Lerner and Colander 1980b).

Collaboration with Abba Lerner made my academic career. Before I collaborated with Abba, I couldn't get my work published. After I started collaborating with Abba I could get published, and became a reasonably well-known economist. I went from being one of the hundreds of young economists trying to make it in the profession on the profession's terms, to being considered an out-of-sync gadfly who had some wild ideas that might be worth listening to. I now had publishers pursuing me, rather than me pursuing publishers. Thereafter, I could get published, not only jointly with Abba but on my own, and I was appointed to Distinguished Chair in my early 30s. So you can see that collaboration has been good to me.

8.2 Collaboration with Harry Landreth

My work with Abba also led to an interest in methodology and how ideas in economics evolved and developed. That led me to another collaboration—this time on a history of thought textbook (Landreth and Colander 1989, 1994, 2001). Harry had been a professor at Miami of Ohio, but had quit when he became a mogul, by which I mean that he earned enough in oil and stocks to not have to work. So he asked himself, what did he really want to do? Dealing with academics was not high on his list. He decided that what he really wanted to do was fish. So he bought two houses—one at Henry's Fork, Idaho, for trout fishing, and the other in the Florida Keys for tarpon fishing. As he described it to me, he had the perfect life.

But he got bored just fishing, and thought that teaching a couple of courses might be fun so he accepted a short-term position at the University of Miami. I happened to be teaching there—it's a long story why—and Harry and I found that we shared a sense of humor and a love of history of economics. I provided comic relief for him and updated him on developments in economics; he provided me with good wine (Harry had a great wine cellar), good food (his wife was a gourmet cook) and some of the best fishing in the world. It was a great trade for me.

Before he had become a mogul, Harry had written a history of economic thought text, which the publishers were pressuring him to revise. But he was hesitant—that was work, and he didn't want work to interfere with a life of fishing; he might miss that next big tarpon. So sitting out fishing we decided it would be fun to revise the text together. So our collaboration began, and it extended into other books and articles (Colander and Landreth 1995, 1996, 1998, 2006).

My collaboration with Harry changed an interest in the history of thought into a second specialty for me. As I read more widely in the history of thought I developed a new and deeper understanding of the profession and how it evolved. So it was a great collaboration for me. It was not so good for Harry, at least to hear him tell the story. He has never forgiven me for having destroyed his perfect life of fishing. But secretly, I think he enjoys the work.

8.3 Collaboration with Arjo Klamer

My growing reputation as a creative gadfly led to a third collaboration—this time with Arjo Klamer, who, having become familiar with my unusual approach to macroeconomics, contacted me to see if he could interview me for a book he was working on. Arjo was a young professor who had just published a well-received "Conversations with Economists" book (Klamer 1983) that explored developments in macro theory by asking top macro researchers about their approaches. It was right at the time that new classical economics was catching on, and Arjo's book received lots of press and discussion. I told Arjo that I would be happy to be interviewed. So he came up to Middlebury where I was teaching, and interviewed me. The interview was never published, but his visit led to an all-day discussion of problems with the profession.

We were soon talking about collaborating on a study exploring the nature of graduate school, and what students thought about it as they were going through it. We decided to survey and interview students at top schools, and we published the results in the then newly created *Journal of Economic Perspectives* (Colander and Klamer 1987) and in a book (Klamer and Colander 1990). Our findings were widely discussed in the profession, and it led to an NSF study of graduate economics education, which came to similar conclusions to our study. So that collaboration led to a third specialty for me—economic education. Not only was I known for my oddball approach to macro theory and policy and for the history of thought, I was now also known as an observer and critic of the economics profession, and a specialist in economic education.

8.4 Collaborations with Critics

The above examples should make it clear that I am a serial collaborator because I love to discuss economics. Those discussions lead to collaborations as I and the person with whom I am discussing jointly come of a conclusion about an issue. Hardly a week goes by without a conversation with other economists leading to an idea for a paper, and sometimes an actual discussion of possibly doing a paper together.

Let me give some recent examples. An Australian economist, Craig Freedman, wrote a long, and somewhat critical, critique of my work, describing me as an economics court jester. (Freedman 2008). It was supposed to be a review of one of my books, but it became a 20-page paper in its own right and was published as a chapter in a book on Chicago methodology. I came upon it and wrote him back that I thought he did a great job—he had understood me. That led to a dinner at the AEA meetings which led to a decision to collaborate on a paper on the Chicago school of economics (Colander and Freedman 2011). The paper is done, but not yet published in part because it is too long, and in part because we are both too lazy to bother sending it in and dealing with editor's and the reviewer's comments. We are considering extending it into a book.

Another current collaborator of mine is Huei-chun Su, whom I met when I sat in on a presentation she gave at a conference in the Netherlands.

Her views on methodology largely coincided with mine and I could see that we had much in common. The next I heard of her was when I was a reviewer for a paper which she had submitted to a journal. The paper took me to task on a couple of issues on which she was right. Her paper cleared up those issues, and I gave it a good review. We met again soon thereafter and started keeping in touch by e-mail. I thanked her for clarifying my work, and we started discussing methodological issues. From those discussions it was clear that she was having trouble getting her work recognized, and it looked as if she could use a couple of publications. So I suggested that we could do a paper together, and she was enthusiastic about it.

I had been asked to do a paper about the field of economics for a volume on the social science profession. I wasn't going to do it, but then I thought that since she could use the publication, that we could do it together to see how we worked together. So we did. After completing that paper, we continued our conversations and saw some articles that we both felt had missed our central point about methodology. So we wrote two more papers together expressing that view and further developing the art/science distinction that is at the heart of my methodological approach. Those papers have now been published. (Su and Colander 2013; Colander and Su 2015) and we have received nice comments from a number of economists on them. We will likely collaborate on more, possibly with some additional young scholars who have also written me critiquing, and further developing, my art/science methodological approach.

8.5 Et al.: Institutionally Imposed Collaboration

Another set of collaborative articles that I have done have been institutionally imposed collaboration. One is appointed to a committee or working group that is asked to put down their views. An example is a working group that looked at the problem of undergraduate economic education (Kasper et al. 1991). This type of collaboration is less satisfying for me. These institutionally imposed "collaborations" can suffer from committeeitus, in which the report says things that none of the authors totally agree on, but which are the only things on which the committee could agree. To avoid committeeitus, I tend to avoid committees, and recently when asked to do a follow-up study on undergraduate economics education, rather than form a committee, KimMarie McGoldrick and I did a joint report (Colander and McGoldrick 2009) and then invited a wide range of others to challenge and criticize it, and published the entirety as a book (Colander and McGoldrick 2010).

8.6 Collaboration with Non-Economists

It isn't only economists with whom I collaborate. As my intended audience has widened beyond just economists, I have begun collaborating more with non-economists. Collaborating with someone outside one's field leads to a different type discussion. Non-economists bring a different frame to an issue, and different ideas are developed. A recent example is my book on complexity and policy that is jointly written with a physicist-turned business executive (Colander and Kupers 2014). It came about like this: We are at a conference and discovered that we shared the view that much of the policy debate at the conference was missing the main point. We were on the same plane after the conference, and we struck up a conversation about our shared interest in complexity theory. That led to a decision to work on a book. The book was well received and it led to more requests for clarifications and shorter presentations of our arguments, so it will likely lead to more collaborations between the two of us.

Another non-economist collaboration I am currently working on is with a venture capitalist. He and I are exploring whether we want to do an article on social entrepreneurship, and its role in the economy. We had met at a conference a few years back, and I had commented on some chapters of a book he was working on. Then, we met again at George Soros' INET conference—composed mostly of left-learning economists. Right after that conference, there was an APEE conference composed mostly of right-leaning economists, which we both also attended. I suspect we were the only two individuals who attended both conferences, which suggested we had something in common.

I learn enormous amounts from these collaborations with non-economists because they have a different knowledge set than I do. Their knowledge set would not help me publish in an economics journal, but it does help with understanding issues and the relevance of my ideas for the real world. Publishing primarily in venues read by economists is highly limiting, so once any academic economist has tenure and narrow publications no longer matter that much, I strongly encourage him or her to think more broadly about collaborators, and publishing.

8.7 Collaboration with the Dead

I have not only collaborated with many living authors but also with a dead one. Let me explain. Early on in my career I was seen as a potential textbook author. Publishers liked my conversational style and my ability to meet deadlines. One of the projects I was offered when I was still young and poor was to revise a social science text whose last remaining author had died about five years earlier. The text, published by Macmillan Publishers, had its origins in the 1930s as a collection of essays put together by some social science professors. It was used in a wide variety of social science courses. Then, in the 1940s, it was changed into an actual textbook with four or five coauthors. In the 1950s, one of those coauthors, Elgin Hunt, took over the book and he continued to revise it until the 1970s when he died.

During this period, much had changed in the teaching of social science. At many colleges the general social science course had been replaced with individual social science courses such as political science, anthropology, economics, sociology, and so on. So sales of the book had declined, but were still substantial in certain geographic areas, which meant that the publishers had a desire to publish a new edition.

They had a problem however. There were no more social scientists; there were only economists, political scientists, sociologists, and so on. So they didn't know whom to get to revise the book. Somehow I came under their radar as someone who had broad interests and who could write. So the editor flew down to convince me to undertake the project. I negotiated a decent advance that paid for the rent of a beautiful apartment on Paradise Island (right behind the Ocean Club) for the summer, along with a typist and other support staff. The publisher also agreed to send me all their latest texts in each of the social sciences, which were about 20 books.

So that summer I revised the text. In the morning I would go out on the beach and read up on a field, and then in the afternoon, I would go back to the apartment and revise the chapter on that field. I would give the written material to a typist, and would edit the typed material in the evening. It made for a very enjoyable summer, and by the end of the summer, I had the first draft of the revision ready to send in. The reviewers liked almost all the revisions, except for those in economics—where they felt that I clearly didn't know what I was talking about. (It was an important lesson for me in textbook writing—many users will like the book better if you simply summarize the standard knowledge, and don't know too much about the field.)

Because the book was so well known, the publishers decided to keep the name of the previous author as the lead author, so the book was by Hunt and Colander (Hunt and Colander 1984, … 2014). The revision did well, and I have kept it up under the coauthorship of Hunt and Colander, even he has been dead for over 40 years. The book is now in its 17th edition, and I believe is the longest lasting textbook in any field.

8.8 The Often Unmentioned Collaborators

The above discussion of collaboration has left out some important collaborators because it has just focused on those people whose name shows up as an author. Any work has many more collaborators than coauthors. All work, including single-authored work, is collaborative. Ideas don't come from nowhere—they come from discussions, challenges to positions and reading. Everyone you have ever read, or spoken with about an idea, is a collaborator, as are peer reviewers and friends who read papers and make suggestions. Some of those show up in the preface, footnotes and bibliography, but many do not.

There is also another type of collaboration that is important. Developing an idea in one's mind is quite different than developing an idea that is publishable. I have outlined 1000s of articles in my mind, and have only tried to turn a small number of them into articles, because developing ideas is fun; turning them into articles is hard work. One reason I have translated as many ideas as I have into articles is due to collaboration—with the unsung heroes of academia—the editors and publishing personnel who massage a draft article into a finished article or a book. Any paper or book has to be massaged and edited numerous times before it is published.

I have been lucky to have some wonderful personal editors—individuals who have edited my papers and to clear up many of the ambiguities. I have my own personal editor who works on my principles of economics textbook, now in its ninth edition; she goes far beyond the role of editor, and develops examples, finds new ideas, finds the latest data, and helps guide my principles book through the publication process. These often unmentioned collaborators make authors seem brighter and more knowledgeable than they are.

8.9 Why Collaborate?

Reasons for collaboration include some combination of the following: (1) gains from trade, (2) collective enjoyment, (3) desire to help someone or to be helped, (4) strategic collaboration and (5) institutionally fostered collaboration. Let me talk about each briefly.

Gains from trade collaboration occur when coauthors bring in different expertise. My collaboration with Buz Brock is an example (Brock and Colander 2000, 2004). Buz and I met when we were discussing the market anti-inflation plan. Buz was one of the few high theorists who engaged the issue and we had some lively conversations on it, and on complexity. Buz is a super mathematician; I can write, and sometimes translate his mathematical understanding into words so more people can understand it. We worked on a policy and complexity book together, but it never came to fruition, but the ideas discussed with him became built into the book that I did with Roland Kupers on complexity and policy.

Collective enjoyment collaboration is always important. My collaboration with Ken Koford is an example. Ken was an economist who was excited about ideas. He was a sounding board for my early ideas, and his enormous knowledge of the literature within and beyond economics would always result in him giving my four of five suggestions to read. We did an early paper together on methodology (Colander and Koford 1979), and then a number of papers on the market anti-inflation plan, and he brought a whole group of individuals in to work on it. It was a joy working with him, and had he not died prematurely, I am sure we would still be collaborating today.

Another enjoyable collaboration is my collaborations with Casey Rothschild (e.g. Colander and Rothschild 2010). He was a young professor who was top of his class at MIT, but, unlike most top graduates, was interested in teaching and in broader ideas as well as technical issues. When he was here at Middlebury we did three papers together, and had he stayed, I am sure we would have done many more. Talking about ideas with someone who is theoretically superb and willing to talk about broad ideas is always a joy.

I collaborate for pleasure more now than I did early in my career, and I expect that the reason why is technology. The Internet allows collaboration over large geographical areas that would not have been possible earlier. When Abba and I collaborated, we had to figure out times to physically get together. Today, while physically seeing the other person is important, it is not mandatory; one can collaborate over the Internet. This is the case in my collaboration with Barkley Rosser and Ric Holt, with whom I have done a couple of books and a number of articles (e.g. Colander et al. 2004, 2010; Rosser et al. 2010). They are great fun to work with, and I expect that I will continue to collaborate with them in the future.

I have already given examples of desire to help someone leading to collaboration. Abba was helping me by writing with me, and I hope that as I have written with younger scholars I have helped them. Collaborations with students and research assistants would also fall under this heading. I have collaborated with many students, and where they have done significant work have been happy to include them as a coauthor with students. One early collaboration with a student was with John Haltiwanger when he was a student—long before he became a well-known economist. He was working for me as a research assistant, and I had written a paper on water elasticity demand, and needed some regressions run. He ran them and we jointly published an article (Colander and Haltiwanger 1979).

Strategic collaboration is a collaboration in which one publishes together in order to make a statement to the profession. An example of that is my paper with Axel Leijonhufvud, Perry Methling, Peter Howitt, Alan Kirman and myself (Colander et al. 2008). It was to serve as a type of manifesto stating our position that any reasonable macro theory had to take about of agent interdependencies in better ways that the then current models were doing. This work can sometimes be institutionally fostered collaboration, as is the case in the Dahlem Report criticizing economists' role in the financial crisis (Colander et al. 2009) but when the group is small and there is general agreement institutionally fostered collaboration can be strategic and enjoyable.

8.10 A Final Comment

I could go on but since I don't have a coauthor, I won't. There is only so much space a single author should take. Collaboration comes naturally. Knowledge advances through discussions and discussions naturally lead to collaborations. It is to be encouraged whether or not it leads to publications.

Bibliography

Brock, W., & Colander, D. (2000). Complexity and policy. In D. Colander (Ed.), *The Complexity Vision and the Economy*. Northampton, MA: Edward Elgar Publishers.

Brock, W., & Colander, D. (2004). Complexity, pedagogy, and the economics of muddling through. In M. Salzano & A. Kirman (Eds.), *Economics: Complex windows*. New York: Springer.

Colander, D., Kirman, A., Follmer, H., Sloth, B., Juselius, K., Haas, A., & Lux, T. (2009). The Financial crisis and the systemic failure of the economics profession. *Critical Review, 21*(2–3), 249–267.

Colander, David and Arjo Klamer. 1987. The making of an economist. *Journal of Economics Perspectives, 1*(2), 95–111.

Colander, D., & Rothschild, C. (2010). The sins of the sons of Samuelson: Vision, Pedagogy and the Zig Zag Windings of Complex Dynamics. *Journal of Economic Behavior and Organization, 74*(3), 277–290.

Colander, David and Craig Freedman. 2011. The Chicago Counter-revolution and the Loss of the Classical Liberal Tradition. *Middlebury College Working Paper*.

Colander, David and Harry Landreth. (1995). *Classic readings in economics*. Ed. Maxi Middlebury. Homewood, IL: Press/Irwin.

Colander, D., & Landreth, H. (1996). *The coming of Keynes to America*. Edward: Elgar.

Colander, D., & Landreth, H. (1998). God, man, and Lorie Tarshis at Yale. In O. Hamuda (Ed.), *Keynesianism and the Keynesian revolution in America*. Northampton, MA: Edward Elgar.

Colander, D., & Landreth, H. (2006). Pluralism, formalism and American Economics. In R. Koppl (Ed.), *Festshrift in Honor of Leland Yeager*. New York: Routledge.

Colander, D., & Su, H.-C. (2015). Making sense of economists' positive-normative distinction. *Journal of Economic Methodology, 22*(2), 157–170.

Colander, D., & Haltiwanger, J. (1979). A comment on the elasticity of demand for water. *Water Resources, 15*(5), 1275–1277.

Colander, D., & Koford, K. (1979). Realitic and analytic syntheses of macro and micro economics. *Journal of Economic Issues, 13*(3), 707–732.

Colander, David and McGoldrick, KimMarie. (2009, May). The Economics Major as Part of a Liberal Education, *American Economic Review*.

Colander, D., & McGoldrick, K. M. (2010). *Educating economists: The teagle discussion on rethinking the economics major*. Northampton, MA: Edward Elgar Publishers.

Colander, D., Howitt, P., Kirman, A., Leijonhufvud, A., & Mehrling, P. (2008). Beyond DSGE models: Toward an empirically based macroeconomics. *American Economic Review, 98*(2), 236–240.

Colander, D., Holt, R., & Rosser, B. (2004). *The changing face of economics*. Ann Arbor, MI: University of Michigan Press.

Colander, D., Holt, R., & Rosser, B. (2010). How to win friends and (possibly) influence mainstream economists. *Journal of Post Keynesian Economics, 32*(3), 397–409.

Colander, D., & Kupers, R. (2014). *Complexity and the art of public policy: Solving society's problems from the bottom up*. Princeton, NJ: Princeton University Press.

Freedman, C. (2008). Court jesters, house gadflies and economic critics. In C. Freedman (Ed.), *Chicago fundamentalism: Ideology and methodology in economics*. Hacknesack, NJ: World Scientific Publishing.

Hunt, A., & Colander, D. (1984, 1987, 1990, 1993, 1996, 1999, 2002, 2005, 2008, 2011, 2014). *Social Science*. Allen and Bacon Publishing Co.

Kasper, H., et al. (1991). The education of economists: from undergraduate to graduate study. *The Journal of Economic Literature, 29*(3), 1088–1109.

Klamer, A. (1983). *Conversations with economists: New classical economists and opponents speak out on the current controversy in macroeconomics*. Totowa, NJ: Rowman and Allanheld.

Klamer, A., & Colander, D. (1990). *The making of an economist*. Boulder and London: Westview Press.

Landreth, H., & Colander, D. (1989). *History of economic thought* (2nd, 3rd, 4th ed.). Boston: Houghton Mifflin and Co.

Lerner, A., & Colander, D. (1979). MAP: A cure for inflation. In D. Colander (Ed.), *Solutions to inflation*. New York: Harcourt Brace Jovanovich.

Lerner, A., & Colander, D. (1980a). There is a cure for inflation. In M. Claudon & R. Cornwall (Eds.), *Incomes policies for the United States: New approaches*. Boston: Martinus Nijhoff.

Lerner, A., & Colander, D. (1980b). *MAP: A market anti-inflation plan*. New York: Harcourt Brace Jovanovich.

Lerner, A., & Colander, D. (1982). Anti-inflation incentives. *Kyklos, 35*(1), 39–52.

Rosser, B., Holt, R., & Colander, D. (2010). *European economics at a crossroads*. Northampton, MA: Edward Elgar Publishers.

Su, H.-C., & Colander, D. (2013). A failure to communicate: The fact-value divide and the Putnam/Dasgupta debate. *Erasmus Journal of Economics and Philosophy, 6*(2), 1–23.

CHAPTER 9

Collaboration With and Without Coauthorship: Rocket Science Versus Economic Science

William A. Barnett

9.1 Introduction

My intellectual origins as an economist are somewhat different from those of most economists. While the words "rocket scientist" are often loosely associated with some economists, I really was a rocket scientist. After receiving my BS in engineering from MIT, before returning to graduate school to acquire my Ph.D. in statistics and economics, I worked as a systems development engineer for Rocketdyne in Los Angeles on the development of the F-1 booster rocket engine for Apollo. That rocket engine, producing 1.5 million points of thrust, was, and still is, the most powerful rocket engine ever built. The engine was used in a cluster of five in the first stage of the Apollo launch vehicle, which was 363 feet tall and weighed six million pounds. The first stage raised the vehicle to 40 miles of altitude at Mach 7 in two and one-half minutes, while burning four and one-half million pounds of propellant.

W.A. Barnett (✉)
Center for Financial Stability, New York, NY, USA

The University of Kansas, Lawrence, KS, USA

M. Szenberg, L.B. Ramrattan (eds.), *Collaborative Research in Economics*, DOI 10.1007/978-3-319-52800-7_9

For the benefit of readers not familiar with Rocketdyne, I provide the first paragraph of the back cover of the authoritative book, Kraemer (2005):

> From the first American orbiting satellite, to Neil Armstrong, and Buzz Aldrin's historical walk on the Moon, virtually every major achievement in American Space history was made possible by a Rocketdyne engine. And, that record has stood true for over forty years, as today the Space Shuttle program continues to rely on engines designed and built by Rocketdyne. This book is the story behind that unprecedented accomplishment. It is the chronicle of success of one team of rocket pioneers who propelled the American space program from trailing the Soviet Union in the 1950s and early 1960s into today's position of leadership in space. It is a story of heroes and even a few villains, but mostly it is a story of triumphant success in the human venture into space. ... The rest of the book is a chronicle of both the author's own memories and experiences as a member of the Rocketdyne team, as well as those of other key members of this elite group, including: ... Bob Biggs. ... This book is a true testament to the human spirit—and to a dedicated and determined team of aerospace engineers who launched a nation into Space.

Real "rocket scientists" virtually never work alone. A modern rocket engine is far too complicated to be developed by one person. Many major advancements in science were produced by Rocketdyne and other contractors working on Apollo, and those contractors sought to employ the most sophisticated engineers and scientists. While I did work on major advances in engineering in collaboration with other engineers, I never published a paper while employed at Rocketdyne. In fact, if I had attempted to do so, I would have gotten into serious trouble. Everything I did at Rocketdyne was classified as "secret." My security clearance explicitly prohibited me from publishing any results or discoveries produced from my work.

While the aerospace industry has long been a major source of unpublished advances in science and engineering, Silicon Valley has more recently become a world center of scientific and engineering advances. The engineers and scientists working there are usually not permitted to publish their work, which is viewed as proprietary to their firms. We academics tend to equate collaboration and coauthorship, as a result of academia's emphasis on publication. That view is likely reflected by other chapters in this volume. But in the physical sciences, a large percent of the most important collaborative scientific research is not, and cannot be, published.

Since my intellectual origins as a scientist go back to my experiences at Rocketdyne, at which all research and development are necessarily collaborative, my publications, since becoming an economist, have usually been coauthored, often with graduate students. But a few of my most important papers were solely authored, such as my paper, Barnett (1980). In that paper, I originated the Divisia monetary aggregates and the modern literature on aggregation-theoretic aggregation over financial and monetary assets.

9.2 Rocket Science

One objective of this chapter is to contrast my experience as a collaborative rocket scientist with my experiences as an academic economist. Indeed, the contrast is sometimes stark.

My immediate supervisor at Rocketdyne was a brilliant engineer by the name of Robert E. (Bob) Biggs. I have been out of contact with him, since I became an economist, although I did see him on television recently being interviewed about the space program. He rose to high levels within that industry, as evidenced by his mention among the "elites" in the back cover quotation reprinted above from Kraemer (2005). You can find his dramatic biography and a paper by him in Fisher and Rahman (2009, pp. 15–26). His paper comprises Chapter 1 of that book and is entitled, "Rocketdyne F-1 Saturn V First Stage Engine." His contributions to the development of the F-1 rocket engine and subsequently to the Space Shuttle main rocket engine were major. When I knew him, he was a very unusual person, early in his career. He had no college degrees, but took night courses at UCLA in mathematics. He had become exceptionally innovative in the use of the Laplace transform in solving difficult problems, but that was by no means his only area of conspicuous expertise. He was very impressive and extraordinarily determined. One of his statements to me at that time was that if coins ever fell out of his pocket at the coffee vending machine, he would leave the coins on the floor, since his time was too valuable to be wasted picking up coins.

There were situations under which I had to talk with machinists in the factory about possible sources of unsolved problems in design or about the production of a device to be used in an experiment. One of the factory workers was an especially nice guy, who I found to be very helpful, when I needed something done by a machinist. I told Bob about him. Bob's reply was "I hate nice guys." Bob was likely the most brilliant engineer I knew at Rocketdyne. But would you expect such a person to be welcomed into academia as a professor? Similarly some of the best known and most successful scientists in Silicon Valley have no college degrees and have never published a paper in a peer-reviewed journal. Indeed real rocket science and economic "rocket scientists" in academia can be very different.

Bob Biggs' immediate supervisor was the F-1 Development Project Engineer, Stuart Mulliken, who in turn worked for the F-1 Project Engineer. The position of Project Engineer is a very powerful position, since he is in control of all of the engineering being done on the engine, with the Development Project Engineer being in charge of the system development engineering on the engine. I worked directly in the Project Office, which included a couple of dozen engineers who were at the center of the F-1 development engineering. Many staff specialists in such fields as thermodynamics and fluid dynamics worked in support groups that did not report directly to a project office and could work on any of the rocket engines being developed by the firm, such as the upper stage J-2 or H-1 rocket engines for Apollo. But any work done on the F-1 rocket engine by such a staff support engineer was under the control of the F-1 Project Engineer, who thereby had direct or indirect control over the work of hundreds of the firm's most brilliant engineers. In my work in the F-1 System Project Office, I often needed to be able to consult with experts in the staff support groups, especially regarding problems with the troublesome turbo pumps, which pumped the fuel and liquid oxygen into the engine's thrust chamber. Bob Biggs knew all of the staff support experts and invariably referred me to the relevant ones, when I needed specialized assistance.

In addition to being a fine engineer, Stuart Mulliken had an exceptionally outgoing and likeable personality, making it easy for him to gain the voluntary and cooperative support of any of the firm's engineers, when needed. He was the best-liked engineer I knew at Rocketdyne. I am sure he did not dislike "nice guys" and would have taken the few seconds to pick up any coins he might have dropped at the coffee vending machine. To my astonishment, when he was at the peak of his power and influence at Rocketdyne, he resigned to become a realtor in Los Angeles. Although he was not trained as an economist, his decision, in retrospect, was based upon a very insightful economic decision. This happened during the 1960s, when real estate was inexpensive in Los Angeles. Many people from the northern USA were moving to Los Angeles, because of the inexpensive real estate. The usual explanation of the low LA housing prices at that time was the lack of need to excavate to build basements for furnaces, since the winters were so mild. For example, I was offered the opportunity to buy a house in Beverly Hills at a low price. I declined, and continued renting an apartment, during the time I lived in California. Evidently my insight into regional economic trends was significantly inferior to Stuart Mulliken's. Considering what has happened to real estate prices since the 1960, I assume that Stuart must now be a very wealthy man.

9.3 Nonlinearity

In terms of methodology, the clearest contrasts between my work at Rocketdyne and my subsequent work as an economist are in terms of the degree of emphasis on nonlinearity and especially emphasis on measurement. At Rocketdyne, I had available vast amounts of experimental data, sometimes acquired at my request. We tested the F-1 rocket engine at Edwards Air Force Base. Rocketdyne's primary test facilities were in the beautiful Santa Susana Mountains at the western border of the San Fernando Valley. That facility was very conveniently located, since Rocketdyne's engineers were in buildings in Canoga Park at the west end of the San Fernando Valley.

The 2850-acre former rocket engine test site is now contaminated by a vast amount of radioactive isotopes and toxic chemicals and is currently undergoing one of the country's most challenging cleanup efforts. But the awesome, thunderous roar produced by the F-1 engine was so overwhelming, that it could have been heard from that high mountain down into the Valley, where residents would have complained or been alarmed. As a result, we instead used a highly secure location in Edwards Air Force Base, far from the nearest city in the central California dessert. Since the USA was under the incorrect impression that it was in a race with the Soviet Union to put astronauts on the moon, Rocketdyne had easy access to enormous amounts of money from NASA contracts to run tests of our rocket engines.

It was clear to me from the results of those tests that linear models could not accurately fit the data. With the availability of only early-generation mainframe computers, estimation of nonlinear models was challenging. But I did have access to a staff of statisticians to help. While estimation of nonlinear models is now much easier than at that time and while the economy is a much more complicated system than any rocket engine, I remain somewhat uncomfortable about the heavy use of linear econometric models by econometricians. However, that difference is minor compared with the difference in emphasis on measurement.

9.4 Measurement

The different emphasis on measurement is very major, especially between macroeconomics and rocket science. In fact, the disturbingly large magnitude of that gap motivated me to become the founder and first president of the new Society for Economic Measurement and is the primary motivation for my recent book, Barnett (2012).

The cost of our data acquisition at Rocketdyne was enormous. The cost of the fuel and oxidizers alone was extreme, along with the other costs of the tests run daily. Our staff of statisticians had particular expertise in the statistical design of experiments. We made extensive use of Latin square designs. In addition, the rocket engines and test stands were heavily instrumented to provide us with extensive data from each test. There is no way that we could successfully have developed that rocket engine without those tests and the thousands of resulting observations on hundreds of variables. In addition, the measurements on those variables had to be made with extraordinary accuracy.

For example, in one project that dominated my research for a year, I needed measurements of the engine's start times and the ability to predict those start times accurately to within a few milliseconds. The needed accuracy of that measurement was determined by NASA and imposed on us. The first stage of the Saturn Vehicle had five F-1 engines clustered to produce a total of 7.5 million pounds of thrust, to get the vehicle off the ground and on its way. The five engines had to start in a particular sequence, with great accuracy. An error of only milliseconds could have caused a catastrophic failure, called the "pogo effect," by which the vehicle would go into harmonic oscillations and break apart.[1] The failure of the vehicle would cause rupture of the fuel and oxidizer tanks and a resulting explosion that would have killed any astronauts unfortunate enough to have been in the command module sitting at the top of the vehicle. If you have ever seen any of the early tests of civilian or military rockets, you likely saw such explosions and thought that the rocket engine had exploded, when in fact the explosion was more likely caused by structural failure of the vehicle from pogo effect oscillations.

"Bifurcation" was discovered by the famous mathematician, Henri Poincaré (1885), for which he won the Gold Medal of the Royal Astronomical Society (1900).[2] Indeed, those explosions were bifurcations. Such phenomena are well known to engineers. Consider, for example, the frequent law suits against automobile manufacturers, resulting from fatalities of drivers or passengers following bifurcations of automobile dynamics. Such bifurcations and resulting catastrophes usually are caused by very small errors in design or manufacture.[3]

In my opinion, here lies the source of the largest gap between rocket science and economic science. In real rocket science, engineers are fully aware of the implications of systems theory, which emphasizes that small changes in data or parameters can cause major changes in system dynamics. The cause is crossing a bifurcation boundary in parameter space. As a result, "errors in the variables" in rocket science are investigated by exploring the effects of small changes of variables in data space on solution dynamics in function space, if the parameters are known. If the parameters are unknown and estimated, then the relevant mapping is from the data space to the space of stochastic processes, since the solution functions are then stochastic processes. By contrast, macroeconomists tend to look upon "errors in the variables" in terms of a mapping from one Euclidean space to another, not from one Euclidean space to a function space. For example, it is common to consider the effect of a small data error on estimates of elasticities of substitution. Small changes in the domain space of that mapping typically produce small changes in the range space of the mapping. Systems theoretic dynamical robustness is a very different matter.

Economic theorists are well aware of the consequences of bifurcation, and many theoretical papers have been published on that subject. But when policy simulations of macroeconometric models are run, they typically are run with the parameters set only at their point estimates. For example, when I was on the staff of the Federal Reserve Board, I never saw such policy simulations delivered to the Governors or to the Open Market Committee with parameters set at any points in the parameter estimators' confidence region, other than at the point estimate. This mind-set suggests to macroeconomists that small errors in data or in parameter estimates need not be major concerns, and hence emphasis on investment in measurement in macroeconomics is not at all comparable to investment in measurement in real rocket science. If macroeconomic policy simulations were conducted at various points within the confidence regions, the sensitivity of dynamical inferences to measurement would become as widely understood in economics as in rocket science.

The confidence regions of the parameter estimators of most macroeconometric models are intersected by bifurcation boundaries, producing a robustness problem for dynamical inferences. See Barnett and Chen (2015), who survey a large number of such bifurcation boundary searches over models spanning all modern classes of macroeconometric models, including recent models with rational expectations, older Keynesian models with adaptive expectations, Euler equation models with deep parameters, open economy models, endogenous growth models, new Keynesian models with Taylor rule or inflation targeting policy equation, linear models and nonlinear models, continuous time and discrete time models, and Marshallian macroeconometric models with industrial free entry, among others. In fact we have not succeeded in finding a single model that is not vulnerable to the problem, as would perhaps not surprise an economic theorist familiar with Grandmont's (1985) early result.[4]

It is tempting to blame central bank economists for this problem, as a result of their vested interest in the ability to provide unqualified policy simulation recommendations to the bank's governors. But in fact academic economists are no less to blame. I have been the editor of the Cambridge University Press journal, *Macroeconomic Dynamics*, since it was founded in 1997. Although that journal has published many papers containing policy simulations with parameters estimated or calibrated at a point, I rarely recall having received a submission that systematically investigated robustness of those dynamical inferences to variations of the parameters within the confidence region around the point estimate.[5]

Of course, it is not necessary to be a "rocket scientist" to recognize that there are serious problems with the availability and quality of macroeconomic data. Media reporters with no knowledge of bifurcation have been complaining about those data for years. For example, the following by Mandel (1994) appeared as the cover story of *Business Week* magazine,

> The economic statistics that the government issues every week should come with a warning sticker: User beware. In the midst of the greatest information explosion in history, the government is pumping out a stream of statistics that are nothing by myths and misinformation.

The following appeared more recently in the *Economist* (2015) magazine: "Established macroeconomists would do well to pay attention. They should start by being much more careful about data."

Indeed, some economists have themselves been observing the problem for decades. Consider, for example, the following from Boulding (1970, p. 233): "We seem to be producing a generation of economists now, whose main preoccupation consists of analyzing data which they have not collected and who have no interest whatever in what might be called a data-reality function, that is, into what extent a set of data corresponds to any significant reality in the world."

9.5 The Federal Reserve

I was a research economist in the Special Studies Section of the Federal Reserve Board in Washington, D.C., for seven years. Sadly that elite research section no longer exists. While some of my most important solely authored papers were published during those years, such as Barnett (1980), collaboration in various forms is common within the Federal Reserve. Federal Reserve economists have easy access to data, assistance, and interaction with other economists. Although collaboration within the Federal Reserve is not comparable to the tightly bound collaboration of engineers within aerospace firms, collaboration within the Federal Reserve does not necessarily lead to coauthorship. For example, the Special Studies Section chief, Peter Tinsley, for whom I worked, was regularly a source of information and inspiration. In addition, he strongly encouraged collaboration and was a valuable source of information about which economists on the Board's staff possessed expertise in areas relevant to my research. But I never coauthored a paper with Peter.

Coauthorship and publication were not constrained at the Federal Reserve to the same degree as at Rocketdyne, since there are no national security clearance issues.[6] Nevertheless, publication is not as unconstrained as in academia. Publication in the Federal Reserve *Bulletin* or in a Federal Reserve regional bank's *Review* goes through a screening procedure at higher levels of the organization. The final published version of the article in the Federal Reserve System publications might differ substantially from the authors' original submission. Screening of publications in professional academic journals was much lighter, but did exist. I do not know whether that is still the case. When screening began at the Board, while I was there, the procedure seemed puzzling.

When I first arrived at the Board, we were free to submit papers to professional journals without any internal review at all. But shortly after I arrived, an internal review requirement was implemented. Prior to submission to a journal, the Federal Reserve Board staff authors had to provide the paper to a high-ranking Board staff officer for review. He invariably marked some changes in wording onto the manuscript. Making those "suggested" changes was mandatory before submission to a journal. I found this review to be puzzling, since those changes rarely were substantive and never altered the nature of my reported research or the conclusions. The changes of wording seemed trivial and harmless. As a result, I asked my section chief, Peter Tinsley, what the purpose of those changes was. The answer was surprising. I will need to provide some relevant background before explaining this paradox.

Prior to the time that I arrived at the Board, one of the staff's best economists, William Poole, left on leave for the Federal Reserve Bank of Boston and then permanently to Brown University. Along with others, he became an outspoken critic of the Federal Reserve, frequently publishing his criticisms in the public media. Peter Tinsley told me that the seemingly harmless censorship was designed to remove or modify sentences that were worded in a manner that Poole might have found to be quotable in the *American Banker*, in which he had a regular byline. Considering how worried the Board and its senior staff were about Poole's publications, I was surprised many years later when his appointment as the president of the Federal Reserve Bank of St. Louis was approved by a subsequent Federal Reserve Board chairman. But it was another time and another place. The time during which the Board and its senior staff were so worried about Poole and the Fed's other critics was the 1970s—a time of intense controversy about inflation.

Although the odd censorship of journal articles at the Board was harmless, and although the economists at the Federal Reserve normally do not have security clearances, there are nevertheless some severe constraints on Federal Reserve employees. The Federal Reserve acquires some data from private-sector suppliers under confidentiality agreements. Any economist who makes any of those data public is in serious trouble. While I was there, an economist supplied to *Consumer Reports* magazine data on interest rates being paid by individual banks throughout the country on deposits. Although any bank will reveal that information, if asked, the "reserve file" that housed that data at the Board was acquired under a confidentiality agreement. When the *Consumer Reports* article appeared, Chairman

Burns asked the FBI to investigate his entire staff to find the person who had provided the data to *Consumer Reports.* The economist who had done that, perhaps believing he had to provide the data under the Freedom of Information Act, was tracked down by the FBI and fired.

There also are security clearance issues at the Federal Reserve, but not of a sort usually evident to researchers. The Federal Reserve senior staff members with access to Federal Open Market Committee (FOMC) material must be very careful. In fact, the Federal Reserve Bank presidents and senior staff with access to the FOMC secure server are subject to background investigation before appointment.

Since Federal Reserve economists publish widely and speak frequently at conferences, it is tempting to believe that the culture and attitudes are similar to those in academia. When I was at the Board, the Staff Director of Monetary Policy had the most powerful position on the Federal Reserve Board's staff. He told us "Never trust academics. They are glory seekers." Considerably more insights of that sort can be found in Barnett (2012).[7]

9.6 Academia

My first academic position was at the University of Texas at Austin. I was never an assistant professor or associate professor. The University of Texas hired me away from the Federal Reserve Board as a full professor with an endowed chair. Academia proved to be another world for me. There were no longer any constraints on what I could publish, and indeed collaboration usually did result in coauthorship. In accordance with the maxim, "publish or perish," the incentive to publish was clear and unconditional. Because of my intellectual origins at Rocketdyne, I immediately began collaboration with other professors and with my own PhD students, some of whom have become famous. For example, Salam Fayyad became the Prime Minister of the Palestinian Authority. In addition, I have always supervised large numbers of PhD dissertations, since I value that kind of interaction to the same degree I did at Rocketdyne, when all work was necessarily collaborative. But unfortunately I have not had access in academia to the kind of experimental data available at Rocketdyne. The potential value of such data became evident to me, when Barnett et al. (1997) conducted a controlled competition among tests for nonlinearity. Robustness of econometric inferences across competing tests was found to be disturbingly low.

Considering how many collaborators and coauthors I have had at the University of Texas, at Washington University, and at the University of Kansas, I find it to be difficult to decide which to mention. Names that immediately come to mind include Apostolos Serletis, Marcelle Chauvet, Melvin Hinich, Ron Gallant, John Geweke, John Keating, Michael Belongia, and my two most productive current Ph.D, students, Liting Su and Guo Chen. With the exception of Mike Belongia, I have coauthored papers with each of those, but indeed my interactions with Mike and his coauthor, Peter Ireland, would rank high in terms of the intellectual influences among us. My work with Paul Samuelson on our book, Barnett and Samuelson (2007), translated into seven languages, was a unique and unforgettable experience. Others with whom I have coauthored or coedited books include Karl Shell, Kenneth Singleton, Ernst Berndt, Halbert White, James Powell, George Tauchen, Andreu Mas-Colell, Jean Gabszewicz, Claude D'Apremont, Bernard Cornet, Maurice Salles, Herve Moulin, Giancarlo Gandolfo, Alan Kirman, Mark Salmon, David Hendry, Svend Hylleberg, Timo Terasvirta, and Carl Chiarella, among others. My discussions with Ilya Prigogine, Nobel Laureate in Physics at the University of Texas, influenced me in profound manners.

9.7 Conclusion

It has been a long road through many lifestyles. The most conspicuous differences among them have been in the nature of collaboration and publication, and the nature of the constraints on them. In terms of which experience was closest to the formal definition of science, in accordance with the "scientific method," there is no question which it was. It was at Rocketdyne, and indeed the work at Rocketdyne was the most exciting I have ever encountered. In terms of which has proven to be the most intellectually rewarding, there also is no question. It is academia. The intellectual freedom provided by academia is unmatched, and the ability to supervise and work with my own Ph.D. students on their dissertations is deeply rewarding. My work at the Federal Reserve Board was somewhere in the middle ground, but was no less important to my life's work and to my development as a scholar.

Finally, it should be observed that institution type does not necessarily dominate collaboration experience. It is not my intention to impute my experiences at three types of institutions to everyone who has worked in central banks, universities, and high-tech private firms. Beyond the influence of the research setting, collaboration tends to be idiosyncratic to personalities, including the nature of the other personalities at the institution. In fact, there is now a highly relevant new field called the "science of team science" (SciTS), dominated by psychologists. That field has its own society, running regular conferences.[8]

Notes

1. Another source of the pogo effect was unstable low-frequency oscillations in combustion in the engine's thrust chamber or of propellant feed at the resonant frequency of the vehicle. This problem was troublesome with the second stage engine, the J-2. With the F-1, the risk was caused by sudden compression of the fuel lines during engine start, especially of the central engine. A consequence could be fluctuations in fuel pressure through feedback.
2. A bifurcation is a fundamental change in the nature of the solution path to a dynamical system, such as change from monotonic stability, to damped stability, or to unstable periodic oscillations. While many bifurcations are from stable to unstable dynamics, soft bifurcations are from one type of stable dynamics to another. There are an infinite number of types of unstable bifurcations, with chaos being a limiting case. But there are also an infinite number of soft bifurcations, such as from periodic damped stability to multiperiodic damped stability. Soft bifurcations can produce dramatically different behavior over finite lengths of time.
3. I first became aware of this problem long ago, while working for the Rochester Products Division of General Motors. Tiny changes in settings or in design could produce dramatic changes in behavior, such as engine stall. The laboratory used to test new designs was instruments for extremely precise measurements.
4. That model was an elementary classical model with rational expectations, continuous market clearing, no rigidities or market failures, perfect competition, and Cobb Douglas consumers and firms, with all solutions being Pareto optimal. Grandmont proved that the parameter space is stratified into an infinite number bifurcation subsets supporting monotonic stability at one extreme, chaos at the other extreme, and an infinite number of multiperiod solutions between. More recent models capable of producing policy relevant

non-Pareto-optimal solutions can produce even more complex forms of bifurcation, as surveyed by Barnett and Chen (1985).
5. Explorations of robustness to parameter estimates produced in different manners are relatively common, but such studies remain about point estimates, not about variations within the confidence region about the estimates. For example, there have been studies of new Keynesian models with Taylor rules or inflation targeting equations under various assumptions about "active" versus "passive" and forward-looking versus backward-looking rules. For surprising results from systematic investigation for bifurcation boundaries within the parameter space of such models, see section 4 of Barnett and Chen (2015).
6. I did not work in the International Finance Division, which had access to CIA data and was subject to higher security constraints than the Division of Research and Statistics.
7. Barnett (2012) won the American Publishers Award for Professional and Scholarly Excellence (the PROSE Award) for the best book published in economics during 2012.
8. See www.scienceofteamscience.org/.

References

Barnett, W. A. (1980). Economic monetary aggregates: An application of index number and aggregation theory. *Journal of Econometrics, 14*, 11–48.

Barnett, W. A. (2012). *Getting it wrong: How faulty monetary statistics undermine the fed, the financial system, and the economy.* Cambridge, MA: MIT Press.

Barnett, W. A., & Chen, G. (2015). Bifurcation of macroeconometric models and robustness of dynamics inferences. *Foundations and Trends in Econometrics,* Vol. 8: No. 1–2, 2015, pp. 1–144. http://dx.doi.org/10.1561/0800000026

Barnett, W. A., & Samuelson, P. A. (2007). *Inside the economist's mind: Conversations with eminent economists.* Malden, MA: Blackwell/Wiley Publishing.

Barnett, William A., A. R. Gallant, M. J. Hinich, J. A. Jungeilges, D. T. Kaplan, and J. J Jensen (1997), "A single-blind controlled competition among tests for nonlinearity and chaos," *Journal of Econometrics,* vol 82, pp. 157–192.

Boulding, Kenneth E. (1970, fall), "After Samuelson, who needs Adam Smith," *History of Political Economy* 2(3), pp. 225–237.

Fisher, S. C., & Rahman, S. A. (eds.) (2009). *Remembering the giants: Apollo rocket propulsion development.* The NASA History Series, NASA History

Division, National Aeronautics and Space Administration, Office of External Relations, Washington, DC.

Grandmont, J. M. (1985). On Endogenous Competitive Business. *Econometrica, 53*, 995–1045.

Kraemer, R. S. (2005). *Rocketdyne: Powering humans into space*, AIAA Education, American Institute of Aeronautics and Astronautics, Reston, VA.

Mandel, M. M. (1994, November). The real truth about the economy: Are government statistics so much pulp fiction? Take a look. *Business Week, 7*, 110–118.

Poincaré, H. (1885). L'Équilibre d'une Masse Fluide Animée d'un Mouvement de Rotation. *Acta Mathematica, 7*, 259–380.

The Economist. (2015). A long way from Dismal. January 10–16, vol. 414, no. 8920, p. 8.

CHAPTER 10

Why We Collaborate in Mathematical Ways

Graciela Chichilnisky

Is it better to write alone? The classical works of economics were authored by one individual. Intellectual work used to be a lonely activity requiring a solitary disposition.

Things have changed. Today intellectual work is no longer a lone contribution: it is gradually becoming a highly social activity. The personality traits of a successful scientist are also changing. The library mouse is disappearing, and is being replaced by collaborators and great communicators. Publish or perish still counts—but who you publish or perish with counts at least as much.[1]

Even in the business world collaboration is increasingly acceptable these days. The first reaction to a new idea or to a new project seems to be to work with others, to collaborate. There is a sense in which collaboration has become more socially acceptable than naked competition. There seems to be a shift in our model of competition that is at the core of capitalism.

What is causing the change?

G. Chichilnisky (✉)
Columbia University, New York, NY, USA

M. Szenberg, L.B. Ramrattan (eds.), *Collaborative Research in Economics*, DOI 10.1007/978-3-319-52800-7_10

10.1 Lonely Work versus Collaboration in the Knowledge Economy

A profound change in the pattern of human productivity is shifting the balance between competition and collaboration. This change is most visible in modern economies where knowledge has become an important input of production. This anticipates changes in the structure of capitalistic economies where naked competition—a zero sum game—used to be the norm. Here we argue that the change has to do with the human brain and how it acquires and improves skills.

10.2 Division of Labor Then and Now

A main rationale for lonely work is the benefits from the "division of labor." This is an attractive paradigm originating from international trade. It argues that if each nation specializes in what they do best and trade with others, everybody is better off.

David Ricardo argued that Portugal was better off by producing wine as it has more sun, and England was better at producing textiles. Both England and Portugal could produce more by specializing and when they traded, they ended up with more wine and more textiles for everybody.

The "division of labor" paradigm is pervasive and was even used to explain the division of labor at home. The classic economist George Becker (1985) argued for a division of labor at home, for men to work in the marketplace and women at home caring for the children. He viewed this as an optimal "division of labor." This "Stone Age" vision of home life had a rational basis. After all, men are better paid than women in the marketplace—women receive about 70 cents for every dollar received by a man. This difference is persistent and consistent, it holds across occupations and through time. It is true in the USA today. There is no Equal Pay Act for American women. But what is cause and what is effect? The arrow can go the other way. If we continue to pay men more than we pay women, then specialization can pay off.

In any case, the Stone Age argument is actually wrong as we will see below. Think of the problem in the context of intellectual work. Each author can specialize in one topic or area and produce more this way, benefitting us all. This is an appealing argument for going it alone. But is it correct? No, I will show it is not. Otherwise there would not be so much collaboration today.

What is wrong with the division of labor? Why not specialize in a single topic and share the knowledge produced with others? What is wrong with traditional international trade where poor nations export raw materials forever and rich nations produce capital goods? What was wrong with women and men in the Stone Age? What is wrong with unbridled capitalistic competition where each does what they do best and trade, as an organizing force? If these appealing arguments hold, where does the appeal of collaboration come from?

New findings discussed below show that division of labor works best only at the beginning of a production process. In a mature activity collaboration is better in ensuring more productivity. This is why things are changing. In the physical and biological sciences, which have been longer at it, collaboration is now the norm. This is why human societies are moving away from the Stone Age, even if admittedly at a slow pace. The rationale and explanation for increased collaboration is in the human brain, on how the human brain acquires and perfects skills.

Let us see how this works.

10.3 How the Human Brain Acquires and Perfects Skills

There is a new finding on how the division of labor evolves through time (Chichilnisky and Eisenberger 2005). It starts from and develops the classic work of Arrow (1963) on the economics of how the brain learns. Arrow pointed out that the more time we spend in a given activity the better we become at doing it. This is called *learning by doing*. Becker (1985) used Arrow's work and assumed that marginal productivity increases with time, which means that the more we learn the faster we can learn in each unit of time. Under these conditions, it is true that each person in the family (man or woman) should specialize as Becker shows—one should specialize in working at home, and the other in the marketplace. Both are more productive, at home and in the marketplace, thus increasing family welfare. As a direct consequence of Becker's assumption, when women's salaries are lower than men's, women should do all the housework. Men should only work in the marketplace. Since in reality women's salaries are lower than men's, historically and currently, Becker's assumption leads directly to a division of labor where women stay at home and men work in the marketplace. Under Becker's assumption the Stone Age and some of the current situation is a rational and efficient solution. But we will see that this is a limited explanation and that things can turn around drastically in a more evolved society where knowledge plays an important role and there is learning by doing.

There is indeed learning by doing in our society, and therefore Becker's assumption is reasonable, but as we will see this is true only up to a point. Human beings produce more when they repeat their tasks and learn from this over time, but they need rest after a number of working hours and there is a decrease in marginal productivity beyond a certain number of hours of work. Accordingly, the time derivative of the home production function is initially positive, but, after a maximum is reached, it starts to decrease since humans cannot increase productivity forever without rest. The same thing occurs when allocating time to an activity. This is critical for the shift through time from division of labor to collaboration.

New results indicate that the gains obtained from the division of labor depend on the shape of the learning-by-doing curve (Chichilnisky and Eisenberger 2005). This shape in turn is determined by how the human brain acquires and perfects skills.

10.4 Findings in Experimental Psychology

There is overwhelming experimental evidence of the learning-by-doing curve in experimental psychology which agrees that the time needed to execute a task $z(t)$ decreases exponentially with the number of trials t. There is an asymptotic limit K due to limitations on neurons' firing, so that we may write

$$z(t) = k + e^{-t}$$

10.5 From Experimental Psychology to Economics

To move from experimental psychology to economics, one identifies time t with the number of trials and the output per unit of time $g(t)$ is identified with the inverse of the time of execution. From the above equation this yields the logistic curve:

$$g(t) = \frac{1}{(k + e^{-t})} \tag{1}$$

illustrated in a special case below (Fig. 10.1):

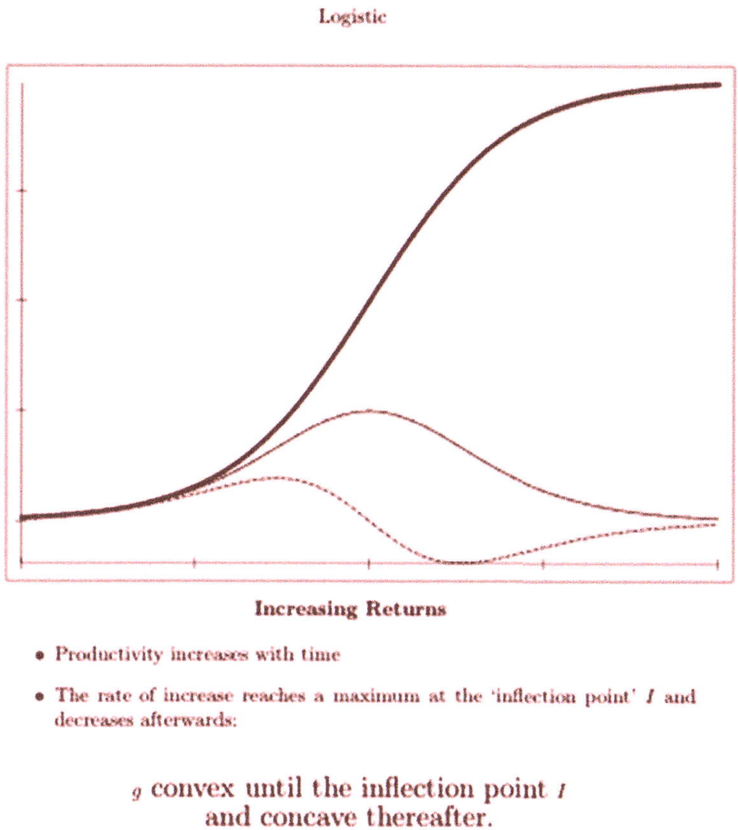

Fig. 10.1 Logistic Curve of Increasing Returns

If $g(t)$ is the amount of a good produced with t hours worked then, as empirically observed, increases in productivity through time $(d/dt)g$ follow a modified quadratic form, increasing initially with t and then decreasing with t as explained above, for example

$$dg/dt(t) = ag - bg^2 \; (a,b > 0) \tag{2}$$

Equation (2) integrates to yield the classic logistic curve that is illustrated above, which has also been used for example to describe the evolution of biological populations over time.

Observe that the first convex part of the logistic (1) is similar to Becker's (1985) assumption and yields similar results. On the other hand the concave part, which occurs after the inflection point I in the logistic curve, is reached, where the derivative goes from positive to negative, yields very different results, as shown below. The inflection point I determines a change from one regime to the other; it appears in the diagram above as the maximum of the quadratic curve illustrated below the logistic, which is the time derivative of g. In the following we assume that production in modern economies has reached the inflection point, an assumption that seems to tally with the evidence. We describe this situation as having achieved higher levels of output.

10.6 Regime Shift in the Learning Curve

There is a regime shift that is validated everywhere in experimental psychology: after a number of trials the curve turns from convex to concave—namely, from what can be described as Becker's shape to Arrow's shape. This shift changes the optimal allocation of resources and decides whether or not division of labor is the optimal solution, as discussed below.

10.7 Solving a Classic Problem of Resource Allocation

A classic problem of resource allocation is how to allocate two resources efficiently between two competing activities. New results on division of labor are that the optimal division of labor depends on the shape of the learning curve:

Theorem 1: (Chichilnisky and Eisenberger 2005)

1. The theorem characterizes the Pareto efficient allocation of two scarce resources between two sectors each of which has logistic production technologies as illustrated in the figure above.

   (i) When the average total effort allocated to a sector is below the inflection point I, that is, $(L1 + L2)/2 < I$, where $L1$ is the time input by the first individual and $L2$ is the time input of the second individual, and I is the "inflection point" in the logistic curve in the diagram, then Pareto efficiency[2] requires specialization, namely it is achieved when $L1 = 0$ or $L2 = 0$.

(ii) However, when the average effort allocated to the sector exceeds 1, $(L1 + L2)/2 > I$, then Pareto efficiency requires equal division of labor within each of the two sectors namely $L1 = L2$.

Why does it matter whether we are in the convex part of the logistic, namely before the inflection point *I*, or in the concave regime namely after *I*?

Here is the reason: by definition of convexity and concavity, the convex regime satisfies (3) below and the concave regime instead satisfies (4) below:

$$\big(g(x)+g(y)\big)/2 > g\big((x+y)/2\big) \tag{3}$$

$$\big(g(x)+g(y)\big)/2 < g\big((x+y)/2\big) \tag{4}$$

In the first (convex) regime prior to *I*, distributing equally the input between the two collaborators yields less output than having one of them specialize (one of them has input *x* and the other has input *0*) because according to (2)

$$g(x/2)\big\langle\big(g(x)+g(0)\big)/2 \text{ or equivalently } g(x)\big\rangle 2g(x/2)$$

The opposite is true in the concave regime because according to (3) more output is produced if the two share the input equally, namely

$$g(x/2) > \big(g(x)+g(0)\big)/2 \text{ or equivalently } g(x) < 2g(x/2)$$

Corollary 1. At higher levels of skill, distributing labor equally between co-workers produces more output for the same total of labor.

10.8 Why Do We Collaborate?

The following proposition follows directly from the above

Proposition 2. At higher levels of output, collaboration is superior in terms to productivity than the division of labour

Lonely work or classic division of labor is the efficient solution with increasing returns or *convexity* (Becker 1985). Becker's learning by doing leads in this case to specialization: for example, some work at home, and others in the marketplace. Indeed, when women salaries are lower than men's, it is efficient that women do housework and men work in the marketplace.

But this first case does not explain why women are working increasingly in the marketplace and, to the point of this note, why collaboration is increasingly frequent.

The reason we find is that at higher levels of input, as it corresponds to modern economies, distributing labor equally between coauthors—or between men and women at home—produces more output for the same total labor.

This is because the more time we work on an activity the more productive we become—however, over time the marginal increase of productivity starts to decrease, and we have a *concave* learning curve (Arrow 1953).

10.9 Conclusion

In an economy with learning by doing, the division of labor is most productive initially, before the inflection point of the logistic. Collaboration becomes a more efficient use of resources, however, later, after the inflection point of the logistic. This is due to the concavity of the learning-by-doing curve at higher input levels.

Notes

1. Exceptions are when one is explicitly required to work alone, such as Ph.D. dissertations and tenure track work, although in the latter cases the quality of one's collaborators seems a positive factor.
2. A Pareto efficient allocation of resources requires that there is no reallocation of the given total resources that makes everybody better off.

Selected References

Arrow, K. J., Barankin, E. W., & Blackwell, D. (1953). Admissible points of convex sets. *Contributions to the Theory of Games, 2*, 87–91.

Arrow, K. (1963). The implications of learning by doing in economics. *Review of Economic Studies.*

Becker G. (1985). Human capital effort and the sexual division of labor. *Journal of Labor Economics.*

Chichilnisky, G., & Eisenberger, P. (2005). Science and the family.

CHAPTER 11

Collaborative is Superadditive in Political Economics

Richard Zeckhauser

The nature of research in economics has changed a great deal in the last century. The locus of expertise has moved from Europe and most notably the UK, to the USA. Books have overwhelmingly been replaced by journal articles and discussion papers, including postings on the web. Grand theorizing and words get much less attention these days; empirical analyses and mathematics get much more. Whereas lone authors were once the norm, the most important research these days usually has multiple authors. This last phenomenon is the subject of this chapter and of this book.

This chapter first presents some numerical evidence on the trend in economics toward multiple authors. Then it provides potential explanations for the profession's move from mostly single-author works to mostly multiple-author works. Subsequent sections present a model of the production process for works with multiple authors. The model informs a discussion of why collaboration might be pursued insufficiently, and of ways to secure maximum value from collaborations.

Let me apologize in advance. A number of the arguments in this chapter are speculative, relying on personal assessments of the nature of the collaborative process. They are based on my own heavily collaborative

R. Zeckhauser (✉)
Kennedy School, Harvard University, Cambridge, MA, USA

M. Szenberg, L.B. Ramrattan (eds.), *Collaborative Research in Economics*, DOI 10.1007/978-3-319-52800-7_11

research career, on anecdotal evidence from others, and on what might be called back-of-the-envelope empirical investigations, accomplished, for example, by scanning the tables of contents of leading journals. This chapter argues that collaborations, particularly those involving individuals with different backgrounds and training, have great potential, much of which is not realized. This chapter makes the general argument that attempting collaborations provides option value; that is, if collaboration looks promising, it can be repeated. To those who are contemplating their first professional collaboration, in the spirit of this chapter my principal advice is: "Try it; you may like it."

11.1 Evidence of Increasing Collaboration

In economics, as in most professions, the ordinary seek to emulate the extraordinary. Those who chronicle the profession also look to the high outliers. Recognizing all the biases entailed, I provide evidence of collaborative activity by the winners of the Nobel Memorial Prize in Economics (Nobel Prize) and by the much younger winners of the John Bates Clark Award. My goal is to examine the trend in collaboration over a period of several decades.

Let us begin with Nobel Prize winners, for whom I expect the number of collaborations to increase over time. However, since the Nobel is awarded to individuals of different ages, holding the year of the prize fixed, I expect older winners, who presumably also worked in their younger years, to have fewer collaborations. Note, we refer to collaborations, not to the number of collaborators. Figures 11.1 and 11.2 show the number of collaborations for Nobel Prize winners for their single most cited and for their ten most cited works, respectively. The upward trend is clear in both graphs. Notably, none of the first ten Nobel Prize winners had any collaborators on their single most cited work. The graph for each winner's three most cited works, not shown, gives a very similar impression.

Let c_i represent the number of collaborative works among the i most cited, $i = 1$ and 10, x_1 the number of years since the first year of the Nobel Prize, and x_2 the Nobelists' ages in the year of the award. The equations giving the number of collaborations are:

$$c_1 = 0.52963 + 0.00682x_1 - 0.00721x_2$$
$$c_{10} = 7.34062 + 0.08931x_1 - 0.08518x_2$$

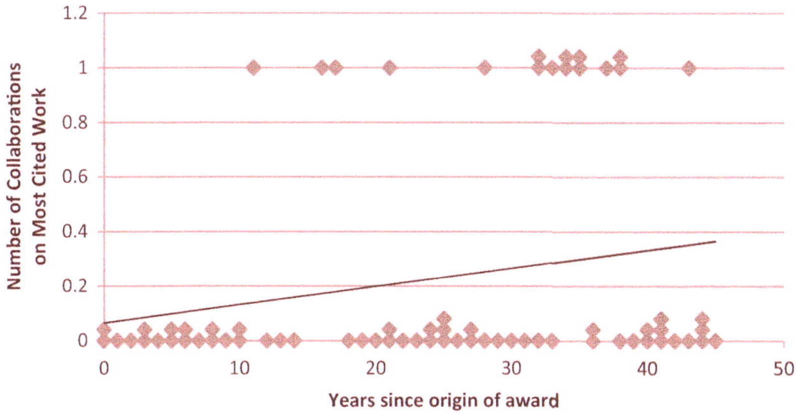

Fig. 11.1 Collaborations on Nobel Prize Winners' Most Cited Work

Fig. 11.2 Number of collaborations Within Nobel Prize Winners' Ten Most Cited Works

For c_1, the number of elapsed years barely misses significance at the 0.05 level ($z = 1.958$); for c_{10} it is significant well beyond the 0.001 level. Age is significant for c_{10} at the 0.05 level, but is not significant for c_1.[1]

For the John Bates Clark Award, the two figures are similar to those for the Nobel Prize (Figs. 11.3 and 11.4).

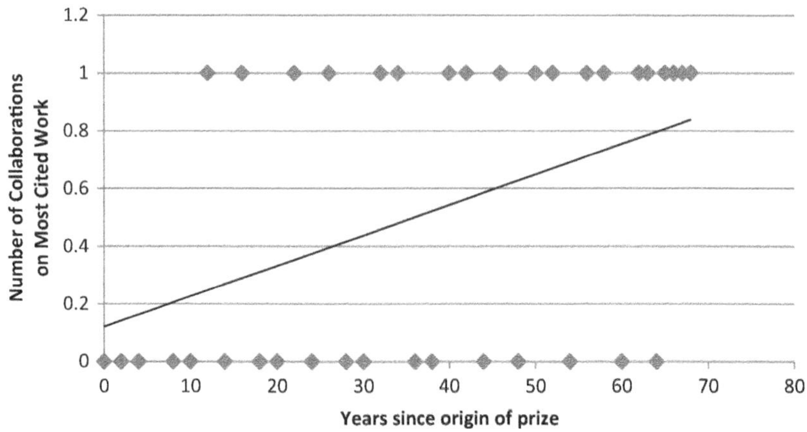

Fig. 11.3 Collaborations on John Bates Clark Award Winners' Most Cited Work

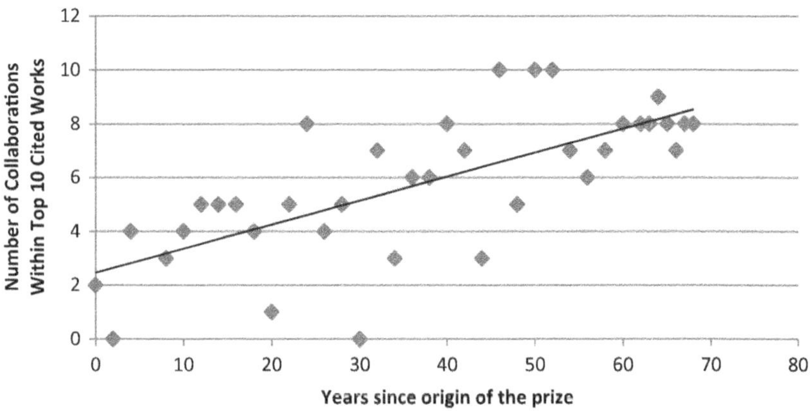

Fig. 11.4 Number of collaborations Within John Bates Clark Award Winners' Ten Most Cited Works

The Clark Award is given to individuals younger than 40; the winners are almost always close to 40 in age. Not surprisingly, age is never a significant explanatory variable; hence x_2 is not included in the regressions below. Let C_i represent the number of collaborative works among the i most cited, $i = 1$ and 10, and x_1 the number of years since the first year of the John Bates Clark Award. The equations giving the number of collaborations are:

$$C_1 = 0.11995 + 0.01056x_1$$
$$C_{10} = 2.45989 + 0.08918x_1$$

For both C_1, years are significant at the 0.005 level; for C_{10}, it is significant at well beyond the 0.00001 level.[2] As we would expect, for both Nobel Prize and John Bates Clark Award winners, the results are much more significant for the ten most cited works, given the greater data available.

Within both these extremely high prestige groups, there has been a strong trend toward increasing collaboration as the years have progressed.[3]

11.2 Explanations for Increasing Collaboration

Why has collaboration become much more the norm in economics? I believe that there are many factors. I shall identify just a few.

The need for specialization. The great economists of olden times mastered many disciplines or at least many areas of economics. Samuelson, Arrow, Friedman, Simon, Becker—to identify just a few American pioneers—were all masters of many realms within economics, and indeed often of realms in related disciplines. However, the advance of the field has called for specialization, as it has in so many domains, such as mathematics and medicine. The great emphasis on empirical work today has made it more effective to work in teams. Whereas a Friedman, a Samuelson, an Arrow, a Simon, or a Becker could make his greatest contributions merely by sitting in his office and thinking, most contemporary stars work with large data sets. When Friedman did turn to empirical work, in his *A Monetary History of the United States, 1867–1960*, he teamed up with Anna Schwartz, a data adept (Friedman and Schwartz 1963).

Two of the original American economics prize winners, Kuznets and Leontief, might seem to be exceptions.[4] They are noted for contributions that led to vast amounts of empirical work. Moreover, both scholars loved delving into real-world numbers. However, their major lasting contributions came from the methods and frameworks they developed individually. Kuznets created a sound basis for national income accounting, and Leontief invented input–output analysis.

Why has economics become both more specialized and more empirical? One possible explanation would be that the problems that are simultaneously important, conceptual, and tractable have disproportionately been solved. A second explanation could be that we now have access to data and the ability to process information in ways that did not exist when our predecessors made their major contributions. This suggests a Says Law of research methodology: when new methods become available, they will be used disproportionately. A third possibility would be that the advent of the personal computer, the Internet, and file sharing has dramatically lowered the cost of collaborative research investigations. When conducting large-scale data-gathering investigations, for example, collaboration is often essential. This has proved particularly true in the burgeoning field of behavioral economics, where data from laboratory and field studies[5] is the raw ingredient required to produce a successful product. A fourth conjecture is that the nature of advancement in the profession has changed. The pressures to publish or perish have become ever greater. And for getting publications out quickly, many hands make swift work.

I will argue that each of these four proposed explanations helps to explain why economics has become more collaborative. The discussion thus far might suggest that the choice to collaborate is a highly rational process; for example, when A and B are deciding whether to work together or work separately, they simply examine the production and credit functions and pick the mode of organization that yields the most value. An alternative model, leading to much the same conclusion, would be that processes akin to natural selection, with just a little support from careful deliberation, play a role. Thus, skirting rational assessment, some economists simply try out various modes of producing research. Strategies that are more successful get more attention, lead to promotions, and drive out inferior methods. Careful deliberation operates when individuals look consciously to imitate the more successful research methods.

Either of these models might lead to optimal research methods, though the second would encounter some lag. The lag might be a product, for example, of the old-dog-new-tricks impediment. Informal evidence indicates that—reflecting time trends—young scholars are much more collaborative than their older colleagues. Those older colleagues may have more trouble adapting and modifying their work habits.

11.3 Superadditivity in Production

We shall talk about researchers with different specialties, that is, different types, below. For now, consider a single type x, for example, a macroeconomist. Let $h(x)$ be what a single researcher can produce alone. Collaboration between two different x's yields output $g(x,x)$. Our concern is whether collaboration is worthwhile, in other words where it is superadditive. Superadditivity can come from better, not merely more, research, and indeed even from less. Superadditivity would be represented as

$$g(x,x) > 2h(x) \tag{1}$$

If this condition holds, then two macroeconomists working together could produce more than twice the output of one macroeconomist working alone. This condition would apply for some individuals on some projects, but not for other individuals or other projects.

11.4 A Model of Collaboration Costs and Benefits

We shall now allow for a second specialty (type), y, to illustrate an econometrician, and the possibility for a mixed collaboration between an x and a y. When shown as arguments in a production function, either variable represents a single researcher.

The concept of positive cross-partial derivatives drives a great number of phenomena in economics. Thus, for the function $z = f(K,L)$, with derivatives indicated by subscripts, such positivity would imply that $f_{KL} = f_{LK} >> 0$. This concept is particularly relevant in production theory. Thus, labor is more productive where capital is relatively more abundant, and vice versa. The same is true, I will argue, with collaboration in economics, and indeed in many realms. Disparate thinkers produce more when they are brought together.[6]

Think of a likely future economics paper, perhaps on the effect on low-skilled workers when the minimum wage is raised dramatically, a question of contemporary policy interest in the USA. I shall simplify discussion by assuming there are two macroeconomists who could get together and write an excellent paper. So, also, could two econometricians. But I would argue that if the collaborations encompassed different specialties, with a macroeconomist and an econometrician in each, the prospect of making major contributions would be greater. I would also argue that the single-specialty collaborations would be more likely to emerge. Macroeconomists disproportionately keep company with macroeconomists, and econometricians with econometricians. Collaborating with one's familiars is easier, and probably more fun, at least at the outset. In economists' terms, it is cheaper.

Collaboration costs are certainly relevant. Benefits, however, are the other weight on the balance scale. Posit the following situation. The two types of researchers, x and y, are equally productive. To be crass, let us say they produce as many top-tier journal articles—when working in a single-specialty collaboration. Thus, output $g(x,x) = g(y,y)$.[7] The output for an x,y collaboration is $f(x,y)$, and we are positing positive cross-partial derivatives, so that

$$f(x,y) >> g(x,x) = g(y,y) \tag{2}$$

To simplify for now, we will assume that, in any collaboration, the participants share the benefits and costs equally. Any collaboration incurs a transaction cost, as in explaining to a partner one's thinking, or as in just agreeing on how to proceed. All collaboration costs will be measured as the total costs to the partnership. Represent those costs for a single-specialty collaboration as k_p. The collaboration cost for a mixed x,y collaboration is k_m, where we expect $k_m >> k_p$. Represent the difference as $k_d = k_m - k_p$. Here k_d might represent the costs of explaining to one's collaborator the underpinnings of one's sub-discipline, of writing a joint paper when the styles of the two fields clash, and so on.

The optimal collaboration decision, assuming a one-time collaboration would be

Single-specialty collaboration if

$$f(x,y) - k_d < g(x,x) = g(y,y) \tag{3a}$$

Mixed collaboration if

$$f(x,y) - k_d > g(x,x) = g(y,y) \tag{3b}$$

Why might researchers not follow Eq. (3)? In particular, why might they continue with single-specialty collaboration when (3b) was satisfied? One possible answer, I believe, relates to hyperbolic discounting. The cost k of engaging in the collaboration is borne up front. We know that immediate costs get disproportionate weight relative to those that come later, a concept that we elaborate on in Section 7.

The strength of my argument that we see too few mixed collaborations in economics comes not so much from one-time collaborations, but from the multiple repeat collaborations that never happen. It may well be that for a single collaboration, k_d is large, so (3a) applies. Indeed, it could be that the first mixed collaboration yields negative value, that $f(x,y) - k_m < 0$. However, the initial k should be thought of as a price of entry. For any collaborators, once they have worked together, the cost of future collaborations will decline. Represent the costs of a particular collaboration in round i to be k_{mi} or k_{pi}. Thus,

$$k_{pi+1} < k_{pi} \tag{4a}$$

and

$$k_{mi+1} < k_{mi} \tag{4b}$$

Let us first consider (4a) by itself, and assume that only single-specialty collaborations are possible. Posit the empirical validity of (4a). If hyperbolic discounting leads researchers to assign to the immediate collaboration excessively high costs relative to the future value of collaborations, there will be too few single-specialty collaborations.

I am asserting a second key empirical fact: the costs of a mixed collaboration decrease faster than those of single-specialty collaboration. That implies that $k_{d+1} < k_d$. In short, even when a mixed collaboration might be less attractive than single-specialty collaboration on a one-time-only basis, as represented by (1a), a mixed collaboration might become preferable if there will be repeat collaborations. Of course, there is no reason why a researcher could not pursue both single-specialty and mixed collaborations, though time ultimately does become a constraint, as can timely subject matter.

In short, collaboration should not be thought of as merely a one-time process. Rather, there is the potential for investment in a collaborative partnership. The first trial with a collaborator may produce a net loss, but as with many investments, it has the potential to pay off over time. Additional factors could reinforce this observation. For example, there could be some equivalent of mutual learning, in which a collaboration yields increasing value over time; that is, $f(x,y)$ or $g(x,x)$ or $g(y,y)$ would increase as the collaboration moves forward. We now turn to another reason why potential long-term collaborations might be worthwhile, though short-term collaborations might not be.

Option value in collaboration. My formulation thus far has ignored uncertainty, a salient feature of research. The potential of collaboration adds a further uncertainty: will coauthors work together effectively? To address this case, I will simplify and talk only about the net value of a unit of the collaboration, v, and will further assume that v stays constant over time, a conservative assumption for the pro-collaboration argument. Here v can be negative and costly or positive and enriching. If v were known, there would be a simple rule: proceed if v is positive. In virtually any real-world partnership, however, v will be unknown. Then, to initiate a collaboration would essentially mean purchasing an option. The implication is that, if the uncertainty regarding v is great, as with any option, it might be worthwhile to proceed even if the expected returns are negative. Uncertainty promotes option value.

Whether one should purchase the option will depend on risk aversion, the potential number of trials, and the discount rate. To simplify, let us assume risk neutrality, two trials, and a zero discount rate. There exists the potential for a collaboration whose payoff is uniform on $[-4, 3]$, implying an expected payoff of $-1/2$ on a single trial. There is a $4/7$ chance that $v < 0$; if so, the researchers will cease collaborating after one period. However, there is a $3/7$ chance that the first trial will reveal that the collaboration is beneficial, that $v > 0$. If so, the average payoff will be $3/2$ in any second trial. Thus, the expected return from the collaboration will be $-1/2 + (3/7)(3/2) = 2/14 = 1/7$. The collaboration will yield positive expected value. If the uncertainty regarding the value of the option is greater, holding its mean payoff fixed, as is true with any option, will increase its value. Thus, if v were uniform on $[-10, 9]$, it would also have an expected payoff of $-1/2$ on a single trial. However, the expected return from two trials together would now be $-1/2 + (9/19)(9/2) = 62/38 = 1\ 12/19$. Of course, if there could be dozens of future trials, the expected value of venturing into collaboration with uncertain payoff would be much greater.[8] Conversely, a positive discount rate and/or risk aversion on the value of the option would diminish its value.

The real world, as would be expected, is much more complicated. It would presumably have the costs of collaboration declining over time, as modeled above. A single trial would not fully resolve the uncertainty about the period payoff to collaboration. Thus, there would be learning over time about the payoff, implying that it might be worthwhile to persist even if the first trial yielded a negative payoff. However, the central point that emerges from thinking about a potential collaboration in terms of purchasing an option is clear: it may be worth venturing a trial with a negative expected payoff in order to learn whether the payoff from future trials will be positive.

Moreover, leaving aside risk aversion and holding the mean payoff fixed, the greater the uncertainty about the payoff is, the more worthwhile it is to try out a collaboration. Empirically, this would seem to suggest, for a reason quite different from those considered above, that mixed collaborations deserve serious consideration. It is likely that uncertainties about their payoffs are greater than for single-specialty collaborations. Given that the future value of such an option would increase with the number of future trials, young scholars should be particularly eager to try out collaborations. That lesson is reinforced if, as posited above, the costs of collaboration decline with time.

11.5 Superadditivity in Credit

Of course, the collaborative authorship approach would only make sense if at least one of the two following conditions existed.

A. The production process was superadditive. That is condition (1); two individuals working together produce more than twice the value of research of the two individuals working alone. (Note the use of the word "value" and not "quantity.")
B. The credit process was superadditive. That is, an individual producing nine papers with two coauthors was more richly rewarded than by alone authoring three papers.

A. Credit in Collaborations. The allocation of credit is one of the most troubling issues in collaborative efforts. Perhaps more accurately, the question should be what practices should be employed, such as in the way authors are listed, to convey credit. Different disciplines have different practices. In economics, authors are usually listed alphabetically, unless there have been disproportionately significant contributions. In psychology, medicine, and many other scientific fields, most collaborative efforts list the principal contributors first and the heads of the labs last, with the heads getting named even if they made no intellectual contribution to that particular project. The disproportionate-contribution principle of economics not infrequently leads to conflict. Collaborator B thinks she has contributed enough more than A to be named first, but A thinks not; he may even think that he has contributed the lion's share. Parceling out credit is particularly difficult if B supplied the theory and A the empirical work, and if, as might seem natural, each rates her/his own realm as more important. Kahneman and Tversky (1979) were listed in that order for "Prospect Theory," but as Tversky and Kahneman (1974) for "Judgment under Uncertainty: Heuristics and Biases." These are their two best-known articles. Richard Zeckhauser, the current author, despite being alphabetically challenged, virtually always lists names on collaborations in alphabetical order. Listing order becomes particularly important when there are many authors on a paper. When A and B write a paper together, usually both authors will be indicated in citations. However, when A, B, C, and D produce a paper, perhaps with authors listed alphabetically, the paper will often be referred to as A et al.

Nevertheless, some highly successful economic teams have now worked out the arrangement of always listing all members alphabetically, even though the contributions of different members may vary considerably from project to project.[9] This approach has two major benefits: (1) It avoids all conflicts over credit and (2) it announces that listing order does not involve contribution fraction.

Departing from the listing question, why is credit likely to be super-additive? That is, when A and B collaborate, why should both of them end up with, for example, 60% of the credit? The answer lies in a straightforward extension of the phenomenon of egocentric biases in availability and attribution.[10] A significant experimental literature has shown that, when assessing credit for a group project, one's own contributions are more easily available than those of collaborators. Thus, individuals tend to assign to themselves greater credit for a successful group project than do their team members. Now consider credit given to two young collaborators, A and B, a theorist and a development economist, both hoping for promotions. When outside evaluation letters are sent out to theorists asking about A, the respondents will be much more familiar with A and will be better able to recognize his contributions. Being more available, A will get disproportionate credit from them for the contribution. The same will be true for B. Her development economist respondents will find her more available, and will give her the lion's share of credit.

Let me add a further speculation following this logic: the phenomenon of superadditive credit will be greater the more disparate the collaborators are. Thus, superadditivity will be more extreme for scholars from different universities, who attended different graduate schools, who have different specialties, and so on. That is because the greater the disparity among collaborators is, the greater will be their differences in availability to the various judges. In a collaboration across fields, not merely specialties, I was fortunate to write *The Patron's Payoff: Conspicuous Commissions in Italian Renaissance Art*, with Jonathan Nelson, an art historian (Nelson and Zeckhauser 2014). Jonathan's colleagues did not have the slightest familiarity with me or with economics and gave him 80% of the credit. My fellow economists were equally unfamiliar with Nelson and art history. They gave me most of the credit, though a few might have examined the deep art history in the book and properly assessed my inadequacies.

In short, I am arguing that, holding the size of the contribution fixed, there will be significant superadditivity in credit just because those who are judging A will know A better and those judging B will know B better.[11] This phenomenon will be more pronounced on average for mixed collaborations. Let me now leave credit aside, and turn to the productivity of collaborations.

11.6 Productivity in Mixed Collaborations in Music and in Economics

Collaborations in Popular Music. Given the statistics for economics presented above, where the trend has been strongly toward more collaboration, it is likely that the great collaborations in economics mostly lie in our future. That gives me latitude to illustrate my main point—that mixed collaborations have strong potential to be superadditive—by drawing on famous collaborations in the field of popular music.[12] Many extremely famous mixed collaborations arise in the field of popular music. Both music and lyrics are required, and a star at lyrics may not be a star at composition. Yet the two must be blended in tight form. The paired names of Gilbert and Sullivan and of Rogers and Hammerstein almost seem inseparable, though Rogers and Hammerstein each had successful collaborations with others. The Gilbert and Sullivan collaboration was not only prolific, with Gilbert on lyrics and Sullivan on music, but also often troubled. The two men had personalities that clashed, and quite differing political orientations, the latter a considerable handicap given that their shows satirized central features of British society.

Lennon and McCartney, often Lennon–McCartney, had the basic songwriting responsibilities for the Beatles. However, their songwriting collaboration was far from typical. Both were skilled at composition and lyrics; many of their collaborative songs were primarily, though rarely exclusively, the work of one or the other, though they were always co-listed as creators.

The Lennon–McCartney collaboration, like that of Gilbert and Sullivan, was mixed in terms of personalities. It was also a mingling in approaches to work. Cynthia Lennon, John's first wife, said: "John needed Paul's attention to detail and persistence. ... Paul needed John's anarchic, lateral thinking."[13]

Mixed Collaborations in Economics. The most famous collaborations of economists, I am confident, have involved diversity along a variety of dimensions beyond specialty, including personality and work habits. For example, Milton Friedman was a highly gregarious, eager debater. He had a remarkable propensity for conceptual formulation, a passion for simplification, and great powers of public persuasion. Anna Schwartz, by contrast, exemplified the quiet scholar. She was known for working exceptionally long hours in her office, where she deployed her remarkable skills in assembling, reviewing, and distilling vast amounts of information.[14]

Two other collaborations that greatly influenced economics deserve mention as mixtures. Von Neumann–Morgenstern represented the pairing of a brilliant mathematician, one of the great minds of the twentieth century, with a highly capable economist. It is doubtful that their monumental *Theory of Games and Economic Behavior* could have been written without both disciplines and both individuals (von Neumann–Morgenstern 1944). Kahneman and Tversky deserve credit for ushering in the behavioral revolution into economics. Though both were eminent scholars in the same field, their personalities differed substantially. Amos had a quick and playful demeanor; he leapt to insights. His manner reminded me of many a leading economist. Danny has the aura of a deeply reflective soul, of a philosopher. He is well possessed of the virtue of slow thinking. To this outside observer, he seemed much more inclined to behavioral tendencies than Amos.[15] One might speculate that to identify basic behavioral phenomena to investigate, Danny would make decisions, and he and Amos would then conducted a post mortem.[16] These remarkable psychologists cross-fertilized the formerly walled-off field of economics. They set the stage for the economists who now regularly collaborate with psychologists and neuroscientists to gain insight into how individuals make economic decisions. [17]

Collaborators of Uneven Prominence, Experience, and Skill. Much collaboration in economics involves individuals of quite different degrees of prominence, for example, faculty members and students, or full professors and junior professors. Within economics, unlike in many scientific disciplines, this rarely involves the unsavory practice of high-status individuals just attaching their names to the works of more junior people who are beholden to them, perhaps because they are thesis advisors. Collaboration across a hierarchy also may entail greater costs than, for example, having two junior faculty members working together, but it may offer the productivity benefits of a mingling of individuals with quite different perspectives on the world or quite different skill sets. Thus, a senior faculty member might bring a broad-based view of the world and the ability to relate a paper to a range of subjects, whereas the junior faculty member might contribute greater energy and technical skill. Superstars often benefit greatly working with lesser known stars, as did von Neumann and Friedman when they collaborated, respectively, with Morgenstern and Schwartz. To return to our model, collaboration is worthwhile if $f(x,y) > h(x) + h(y)$; and that holds true even if $h(x)$ is extremely large relative to $h(y)$.

Size of Teams. Casual empiricism suggests that the size of teams has grown alongside the frequency of collaboration in economics. Intuitively, the forces that make two heads better than one, are likely to raise the comparative advantage of three heads relative to two, and so on. The limiting factor is that coordination costs probably rise more than linearly with the size of the team. Just as there is an optimal scale for a firm, depending on its product, there is an optimal size for a collaborative team addressing a particular problem. In some disciplines, collaborative teams can be extremely large, a phenomenon not yet apparent in economics. As an extreme example, a May 2015 paper in *Physical Review Letters* reported on findings from the Large Hadron Collider regarding the Higgs boson; it listed 5154 coauthors (Aad et al. 2015).

11.7 Suboptimal Levels and Modes of Collaboration, Some Behavioral Explanations

Hyperbolic discounting, mentioned above, is a descriptive concept arguing that, in practice, individuals employ discount rates that decline as they project to a more distant future. One version of this model posits that there is a big discount between current period 1 and period 2; however, after that per-period discount rates are both much lower and constant. Thus, an individual might insist on $125 in a month in exchange for $100 today, but for $t > 1$ would exchange $100 for month t in the future for $102 in month $t + 1$.[18] There is considerable empirical evidence for such behavior. For example, it represents the underpinning of the propensity to procrastinate on worthwhile projects that incur an up-front cost, since that cost will be "overvalued" relative to future benefits.

Collaboration is just such a worthwhile project entailing up-front costs. For more diverse collaborations, those up-front costs are greater as, for example, the theorist learns to speak the language of the development economist. If the discount factor from today to tomorrow is large enough, a worthwhile collaboration will never happen. One might argue that if one really feels this discount, then the collaboration should not happen. That argument would appeal to those who think that the descriptive (of reality) should necessarily be normative. That is a view that I reject.[19] We have many natural tendencies that we would like to overcome, such as failing to watch the ball in tennis, leaning uphill when skiing, or overspending instead of saving. Often knowledge of such tendencies is sufficient to put one on a path to overcome them. That is the purpose of this section, which seeks to encourage readers to collaborate when they might not otherwise do so.

There is a second behavioral shortcoming, much less documented than hyperbolic discounting, that also leads to inadequate steps into new and, particularly, mixed collaborations. The failure to recognize option value is a costly deficiency in most people's intuitive apparatus. For example, a physician puts a 50-year-old man on a statin drug, expecting on average a 25% reduction in his cholesterol reading. The reduction proves to be 19%. Yet the doctor and patient usually continue with the same drug, although an alternative statin might achieve the 25% reduction. The trial period is brief, the individual will be on the statin for the rest of his life, and there are many slightly different cholesterol-lowering statins available. The option value of trying a second statin is not recognized.

Similarly, the success of collaboration with a new partner is a highly uncertain venture. Maybe the partners will not work well together. Maybe their ideas will clash. Maybe the new partner will prove to be a shirker. But then again, maybe the collaboration will lead to significant success, and then further collaborations can be undertaken with the same partner. Holding the expected payoff fixed, the more uncertain the payoff, the greater the value of the option.[20]

11.8 Conclusion

Economics is moving strongly toward more collaborative production. That is significantly due to the evolving nature of the field, away from seminal achievements by individuals who worked across broad swaths of the field, and toward much more specialized investigations requiring more technical skills, more data gathering, and more heavy lifting requiring teams of investigators. In this regard, economics is following the trajectory of many experimental sciences in which research teams are now the overwhelmingly predominant mode of production.

This chapter provided evidence on this trend toward collaboration by looking at the output of the most celebrated economists, those who won the Nobel Prize and the John Bates Clark Award. It then laid out a conceptual model of the collaboration process. It highlighted various famous collaborations, examined the advantages of mixed collaborations, and identified factors that might inhibit the use of collaborations.

This author's advice, as stated at the outset, is: Collaboration—try it; you may like it.

Notes

1. The respective standard errors for the coefficients on x_1 and x_2 are 0.00349 and 0.00572 for c_1, and 0.02094 and 0.03439 for c_{10}.
2. The respective standard errors for the coefficients on x_1 are 0.00365 for c_1 and 0.01507 for c_{10}.
3. A conceivable alternative explanation, of course, is that the award committees previously were much more oriented toward single-author work. However, I have found no evidence to that effect.
4. Of these seven mentioned early pioneers, only Arrow is still among us. Now in his mid-90s, he continues dispensing sought after insights.

5. Field studies oriented toward behavioral explanations are particularly prevalent in development economics. Senior scholars often engage a cluster of junior collaborators to conduct such investigations.
6. See *The Difference: How the Power of Diversity Creates Better Groups, Firms, Schools, and Societies*, by Scott E. Page (2007), which posits that, because diverse groups of people bring to groups or organizations more or different ways of seeing problems, they produce better ways of solving them. The book pays considerable attention to intellectual problems.
7. Given that research is involved, output should really be thought of in stochastic terms, so these production functions might be expected values. Given the competitive nature of much of research, it might even be that greater uncertainty in output is beneficial. And, of course, the value of output is some function of both quality and quantity. The reader is asked to forgive the simplifications here, which do not obscure the basic argument.
8. A more sophisticated formulation would allow for an error term about v with each trial. Thus, there would be further, but steadily reduced, learning after the first period.
9. For example, James Choi, David Laibson, and Brigitte Madrian had produced 22 joint articles and 11 book chapters as of August 2015, a number in conjunction with other authors. They always employed alphabetical order when it was just the three of them.
10. A pioneering article is "Egocentric Biases in Availability and Attribution," by Michael Ross and Fiore Sicoly (1979).
11. This will even be true for two people in the same specialty if A is at University C and B is at University D.
12. Of course, the empirical researchers among the readers will object to a selection effect. The individuals would never have gotten famous for collaborating had they not had a successful collaboration.
13. Quoted in "The Power of Two," by Joshua Wolf Shenk (2014).
14. Milton Friedman also greatly enjoyed engaging with numbers. Private communication with Jan Friedman Martel, Milton's daughter, August 6, 2015. The nature of his collaboration with Schwartz reflected comparative advantage.
15. Kahneman (2011) remarks on a productive style difference with his within discipline coauthor: "Amos was the more logical thinker,

with an orientation to theory and an unfailing sense of direction. I was more intuitive and rooted in the psychology of perception, from which we borrowed many ideas." *Thinking, Fast and Slow*, p. 6.

16. Michael Lewis, who is writing a book on their collaboration, concurred in this speculation.
17. Richard Thaler (2015), *Misbehaving: The Making of Behavioral Economics*, delightfully recounts much of the story of the penetration of the economics fortress and the subsequent cross-disciplinary collaborations.
18. David Laibson (1997).
19. It is disturbing that some bands of behavioral economists argue that what is descriptive should be defined as normative, though—like all behavioral economists—they delight in poking holes in the more traditional economic view that what theory says is normative will also be descriptive; that is, that decision makers are rational.
20. I am simplifying by leaving aside risk aversion. However, it is not likely to be a major consideration since the participants are not making a major commitment.

References

Aad, G., et al. (ATLAS Collaboration, CMS Collaboration) (2015). Combined measurement of the Higgs Boson Mass in *pp* collisions at $\sqrt{s}$ =7 and 8 TeV with the ATLAS and CMS experiments." *Physical Review Letters*, 114, 191803.

Friedman, M., & Schwartz, A. J. (1963). *A monetary history of the United States, 1867–1960*. Princeton, NJ: Princeton University Press.

Kahneman, D. (2011). *Thinking fast and slow*. New York: Farrar, Straus and Giroux.

Kahneman, D., & Tversky, A. (1979). Prospect theory: An analysis of decision under risk. *Econometrica, 47*(2), 263–292.

Laibson, D. (1997). Golden eggs and hyperbolic discounting. *Quarterly Journal of Economics, 112*(2), 443–478.

Nelson, J. K., & Zeckhauser, R. J. (2014). *The Patron's payoff: Conspicuous commissions in Italian Renaissance Art*. Princeton, NJ: Princeton University Press.

Page, S. E. (2007). *The difference: How the power of diversity creates better groups, firms, schools, and societies*. Princeton, NJ: Princeton University Press.

Ross, M., & Sicoly, F. (1979). Egocentric biases in availability and attribution. *Journal of Personality and Social Psychology, 37*(3), 322–336.

Shenk, J. W. (2014, July/August). The power of two. *The Atlantic*.

Thaler, R. (2015). *Misbehaving: The making of behavioral economics*. New York: W.W. Norton & Co..
Tversky, A., & Kahneman, D. (1974). *Judgment under uncertainty: Heuristics and biases. Science, 185*(4157), 1124–1131.
von Neumann, J., & Morgenstern, O. (1944). *Theory of games and economic behavior*. Princeton, NJ: Princeton University Press.

CHAPTER 12

"Heinz" Harcourt's Collaborations: Over 57 Varieties

G.C. Harcourt

12.1 Introduction

Until Michael and Lall asked me to contribute a chapter to their volume on collaboration I had not realised what a collaborator I was, nor that I was one of so many varieties. Their letter sent me to my CV which led me in turn to classify my joint efforts into categories: of people collaborated with and of what forms the collaboration took. The latter includes books co-authored or co-edited; co-authored articles and review articles; notes; reviews; edited volumes of selected essays; and chapters in volumes. If I ignore items accepted but not yet published, I have collaborated 92 times with 104 collaborators. (To add perspective, I have published 30 books and over 400 articles, review articles, notes, chapters in edited volumes

I thank, but in no way implicate, Wendy Harcourt, Prue Kerr and Peter Kriesler for comments on a draft of the chapter.

G.C. Harcourt (✉)
UNSW Australia, Sydney, Australia

M. Szenberg, L.B. Ramrattan (eds.), *Collaborative Research in Economics*, DOI 10.1007/978-3-319-52800-7_12

and reviews.) In the total are 17 books, two co-authored, 15 co-edited, including three editors of volumes of selected essays, with 22 collaborators; 16 articles involving 17 collaborators; four review articles with four collaborators; 12 notes with 15 collaborators; 35 chapters in books with 37 collaborators; and two reviews with two collaborators.

The person I have collaborated with longest and most is Prue Kerr—13 times, consisting of three books and ten chapters in books. Next is Peter Kriesler—one book, five articles and seven chapters in books. Claudio Sardoni and Avi Cohen are equal third, both four times. With Claudio, I have one book and three chapters in books; with Avi, I have one article, one note and two chapters in books.[1]

The rest of the chapter contains reflections on why and what I have done with others. I start by saying that my personal and working life has been greatly enriched by these joint happenings, whereby I have both made new friends and deepened already established friendships.[2]

My collaborators may be classified into two broad categories: first, present or past graduate students; second, internal or external colleagues. Three of my principal collaborators—Prue Kerr, Peter Kriesler and Claudio Sardoni—were my students: Prue as an undergraduate at The Flinders University of South Australia, a Master's student at Adelaide University and a Ph.D. student at Cambridge University. I examined Peter's Master's Degree for Sydney University,[3] supervised his doctoral dissertation at Cambridge and we are now colleagues at the School of Economics of the University of New South Wales (UNSW Australia) in Sydney. Claudio did his Ph.D. with me at Adelaide.[4]

12.2 Early Collaborations

My first ever published article was jointly authored with Duncan Ironmonger. The title was "Pilot survey of personal savings". It was published in the *Economic Record* in May 1956, and was a summary of the contents of my Master's Degree at Melbourne University. By then I was a doctoral student in Cambridge so I did not write directly one word of the article. Duncan and I had been undergraduates together at Melbourne and, when I worked on my Master's project, he was the expert advisor from the Australian Bureau of Census and Statistics on the stratified sampling method I used to gather data for the project, so he was the ideal co-author.

After being a research student at Cambridge (1955–58), I worked principally at Adelaide (1958–63; 1967–82), Cambridge (1963–66; 1972–73; 1980; 1982–2010) and the University of Toronto (1977; 1980). Since August 2010 I have been a Visiting Professorial Fellow at the UNSW, Australia. In August 2016, I became an Honorary Professor. Overwhelmingly all of my collaborations have been with people at one or other of these four centres.

12.3 First Adelaide Years

In my first six years at Adelaide, 1958–63, before I went on study leave to Cambridge, my first collaboration was with Allan Barton, my great friend from Melbourne and Cambridge days, who was then at Adelaide. Allan was a whiz kid on many things, including detailed accounting procedures and taxation measures. I had a chapter on investment allowances in my Cambridge dissertation and we adapted the arguments there to propose for Australian primary producers, investment allowances in the place of accelerated depreciation allowances and/or cash grants, see Barton and Harcourt (1959). I suspect this policy proposal fell on deaf ears even though Australian primary producers were well represented in the Federal and State Parliaments through the then Country Party.

With Jim Bennett, who was a Lecturer in the Commerce Department at Adelaide (members of the Economics and Commerce Departments worked very closely together[5]). Jim had spent some time at MIT (the other Cambridge) and we combined to write a short paper, "Taxation and business surplus", published in the *Economic Record* in August 1960. I now regard it as the silliest paper I have ever published because it tries to combine two irreconcilable approaches to economic analysis: not Jim's fault, I hasten to add, but mine. It did have the amusing consequence that if only long-period normal profits were being received, companies using our measure of surplus for taxation purposes would pay no tax, as Peter Swan, an unreconstructed Chicago economist and friend of mine at UNSW, once had great glee in pointing out to me.

I first met Donald Whitehead in the 1950s when he was at Nuffield College, Oxford—he was the Oxford Secretary of the London, Oxford, Cambridge research students' seminar which met once a term in one of these three places. I was the Cambridge Secretary. Donald was a star, the life and soul of the graduate students and Faculty at Nuffield. In the 1950s I recommended to Peter Karmel, then Professor of Economics at Adelaide, that Donald be considered for a Lectureship in Economic Development at Adelaide, to which he was duly appointed. Oxford life for Donald had not been conducive to publication as opposed to teaching and in-depth discussions, so to get Donald started on what subsequently became an impressive list of publications before his far too early death at the age of 49 in 1980, we wrote together the chapter on "The wool textile industry" in Alex Hunter's pioneering edited volume, *The Economics of Australian Industry*, Hunter (1963). Donald's part of the chapter is far more interesting and innovative than mine.

The same is true of my collaboration with one of my Australian mentors, the late Russell Mathews, on the chapter on "Company Finance" for Ron Hirst and Bob Wallace's now classic edited volume, *Studies in the Australian Capital Market* (1964). Russell at this time was Professor of Commerce at Adelaide. His pioneering work with John Grant on inflation and company finance which culminated in their 1958 book had greatly influenced the approach I took in my Cambridge dissertation; in effect, I did a "Mathews and Grant" for UK companies. I adapted their analysis to include insights I had obtained from Joan Robinson's *magnum opus*, *The Accumulation of Capital* (1956) which I had studied intensively while at Cambridge, see Harcourt (2001a), 7–8.

The most important joint project arising from those first years at Adelaide was the beginnings of what became my first book, *Economic Activity* (1967). It was written jointly with Peter Karmel and Bob Wallace. Peter had developed a superb, if demanding, first-year course, "Outlay", which was basically a rigorous introduction to the economics of Keynes. When he was appointed the first Vice Chancellor of the newly established Flinders University of South Australia in the early 1960s, he asked me to take over the Outlay course and generously lent me his very full set of lecture notes.

As I lectured, I began to realise that there was no suitable textbook which took our approach to the issues, so I suggested to Peter that we write one based on our lectures. As I was going on study leave in August 1963, Bob Wallace took the course over from me and also came on board as a third author. Bob had taught me in Melbourne and was a major reason why I wanted to come to Adelaide.[6] He and Peter had written a "way before its time" article, "Credit-creation in a multi-bank system" (1962), published in the first ever issue of *Australian Economic Papers*, and his deep understanding of the integration of monetary and finance processes with real processes in systemic analysis served to more than make up for my deficiencies as a real man, not a money man.

12.4 Cambridge in the 1960s

Soon after I returned to Cambridge, to my utmost astonishment, I was invited by Joan Robinson to apply for a Lectureship. I was interviewed and appointed in November 1963 (the day after President Kennedy was assassinated). I had a moral duty to return to Adelaide, so I asked for and received three years leave without pay in order to take up the Lectureship and subsequently a Fellowship at Trinity Hall.

When my appointment was announced in the Cambridge University *Reporter*, the Cambridge University Press wrote to me to ask me whether I had any books on the go. I did not realise that such a distinguished Press liked textbooks but they jumped at the chance to publish what became *Economic Activity* (1967), as did I and its other two authors. I wrote the first drafts during my years at Cambridge and I spent a wonderful summer at Stanford in 1965 with Bob Wallace and his family (he was on leave there) writing second drafts. I had brought a bottle of fine brandy with me and Californian public radio played classical music continuously. It should be possible to find more mellow and poetic passages in the book as the combination of brandy and music made their impact on our composition as the Californian evenings drew in.

When Robin Matthews left Cambridge to take up the Drummond Chair at Oxford in 1965 (succeeding John Hicks), he asked me to take over his Part I Lectures on the economics of Keynes. I told the undergraduates that 30 years ago Keynes was lecturing to a select group of undergraduates from the proof sheets of *The General Theory*. I added that I was not Keynes and nor were they as select a group of undergraduates, but I was going to give a course of lectures on the economics of Keynes from the manuscript of the emerging book. The most distinguished pupil who attended the lectures at that time is Mervyn King, a former Governor of the Bank of England and now Lord King. Three times in semi-public he has praised the lectures as the ideal introduction to systemic analysis of the economy. I really must get this from him in writing.

Economic Activity was published in 1967; for a while it was used widely in Australia and overseas and Paolo Sylos-Labini at La Sapienza in Rome arranged for an Italian translation which was published in 1969.

As well as *Economic Activity*, another volume was published by Cambridge as a result of my time there, this time jointly edited. R.H. (Bob) Parker, the distinguished historian of accounting, and I had been colleagues at Adelaide before he went, first, to the University of Western

Australia and subsequently to the University of Exeter. He asked me to join him in editing a selection of readings in the concept and measurement of income. The selection was published in 1969, a selection that John Hicks subsequently was to describe as a classic. Bob was undeniably the senior editor—hence Parker and Harcourt and his important section of the Introduction—but I did contribute a section based on my earlier work on historical and replacement cost accounting. We also reprinted in the selection what has become my second best-known publication, "The Accountant in a Golden Age".

The paper was first published in *Oxford Economic Papers* in 1965. The research project on which it was based started when I was in Adelaide. Harold Lydall (who succeeded Peter Karmel as the George Gollin Professor) was puzzled by some findings he had made when comparing accounting rates of profit with economic ones. He asked me to see if I could find the cause(s) of his puzzles. I was helped most in this pursuit in Adelaide by Deane Terrell, my first ever Honours student there,[7] who had recently returned from Oxford and MIT, and was now a Lecturer at Adelaide, and subsequently by Dr Lucy Slater, the whiz kid programmer at the Department of Applied Economics (DAE) in Cambridge. They ran the simulations from which my findings arose because my meagre grasp of algebra would not allow me to work out the general case. This was done later in the 1980s by Franklin Fisher, see Fisher and McGowan 1983, Fisher, 1984, when he appeared as a witness for IBM in US v IBM to argue that IBM may not be making monopoly profits, or if it were, this could not be inferred from the use of accounting data. In effect, we had asked the same question: if we know what the "true" economic rate of profit is (as we would in a Golden Age), would an accountant let loose in a Golden Age with his/her conventional tools give us the right, that is, same, answers? My simulations of various possible scenarios and Fisher's elegant algebra both showed conclusively that the answer was "no", often by large orders of magnitude. So in a sense Fisher and I had collaborated by osmosis even though he was not aware of my article when he wrote his 1983 one, see Fisher 1984, where he replies to his critics.

Soon after I arrived in Cambridge in September 1963 I met Vince Massaro. Vince was a graduate of Notre Dame, he wrote his Ph.D. dissertation on the immiserisation of wage-earners thesis in Marx's *Capital*, he was the son of Sicilian migrants, a devout Roman Catholic much influenced by the pacifist Roman Catholic Dorothy Day, so naturally he was awarded a NATO Fellowship to come to Cambridge to study the writings of Joan Robinson and Piero Sraffa.

I had had a look at Sraffa's 1960 classic, *Production of Commodities by Means of Commodities*, while in Adelaide. I was completely bamboozled by it but I was determined to study it in depth during my leave. I suggested to Vince that we work together on this project which we did over the academical year 1963–64. Piero had looked after the Cambridge research students in the 1950s and I had come to know him then. He also loved to meet Italians and Italian speakers so Vince often went to see him in his rooms in Trinity.

The result of our collaboration were two papers—"A note on Mr Sraffa's sub-systems" in the *Economic Journal* (1964a) and a review article of *Production of Commodities* in the *Economic Record* (1964b). We had the great advantage of clearing what we wrote with Piero himself so that our note and review article may be claimed to be definitive because Piero finally gave us the OK to go ahead and submit them, though not before some terrific dramas, see Heertje (1999, 50–53). Vince and I became and remain firm friends—I was the best man at his wedding in Cambridge to Denise; she worked at the *DAE* and Vince courted her when he was in Cambridge (sadly, Vince died last year.).

Another collaborator in Cambridge at this time with whom I formed a lifetime friendship is Geoffrey Whittington. He was a research officer in the *DAE* working on a collection of UK accounting data, the collection of which had started at the National Institute in London (it was the data on which the empirical parts of my 1950s Ph.D. dissertation were based). Geoff worked in collaboration with the pioneering work of Ajit Singh and Gay and Geoff Meeks on the behaviour of UK companies, especially the implications of their take over activities. Geoff was an outstanding applied economist who had advanced accounting qualifications in his considerable armoury. He and I wrote a paper, Harcourt and Whittington (1965), that commented on the irrelevancy of the British differential profits tax in an article that had been written by A. Rubner and published in the *Economic Journal* in 1964, a journal that then would have been classified as a "brownie point" outlet had there been RAEs operating—which, thank goodness, there were not. It was Geoff's first publication.

Since then, Geoff and I have collaborated twice. He was the third editor of the second edition of Parker and Harcourt, published by Philip Allan in 1986. Part of his contribution was to remove the section of essays on depreciation that had appeared in the first edition and included "The

Accountant in a Golden Age", thanks, pal. We also wrote a joint chapter on the concepts of income and capital for John Creedy's edited volume, *Foundations of Economic Thought* (1990).

We linked the accountants' concept of a going concern to the "vision" of capitalism that sees the capitalist classes (all three) as the driving forces of the capitalist mode of production, as opposed to the mainstream "vision" which has the consumer queen in the driving seat. Which "vision" dominates has important implications for the concept of replacement costs to be used in replacement cost accounting reforms to which Geoff contributed hugely over his working life and which were also part of my Ph.D. dissertation and subsequent projects.

Though I did not write any more joint articles or books in Cambridge during the 1960s, I was enormously helped with my single author publications by many colleagues there. I would especially like to single out Maurice Dobb, the kindest and most supportive of men, who responded more than fully and in beautiful handwriting[8] to requests for help; Esra Bennathan, whose enthusiastic encouragement and friendship I value deeply; Bob Rowthorn, to my mind, the most fertile and sharpest mind of the younger people then at Cambridge; Ken Arrow and Bob Solow, who were on leave in Cambridge when I was and who brought their great skills to bear on some technical puzzles that had had me foxed; and, last but not least, Joan Robinson who took a great interest in whatever I was doing and usually approved of it—which was just as well as disagreeing with her was not an easy or forgettable past time.

12.5 Return to Adelaide 1967–72

I left Cambridge for Adelaide at the end of 1966 to begin another exciting phase of my life. I immediately became deeply involved in the anti-Vietnam War movement in South Australia (Australia and New Zealand were the USA's only "respectable" allies in that most immoral of wars) and I averaged two and a half days a week on anti-war activities for the next eight years.

As far as my academic life was concerned, a career-changing event occurred in 1968. Mark Perlman was visiting Melbourne University. He had recently been appointed the founding editor of the newly established *Journal of Economic Literature* (*JEL*). While in Melbourne, the author he had commissioned to write the survey article (on capital theory) for the second issue let him know he could not do it for fear of offending his patrons. Wilfred Prest, who was Professor of Economics at Melbourne then and when I was an undergraduate, suggested to Mark that I might be an appropriate replacement—he thought from what he knew of me as an undergraduate that I could be good at explaining what other people had written. Perlman visited me in Adelaide in August and after a hard day's sell I agreed to write the survey—I had no patrons to offend!—and to deliver a first draft by the end of the year.

So I took temporary "leave" from my anti-war activities (with the blessings of my comrades in the movement) and retired behind a door which prior to that I always left open for colleagues and students to drop in for chats. I put a notice on the door "Man at work", which someone thoughtfully altered to "Maniac...".

As the project in its totality threatened to overwhelm me, I decided to write working paper drafts of segments of the survey. I sent these to about 30 friends around the world, some of whom were sympathetic to the approach of Cambridge, England, to the then ongoing controversies in capital theory between the two Cambridges (Mark had asked that in the survey I concentrate on the issues involved), others who were not sympathetic, but as friends sent me invaluable comments and criticisms. I sent off the draft on time, then revised it in the light of Mark's feedback and the final version was published in the June 1969 issue of the *JEL*. The list of people thanked in the opening footnote is in a sense a mini *Who's Who* of the profession at the time. I singled out Joan Robinson for her comments and great encouragement which kept me going. I especially thanked Pippa Simpson for her expert mathematical advice, without which I would have been even more lost than I obviously had been in the jungle of squiggles that characterises most modern economic theory.

One of the people whose comments were most helpful to me was Mario Nuti who was then teaching at Cambridge. A by-product of sending out the working papers was that Frances Welch, Mario's partner, was at the time the Economics Editor of Cambridge University Press. She came to know of them and as a result commissioned me to write for the Press a book of the survey. It was published in 1972, a pleasing by-product of what I like to think of as bedside reading. Though I did not implicate anyone in the views I took in the survey, this whole experience of willing collaboration is a leading highlight of my working life.

Mark Perlman and I became firm friends. He wrote a Foreword to a selection of my essays, Harcourt (1995a), published by Edward Elgar in the Economists of the Twentieth Century series that Mark edited with

Marc Blaug. I was delighted to be a joint editor with Hank Lim and Ungsuh Park, two of his former doctoral students, of his *Festschrift* volume, most appropriately titled *Editing Economics* (2002). When he retired as editor of the *JEL* in 1980, I organised a round robin letter signed by 36 AEA members located all around the world, which was sent to Moses Ambrovitz who succeeded him. It thanked Mark for his outstanding, fearless and liberal editing, see Lim et al. (2002), 3–4.

I spent the academical year 1972–73 as a Visiting Fellow at Clare Hall, Cambridge, where the Harcourt family overlapped with the Asimakopulos family—Tom was also a Visiting Fellow. Tom and I had been Ph.D. students at King's in the 1950s. We were both close friends of Keith Frearson who had taught me at Melbourne and who was then a graduate student at Cambridge. In 1955–56, we went to Joan Robinson's lectures on what was to become *The Accumulation of Capital* (1956). Keith was enthralled, Tom was irritated by her criticisms of MIT economists, and I was mystified, not least because when she came to a crucial point in the argument, she dropped her voice so much that she went unheard, at least by me. In the 1960s, Tom went on leave to MIT. Listening to Bob Solow's lectures, the scales fell from his eyes, he twigged what Joan had been on about and from then on became one of her most devoted (but always critical when justified) disciples. I had published in *Australian Economic Papers* one of the first fruits of Tom's conversion, see Asimakopulos (1969a, 1969b).

At Clare Hall, Tom and I decided to write a book on economic growth reflecting the Cambridge approach. The economics editor of Allen and Unwin had been urging me for some time to write such a book. I said I would if he gave me lunch at his London Club (The Reform). In the event, he had to fork out for two lunches and we never did get to write that book. We did, however, collaborate on a note, "Proportionality and the neoclassical parables", which was published in the *Southern Economic Journal*, Asimakopulos and Harcourt (1974). It was a comment on Charles Ferguson's Presidential Address to the Southern Economic Association, Ferguson (1972). Our note established clearly why only the "corn" model produced results that were consistent with the central neoclassical view that all prices are indexes of scarcity; in *n* commodity models the "agreeable" parables reflecting this intuition were not generally applicable. The technical skills and extreme clarity of the exposition are overwhelmingly due to Tom, whose teaching and written work had these traits in abundance. Until Tom's untimely death in 1990, we regularly exchanged and commented on our ongoing research papers. My evaluation of Tom the person and the economist may be found in, for example, Harcourt (1991) (2008).

After Tom died, a week-long conference in his honour was held at the Levy Institute of Bard College in Up State New York in 1992. The papers given at the conference formed the basis of the volume, *Income and Employment in Theory and Practice* (1994) that Alessandro Roncaglia, Robin Rowley and I edited for Macmillan. Unbeknownst to me at the time of the conference, I was actually dying from the onset of type 1 diabetes. Most fortunately, Esther and Hy Minsky—Hy had diabetes—were at the conference and, realising that something was wrong, took my blood sugar level on Hy's machine. It went off the Richter scale and I ended up in Emergency at the hospital in Up State New York. I often remark that, except for the Minskys's timely intervention—my Minsky moment—the participants could have stayed on for another day for a conference in my honour and so spread the overheads.

12.6 Collaboration in Adelaide in the 1970s

In Adelaide in the 1970s I supervised some outstanding Master's and doctoral students, with some of whom I collaborated. Peter Kenyon came to Adelaide in 1974, after finishing his undergraduate course at Monash University in Melbourne, to do a Master's degree under my supervision.

In my last year at Cambridge I had written a paper, "Pricing and the investment decision", in which I tried to analyse the determination of the size of the mark-up by a price leader in an oligopolistic market structure, whereby discretion in setting prices was directed towards raising internal funds with which to finance planned investment expenditure. The paper was rejected by the *Oxford Bulletin of Economics and Statistics.* I was able to deduce from one of the referees' reports that a referee had been G.B. Richardson, an unsung hero of the British and, indeed, the world economics professions. (Moral: never let your initials be put on your referee report.) He liked the project but detected a logical flaw which vitiated my arguments.[9]

I put the paper on the back burner but I suggested to Peter that he work on these and other issues in post-Keynesian price theory for his Master's thesis. In 1974 I had a serious operation which put me in hospital for three weeks. On the day I was discharged Peter was giving a progress report on his research. I went from hospital to his seminar on the way home. Listening to his report, the solution to the logical problem suddenly came to me so when I went home, in a state of euphoria, I sketched the theoretical arguments and gave them to Peter to put the scholarship around them. We submitted the resulting paper to the *Economic Journal* (then edited by David Champernowe and Brian Reddaway) because I thought that Brian would like the "down-to-earth" nature of our analysis. Alas, neither he nor the referees did like the paper and he asked Champ to write the rejection letter. He told Champ he was embarrassed to do so because he and I were such good friends. Champ wrote ruefully in the letter, "where did that leave him?!".[10]

Bruno Frey, who I had met at Cambridge, was then editor of *Kyklos*. He had often asked me to submit a paper to the journal so I suggested to Peter that we send our paper to him. It was quickly accepted "as is", it was published in 1976 and is now regarded as a classic in the post-Keynesian literature on pricing, see, for example, Coutts and Norman (2013).

As I mentioned above, Prue Kerr, having been an undergraduate student of mine at Flinders, came to Adelaide in the 1970s to write a Master's thesis under my supervision on the characteristics of the Cambridge School of Economics, especially in relation to Marx. Prue's outstanding thesis (both examiners praised its maturity and deepness of thought and analysis) and our discussions while it was being written mark the beginning of our long-lasting, still ongoing friendship, collaboration and my education in what Marx was on about. (As I have often written, Marx's *Capital* was the only "great work" I could not make head nor tail of when as an undergraduate I did History of Economic Thought in 1952.) As far as Marx and Prue are concerned, our collaboration culminated in one of my favourite essays—our joint chapter on Marx, Harcourt and Kerr (2001), written for Malcom Warner's *International Encyclopedia of Business and Management* (2001), all his readers needed and wanted to know about the great man.

Prue left Adelaide in the late 1970s to do the M.Phil in Economics at Cambridge where, some years later, I became her Ph.D. supervisor. Prior to this in 1980–81, she edited my first selection of essays, *The Social Science Imperialists*, published by Routledge in 1982.

Education in Marx and collaboration were also added to in the 1970s by my supervision of Allan Oakley's fine Ph.D. dissertation on the formation of Marx's views up to the writing of *Capital*. It subsequently became the basis of three outstanding volumes, Oakley (1983), (1984), (1985). Claudio Sardoni came to Adelaide on an Italian scholarship and wrote his dissertation on Marx and Keynes on recession, showing that when they examined the same issues they mostly came up with same answers, adjectives aside. I quote below from the Foreword I wrote to the book based on the dissertation, Sardoni (1987). After noting that "I learnt more from Claudio than he ever did from me", I wrote that his book was "a fine example of analytical history which gives readers the feel both for what their great predecessors achieved and for what is the appropriate framework within which to continue their work ... the book is an absorbing story of theories which were not only relevant in their authors' days, but in ours too" (xi).

Claudio and I were subsequently to write three joint chapters for edited books. The first was "Keynes's vision: method, analysis and tactics" in John Davis's volume *The State of Interpretation of Keynes* (1995). The second was our chapter, "*The General Theory of Employment, Interest and Money*: three views", in the *Festschrift* volume for Paul Davidson edited by Philip Arestis (1997). The third was "George Shackle and Post-Keynesianism", a chapter in the memorial volume for George edited by Peter Earl and Stephen Frowen (2000).

In the chapter for Davidson's *Festschrift* we compared and contrasted the interpretations of *The General Theory* to be found in two great biographies of Keynes—Moggridge (1992) and Skidelsky (1983, 1992, 2000)—with those of Paul Davidson over many years. Paul and Skidelsky both had a post-Keynesian interpretation, not a view Don Patinkin ever accepted. Claudio and I thought that Skidelsky's chapters on *The General Theory* contained deeply incisive and correct understanding of the significance of the contributions of Keynes's *magnum opus*. Moggridge documents superbly the making and the aftermath of the book and of its contents. We praised Paul's painstaking, evidence-based, accounts in many places of Keynes's essential insights. Paul built substantially on these in his own contributions to our understanding of modern monetary production economies. Claudio's understanding of the messages in primary sources together with his analytical skills greatly enriched the narratives of the chapters. I was also delighted to find that Shackle's biographers, Peter Earl and Bruce Littleboy, stated that Claudio and I got it right in our discussion of George Shackle and post-Keynesianism, see Earl and Littleboy (2014), 39.

In 1992 Claudio edited for Routledge a selection of my essays from the previous 30 years, entitled *On Political Economists and Modern Political Economy*. Routledge had previously published the first volume of my selected essays in 1982, *The Social Science Imperialists*, which, as I noted above, Prue edited. In 1986, Omar Hamouda edited a further selection,

Controversies in Political Economy, which was published by Wheatsheaf Books. So I have been three times more fortunate with editors than was Ricardo who had Piero Sraffa; or rather, one and a half times as Piero's extraordinary edition of Ricardo's works and correspondence was latterly done with the collaboration of Maurice Dobb.

12.7 Collaboration in Canada

Another major collaboration arose from two visits I made to the University of Toronto in the winters of 1977 and 1980. Jon Cohen and I edited a *Festschrift* volume for Lorie Tarshis, *International Monetary Problems and Supply-side Economics* (1986), published by Macmillan. The title takes in issues that were very much on Lorie's mind at the time. We presented the copy to him as a (pleasant, we hope) surprise at a conference in his honour held in Toronto.

I had come to know Sue Howson and Don Moggridge in Cambridge in the 1970s. Don was then a Lecturer in the Faculty and a Fellow of Clare; he had taken on the gigantic task of editing Keynes's papers alongside Austin Robinson and Judith Allen. Don was a Canadian and decided to return to Canada in the late 1970s to the University of Toronto (U of T). Lorie, a Canadian and a graduate of the U of T, had subsequently attended Keynes's lectures in the 1930s when Keynes was making *The General Theory*. After the Second World War Lorie taught at Tufts and then at Stanford where I first met him in 1965. In the 1970s Lorie decided to return to Canada, sickened by the growing tide of illiberalism in the USA, and by the war in Vietnam. A department of economics principally staffed by a group of very bright young scholars including Sue and Don had been set up as an outreach Campus of the U of T 20 minutes out from downtown Toronto, Scarborough (known to us all as Scarberia). Lorie was the wise guiding chair. Through Sue and Don I was invited there in 1977 and subsequently I was asked to come for a semester every two years.

In 1977 while I was in Toronto, my greatest Australian friend and mentor, Eric Russell, tragically died in Adelaide after a game of squash. Jon Cohen was also at Scarborough. He had similar traits to Eric's and became my greatest friend there. We both were tremendous admirers of Lorie, for why see, for example, Harcourt (1995c), so we set about preparing the *Festschrift* for Lorie. This was one of the most enjoyable collaborations of my life, working with one friend in order to honour another by commissioning contributions from other mutual friends and admirers of Lorie. They provided fine chapters with which we believe (hope) Lorie was well pleased.

It was through Jon that I came to meet his namesake Avi Cohen who lived near Jon and Lorie and taught at York University. Avi had been a graduate student of Don Harris at Stanford (Don was a close friend of Joan Robinson and mine). Avi and I had a mutual interest in controversies in capital theory. I persuaded him to spend a year's leave (1980) at Cambridge as a Visiting Fellow of Clare Hall, one of my four Cambridge colleges. From this our sustained collaboration and friendship grew.

When Timothy Taylor, the managing editor of the *Journal of Economic Perspectives*, one of the few journals left that all economists can both read and gain sustenance from, asked me in the early noughties to write about the Cambridge–Cambridge capital theory controversies for the journal's Retrospectives section, I asked that it be a joint paper with Avi. Otherwise I felt I would be trespassing on the understanding of the issues concerned that I had learned from him. The upshot was the paper "Whatever happened to the Cambridge capital theory controversies?" (2003). In it we argued that the 1950s to 1970s debates were but the latest in a series of such debates about similar issues dating back at least to Böhm-Bawerk, J.B. Clark, Irving Fisher and Thorstein Veblen at the turn of the last century. We set out the arguments and results involved and the unsolved issues between the two camps about the significance of the results.

At about this time Edward Elgar approached me to edit volumes of readings in capital theory. I asked him whether Avi could be a co-editor and as well could we follow the model of the book on readings in capital and growth, which was published by Penguin in 1971 and which I had co-edited with Neil Laing, a colleague of mine at Adelaide. Neil took an independent and original though basically neoclassical approach to the issues. The idea was that by me writing an introduction to the readings with a Cambridge, England, stance and Neil, another, neoclassical one, readers, principally students, would not only have the differences set out but would also have primary evidence in the readings to enable them to make up their minds on where they stood on the issues.

I had come to know Christopher Bliss at Cambridge in the 1960s. Though we did not agree on the capital theory debates he had been a great help to me with his comments on the working papers for the *JEL* survey. Moreover, his 1975 monograph on capital theory and the distribution of income, Bliss 1975, is one of the finest works of scholarship in modern economics. So I asked Edward could Chris also be a joint editor and contribute a Laing-like introduction to the volumes while Avi and I wrote the other, “correct”, introduction.

The three volumes were published in 2005, Bliss et al. (2005). In retrospect I realise I made a serious tactical error, one which I avoided when collaborating with Neil, whose surname started with a first letter lower in the alphabet than mine—hence Harcourt and Laing with my introduction coming first. In the 2005 volumes I am relegated in citations to Bliss et al. (eds) and Chris has first bite of the cherry at persuading readers who is right, as his introduction also comes first. Nevertheless, despite some dramas and hissy fits on the way, the final product is one we could be proud of and the editors especially appreciated David Laidler’s endorsement of the volumes. David is one of the finest scholars in our trade so it was reassuring that he wrote that our “collection addresses the topic’s intrinsic difficulties head on. [Moreover] because it is beautifully balanced and thoughtfully organised it makes the many complexities of capital theory accessible to anyone willing to make the effort to work through it. And that ought to be all of us”.

In 2010, Marc Blaug and Peter Lloyd edited a volume, *Famous Figures and Diagrams in Economics*. Avi and I wrote/drew the chapter on capital-reversing and reswitching. As has become our practice, I sketched the first draft (it is published in Harcourt (2012b)) and Avi provided the scholarship and analytical polish. We used the relevant diagrams from my 1972 book to give them the chance to go down in history—but, as far as I know, none of the reviews of the Blaug Lloyd volume have mentioned our chapter.

As I write (March 2015) Avi and I are following the same procedure in order to produce 1800 words on the Cambridge debates for Cyrus Binha and Chuck Davis’s edition of *Global Economics: Encyclopedia of Crisis and Transnational Change*. (We still do not know the final outcome of the volume.)

12.8 Further Collaboration in Adelaide

When in Cambridge in the 1960s I published a paper, Harcourt (1966), in *R.E. Studs* (my only ever excursion into what Dennis Robertson called “The Green Horror”) on biases in empirical estimates of values of the elasticity of substitution of CES production functions. It was a satirical paper (though one referee thought it serious econometrics that failed); it included making up imaginary scenarios to see whether the econometric methods used in the CES literature in fact established "true" values or were subject to arbitrary biases because the theoretical models behind the specifications, especially the variables they contained, did not match those of the actual processes that threw up the data used.

Subsequently, I collaborated in Adelaide with Al Watson and Peter Praetz on a similar project. We argued that one of the joys of living in the age of computers was that it allowed economists to play God—we could make up worlds with known parameter values and then see whether econometric methods actually provided unbiased estimates of these values. Fred Gruen and Allan Powell had published an important article in the *International Economic Review*, Powell and Gruen (1970), the last in a series of papers on econometric estimates of constant elasticity of transformation functions, in order to get a handle on supply responses in Australian agriculture. The "Trinity from Adelaide" wrote a comment on their article, using a Monte Carlo experiment to argue that their method was not successful. My only contribution was to pose the question and suggest the approach. Al and Peter as excellent econometricians then took over.

Our comment, Watson, Praetz and Harcourt (1970), led to a cross reply from Allan and Fred, together with comments by Ray Byron (who had been a referee) that visited a plague on all our houses, see Powell and Gruen (1970), Byron (1970a, 1970b).[11]

12.9 Twenty-eight Years in Heaven: Return to Cambridge in 1982

Joan and I returned to Cambridge in 1982 for 28 wonderful years in the Faculty (I retired in 1998 but visited the Austin Robinson building a couple of days a week after that) and in Jesus, literally Heaven on Earth. As for collaboration, I first mention the cooperative editorial board of the *Cambridge Journal of Economics (CJE).* I had been associated with The *CJE* since it started in 1977. The editorial board met every Friday for a working lunch in which the editors accepted, rejected or gave another chance to would be authors. Despite our often heated arguments—I hold the record for the greatest hizzy-fit when I smashed a tea cup on the table, exasperated by a highly predictable response by Tony Lawson to my assessment of a paper (we now use paper cups)—I looked forward to each Friday and I count the members of the editorial cooperative among my best and closest friends.[12]

I also contributed to Memorial Issues for the Cambridge greats who had died. Gabriel Palma, one of my closest friends, and I wrote the Introduction to the *Memorial issue* for Richard Kahn, Harcourt and Palma (1994).

Before I discuss my many years of collaboration with Prue Kerr then and now, I discuss other collaborations from this period. The first is my only excursion into *Economic Letters*, then the counterpart in economics of *Nature* in the natural sciences. I met Mohammed Dore in Canada and later in Cambridge. We discussed his search for the best form of taxation of exhaustible resources when the market structure in which the output was sold was oligopolistic. I suggested that a sales tax would be preferable to a profits tax. He adapted a model by Partha Dasgupta and others to establish a neat expression for the tax which contained the price elasticity of demand as the key parameter, see Dore and Harcourt (1986). He did all the squiggles and exposition but insisted, most generously, that I be a joint author.

After the note was published, I received a letter from an economist based in Sweden. It said in effect that until he read the note he had always admired my economic intuition and sensible use of maths, both characteristics, he argued, were now conspicuous by their absence in the *Economic Letters* note. Mohammed took him on; there was an acrimonious but inconclusive exchange of letters. I showed the exchanges to Bob Rowthorn who said "You're all wrong!"

Next, in the early 1980s at the annual Trieste international summer school for mavericks, I met Omar Hamouda, a doctoral student at McGill of my friend Athanasios (Tom) Asimakopulos. During the after-lunch siesta, I read and commented on drafts of Omar's dissertation on John Hicks's writings. Thus began a collaboration with Omar who regularly visited Cambridge. He edited the second volume of my selected essays, Harcourt (1986), and we wrote a joint survey article on post-Keynesianism for the *Bulletin of Economic Research*, subtitled "From criticism to coherence?" It has become a much cited article. In it we argued for a "horses for courses" approach to economic theorising and applications—hence the question mark following coherence. We included Piero Sraffa's classic contributions under the rubric of post-Keynesianism. This is still a controversial proposition, see Harcourt and Kriesler (2013), vol 1, Introduction and Chaps. 2–4.

Luigi Pasinetti and I became friends when we were Ph.D. students at Cambridge. Subsequently we were colleagues at Cambridge in the 1960s. We read and commented on each other's papers. Luigi often asked my advice about the tone of his replies to criticisms of his work by, for example, Frank Hahn and James Meade. I believe I helped him get the logic across more clearly by toning down polemical asides! Mauro Baranzini, who was a friend and admirer of Luigi, suggested to me that we prepare a *Festschrift* volume, Baranzini and Harcourt (1993), for Luigi's 60th birthday in 1990 (Luigi had returned to Italy by then). We started five years beforehand and presented it to him in 1993, three years after his birthday (Economics is not an exact science.) Mauro and I wrote a long chapter analysing Luigi's many original contributions, providing the evidence for our claim that he is probably the last of the great system builders in our increasingly Balkanised Trade. The wide range of topics in the chapters of our distinguished cast of contributors back up this claim. We celebrated with the recipient at a dinner party at the Graduate Centre in Cambridge ("the Grad Pad"). The Vice Chancellor was having dinner at the next table and when I told him why we were there, he presented us with a bottle of the best champagne—we do things in style in the Ancient Universities.

The National Bureau of Economic Research celebrated its first 50 years of existence with a volume edited by Berndt and Triplett in 1990. Lars Osberg, the review editor of the *Review of Income and Wealth*, who I had come to know in Canada and Cambridge, asked me to write a review article of the volume. I asked Mike Kitson, a colleague of mine at Cambridge who had worked with Nicky Kaldor in the *DAE*, to be a co-author, an inspired request, Mike contributed some of the most important sections of our review article, including a masterly account of the difference in the approaches of the NBER and those of Cambridge.

> "The neoclassical approach is a way of doing economics, it is not *the* way. The Cambridge approach is one alternative; an approach, however imperfect, which tries always to place great emphasis on the complexities of the real world. Reliable measurement is dependent on relevant theoretical hypotheses. The neoclassical approach, displayed in this volume, provides clarity and internal consistency. An alternative Cambridge approach, sceptical of the ability of markets to clear, would more readily accept that individual and collective actions are affected by institutions and political and social forces. The resulting picture of the world that emerges may be less-defined but also perhaps less distorted". Harcourt and Kitson (1993), reprinted in Harcourt (2001), 233–34, emphasis in original: this is pure Kitson.

One of my favourite papers was written with my Brazilian Ph.D. student, Jorge Araujo.[13] A friend of mine, Mike Lawlor, one of the finest

Keynes scholars I have ever met, came across in Keynes's papers in the King's Archives, a three-way correspondence between Maurice Dobb, Joan Robinson and Gerald Shove on whether an economy could grow if the firms in it were only receiving normal profits. Jorge went meticulously through the correspondence (like Prue he is a born researcher in archives) and then set out beautifully the formal analysis of what became our article, Araujo and Harcourt, (1993); Harcourt (1995), rigorously establishing our combined intuitions concerning the issues involved. We ended up using diagrams and analysis developed by Paul Davidson (1972) and Don Harris (1975, 1978). These provided solutions to the issues raised and helped to illustrate the transition in and development of Joan Robinson's approach from its Marshallian–Keynesian starting point to her mature stance in which the classicals, Marx, Keynes, Sraffa and Kalecki came to dominate her approach and views. It also illustrated what fine and subtle minds the three correspondents had.

One of my most enjoyable and, I believe, important, collaborations was with a gifted New Zealand economist, Paul Dalziel. I sponsored his visits to Cambridge in the 1980s and 1990s. Paul is not only a gifted technical scholar but also a courageous moral person with fine ideals based on his Christian faith. He and his wife, Jane Higgins, were virtually the only voices crying in the wilderness protesting against the extreme monetarist neoliberal policies implemented in New Zealand in the latter part of the 20th century. Paul complemented his compassionate religious ideals with an increasing interest in, and mastery of, post-Keynesian analysis—hence his visits to Cambridge.

In 1993 James Meade published in the *Economic Journal* an account of his role in the "Cambridge circus" in the development of the analysis of Richard Kahn's classic 1931 *Economic Journal* article on the multiplier. Meade analysed the multiplier process through the leakage into saving through the marginal propensity to save (s) rather than the build-up in expenditure through the marginal propensity to consume (c). Meade's multiplier formula, $1/s$, became known as "Mr Meade's relation". Both Kahn and Meade emphasised the central Keynesian insight that, logically, investment leads and saving follows. Meade put it vividly in Meade (1975), 82, when he pointed out that the essence of the Keynesian revolution was that Keynes changed our view of the world from one of a saving dog wagging an investment tail to the other way around.

In 1980 Feldstein and Horioka published an influential article in the *Economic Journal* in which they argued that, for the world as a whole, it was saving not investment which led, thus returning to a pre-Keynesian view. I suggested to Paul that we should take them on, adapting the analysis of Meade's 1993 article—process/period analysis in a closed economy model—to an open economy model of the world as a whole in which domestic saving and international capital movements were taken into account in our confirmation of the Kahn, Keynes, Meade insight. When I write "our", it was Paul who provided the elegant formal analysis.

We sent our draft to James and he wrote agreeing with what we had done and providing in one succinct paragraph (which he kindly allowed us to include in our note) what it eventually took us 15 printed pages to establish! After an unsatisfactory round of exchanges with the *Economic Journal*, our note was finally published in the *Cambridge Journal of Economics* in 1997 (it is reprinted in Harcourt (2001)).

Another important collaboration was with my long-time Australian friend, Peter Riach, who left Australia for the UK at much the same time as I did in the 1980s. Peter became Professor and Head of the Department of Economics at De Montfort University. He hit upon a wonderful project. Noting that famous composers often died leaving unfinished scores which others then finished, he referred to Keynes's promise to Ralph Hawtrey in 1936, never fulfilled because of illness, the Second World War and his early death, to write "some footnotes" to *The General Theory*, see Harcourt and Riach (1997), xiv. Peter suggested we commission a cast of scholars of Keynes of all varieties to write chapters on what they thought Keynes would have written in the late 1930s and why they themselves had subsequently worked on the aspects of Keynes's insights that they had.

The project resulted in *A* "Second Edition" *of The General Theory*, two volumes, published by Routledge in 1997 (and subsequently translated into Japanese with an introduction by the late Hirofumi Uzawa whom I greatly liked and admired, see Harcourt (2014)). The chapters in volume 1 mirror the original chapters in *The General Theory*, those in volume 2 are overwhelmingly post-*General Theory* and Keynes's death. Volume 2 also contains what is probably Jim Tobin's last considered views on the significance of *The General Theory*, Tobin (1997). Some of our authors chose to write at least the first sections of their chapters as J.M. Keynes, which they did very well. As well as writing the Introduction with Peter, I collaborated with Wylie Bradford, one of my best-ever doctoral students at Cambridge, to write on "Units and definitions", Chap. 7. Again alphabetical order is the correct index of the depth of contribution.

E. Roy Weintraub wrote a rather embittered and unfair review of the volumes in the *Economic Record*, Weintraub (1998). Among other things he wrongly classified all our contributors as post-Keynesians (about whom he has a thing) and he denied our volumes any place at all in the canon of respectable, proper HET. In contrast, Tony Thirlwall, a self-declared unreconstructed Keynesian, published a delightful and cleverly amusing review article in the *JPKE*, writing as JMK resurrected, Thirlwall (1999). The late Bernard Corry, a great HET scholar, also published a pleasingly fair minded favourable review in the *Manchester School*, Corry (2000), not long before he died.

Bertram Schefold took over as general editor of a prestigious German HET series. He asked me to contribute a chapter on the representative firm and increasing returns debates of the 1920s in the *Economic Journal*, starting with John Clapham's empty economic boxes (1922) and ending with the 1930 symposium edited by Keynes, containing articles by Dennis Robertson, Gerald Shove and Piero Sraffa. I asked Stephanie Blankenburg, whose fine M.Phil dissertation on Gramsci and Kalecki I had supervised (this was the beginning of our now long-standing friendship), to collaborate with me. The result, Blankenburg and Harcourt (2001), was that I wrote on the actual debates and Stephanie drew out their implications for a critique of modern endogenous growth theory, ideas she had developed in one of the essays of her Ph.D. dissertation.[14] The English version, "The representative firm and increasing returns: then and now", was later published in 2007 in a volume edited by Philip Arestis, Michelle Baddeley and John McCombie (and published by Edward Elgar). Again alphabetical order has nothing to do with authorship order for I would have insisted that Stephanie be first, as her deep insights, criticisms and analysis are startling.

12.10 Collaboration on Visits to OZ

While we were in Cambridge from 1982 on, Joan and I always returned each year to Australia for a month or more, as befits "A Cambridge economist *but* an Australian patriot", see Hatch and Petridis (1997). From 1997 on our main port of call was the School of Economics at UNSW, mainly because Peter Kriesler was there. One of my UNSW colleagues was Mehdi Monadjemi who had done his doctorate with the late John Cornwall, an outstanding post-Keynesian scholar. John and I had been friends since we met in Cambridge in 1963. When Mark Setterfield, who had been a pupil of Peter and mine at Cambridge and then had been John's doctoral student at Dalhousie, asked me to contribute a chapter to a *Festschrift* for John, Setterfield (1999), I asked Mehdi to join me. Our chapter was entitled "The vital contributions of John Cornwall to economic theory and policy: a tribute from two admiring friends on the occasion of his 70th birthday", Harcourt and Monadjemi (1999). I surveyed John's contributions and insights and Mehdi supplied a case study on the role of housing and its finance over the trade cycle, a study arising from his dissertation and an ideal complement to my overview.

12.11 In Cambridge From 1982 On

My principal intellectual reason for returning to Cambridge in 1982 was to attempt to document the contributions of those who had worked with Keynes—Richard Kahn, Austin and Joan Robinson, James Meade, Piero Sraffa—or who had been greatly influenced by him—Nicky Kaldor, David Champernowe, Brian Reddaway, Dick Goodwin, Dick Stone and in my generation, especially Luigi Pasinetti. By 1982 the first group had become elder statespersons and were to die in the 1980s and 1990s—indeed, only Luigi and I are now alive! I had been writing oral histories and essays in intellectual biography since the 1970s. Drawing on this background, in 1990s I collaborated with my colleagues and friends, Allan Hughes and Ajit Singh, to publish short obituary tributes to Austin Robinson, Harcourt, Hughes and Singh (1993), and to the great Indian economist, Shukhanoy Chakravarty, who had spent time in Cambridge and who had died tragically young in his mid-50s, see Harcourt and Singh (1991).

I came to know Dick Stone in the 1960s when he and Allan Brown were running the Cambridge growth project team. To my delight he told me how much he liked *Economic Activity*, the proof sheets of which he had read in the *DAE* Library. One of my oral histories was based on conversations I had with Dick in the 1980s (it was subsequently published in Harcourt (1995)). I was the obituary editor of the *Economic Journal* for eight years. When Dick died in 1991, I asked Hashem Pesaran to write Dick's obituary for the journal. Subsequently we made it a joint obituary, a complementary combination of Hashem's great technical strengths and his appreciation of Dick's outstanding technical contributions with my evaluation of Dick the person, see Pesaran and Harcourt (2000). Our obituary article has been well received by the profession, especially by those who knew and admired its subject, and it is often cited and downloaded.

Ever since the publication in the *JEL* in 1969 of my article on the Cambridge–Cambridge capital theory controversies, I have often been asked/commissioned to write survey articles. One of those—it is on post-Keynesianism—was commissioned for Shri Bhagwan Dahuya's series, *The Current State of Economic Science.* I had come to know Luke Spajic, a graduate student at Cambridge, and we had had many discussions on issues in banking and finance, issues on which he was knowledgeable and I, a tyro but a keen learner. So I asked Luke to combine with me whereby I would write on the real aspects and he on those relating to banking and finance, especially the theory of endogenous money. Of course, we stressed that one of Keynes's greatest insights was that the real and money must be integrated from the start in the analysis of a monetary production economy. This did not preclude another core insight, this from our founder Adam Smith, of the advantages of specialisation and the division of labour. The survey was published in 1999.

Robert Skidelsky's superb three-volume biography of Keynes (1983, 1992, 2000) was being written and published while I was in Cambridge. Skidelsky was a close friend of the Kaldors and stayed with them for much of the time while he was writing volumes 2 and 3. I came to know him and we had many discussions on matters Keynes. So when volume 3 was published, I decided to write a review article of the three volumes. Before this I had examined an outstanding Ph.D. dissertation Sean Turnell had written at Macquarie University in Sydney. Sean and I became close friends when I sponsored his first visit to Cambridge as a Visiting Fellow at Wolfson College.

I suggested to him that we make the review article a joint effort. I would write the first draft of our evaluation of volumes 1 and 2, he, that of volume 3. This division of labour reflected our comparative advantages: my knowledge of Cambridge social groupings and the intricate goings on of the Bloomsbury circle of whom Keynes was a key member[15] and my many years of teaching and writing about Keynes's books and articles. Sean was a whiz kid on international trade, capital movements and institutions and so Keynes's roles at Bretton Woods and in post-war reconstruction were very much his cup of tea.

In the event our review article took over four years to write and came to 16,000 words (after all Skidelsky had written three large volumes). We had intended it for the *Cambridge Journal of Economics* but the referees and editors felt otherwise.[16] So we sent it to Jayati Ghosh, a former doctoral student of mine at Cambridge in the 1980s,[17] who is closely associated with the *Economic and Political Weekly*, the influential and widely read Indian journal. It was quickly accepted, see Harcourt and Turnell (2005), but we had to prune it, so losing some relevant, dispensable for this purpose, footnotes. The unexpurgated version is the title essay of a selection of my essays, Harcourt (2012a), published by Palgrave Macmillan.

Our evaluation of Skidelsky's volumes was highly favourable, especially on Skidelsky's take on what happened at Bretton Woods and the disastrous consequences of this for the survival of the Bretton Woods institutions in the post-war period. We also especially liked Skidelsky's deep understanding of the meaning and relevance of *The General Theory*. (Don Patinkin had criticised him for adopting a post-Keynesian interpretation, see Skidelsky (1992), xi, a criticism up with which we would not put.) We did part company with the author over his evaluation of the criticism by Étienne Mantoux (1945; 1952) of the theoretical and applied analysis in *The Economic Consequences of the Peace*, Keynes (1919; *C.W.*, vol II, 1971). Mantoux wrote his book after *The General Theory* had been published and criticised Keynes's use of the pre-*General Theory* quantity theory of money framework with its implicit assumption of full employment which made the problem of reparations, economically anyway, seem more serious than it in fact was. He wrote as if he were *Lord Keynes* after *The General Theory* criticising *Mr Keynes* before *The General Theory*.

In footnote 17 I mentioned Terry O'Shaughnessy. Terry is an Australian from Adelaide whom I first met in the anti-Vietnam War protests in the 1960s and 1970s. He was then an engineering undergraduate and a member of Christians for Peace. He subsequently became a Communist—Australia then had three communist parties, Russian, Chinese and intellectuals, all meeting in their own separate telephone booths. Terry belonged to the last and was a journalist on their newspaper. He did a Master's Degree in Political Thought at Macquarie and subsequently came to Cambridge to do the M.Phil in Economics and then a Ph.D. which I supervised.

At this time there was a bitter dispute about whether *The General Theory* was set in the short period or the long period, with Richard Kahn and Joan Robinson arguing for the first, Pierangelo Garegnani, John Eatwell and Murray Milgate, for the second view. Terry and I wrote a paper on this theme, Harcourt and O'Shaughnessy (1985), for the Keynes Centenary Conference at the University of Kent, that resulted in a volume, *Keynes and his Contemporaries*, which I edited, Harcourt (1985). We came down on the side of the short-period interpretation, a correct but dangerous stance.

12.12 Prue Kerr and I

As well as Prue and I collaborating on Marx, we wrote a chapter, "The Mixed Economy", for the 1980 volume, *Labor*, edited by Jane North and Pat Weller. The arguments of our paper were fed by me into Discussion Paper No. 6 of the series of discussion papers put out by the ALP National Committee of Enquiry which was set up in the late 1970s to find out why the Labor Party had fared so badly in Federal elections after the dismissal of the Whitlam government in 1975 by the Governor General, a shameful act which greatly divided the Australian community. We contributed a package deal of economic policies, which, I like to think, Bob Hawke, the incoming ALP Prime Minister in 1983, implemented for a good half hour after coming into office. The government did put into place the Accord, an incomes policy designed to fit in with the then characteristics and institutions of the Australian labour market which Eric Russell, Wilfred Salter and others had developed since the 1950s, see Harcourt (2001b).

Prue and I reckon that between us we have written over 100 essays on the theme of Joan Robinson and her circle. In 2009, our intellectual biography of Joan was published in Tony Thirlwall's series with Palgrave Macmillan, "Great thinkers in economics". Though very much a joint work, the first drafts of the 12 chapters were divided equally between us. I wrote the chapters on most of Joan's major books—*The Economics of Imperfect Competition* (1983), *Introduction to the Theory of Employment* (1937a), *Essays in the Theory of Employment* (1937b), *The Accumulation of Capital* (1956), *Economic Heresies* (1971) and *Introduction to Modern Economics* (1973), her introductory textbook co-authored with John Eatwell. Prue wrote on Joan Robinson's contributions to Marxian economics, concentrating especially on her exchanges with Maurice Dobb while she was writing her 1942 *Essay on Marxian Economics.* Prue also wrote on Joan's pre-war and wartime essays and addresses on the BBC concerning left-Keynesian theory and policies for the war and post-war years. One of Prue's chapter was on the three books Joan wrote for the general reader, *Economic Philosophy* (1962), *Economics: An Awkward Corner* (1966) and *Freedom and Necessity: An Introduction to the Study of Society* (1970). Prue wrote the chapter that centres around Joan's 1978 book on development economics, a book we both admired. I wrote the chapters on Joan's role in the run up to the publication of *The General Theory* and after, and on *The Accumulation of Capital* and the Cambridge–Cambridge capital theory debates. The Introduction and Conclusion were combined efforts.

Our book was the culmination of decades of work, in which we published Introductions to some major volumes as well as articles and chapters in books. These include the entry on Joan in *The International Encyclopedia of the Social and Behavioural Sciences*, Smelser and Baltes (2001), our "General Introduction" to the five volumes of essays on Joan in Routledge's series, *Critical Assessments of Leading Economists* (2002), in which we included an essay, "On Joan Robinson and China", co-authored with Pervez Tahir. Pervez had been my Ph.D. student at Cambridge; he wrote on Joan's contributions to development economics, Tahir (1990a). Subsequently he was the 1990 Joan Robinson Memorial Lecturer at Cambridge where he wrote a comprehensive manuscript on what Joan had written on China. Our chapter presents the gist of his findings, Tahir (1990b). Also in 2002, we co-authored the Introduction to the Palgrave Archive Edition of Joan's books. In 2003, we published "Keynes and the Cambridge School" in *A Companion to the History of Economic Thought*, edited by Warren Samuels, Jeff Biddle and John Davis. In 2010 we had a chapter, "*The Accumulation of Capital* over 50 years on" in Stefano Zambelli's *Festschrift* for our great pal, Vela Velupillai. We drew on this for our "Introduction" to the republication of her 1956 *magnum opus* in the Palgrave Classic Economics Series, published in 2013. In 1956, as a graduate student, I had locked myself up with her book for a term and then read a paper on it to the research students' seminar, spread over two meetings. Joan came to the third to answer our questions. Alas, during our many moves since then, I lost the paper. I would dearly have liked to have compared its findings with our evaluation over 50 years on. Prue and I are now working on the entry on Joan Robinson for Harald Hagemann and Bob Dimand's *The Elgar Companion to John Maynard Keynes*.

Prue is an expert scholar in Archives, ably gathering relevant material to provide evidence to back up her extremely subtle analysis of issues and people. I have a huge file of our correspondence over the decades. I never cease to be amazed by the subtlety of her thought and her writing. She is able to penetrate to the core of difficulties and explain them with highly intelligent clarity. In many respects, she is the Virginia Woolf of economic analysis—intuitive, deep, innovative. Furthermore, she has a sure feel for context combined with balanced, if often unexpected, evaluations. To have collaborated with such a multi-talented person is one of the most pleasant and rewarding experiences of my life as an economist. Furthermore, her close friendship with Joan (Harcourt) and myself has enriched our lives for nearly 50 years.

Overlapping my last period in Cambridge and now, time at UNSW was a most exciting collaboration with Peter Nolan, my long-time friend and colleague at Jesus. Both of us are friends of Amiya Bagchi, the distinguished Indian economist and historian, who had been a Fellow of Jesus in the 1960s. When I was asked to contribute a chapter to a *Festschrift* for him, I asked the editors that Peter and I co-author it. As I have often mentioned, the article that most influenced me as an undergraduate and ever after is Kurt Rothschild's 1947 classic in the *Economic Journal*, "Price theory and oligopoly". As a radical from the 1960s on, I was also familiar with the writings of Stephen Hymer who had been Charles Kindleburger's doctoral student at MIT and who was a guru of the left until his tragic death in a car accident when he was only 40 years old.

Both Rothschild and Hymer had predicted what would be the likely outcomes in the market structures of capitalism over the long haul—Rothschild, a world of giant multi-national oligopolies, Hymer, one of monopolies. Peter has a huge set of case studies of large multi-national companies. We used these as the empirical evidence to test who of our heroes was closest to the truth in our chapter, Harcourt and Nolan (2009), which we subtitled "Kurt Rothschild and Stephen Hymer revisited". Rothschild won.

12.13 At the School of Economics UNSW, 2010–

I come now to post-Cambridge years at the School of Economics at UNSW where Peter Kriesler, John Nevile and I have collaborated on many papers. They are mostly concerned with post-Keynesian theory and policy but there are also historical essays on Kalecki and Joan Robinson, Harcourt and Kriesler (2011), Kalecki and Rosa Luxemburg, Harcourt and Kriesler (2013a) and Harrod and Fel'dman, Kriesler and Harcourt (2015).

In the second half of 2007, Michael Szenberg and Lall Ramrattan asked me to edit *The Oxford Handbook of Post-Keynesian Economics* for Oxford University Press, USA. I started on this mammoth task during my last years at Cambridge. In the first half of 2010 I asked Peter to be a joint editor—Peter is noted for his editorial skills and expertise with computers, the internet and so on. (I am hopeless with anything mechanical, having only recently graduated from a quill pen to a biro. In Cambridge I was completely dependent on a succession of long-suffering Fellows Secretaries—and now paid "Internet slaves" who are usually graduate students at UNSW—to "do" my emails.) The result has been six years hard (but loving) labour culminating in our two-volume handbook, Harcourt and Kriesler (2013b). Many of my former collaborators are, of course, to be found in the volumes. The volumes themselves, to our great relief, so far have been favourably reviewed, notably by Steven Pressman in the *JEL* (2014) and by Renée Prendergast in *ELRR* (2015).

In 2013, Palgrave Macmillan published *Financial Crises and the Nature of Capitalist Money: Critical Developments from the work of Geoffrey Ingham* which was co-edited by Jocelyn Pixley and myself. Geoff Ingham and I were colleagues and friends for many years at Cambridge, first within the Faculty of Economics which used to be proud of its team of sociologists until the squiggle merchants took over and booted them out, and then in the Faculty of Social and Political Sciences. I had been a sort of midwife to the making of Geoff's groundbreaking book, *The Nature of Money* (2004). I came to know Jocelyn at UNSW and I wrote a most favourable review of her splendid book on emotions in finance, Pixley (2004), see Harcourt (2005). We both are foundation members of the Geoffrey Ingham fan club.

Jocelyn had the innovative idea of getting economists and sociologists inside one set of covers to discuss and develop Ingham's ideas, especially in the light of the recent and ongoing financial crisis. As the word "no" is missing from her vocabulary, she insisted that I be a co-editor rather than just helping her as she put the volume together. The climax was a great two-day conference in Geoff Ingham's honour at his college, Christ's, in August 2013, at which the volume was launched and the contributors talked to their chapters. As Geoff had long been wine steward at Christ's we naturally celebrated our scholarship in the only way Oxbridge understands, that is to say, scholarship has always been born and celebrated there in food and drink.

12.14 Post-Keynesians from Down Under

I had promised Joan (Harcourt) that the *Oxford Handbook* would be my last major project. However, I had in mind a smaller project, preparing a volume of selected essays to take me into double figures on this score. Peter Kriesler pointed out to me that he and I had collaborated on many papers since I had come to UNSW and that he had also collaborated for many years with John Nevile at UNSW and Joseph Halevi of Sydney University. He suggested that we put together four volumes of *Selected Essays by Post-Keynesians from Down Under*, under the rubric of theory and policy from an historical perspective.

Palgrave Macmillan had responded favourably to my initial proposal for a tenth volume and they then readily agreed to the larger project. The four volumes were published at the beginning of 2016. These collaborations have always been rewarding. In general we agree but, if we do not, we argue matters through either to reach an agreed position or, occasionally, to put in a dissenting footnote. The four volumes contain joint essays by Peter, John and Joseph written over many years and mine since 2010. One pleasing offshoot is to be able to bring together in one place Joseph's remarkable contributions over an extraordinary range to the political economy of our time, contributions that have never been properly appreciated, possibly not even known about, by his Philistine colleagues at Sydney.

At UNSW I share a room with John Nevile who has been at the University for more than 50 years, having joined as Professor of Economics in the 1960s. There was a splendid conference to celebrate John's 80th birthday and his many outstanding contributions to our trade and to University and Australian life generally. Peter Kriesler, John Langmore, a long-time friend of John and mine, and I gave a paper which was subsequently published in the Special Issue in honour of John Nevile in the *Economic and Labour Relations Review* (John has been associated with the journal since its inception). The title of our article, "Faith, works and talents entwined: driving forces behind John Nevile's contributions" (2013), says it all.

As I noted, Allan Barton was one of the first persons with whom I wrote a joint article. Allan died in 2012. He was one of the most selfless persons I have ever met. A negative by-product of this was that he never found the time to publish his Cambridge dissertation on the multi-product firm, Barton (1961). I repeatedly nagged him to do so because it anticipated by many years ideas subsequently made well known by Oliver Williamson and others. When Allan died, Selwyn Cornish, Richard Holden and I prepared an obituary tribute to him for the *Economic Record*. Richard, a fine scholar with a detailed and deep knowledge and understanding of the issues of Allan's dissertation, confirmed in our obituary how far ahead of his time Allan had been.

The *Economic Record* has a rule of thumb: 1000 words for obituaries of the greats, 500 for the also rans. The editorial board decided in their (lack of) collective wisdom that Allan, who held Chairs of Accounting at Macquarie and the ANU, who had also been the most successful ever Treasurer of the ANU and who greatly influenced the structure of government accounts and methods used, fell in to the latter category, see Cornish, Harcourt and Holden (2013). The unexpurgated version of our tribute is published in Volume Three of *Post-Keynesians from Down Under*.[18]

12.15 Conclusion

So that is it, an account of a lifetime of much collaboration and deepening friendship combined. The great satisfactions of an academic life may never be able to be fitted comfortably, if at all, into the mainstream model of individual behaviour but as a source of life enrichment in this "veil of tears", they are hard to beat. Especially is this true of my generation who coincided with the Golden Age of Academia. Many readers no doubt will detect a Pollyanna gloss on what I have written. If so, too bad, for that is how I see it.

G.C. Harcourt
UNSW Australia
October 2016

Notes

1. Peter and Avi are coming up fast on the rails if accepted but not yet published items are included.
2. I have not included in the text but I would like to mention that I prize being asked (or offering) to write Forewords to books and commenting on drafts of articles and books. I have no detailed idea of how often I have done this, but I am sure it runs into hundreds.
3. It subsequently became the basis of his well-received book with Cambridge University Press, *Kalecki's Microanalysis* (1987), to which I wrote a Foreword.
4. It was the basis of his fine book, *Marx and Keynes on Economic Recession*, published in 1987. He published a second edition including Kalecki, in 2011. It is entitled *Unemployment, Recession and Effective Demand*. I wrote Forewords to both books. Some years later in Cambridge, he met and subsequently married our oldest child, Wendy.
5. Australian economics as well as commerce undergraduates have always had to take accounting courses, most sensibly so, since it may be argued that a necessary if not sufficient condition for the

rise of capitalism was double-entry bookkeeping, a conjecture now conclusively and delightfully established in Jane Gleeson White's prize-winning volume, *Double Entry* (2011). The script of an interview I did with Jane, which was a hit on the ABC's "Big Ideas" programme, is published as Gleeson White and Harcourt (2012).

6. I had gone as an honours student to Bob's first ever set of lectures (on international trade). Bob came to Adelaide after two years at Oxford, and he, and then I, encouraged many others to come to Adelaide.
7. Much more importantly, Deane was Captain of the University of Adelaide Australian Rules Football team for which I played.
8. Maurice always sent handwritten versions of his manuscripts to publishers because he did not trust typists to get his punctuation right.
9. During one of our many moves, I lost the file containing the "go to whoa" correspondence and drafts associated with the paper so I cannot now check exactly what the flaw was—I think it had something to do with inconsistent time periods associated with price setting and investment planning.
10. See my essay, Harcourt (1995b; 2012b) in Shepherd (ed), *Rejected* (1995) for a full account of the making of the paper and Harcourt (2004) and Harcourt (2012), respectively, for my tributes to Brian and Champ, alas, both now dead.
11. It was Ray who christened us "The Trinity from Adelaide", Byron (1970b, 576), a wry comment which cost him a chair of econometrics at the University of Western Australia. The Head of the UWA Economics Department who interviewed Ray for the post was an evangelical Christian. He was scandalised that anyone would blaspheme in the pages of the *Record*, a charge to which Ray, a fiery red-haired person of Irish descent, did not take to kindly, to say the least. When he blamed me for him missing out, I told him that he was much better off in his post of Reader at the ANU.
12. In June 2011, the journal hosted a conference in Cambridge in honour of my 80th birthday on "The future of capitalism". The Special Issue arising from the conference was published in November 2014. It includes a "blush-making" intro by Stephanie

Blankenburg and among the excellent papers, Costis Repapis's take on developments in economics over the last 50 and more years as seen through my over 100 reviews covering the period.

13. I was lucky enough to have six wonderful Brazilian doctoral students at Cambridge, and to visit Brazil twice.
14. I regard her dissertation as the equal best dissertation I have ever examined and/or read.
15. Noel Annan once quipped that the Bloomsbury circle lived in squares and loved in triangles.
16. A necessary but not sufficient condition to be an editor is to have one or more articles rejected by the journal. I have been necessary more than once.
17. Jayati, Peter Kriesler and Terry O'Shaughnessy, another of my Cambridge Ph.D. students, were the rapporteurs at the Keynes Centenary Conference in King's in 1983. Our mutual efforts—I was very much the junior partner—recorded the discussions at that never-to-be-forgotten gathering, see Worswick and Trevithik (1983)
18. For completeness, I should mention that I have written joint reviews, been interviewed for articles in journals, and I collaborated with Peter Kriesler and Craig Friedman on a chapter for Ed Nell's *Festschrift*, Forstater and Mongiovi (2014), and with Jan Toporowski on an article, "The lender of last resort and capital market stability" (2003). Craig, Peter and Jan were definitely the senior partners.

Collaborations

Books

(with P.H. Karmel and R.H. Wallace), *Economic Activity*, (Cambridge: Cambridge University Press, 1967). (Italian Edition, 1969), pp.xi + 324.

(with R.H. Parker, eds), *Readings in the Concept and Measurement of Income*, Cambridge: Cambridge University Press, 1969). (Second edition, with G. Whittington, Philip Allan, 1986), pp. viii + 402.

(with N.F. Laing, eds) *Capital and Growth, Selected Readings*, (London: Penguin, 1971), reprinted 1973. (Spanish edition, 1977), pp.viii + 383.

The Social Science Imperialists. Selected Essays. G.C. Harcourt. Edited by Prue Kerr, (London: Routledge and Kegan Paul, 1982), pp.vii + 423. Reprinted in the Routledge Library Editions Series in 2003.

(with R.H. Parker and G. Whittington, eds), *Readings in the Concept and Measurement of Income* (2nd ed., Oxford: Philip Allan, 1986), pp. vii + 371.
(with Jon Cohen, eds.), *International Monetary Problems and Supply-Side Economics: Essays in Honour of Lorie Tarshis* (London: Macmillan, 1986), pp.viii + 162.
Controversies in Political Economy, Selected Essays by G.C. Harcourt. Edited by O.F. Hamouda (Brighton: Wheatsheaf Books Ltd, 1986), pp.293.
On Political Economists and Modern Political Economy. Selected Essays of G.C. Harcourt, Edited by Claudio Sardoni. (London: Routledge, 1992), pp.xi + 428. Reprinted in the Routledge Library Editions Series in 2003.
(with Mauro Baranzini, eds) *The Dynamics of the Wealth of Nations. Growth, Distribution and Structural Change. Essays in Honour of Luigi Pasinetti* (Basingstoke, Hants: Macmillan, 1993), pp.xiii + 424.
(with Alessandro Roncaglia and Robin Rowley, eds), *Income and Employment in Theory and Practice* (Basingstoke, Hants: Macmillan, 1994), pp.xviii + 293.
(with P.A. Riach, eds), *A 'Second Edition' of* The General Theory, 2 Vols. (London, Routledge, 1997), pp.*li* + 503, *xlix* + 400. Japanese translation with a Foreword by Hirofumi Uzawa, 2005.
(with Hank Lim and Ungsuh K. Park, eds) *Editing Economics. Essays in Honour of Mark Perlman* (London: Routledge, 2002) pp. xii+314.
(with Prue Kerr), *Joan Robinson. Critical Assessments of Leading Economists,* 5 vols. (London: Routledge, 2002) xli+373; vii+308; vii+405; vii+508; viii+528.
(with Christopher Bliss and Avi J. Cohen, eds) *Capital Theory,* 3 vols (Cheltenham, Glos., UK and Northampton, Mass., USA: Edward Elgar Publishing Limited), 2005, pp. lx + 564; x + 515; viii + 522.
(with Prue Kerr) *Joan Robinson,* Houndmills, Basingstoke, Hampshire: Palgrave Macmillan, 2009, pp.x + 270.
(with Peter Kriesler, eds) *The Oxford Handbook of Post-Keynesian Economics. Volume 1: Theory and Origins,* New York: Oxford University Press, 2013, pp. xii + 623. *Volume 2: Critiques and Methodology,* pp. x + 516.
(with Jocelyn Pixley, eds) *Financial Crises and the Nature of Capitalist Money. Critical Developments from the Work of Geoffrey Ingham,* Houndmills, Basingstoke, Hampshire: Palgrave Macmillan, 2013, pp. xvii + 329.
(with Joseph Halevi, Peter Kriesler and JW Nevile) *Post-Keynesian Essays from Down Under: Theory and Policy from an Historical Perspective. Volume 1: Essays on Keynes, Harrod and Kalecki,* Houndmills, Basingstoke, Hampshire, Palgrave Macmillan, 2016, pp. xii+366. *Volume 2: Essays on Policy and Applied Economics,* pp. xiv+434. *Volume 3: Essays on Ethics, Social Justice and Economics,* pp. xii+320. *Volume 4: Essays on Theory,* pp. xiv+525.

Articles

(with Duncan Ironmonger), "Pilot Survey of Personal Savings", *Economic Record.* Vol.32, May 1956, pp.106–18.

(with A.D. Barton), "Investment Allowances for Primary Producers" *Australian Journal of Agricultural Economics.* Vol.3, December 1959, pp.12–18.

(with J.W. Bennett), "Taxation and Business Surplus". *Economic Record.* Vol.36, August 1960, pp.425–8.

(with A.S. Watson and P.D. Praetz), "The C.E.T. Production Frontier and Estimates of Supply Response in Australian Agriculture", *Economic Record.* Vol. 46, December 1970, pp.553–63.

(with Peter Kenyon), "Pricing and the Investment Decision", *Kyklos*, 29, Fasc. 3. Vol.29, 1976, pp.449–77.

(With O.F. Hamouda), "Post Keynesianism: From Criticism to Coherence?" *Bulletin of Economic Research.* Vol.40, January 1988, pp.1–33.

(with J.A.T.R. Araujo), 'Maurice Dobb, Joan Robinson and Gerald Shove on Accumulation and the Rate of Profits', *Journal of the History of Economic Thought*, 15, Spring, 1993, pp. 1–30, Revised version "Accumulation and the Rate of Profits: Reflections on the issues raised in the correspondence between Maurice Dobb, Joan Robinson and Gerald Shove" in G.C. Harcourt, *Capitalism, Socialism and Post-Keynesianism. Selected Essays of G.C. Harcourt* Aldershot, Hants; Edward Elgar, 1995, pp. 79–106.

(with M.H. Pesaran), "Life and Work of John Richard Nicholas Stone, 1913–1991", *Economic Journal*, Vol. 110, February, 2000, pp.F146–65

(with John Grieve Smith), "The economic policies of Gordon Brown and the Treasury. Stability for what?", *Soundings*, Issue 20, Summer 2001, pp. 57–63.

(with Avi. J. Cohen), "Whatever Happened to the Cambridge Capital Theory Controversies?", *Journal of Economic Perspectives*, Vol. 17, No. 1, Winter 2003, pp. 199–214.

(with Peter Kriesler), "The enduring importance of *The General Theory*", *Review of Political Economy*, vol 23, No 4, 2011, pp. 503–519.

(with Jane Gleeson-White), "Double entry book keeping: a conversation", *Economic and Labour Relations Review*, Vol 23, No. 23, September, 2012, pp. 89–104.

(with Peter Kriesler and J. W. Nevile), "Exchange rates and the macroeconomy in an era of global financial crises, with special reference to Australia", *Economic and Labour Relations Review*, Vol 24, No. 1, March, 2013, pp. 51–63.

(with Peter Kriesler and John Langmore), "Faith, works and talents entwined: Driving forces behind John Nevile's contributions", *Economic and Labour Relations Review*, Vol 24, No. 2, June, 2013, pp. 228–37.

Review Articles

(with Vincent G. Massaro), "Mr. Sraffa's *Production of Commodities*". *Economic Record.* Vol.40, September 1964, pp.442–54.

(with Bruce McFarlane), "Economic Planning and Democracy", *Australian Journal of Political Science*, 25, November, 1990, pp.326–32.

(with Michael Kitson), "Fifty Years of Measurement: A Cambridge View", *Review of Income and Wealth*, Series 39, No. 4, December 1993, pp.435–47.
(with Sean Turnell), "On Skidelsky's Keynes", *Economic and Political Weekly*, XL, November 19, 2005, pp. 4931–46.
(with Peter Kriesler), "Post-Keynesian theory and policy for modern capitalism", *Journal of Australian Political Economy*, No.75, Winter, 2015,pp. 27–41.
(with Peter Kriesler and JW Nevile), "Macroeconomic policy for the real world: A Post-Keynesian perspective", *Economic Papers*, Vol 34, No 3, September 2015, pp. 108–117.

Notes

(with Vincent G. Massaro), "A Note on Mr. Sraffa's Sub-Systems", *Economic Journal*. Vol.74, September 1964, pp.715–22. (Reprinted in French in Gilbert, Farcarello and Phillipe de Cavergne (eds.) *Une nouvelle approche en économie politique? essais sur Sraffa*, (Paris: Economica 1977), pp.53–61).
(with G. Whittington), "The Irrelevancy of the British Differential Profits Tax: A Comment", *Economic Journal*. Vol.75, June 1965, pp.373–8.
(with A.S. Watson and P.D. Praetz), "Reply to Powell and Gruen, and Byron", *Economic Record*. Vol.46, December 1970, pp.574–5.
(with A. Asimakopulos), "Proportionality and the Neoclassical Parables", *Southern Economic Journal*. Vol.40, March 1974, pp.481–3.
(with M.H.I. Dore), "A Note on the Taxation of Exhaustible Resources under Oligopoly", *Economic Letters*, Vol.21, No 1, May 1986, pp.81–84.
(with B.J. McFarlane), "A Reply to Osiatynski", *Australian Journal of Political Science*, Vol. 26, No. 3, November, 1991, pp.355–56.
(with Ajit Singh) "Sukhamoy Chakravarty, 26 July, 1934–22 August, 1990", *Cambridge Journal of Economics*, 15, 1991, pp.1–3.
(with A. Hughes and A. Singh), "Austin Robinson, 20 November 1897–1 June 1993: An Appreciation", *Cambridge Journal of Economics*, Vol. 17, No. 4, December 1993, pp.365–68.
(with Gabriel Palma), "Introduction", *Cambridge Journal of Economics*, Vol. 18, February 1994, pp.1–2.
(with Paul Dalziel) "A Note on `Mr Meade's Relation' and International Capital Movements", *Cambridge Journal of Economics*, Vol.21, September 1997, pp.621–31.
(with Avi Cohen), "Response from Avi J. Cohen and G. C. Harcourt", *Journal of Economic Perspectives*, Fall 2003, vol. 17, 232–3.
(with Selwyn Cornish and Richard Holden) "Allan Barton 1933–2012: A Tribute", *Economic Record*, volume 89, No. 285, June, 2013, p.283.

Chapters in Books

(with D.H. Whitehead), "The Wool Textile Industry", Chapter 13 of A. Hunter (ed.), *The Economics of Australian Industry* (Melbourne: Melbourne University Press, 1963), pp.419–59.

(with R.L. Mathews), "Company Finance", Chapter 9 of R.R. Hirst and R.H. Wallace (eds), *Studies in the Australian Capital Market*, (Melbourne: F.W. Cheshire, 1964), pp.377–424.

(with P.M. Kerr), "The Mixed Economy", Chapter 14 in Jane North and Pat Weller (eds.), *Labor*, (Sydney: Ian Novak, 1980), pp.184–95.

(with T.J. O'Shaughnessy), "Keynes's Unemployment Equilibrium: Some Insights from Joan Robinson, Piero Sraffa and Richard Kahn", in G.C. Harcourt (ed.), *Keynes and his Contemporaries. The Sixth and Centennial Keynes Seminar held at the University of Kent at Canterbury 1983*, (London: Macmillan, 1985), pp.3–41.

(with G. Whittington), "Income and Capital", Ch. 7 of John Creedy (ed.), *Foundations of Economic Thought*. Oxford, Basil Blackwell, 1990, pp.186–211.

(with Claudio Sardoni), "George Shackle and Post Keynesianism" in Peter E. Earl and Stephen F. Frowen (eds), *Economics as an Art of Thought. Essays in Memory of G.L.S. Shackle* (London: Routledge, 2000) pp.76–100.

(with Claudio Sardoni) "Keynes's Vision: Method, Analysis and 'Tactics' "in J. Davis (ed.), *The State of Interpretation of Keynes*, Norwell, Mass., Kluwer, 1995, pp. 131–52.

(with P. Kerr) 'Marx, Karl Heinrich (1818–83)' in Malcolm Warner (ed), *International Encyclopedia of Business and Management*, (London: Routledge, 1996, pp.3388–95). 2nd edition, Vol. 5, 2001, pp. 4355–62. Reprinted in William Lazonick (ed.) *The IEBN Handbook of Economics*, London: Thomson, 2002, pp.674–80.

(with Claudio Sardoni), "*The General Theory of Employment, Interest and Money*: Three Views", Chapter 1 of Philip Arestis (ed.), *Keynes, Money and the Open Economy. Essays in honour of Paul Davidson*, Vol. 1, Cheltenham, Glos: Edward Elgar, 1996, pp. 1–13.

(with P.A. Riach), "Introduction" in Harcourt and Riach (1997), Vol. 1, pp.xiv-li; Vol. 2, pp.xii-xlix.

(with Wylie Bradford) "Units and Definitions", Ch.7 of Harcourt and Riach (1997), Vol.1, pp.107–31.

(with Prue Kerr) "Robinson, Joan, as an Interpreter of the Classical Economists: Mrs Robinson and the Classics" in Heinz D Kurz and Neri Salvadori (eds) *The Elgar Companion to Classical Economics L-Z*, Cheltenham, UK: Edward Elgar, 1998, pp. 324–328.

(with Mehdi Monadjemi) "The Vital Contributions of John Cornwall to Economic Theory and Policy: A Tribute from Two Admiring Friends on the Occasion of

His 70th Birthday" in Mark Settafield (ed.), *Growth, Employment and Inflation. Essays in Honour of John Cornwall*. Houndmills, Basingstoke, Hants: Macmillan, 1999, pp. 10–23.
(with L.D. Spajic), "Post-Keynesianism", in Shri Bhagwan Dahuya (ed.), *The Current State of Economic Science*, Volume Two, Rohtak, Spellbound Publications, 1999, pp. 909–34.
(with Stephanie Blankenburg), "Die Debatte über das repräsentative unternehmen und zunehmende Skalenerträge in den zwanziger Jahren", in Bertram Schefold (ed.), *Vademecum zu der Keanischen Debatte über Kosten, Wettbewerb und Entwicklung*, (Düsseldorf, Verlag Wirtschaft un Finanzen ein Unternehmen der Verlagrsgruppe Handelsblatt GmbH, 2001), pp. 57–97.
English version published in Philip Arestis, Michelle Baddelely and John S. L. McCombie (eds), *Economic Growth, New Directions in Theory and Policy*, Cheltenham, UK, Northampton, USA: Edward Elgar, 2007, pp.44–64 as "The representative firm and increasing returns: then and now".
(with Prue Kerr), "Joan Robinson (1903–83)" in N. Smelser and P. Baltes (eds.) *International Encyclopedia of the Social and Behavioral Sciences*, (Oxford, Elsevier, 2001), pp. 13375–9.
(with Prue Kerr), "General Introduction" to *Joan Robinson. Critical Assessments of Leading Economists*, 5 vols., edited by Prue Kerr with the collaboration of G.C. Harcourt, (London, Routledge, 2002), pp. 1–32.
(with Pervez Tahir and Prue Kerr), "On Joan Robinson and China", Ch. 13 of *Joan Robinson. Critical Assessments of Leading Economists*, Vol. 5, edited by Prue Kerr with the collaboration of G.C. Harcourt, (London, Routledge, 2002), pp.267–80.
(with Prue Kerr), "Introduction" to the Palgrave Archive edition of JOAN ROBINSON, *Writings on Economics*, 7 vols., (Houndmills, Basingstoke, Hants., Palgrave, 2002), pp. v-xxxi.
(with Prue Kerr), "Keynes and the Cambridge School", ch. 22 of Warren J. Samuels, Jeff E. Biddle and John B. Davis (eds), *A Companion to the History of Economic Thought*, Malden, USA, Oxford, UK: Blackwell Publishing, 2003, pp. 343–59.
(with Craig Freedman and Peter Kriesler), "Has the Long-Run Phillips Curve Turned Horizontal?", in George Argyrous, Mathew Forstater and Gary Mongiovi (eds) *Growth, Distribution and Effective Demand. Alternatives to Economic Orthodoxy*, (Armonk, New York, London, England, M.E. Sharpe, 2004), pp. 144–62.
(with Jan Toporowski), "The Lender of Last Resort and capital market stability", *Cahiers d'économie politique*, No. 45, L'Harmatton, 2003, pp. 162–74.
(with Sean Turnell), "Some Reflections on Keynes, Policy and the Second World War", in Tony Aspromourgos and John Lodewijks (eds) *History and Political Economy. Essays in Honour of P.D. Groenewegen*, (London and New York, Routledge Taylor and Francis Group, 2004), pp. 236–44.

(with Avi J. Cohen), "Introduction: Capital Theory Controversy: Scarcity, Production, Equilibrium and Time" in Christopher Bliss, Avi J. Cohen and G C. Harcourt (eds) *Capital Theory, Volume I* (Cheltenham, Glos., UK and Northampton, Mass., USA, Edward Elgar Publishing Limited), 2005, pp. xxvii–lx.

(With P.H. Nolan) "Price theory and multinational oligopoly: Kurt Rothschild and Stephen Hymer revisited", Chapter 10 in Manoj Kumar Sanyal, Mandira Sanyal and Shahina Amin (eds), *Post-Reform Development in Asia: Essays for Amiya Kumar Bagchi*, Orient Black Swan, 2009, pp. 263–288.

(With Prue Kerr), "*The Accumulation of Capital* over 50 years on", Chapter 19 in Stefano Zambelli (ed.), *Computable, Constructive and Behavioural Economic Dynamics. Essays in Honour of Kumaraswamy (Vela) Velupillai.* London and New York: Routledge, 2010, pp. 291–317.

(with Avi J. Cohen) "Reswitching and reversing in capital theory", Chapter 24 in Mark Blaug and Peter Lloyd (eds), *Famous Figures and Diagrams in Economics*, Cheltenham, UK, Northampton, MA, USA: Edward Elgar, 2010, pp. 191–98.

(with Peter Kriesler) "The influence of Michal Kalecki on Joan Robinson's approach to economics", Chapter 9 in Philip Arestis (ed.), *Microeconomics, Macroeonomics and Economic Policy. Essays in Honour of Malcolm Sawyer*, Houndmills, Basingstoke, Hampshire, Palgrave Macmillan, 2011, pp. 153–169.

(with Peter Kriesler) "Introduction" to *The Oxford Handbook of Post-Keynesian Economics*, Volumes 1/2, 2013, pp.1–44.

(with Peter Kriesler) "Michal Kalecki and Rosa Luxemburg on Marx's Schemes of Reproduction: Two incisive intrepreters of capitalism" in R. Bellofiore, E. Karwowska and J. Toporowski (eds) *The Legacy of Rosa Luxemburg, Oskar Lange and Michal Kalecki, Volume I*, Houndmills, Basingstoke, Hampshire, Palgrave Macmillan, 2013, pp.9–18.

(with Prue Kerr) "Introduction" to Joan Robinson, *The Accumulation of Capital*, 3rd Edition, in the Palgrave Classic Economics Series, Basingstoke, Hampshire, UK, 2013, pp. vii-xxx.

(with Peter Kriesler) "The Failure of Economic Planning: The Role of the Fel'dman Model and Kalecki's Critique", Chapter 1 of Jan Toporowski and Lukasz Mamica (eds), *Michal Kalecki in the 21st Century*, Houndmills, Basingstoke, Hampshire: Palgrave Macmillan, 2015, pp. 9–25.

(with Peter Kriesler) "On Ricardo and Cambridge", Chapter 10 of Jerry Courvisanos, James Doughney and Alex Millmow (eds), *Reclaiming Pluralism in Economics: Essays in Honour of John E. King*, Oxford and New York: Routledge, 2016, pp. 150–167.

(with Craig Freedman, Peter Kriesler, and J.W. Nevile) "How Friedman became the anti-Keynes" in Robert A. Cord and J. Daniel Hammond (eds) *Milton Friedman: Contributions to Economics and Public Policy*, Oxford: Oxford University Press, 2016, pp.607–630.

Reviews

Harcourt, G.C. and B.J. McFarlane (1990) "Review of *Political Essays* by H. Stretton" *Australian Journal of Political Science*, 25, 356–8.

Harcourt, G.C. and K. Sheridan (1972), "Review of *Structural Change in Japan's Economic Development* by M. Shinohara", *Economic Journal*, 81, 1002–4.

Other References

Arestis, P. (Ed.). (1996). *Keynes, Money and the Open Economy. Essays in honour of Paul Davidson, Vol. 1*. Cheltenham, Glos: Edward Elgar.

Arestis, P., Palma, G., & Sawyer, M. (Eds.). (1997). *Capital Controversy, Post-Keynesian Economics and the History of Economics. Essays in honour of Geoff Harcourt. Volume one*. London: Routledge.

Asimakopulos, A. (1969a). A Robinsonian growth model in one-sector notation. *Australian Economic Papers, 8*, 41–58.

Asimakopulos, A. (1969b). A Robinsonian growth model in one-sector notation: an amendment. *Australian Economic Papers, 8*, 171–176.

Barton, A.D. (1961). "A contribution to the theory of the multi-product firm", unpublished Ph.D. dissertation, Cambridge.

Berndt, E. R., & Triplett, J. E. (eds). (1990). *Fifty Years of Economic Measurement: The Jubilee of the Conference on Research on Income and Wealth, Studies in Income and Wealth* (Vol. 54). Chicago and London: University of Chicago Press.

Blankenburg, S. (2014). Introduction. *Cambridge Journal of Economics, 38*, 1295–1305.

Blaug, M., & Lloyd, P. (2010). *Famous Figures and Diagrams in Economics*. Cheltenham, UK: Edward Elgar.

Bliss, C. J. (1975). *Capital Theory and the Distribution of Income*. Amsterdam: North-Holland.

Byron, R. P. (1970a). The bias in the Watson-Harcourt-Praetz variant of the C.E.T. production frontier. *Economic Record, 46*, 567–573.

Byron, R. P. (1970b). A rejoinder to the Trinity. *Economic Record, 46*, 576–577.

"Contemporary capitalism and progressive political economics: contributions to heterodox debates about economic method, analysis and policy". (2014). *Cambridge Journal of Economics, 38*, 1295–1540.

Clapham, J. H. (1922). Of empty economic boxes. *Economic Journal, 22*, 305–314.

Corry, B. (2000). Review of Harcourt and Riach (eds), *A 'Second Edition' of The General Theory*, 2 vols, 1997. *Manchester School, 68*, 627–628.

Coutts, Ken and Neville Norman (2013). "Post-Keynesian approaches to industrial pricing: a survey and critique", Chapter 18 of Harcourt and Kriesler (eds) (2013), *The Oxford Handbook of Post-Keynesian Economics, vol 1*, 443-66.

Davidson, Paul (1972). *Money and the Real World*, London: Macmillan, 2nd Edn 1978.
Earl, P. E., & Littleboy, B. (2014). *G.L.S. Shackle*. Houndmills, Basingstoke, Hampshire: Palgrave Macmillan.
Feldstein, M., & Horioka, C. (1980). Domestic saving and international capital flows. *Economic Journal, 90*, 314–329.
Ferguson, C. E. (1972). The current state of capital theory: a tale of two paradigms. *Southern Economic Journal, 39*, 160–176.
Fisher, F. M., & McGowan, J. J. (1983). On the misuse of using accounting rates of return to infer monopoly profits. *American Economic Review, 73*, 82–97.
Fisher, F. M. (1984). The misuse of accounting rates of profits: reply. *American Economic Review, 74*, 509–517.
Gleeson-White, J. (2011). *Double Entry*. Sydney: Allen and Unwin.
Heertje, A. (ed). (1999). *The Makers of Modern Economics, Vol. IV*. Cheltenham, UK/Northampton, USA: Edward Elgar.
Hatch, John and Ray Petrides (1997), A Cambridge economist *but* an Australian patriot, Chapter 1 in Arestis *et al* (1997), 1–10.
Ingham, G. (2004). *The Nature of Money*. Cambridge: Polity Press.
Kahn, R. F. (1931). The relation of home investment to unemployment. *Economic Journal, 41*, 173–198.
Keynes, J. M. (1919). *The Economic Consequences of the Peace*, London: Macmillan, *C.W.*, vol. *II, 1971*.
Keynes, J. M. (Ed.). (1930). Increasing returns and the representative firm: a symposium. *Economic Journal, 40*, 79–116.
Kriesler, P. (1987). *Kalecki's Microanalysis: The Development of Kalecki's Analysis of Pricing and Distribution*. Cambridge: Cambridge University Press.
Mantoux, É. (1945; 1952), *The Carthaginian Peace or The Economic Consequences of Mr. Keynes*, with an Introduction by R.C.K. Enson and a Foreword by Paul Mantoux, New York: Charles Scribner's Sons.
Mathews, R.L. and J. McB. Grant (1958), *Inflation and Company Finance*, Sydney: The Law Book Company of Australasia.
Meade, J.E. (1975), "The Keynesian revolution", Ch 10 in M. Keynes (ed.) (1975), *Essays on John Maynard Keynes*, Cambridge: Cambridge University Press.
Meade, J. E. (1993). The relation of Mr Meade's relation to Kahn's multiplier. *Economic Journal, 103*, 664–665.
Moggridge, D. E. (1992). *Maynard Keynes: An Economist's Biography*. London: Routledge.
Oakley, A. (1983). *The Making of Marx's Critical Theory: A Bibliographical Analysis*. London: Routledge and Kegan Paul.
Oakley, Allen (1984), *Marx's Critique of Political Economy. Intellectual Sources and Evolution. Volume I: 1844–1860*, London: Routledge and Kegan Paul.
Oakley, Allen (1985), *Marx's Critique of Political Economy. Intellectual Sources and Evolution. Volume II: 1861 to 1863*, London: Routledge and Kegan Paul.

Powell, A. A., & Gruen, F. H. (1968). The constant elasticity of transformation production frontier and linear supply system. *International Economic Review, 9*, 315–328.
Powell, A. A., & Gruen, F. H. (1970). Biases in the estimation of transformation elasticities: a rebuttal. *Economic Record, 46*, 564–566.
Prendergast, R. (2015). Review of G.C. Harcourt and Peter Kriesler (eds), *The Oxford Handbook of Post-Keynesian Economics*, 2 vols (2013), Oxford: Oxford University Press. *Economic and Labour Relations Review., 26*(2), 355–362.
Pressman, S. (2014). Review of Harcourt and Kriesler, 2 vols (2013). *Journal of Economic Literature, 52*, 853–855.
Repapis, C. (2014). The scholar as reader: the last 50 years of economic theory as seen through G.C. Harcourt's book reviews. *Cambridge Journal of Economics, 38*, 1517–1540.
Robinson, Joan (1933), *The Economics of Imperfect Competition*, London: Macmillan, 2nd edn 1969.
Robinson, Joan (1937a), *Introduction to the Theory of Employment*, London: Macmillan, 2nd edn 1969.
Robinson, Joan (1937b), *Essays in the Theory of Employment*, Oxford: Basil Blackwell, 2nd edn 1947.
Robinson, Joan (1942), *An Essay on Marxian Economics*, London: Macmillan, 2nd edn 1966.
Robinson, J. (1956). *The Accumulation of Capital*, London: Macmillan, 2nd edn 1965, 3rd edn 1969. *Palgrave Classics in Economics, 2013.*
Robinson, J. (1962). *Economic Philosophy*. London: Watts and Co..
Robinson, J. (1966). *Economics: An Awkward Corner*. London: Allen and Unwin.
Robinson, J. (1970). *Freedom and Necessity: An Introduction to the Study of Society*. London: Allen and Unwin.
Robinson, J. (1971). *Economic Heresies: Some Old-fashioned Questions in Economic Theory*. London: Macmillan.
Robinson, J. (1978). *Aspects of Development and Underdevelopment*. Cambridge: Cambridge University Press.
Robinson, J., & Eatwell, J. (1973). *Introduction to Modern Economics*. Maidenhead: McGraw-Hill.
Rothschild, K. W. (1947). Price theory and oligopoly. *Economic Journal, 57*, 299–320.
Rubner, A. (1964). The irrelevancy of the British differential profits tax. *Economic Journal, 74*, 347–359.
Sardoni, C. (1987). *Marx and Keynes on Economic Recession. The Theory of Unemployment and Effective Demand*. Brighton: Wheatsheaf Books Ltd..
Sardoni, C. (2011). *Unemployment, Recession and Effective Demand*. In *The Contributions of Marx, Keynes, and Kalecki*. Cheltenham: Edward Elgar.
Shepherd, G. B. (Ed.). (1995). *Rejected, Leading Economists Ponder the Publication Process*. Sunlakes Arizona: Thomas Horton and Daughters.

Skidelsky, R. (1983), *John Maynard Keynes. Volume One. Hopes Betrayed, 1853–1920*, London: Macmillan.

Skidelsky, R. (1992). *John Maynard Keynes, Volume Two.* In *The Economist as Saviour, 1920–1937.* London: Macmillan.

Skidelsky, R. (2000). *John Maynard Keynes, Volume Three, Fighting for Britain, 1937–46.* London: Macmillan.

Sraffa, P. editor with the collaboration of M.H. Dobb, 11 vols. (1951–1973). *The Works and Correspondence of David Ricardo.* Cambridge: Cambridge University Press.

Sraffa, P. (1960). *Production of Commodities by Means of Commodities. Prelude to a Critique of Economic Theory.* Cambridge: Cambridge University Press.

Tahir, P. (1990a), "Some aspects of development and underdevelopment: critical perspectives on Joan Robinson", unpublished Ph.D. dissertation, University of Cambridge.

Tahir, P. (1990b), "Making sense of Joan Robinson on China", mimeo, Cambridge.

Thirlwall, A. P., & Keynes, J. M. (1999). A 'Second Edition' of Keynes' General Theory. *Journal of Post Keynesian Economics, 21*, 367–386.

Tobin, James (1997), "An overview of *The General Theory*", Ch 25 of Harcourt and Riach, vol 2 (1997), 3–27.

Wallace, R. H., & Karmel, P. H. (1962). Credit creation in a multi-bank system. *Australian Economic Papers, 1*, 95–108.

Articles et al. by G.C. Harcourt:

"The Accountant in a Golden Age", *Oxford Economic Papers.* Vol.17, March, 1965, pp.66–80. (Reprinted in R.H. Parker and G.C. Harcourt (eds), *Readings in the Concept and Measurement of Income* (Cambridge: Cambridge University Press, 1969, pp.310–25).

"Biases in Empirical Estimates of the Elasticities of Substitution of C.E.S. Production Functions", *Review of Economic Studies.* Vol.33, July 1966, pp.227–33.

"Some Cambridge Controversies in the Theory of Capital", *Journal of Economic Literature.* Vol.7, June 1969, pp.369–405. Reprinted in Italian in G. Nardozzi and V.Valli (eds), *Teori Dello Sviluppo Economico* (Etas Kompass, 1971).

Some Cambridge Controversies in the Theory of Capital, (Cambridge: Cambridge University Press, 1972). (Italian edition, 1973; Polish edition, 1975; Spanish edition, 1975; Japanese edition, 1980). Reprinted, Gregg Revivals Series (Mark Blaug, editor), 1991, pp.x + 272.

(Ed.), *Keynes and his Contemporaries. The Sixth and Centennial Keynes Seminar held in the University of Kent at Canterbury 1983.* (London: Macmillan, 1985), pp.vi + 195.

Post-Keynesian Essays in Biography: Portraits of Twentieth Century Political Economists (Basingstoke, Hants: Macmillan, 1993), pp.xiv + 173.

Capitalism, Socialism and Post-Keynesianism. Selected Essays of G.C. Harcourt. (Cheltenham, Glos., Edward Elgar, 1995), pp.xii + 247.

"'Horses for Courses': The Making of a Post-Keynesian Economist", in Arnold Heertje (ed.) *The Makers of Modern Economics, Vol. IV*, Cheltenham, UK; Northampton, USA: Edward Elgar, 1999, 32–69.

50 Years a Keynesian and Other Essays (London: Palgrave, 2001a), pp.xii + 364.

Selected Essays on Economic Policy (London: Palgrave, 2001b), pp.xvi + 354.

The Structure of Post-Keynesian Economics. The Core Contributions of the Pioneers, Cambridge: Cambridge University Press, 2006, pp. x + 205.

On Skidelsky's Keynes and Other Essays. Selected Essays of G. C. Harcourt, Houndmills, Basingstoke, Hampshire, Palgrave Macmillan, 2012a, pp xi+342.

The Making of a Post-Keynesian Economist. Cambridge Harvest, Houndmills, Basingstoke, Hampshire, Palgrave Macmillan, 2012b, pp x+273.

"Eric Russell, 1921–77: A Great Australian Political Economist (The 1977 Newcastle Lecture in Political Economy) Research Report No 36, pp.iii + 26), reprinted in Harcourt (2001b).

"Athanasios (Tom) Asimakopulos, 28 May 1930–25 May 1990: A Memoir", *Journal of Post Keynesian Economics*, Vol. 14, No. 1, Fall, 1991, pp. 39–48.

"Lorie Tarshis, 1911–1993: In Appreciation", *Economic Journal*, Vol. 105, September, 1995, pp.1244–1255.

"Hirofumi Uzawa 1928–2014: A Personal Tribute", *Economic and Labour Relations Review*, Volume 25, Issue 4, December 2014, 629–30.

"'Horses for Courses': The Making of a Post-Keynesian Economist" in Arnold Heertje (ed.), *The Makers of Modern Economics*, Volume IV, Cheltenham, UK; Northampton, MA, USA: Edward Elgar, 1999, pp. 32–69.

"Contemporary Capitalism and Keynes's General Theory" in Jan Toporowski (ed.) *Political Economy and the New Capitalism, Essays in honour of Sam Aaronovitch*, London, Routledge, 1999, pp.15–22.

"Asimakopulos, Athanasios (Tom) (1930–1990)", in Philip Arestis and Malcolm Sawyer (eds), *A Biographical Dictionary of Dissenting Economists*, Second Edition, Cheltenham, UK, Northampton, MA, U.S.A., 2000, pp. 7–17.

"David Gawen Champernowne, 1912–2000: in appreciation", *Cambridge Journal of Economics*, Vol. 25, July, 2001, pp. 439–42.

"Reddaway, William Brian (1913–2002)", in Donald Rutherford (ed.), *The Biographical Dictionary of British Economists, Volume 2, K-Z*, (Bristol, Thoemmes Continum, 2004), pp. 998–1003.

"The Contributions of Tom Asimakopulos to Post Keynesian Eonomics", Chapter 5 in L. Randall Wray and Mathew Forstater (eds), *Keynes and Macroeconomics after 70 Years, Critical Assessments of The General Theory*, Cheltenham, UK; Northampton, MA, USA: Edward Elgar, 2008, pp. 64–79.

CHAPTER 13

Coauthors and Collaborations in Labor Economics

Ronald G. Ehrenberg

This personal reflective chapter summarizes and explains why the frequency with which I have coauthored research has varied over my career and discusses the reasons that my coauthored publications and collaborations have arisen. The reasons include research that arises from casual conversations with colleagues; the sharing of data both as a donor and as a recipient; invitations to participate in large-scale projects; the division of labor and working with people with complementary skills and personalities; educating graduate and undergraduate students and the desire to give the former a leg up in the job market and to encourage the latter to pursue doctoral study; discussions with my wife about issues she faced as a teacher and administrator in public K12 education; and efforts to magnify my impact on an area of study by convening conferences, commissioning papers, and seeing conference volumes through to publication.

*Irving M. Ives Professor of Industrial and Labor Relations and Economics, Stephen H, Weiss Presidential Fellow, and Director of the Cornell Higher Education Research Institute (CHERI) at Cornell University. CHERI was supported by the Andrew W. Mellon Foundation

---

R.G. Ehrenberg (✉)
Cornell University, Ithaca, NY, USA

M. Szenberg, L.B. Ramrattan (eds.), *Collaborative Research in Economics*, DOI 10.1007/978-3-319-52800-7_13

for almost 20 years and I am grateful to the Foundation for its long-term support which made many of my publications over the period possible. I am also grateful to Orley Ashenfelter and Dan Hamermesh for their comments on an earlier draft and to Ali Olsewski, a Cornell graduate of the class of 2016, for her assistance in helping me tabulate and analyze the data that I used in this paper. Finally, I owe many thanks to Michael Szenberg, editor-in-chief of the *American Economist* from 1972 to 2011, for encouraging me to write this paper.

13.1 Introduction and Patterns to Explain

It is hard for me to believe that I am now 70 years old and in my 46th year as a publishing economist and more recently a higher education scholar. It is even harder for me to believe, as I scan my vita, the number of things I have written and the number of different people with whom I have coauthored pieces.

Table 13.1 is a summary of my publishing career and my coauthors as of May 2016. My publication counts include articles in academic journals (including proceedings volumes and comments), chapters in books, articles in science, economics and higher education magazines and newspapers (*Scientific American*, *Regulation*, *Academe*, *Trusteeship*, and *Change* are examples), and books that I authored or coauthored. In the first column, for my career to date (as of May 2016), and in subsequent columns, for each five-year interval,[1] I indicate the number of publications, the number and share of these that were coauthored and the number that were coauthored by faculty (including visiting faculty and postdocs) at my own institution, my graduate students and former graduate students, my undergraduate students, faculty at other institutions, my wife and one of my sons, and other individuals.[2]

About 60% of my publications have been coauthored. But, contrary to the pattern observed by Dan Hamermesh (2015) for a set of 79 prominent labor economists, my propensity to coauthor has not increased monotonically with age. During the first five years of my career, all my publications were sole authored because, while on the faculty at the University of Massachusetts, I had few colleagues with similar interests and very few graduate students.[3] After I moved to Cornell in 1975, my access to colleagues with similar interests and to graduate students dramatically increased. As a result during the next 25 years, over 74% of my publications were coauthored. However, after 1999, my share of coauthored publications fell to about 49%.

Table 13.1 Numbers of publications with coauthors (share with coauthors)

Year	*1970–2016*	*1970–74*	*1975–79*	*1980–84*	*1985–89*	*1990–94*	*1995–99*	*2000–04*	*2005–09*	*2010–16*
Number of publications	173	9	15	21	17	14	18	32	24	23
No. w/Coauthors	103 (0.60)	0 (0)	13 (0.87)	16 (0.76)	13 (0.76)	12 (0.86)	11 (0.61)	14 (0.44)	13 (0.54)	11 (0.48)
No. w/Grad Coauthors	57	0	2	10	7	8	7	7	9	7
No. w/Undergrad Coauthors	13	0	1	0	0	0	0	7	3	2
No. w/Own Institution Faculty Coauthors	29	0	3	8	6	2	0	0	5	5
No. w/Own Institution Other Coauthors	6	0	0	0	1	2	1	2	0	0
No. w/Other Faculty Coauthors	16	0	5	1	1	1	4	2	0	2
No. w/Other Coauthors	8	0	0	0	0	0	0	1	2	5

Totally 57 of the coauthored publications have at least one current or former graduate student as a coauthor, 13 have at least one undergraduate student as a coauthor, 29 have at least one faculty member at my own institution as a coauthor, and 16 have at least one faculty member at another institution as a coauthor. I have also coauthored papers with administrators and staff at my own institution, with my wife and one of my sons, and with individuals at other institutions who are not faculty members, including colleagues at the Andrew W. Mellon Foundation.

The number of different individuals with whom I have worked is large. The 81 different coauthors of the 173 publications include 35 different graduate students, 11 different undergraduate students, 18 different faculty and administrative colleagues at Cornell, and 15 different individuals at other institutions.[4]

The pattern of where my publications appear has changed over time. Table 13.2 shows the shares of my publications, each period and in total, that were in articles in academic journals, chapters in books, books, and articles in science, economics and higher education magazines. As I was returning to my faculty position after serving as a Cornell vice president from 1995 to 1998, I received some advice from a former provost at another university, who told me that life after administration is great but the experience makes you a different person and you have to do different things. I decided that, in addition to conducting econometric research on higher education issues, I wanted to write more policy-related pieces and publish them in places where I could influence how people think about

Table 13.2 Does the pattern of publications change over time?

Number publications	*Period*	*Journal articles*	*Chapters*	*Magazines*	*Books*
173	1970–2016	94 (0.54)	38 (0.22)	29 (0.17)	12 (0.07)
9	1970–74	7 (0.78)	0 (0)	0 (0)	2 (0.22)
15	1975–79	11 (0.73)	2 (0.13)	0 (0)	2 (0.13)
21	1980–84	14 (0.67)	4 (0.19)	0 (0)	3 (0.14)
17	1985–89	7 (0.41)	8 (0.47)	0 (0)	2 (0.12)
14	1990–94	7 (0.50)	4 (0.29)	2 (0.14)	1 (0.07)
18	1995–99	11 (0.61)	2 (0.11)	5 (0.28)	0 (0)
32	2000–04	12 (0.38)	8 (0.25)	11 (0.34)	1 (0.03)
24	2005–09	12 (0.50)	7 (0.29)	5 (0.21)	0 (0.00)
23	2010–16	13 (0.57)	3 (0.13)	6 (0.26)	1 (0.04)

higher education. During the past 22 years, I have written 27 articles that have appeared in more popular higher education outlets.

Does where a publication appears influence whether a coauthor was involved? A logit analysis reported in the first column of Table 13.3 shows that when the probability that a publication has a coauthor is assumed to depend only on a time trend and the type of publication (publications in journals are the omitted category), my publications in magazines are less likely to have coauthors. However, once one controls in the second column for whether the publication includes econometric research or the development of a formal theoretical model, where the publication appeared ceases to matter. The only variable which proves to be a predictor of having a coauthor is if the publication involved an econometric study. Therefore the decline in the share of my publications that were coauthored after 1999 reflect my authoring more policy related and thought pieces (regardless of where they were published) and fewer econometric studies.

Dan Hamermesh found in his sample that the number of coauthors on each coauthored publication trended upward over time. As Table 13.4 indicates, this is true also in my personal case. I attribute the growth in the number of my coauthors per coauthored piece to the growing number of graduate research assistants to whom I had access, to my more recent involvement of undergraduate students in research, and to the increased ease of simultaneously collaborating with multiple people in different

Table 13.3 Logit equations for the probability of a publication being coauthored

Ind. Var.	*Coefficient (std. error)*	*Coefficient (std. error)*
CHAP	−0.419 (0.394)	0.441 (0.576)
MAG	−0.880 (0.455)**	0.449 (0.662)
BOOK	−0.074 (0.661)	0.744 (0.935)
YEAR	−0.013 (0.014)	0.015 (0.020)
ECONO		3.617 (0.506)*
THEORY		0.314 (0.875)
Pseudo R^2/N	0.030/173	0.367/173

*(**) coefficient is statistically significantly different from zero at the 0.05 (0.10) level of significance

where, CHAP = 1 if chapter, = 0 otherwise; MAG = 1 if magazine article, = 0 otherwise; BOOK = 1 if book, = 0 otherwise; (the omitted category is journal articles); ECONO = 1 if an econometric study, = 0 otherwise; THEORY = 1 if the publication develops a theoretical model, = 0 otherwise; YEAR—time trend

Table 13.4 Number of coauthors per coauthored paper*

Period	*Mean number of coauthors*
Entire career to date	1.635
1975–79	1.308
1980–84	1.25
1985–89	1.385
1990–94	1.583
1995–99	1.455
2000–04	1.714
2005–09	2.000
2010–16	2.545

*No coauthored papers were written during the 1970–74 period

places that changes in technology, most recently the development of the internet, have facilitated.

13.2 The Whys and Whos of Coauthors

During 1971–72, my first year at the University of Massachusetts, I was invited to give a seminar at Princeton by Al Rees (then Director of the Industrial Relations Section at Princeton) and met Orley Ashenfelter, one of the true giants in the field of labor economics. While we discussed my paper prior to the seminar, Orley pointed out an error in it. The paper presented the first empirical estimates of the wage elasticities of demand for state and local government employees, with a view toward making policy statements about whether there were any market forces that might limit the ability of emerging public sector unions to win large wage increases for their members. Its underlying theoretical model was based upon a variant of the Stone–Geary utility function[5] that allowed public decision-makers' utility to be a function only of increments in public sector employment levels above multiples (less than one) of previous employment levels (to capture incremental budgeting). Orley quietly explained to me that if I really believed that a Stone–Geary utility function was the correct specification, there was nothing for me to estimate because this utility function implied that all the own wage elasticities of demand were minus one.

We then went into the seminar where Orley remained absolutely silent and allowed me to explain that the model was meant only to heuristically motivate the empirical research and that the empirical specifications should not be interpreted as being derived directly from the model. My paper was ultimately published in the *American Economic Review*.[6] Using my data and a more flexible system of demand equations that could be explicitly derived from another form of utility function, Orley and I went on to write my first coauthored paper and it was published in a volume edited by Dan Hamermesh.[7] Orley also invited me to work with him as a consultant in Washington, DC in 1972–73 where he was heading up the Office of Evaluation of the US Department of Labor. My experiences working with him led me to focus much of my early research on analyzing the effects of labor market legislation and policies.

Dan, who I first met in 1968 and who became a lifelong friend, was directly responsible for my second coauthored paper. Following in the tradition of Gary Becker's household allocation of time model and Michael Grossman's paper on the allocation of time and money to investments in health capital over the life cycle, Dan coauthored the first paper by an economist on the economics of suicide in 1974.[8] Being a relatively competitive person in my youth, even with friends, I wondered what I could do to "top" Dan's paper. While talking at a party to Corry Azzi, who was visiting the University of Massachusetts, we decided as a joke to work on a model in which individuals make decisions on allocating time each period to the labor market and to religious activities, with the goal of maximizing consumption during both their lifetimes and in the afterlife.[9]

What started out as a joke soon became a serious research effort, as we found there were a variety of empirical observations about participation in religious activities that psychologists and sociologists had made, with different explanations provided for each observed regularity. Shortly thereafter we had developed a lifecycle household allocation of time model that could explain all of these observations plus others and then empirically tested the model. Our resulting paper, which is still one of my most highly cited works, led ultimately to the development of a new, now thriving, subfield that addresses the economics of religion.[10]

Other coauthored work quickly followed as a result of my relationship with Orley. While in DC, I learned about Ron Oaxaca, a recent Princeton PhD student of Orley and Al's, who was teaching at a Canadian university. We quickly hired Ron at the University of Massachusetts and together he and I wrote the first theoretical and empirical paper that applied my dissertation advisor Dale Mortensen's theory of job search to estimate the impact of unemployment insurance benefits on unemployed workers' durations of unemployment and post unemployment earnings.[11] We both soon left the university, Ron going to the University of Arizona and me to Cornell, and sadly we never worked on other issues together.

I also met Bob Smith, a Stanford PhD, who, on leave from the University of Connecticut, was also working with Orley. Orley and Al had been appointed a two-person visiting committee to advise the Dean of the ILR School at Cornell on how to move its then institutional labor economics group toward the new breed of empirical micro labor economists. They recommended a list of people to hire. After Dan, who was first on the list, turned Cornell down, the next two offers were made to Bob Smith and me. Although Dan and I have only coauthored one short piece during our careers, his impact on my career by his not accepting the Cornell offer was extraordinary.[12]

Bob and I have now been Cornell colleagues for over 40 years. While we coauthored five empirical papers together early in our careers, our most enduring collaboration was the writing of our textbook, *Modern Labor Economics*, whose first edition appeared in 1982.[13] Our students at Cornell back then were not very interested in formal mathematics and so our goal was to write a text that explained theories heuristically (without lots of math) and then concentrated on applying the theories to illustrate the usefulness of labor market models in understanding proposed policy changes and the evolution of labor market institutions.

Writing a textbook in any field is a daunting challenge because one's interests may only be in subsections of the field. Our collaboration was facilitated by our different interests. For example, I wrote the first draft of our chapters on labor demand and Bob wrote the first draft of chapters on labor supply. I wrote about the economics of collective bargaining in the private and public sectors and Bob wrote about compensating wage differentials and contract models. But more than differences in our topical interests, our collaboration was facilitated by the differences in our personalities. Throughout my career I have had days of extreme productivity and other days in which I sit around my office and accomplish nothing. Bob is a very steady person and, by working together, he "evened" out my fluctuations in productivity. So differences in personality types may also facilitate collaboration.

Our textbook is now in its 12th edition and it remains the leader in the field. But the last edition that I had anything to do with was published in the mid-1990s. From 1995 to 1998 I served as Cornell's Vice President for Academic Programs, Planning, and Budgeting, and when I returned to the faculty my interests were focused much more narrowly on the economics of higher education. Since then Bob has revised the book every three years on his own and kept my name on it for "branding" purposes. *Modern Labor Economics* is by far "my" most highly cited work and it is only fair that I publicly thank Bob for the impact his revisions have had on my reputation.

During the first 12 years of my career, I worked hard at staying at the frontier of econometrics and tried to use a new (to me) econometric technique in each paper that I wrote. But I had a revelation (unrelated to my work on the economics of religion) when I attended a weeklong course on longitudinal data models taught at NORC at the University of Chicago during the summer of 1982. As I sat through the lecture presented by distinguished scholars, including economist Gary Chamberlain (then at Wisconsin), I realized that I did not have the time or energy to both focus on economic issues that interested me and to stay at the frontier of econometrics methods. Gary had brought a PhD student from Wisconsin named George Jakubson with him to serve as the teaching assistant in the class and I realized it made sense for us to try to hire at Cornell younger colleagues who had skills such as George had to help train our PhD students and to work with me on empirical projects.

The next year we actually hired George and he is the Cornell colleague with whom I have coauthored the largest number of research publications. These have included a book on the impact of advance notice provisions for layoffs in union contracts on displaced workers labor market outcomes (which was cited in the debate that led to the enactment of the WARN legislation), a paper on who bears the cost of university expenditures out of institutional funds on research, two papers on PhD students' times to degree and completion probabilities, a paper on whether the gender mix of academic leaders influences the rate at which academic institutions diversify their faculty across gender lines, and a paper evaluating the Mellon Mays Undergraduate Fellowship Program of the Andrew W. Mellon Foundation.[14]

During the late 1980s, William Bowen, then President of the Andrew W. Mellon Foundation, began the Foundation's support for the economics of education by making a grant to the National Bureau of Economic Research (NBER) for a volume on the economic challenges facing higher education. Charles Clotfelter from Duke was asked by the NBER to head up the project and Charlie, who had read some of my early papers on higher education but had never met me, invited me to join him on the project. Together with Malcolm Getz and John Siegfried from Vanderbilt, we produced what became my first coauthored book on the economics of higher education.[15] While Charlie and I never coauthored another piece, he went on to direct, and I to participate in, a working group on the economics of higher education that met regularly at the NBER for almost 20 years. Many members of this group were current or former higher education administrators including Charlie and Gordon Winston from Williams; both Charlie and Gordon became very close friends of mine. My discussions with members of the group helped to shape much of my subsequent research agenda, even though these discussions only occasionally led to coauthored work.

The financial support that I have received for the Cornell Higher Education Research Institute (CHERI) from the Andrew W. Mellon Foundation was for many years unrestricted; this allowed me to address whatever research issues I felt were important. However, around 2002 Bowen called and told me that the Foundation was in the process of evaluating a major ten-year program of theirs to improve doctoral education in the humanities called the *Graduate Education Initiative*, which had cost the Foundation over $85 million dollars.

They had been collecting administrative data for about 100 treatment and comparison departments involved in the program for ten years before the program began and for each year of the program's duration on students' characteristics and their annual sources of support and progress toward their degree. The Foundation was now going to collect retrospective data on students' views of their doctoral program characteristics and their early career outcomes after they left or completed their programs. Bowen asked if I would be interested in helping to design the retrospective survey and then to conduct an evaluation of what the impact of the program had been on times to degree and completion rates and on what had been learned about the characteristics of doctoral programs that facilitated student success, if they provided me with supplementary funds for several years for a postdoctoral fellow.

I jumped at the opportunity and embarked on an eight-year collaboration with Harriet Zuckerman, a very distinguished sociologist who was the senior Vice President of the Foundation, Sharon Brucker, the researcher at the Foundation who was in charge of the databases, and Jeff Groen, a new University of Michigan PhD in economics who assumed the postdoc position with me. Many preliminary publications and econometric papers later, we published our book summarizing what we had learned in 2010.[16]

Sometimes coauthorship arises because you get the rare opportunity to participate in a major data collection effort and evaluate an important program.

One of the true pleasures of my life has been my interactions with PhD students in economics and education, many of whom have become lifelong friends. To date, I have chaired the dissertation committees of 45 completed PhDs and served on the committees of numerous other PhD students. I have worked with these students on research to enhance their graduate education, to hopefully give them a leg up in the job market by coauthoring with them, and to increase my own research productivity. During the early years, I taught them econometric research methods; now I depend upon many younger colleagues at Cornell, including George, to do this for me.

For the first 25 years of my career, I had a self-imposed rule that I would not coauthor with any graduate student after he or she had received a PhD. In retrospect, my publication record might have been much longer if I had continued to take advantage of all the human capital that I had helped to create. But, I felt that it was important for former students to create their own research programs and to make clear to the world that they were separated from their former advisors and "flying" on their own.

The rule was bent while I was a Cornell vice president. I had previously written a paper with Dominic Brewer, while he was a PhD student, on the early career labor market returns to attending a selective private academic institution.[17] That paper was based on longitudinal data from students graduating from high school in the 1970s. Dominic and Eric Eide, a colleague he had met after receiving his degree, decided to extend the analysis to include a later cohort of students to see if the earnings advantage to going to a selective institution had persisted or grown over time and, in a second paper, to see if attendance at a selective private institution also enhanced the probability that college graduates enroll in graduate and professional degree programs.

Knowing that I was busy administering, Dom invited me to be a coauthor with the understanding that my role would only be to comment on drafts that Eric and he wrote.[18] Put simply, Dom wanted to help me maintain my research productivity during my administrative hiatus. Since that time, I have occasionally broken my rule, coauthoring two additional papers with him, and two papers with three other former PhD students. Dom, who is now the Dean of the Steinhardt School of Culture, Education, and Human Development at New York University, is the individual with whom I have coauthored the largest number of papers (ten) during my career.

The two later papers that I wrote with Dom came about when I was invited by a Cornell colleague, psychologist Steve Ceci, to chair a team of scholars with diverse disciplinary backgrounds to write a review paper for a psychology journal surveying what we know about the impact of class size on student performance. An incentive to do this was the commitment that a popular version of the paper would be published in *Scientific American*, which has a monthly circulation of over 450,000.

Realizing that more people would read that version than the sum of everything else that I had written during my career, I immediately agreed and suggested that Dom, who then was a vice president and Director of Education Research at the Rand Corporation, be added to the team. He was added and the committee of editors choosing the team also selected a sociologist, Adam Gamoran from the University of Wisconsin, and a Canadian statistician, J. Douglas Willms. I had never previously met either Adam or Doug. Over about a year, via email and conference calls, we developed an outline for the papers, took turns writing sections, and then revised and finished the work.[19] While subsequently I met, and served on a National Research Council committee with Adam, to this day I still have not met Doug. Sometimes coauthors can be strangers.

In actuality, while I was a Cornell vice president I was able to continue my research because I supervised the office of institutional research and I figured out ways to conduct research that was both relevant for decision-making at Cornell and had academic value. I wrote papers with colleagues in the office on how Cornell was responding to the elimination of mandatory retirement for tenured faculty and on the 1990s National Research Council ratings of PhD programs.[20] Earlier in my career, having served on many faculty committees relating to the economics of higher education and developing close relations with many university administrators, I also wrote a paper with Cornell's Dean of Admissions and Financial Aid on the "death" of need-based financial aid policies.[21]

Sometimes collaborations arise because of who has the data. I met James Monks, now a faculty member at the University of Richmond but then a researcher at the Consortium of Financing Higher Education (COFHE), at a NBER Higher Education Working group meeting in the mid-1990s. We began to talk about whether the USNWR rankings of colleges might influence institutions' admissions outcomes. COFHE is a consortium of over 30 selective private colleges and universities and Jim had access to confidential longitudinal data on admissions outcomes that COFHE collected. A collaboration quickly developed between us; he and I specified estimating equations, he did all the empirical analyses at COFHE preserving the confidentiality of the data, and we wrote the first empirical paper on how the USNWR rankings influence admissions outcomes.[22]

To take another example relating to who has the data, as a labor economist I believe that in competitive labor markets compensating wage differentials exist for favorable and unfavorable job characteristics. If an academic institution offered its assistant professors a high probability of ultimately receiving tenure, which is a favorable job characteristic, it should, according to labor market theory, be able to pay its assistant professors lower starting salaries than otherwise comparable institutions that offered lower probabilities of being granted tenure. But no one had ever empirically tested this proposition.

I knew that two former Northwestern economics PhD students of more recent vintage than me, Rachel Willis (University of North Carolina) and Paul Pieper (University of Illinois at Chicago), had collected data on the careers of all economists who had received PhDs in economics from US universities during the decade of the 1970s. With their data, I would be able to compute the probability that new PhDs who had taken first jobs as assistant professors at an economics department during the 1970s received tenure at either that department or a department of equal or better quality. I invited them to work with me on a project. We coupled their data with data on starting salaries of new assistant professors at each doctoral level economics department during the 1970s, which the American Economic Association provided to us under conditions of strict confidentiality, and estimated equations that showed that compensating wage differentials for tenure probabilities exist in academia, at least for economics faculty. Other factors held constant, higher probabilities of receiving tenure were associated with lower starting salaries for assistant professor in economics.[23]

Sometimes my coauthors were family members. As the son of two New York City public school teachers and the husband of a woman whose career in public K12 education spanned teaching, school administrative, and district-wide administrative positions, culminating in her serving for nine years as a superintendent of a large high-performing suburban school district in the Albany NY area, I have always been interested in K12 education and have a stream of publications on K12 topics.

Several issues that my wife Randy brought home from her work led directly to coauthored publications with her. When she was a middle school vice principal, her school district offered an early retirement incentive program but did not allow teachers to "buy out" their unused sick leave days at retirement. She observed that an unusually large number of older teachers were frequently absent on Fridays and Mondays that year and she was concerned about the impact of their absences on students.

Her concern led us to collect district-level data for school districts in New York State and conduct an econometric study on how teacher absenteeism depends upon provisions in districts' collective bargaining agreements, on how teachers' absenteeism influences students' absenteeism, and on how teachers' and students' absenteeism influence students' test score performance. We were aided in our research by our older son Eric, then a high school senior, who helped me to code school district contracts, which were on file in Albany, for which he was added as a coauthor. Another coauthor, who did most of the econometric work, was graduate student Dan Rees, son of Al Rees.[24] Dan, I am proud to report, is now the editor of the *Economics of Education Review*.

Another time, back in the mid-1980s, when the debate over merit pay for teachers was just beginning, my wife wondered why there was no discussion of merit pay for school administrators. As a researcher who was aware of the literature on the incentive effects of compensation agreements for corporate CEOs, it immediately struck me that we could do a study to see if school superintendents in New York State were rewarded for performance. This study required us to econometrically define performance measures (such as keeping test scores higher than predicted and keeping expenditures per student lower than predicted given the characteristics of the district) and to see how such measures impacted upon school superintendents' compensation in their current positions and their mobility to higher paying and/or larger districts. Because we had longitudinal data, we were also able to observe, from knowledge of which superintendents were moving, whether knowing who the superintendent was in a district appeared to influence the school district's performance. Again our empirical research was conducted primarily by a PhD student, Richard Chaykowski, who is now a professor at Queens University in Canada.[25]

Still a third joint project with my wife resulted from when she was being interviewed for her school superintendent position in the spring of 2001. Five school board members from the district came to Ithaca, where she was then the Deputy Superintendent of Schools, to interview practically everyone in the community and to also meet with me. At dinner that evening, one of the board members mentioned that the district had never lost a school budget vote; in New York State, taxpayers vote on school budgets each spring. That immediately led us to wonder if there was a literature on school budget vote success and ultimately, my wife and I, along with Cornell undergraduate student Chris Smith and PhD student Liang Zhang, wrote an empirical paper on the determinants of school budget vote success.[26] As an experienced administrator, my wife understood division of labor and delegation; she and I developed the ideas and the students did the work. Other papers I wrote on K12 education issues arose from topics we had talked about but, due to constraints on her time, on which she chose not to work on with me.

Without access to many graduate assistants at the University of Massachusetts, I began my first paper with an undergraduate coauthor while I was there. I was interested in whether local union building trade leaders called chief business agents were rewarded for their performance. They perform many functions but negotiating labor contracts is an important role. Data on the wages scales of different building trade unions (carpenters, painters, etc.) by city were published regularly and I wondered if these business agents' salaries were tied to how high their members' wage scales were as compared to the same trade's wage scales in other cities and the wage scales of other trades in the same city.

Data on the salaries of the chief business agents were available in the 1970s only in paper form at the Labor-Management Services Administration offices at the US Department of Labor in Washington, DC. A bright undergraduate student was going down to DC for a semester on an internship and, with the promise of being a coauthor, he spent his lunch hours for several months copying this information for us. He and I worked on the econometric analyses when he returned. Our paper was published in 1977 after I arrived at Cornell; by then he was a graduate student at Northwestern.[27]

Over the next 20 years, flush with graduate research assistants, I produced many PhD students, but very few of our ILR undergraduate students went on for PhDs in economics.[28] When I returned to the faculty after my stint as a Cornell vice president, I also decided that if I cared about the flow of future PhDs in economics and related fields it was important for me to involve undergraduate students in research early in their academic careers. I have described how I do this elsewhere, but partially it involves my being able to hire undergraduate students as research assistants through the funding for CHERI that I have received from the Andrew W. Mellon Foundation and other sources.[29] Since 1998, I have employed over 50 Cornell undergraduate students as research assistants and written 12 papers that have had at least one undergraduate coauthor, with ten different undergraduate students being coauthors of these papers. My most frequent undergraduate coauthor is Chris Smith, who went on to receive a PhD in economics at MIT and is now an economist at the Board of Governors of the Federal Reserve System in Washington, DC. Eight of my other undergraduate CHERI research assistants have either received PhDs in economics or public policy, or are currently enrolled in PhD programs in these fields.

The count of my coauthored papers with undergraduate students is smaller than it should be because I "gave away" one coauthored paper to the two undergraduate students working on it. I had obtained data from Cornell on the number of PhD students that each Cornell faculty member had supervised over a seven-year period and planned to conduct analyses of how and why the Gini coefficient for the inequality of faculty workloads in supervising PhD students varied across disciplines at Cornell and why faculty productivity in supervising PhD students within a discipline varied across individual faculty members.

The students working on the paper got so excited about doing the research that I realized, especially since the marginal value of an additional publication or citation was so low to me at that stage of my career, that they really did not need me to be a coauthor. They completed the project on their own, working on responding to referees' comments, even after they had graduated, that included implementing econometric methods with which I was unfamiliar. The paper was accepted for publication[30] and while I cannot list it on my vita, I am very proud of it. Based at least partially on that paper, one of the coauthors, Peter Crosta, was accepted at, and went on to receive a PhD in the economics of education from Columbia Teachers College.

13.3 Collaboration Without Being a Coauthor

About 20 years into my career, I realized that one's impact on an area of study can be magnified if one serves as a convener of a conference with a set of commissioned papers on an important topic, and then sees the conference through to publication. Over the years I have edited or coedited 11 conference volumes or journal symposia. Sometimes I have had a sole-authored or coauthored paper within the volume, but the impact of each of these volumes has been much greater than the impact of my own paper.

Table 13.5 contains a listing of the 11 volumes and symposia, which are not included in the publication counts found in Table 13.1. Several had a coeditor who helped me to organize the underlying conference and edit the volume. These coeditors include a Cornell faculty colleague (Fran Blau), a faculty member at another university (Paula Stephan), a university President (F. King Alexander), the Director of the TIAA-CREF Institute (Madeleine d'Ambrosio), and a colleague from the National Research Council (Charlotte Kuh). Six of the last seven resulted from conferences that I organized at the Cornell Higher Education Research Institute.

The last, the symposium on "Persistence Rates in STEM Field Majors," consisted of five papers; three of them were authored by PhD students of mine who were graduate research assistants at CHERI. I helped to design each of the studies and initially planned to be listed as the second coauthor of each of the papers. But as the students got into the research, I realized that they did not need my help in finalizing the design of the studies and conducting the empirical research. I also made the judgment that a sole-authored publication might mean more to them than being the first

Table 13.5 Edited conference volumes and symposia

Ehrenberg, R.G. (Ed.). (1990). *Do Compensation Policies Matter?* Ithaca NY: ILR Press.
Ehrenberg, R.G. (Ed.). (1994). *Choice or Consequences: Contemporary Policy Issues in Education.* Ithaca NY: ILR Press.
Ehrenberg, R.G. (Ed.). (1997). *The American University: National Treasure or Endangered Species.* Ithaca NY: Cornell University Press.
Blau, F.D. and Ehrenberg, R.G. (Eds.). (1997). *Gender and Family Issues in the Workplace.* New York NY: Russell Sage.
Alexander, F.K. and Ehrenberg R.G. (Eds.) (2003). *Maximizing Resources: Universities, Public Policy and Revenue Production.* San Francisco CA: Jossey Bass.
Ehrenberg, R.G. (Ed.). (2005). *Governing Academia.* Ithaca NY: Cornell University Press.
Ehrenberg, R.G. (Ed.) (2007). *What's Happening to Public Higher Education?* Baltimore MD: Johns Hopkins University Press.
Stephan, P.E. and Ehrenberg, R.G. (Eds.). (2007). *Science and the University.* Madison WI: University of Wisconsin Press.
d'Ambrosio, M.D. and Ehrenberg, R. G. (Eds.). (2008). *Transformational Change in Higher Education: Positioning Colleges and Universities for Success.* New York NY: TIAA-CREF Series on Higher Education.
Ehrenberg, R.G and Kuh, C.V. (Eds.). (2009). *Doctoral Education and the Faculty of the Future.* New York NY: Cornell University Press.
Ehrenberg, R.G. (Ed.). (2010). Symposium: Persistence rates in STEM field majors. *Economics of Education Review* 29 (6), 888-946.

author of a joint publication with me. So, again given that the marginal value to me of additional publications and citations clearly was approaching zero, I removed my name from those papers and thus have three fewer coauthored papers with my graduate students listed on my vita than I could have had. Some colleagues have suggested to me that having a joint paper with a distinguished senior faculty member might be worth more to a PhD student in the job market than having a sole-authored paper on their own; however, all three of these PhD students wound up with jobs at universities (Table 13.6).

Collaborations are not limited to publications. Every other year since 2000, my dear friend Michael Olivas, Distinguished Chair of Law at the University of Houston Law Center and Director of the Institute for Higher Education Law and Governance, has hosted a Higher Education Finance Round Table at which six to eight young scholars in the fields of college economics and higher education finance are invited to spend an intense three-day mentoring session with Michael in Houston. It was my great pleasure to serve as a faculty member in that program from 2000 to 2014 and through that experience I met and helped to mentor a large number of young scholars, many of whom have gone on to become leaders in their fields.[31]

13.4 Concluding Remarks

As this chapter has shown, my coauthors and collaborations have arisen for many reasons. To enumerate just a few, these include conversations with faculty colleagues and colleague elsewhere about research by others or policy issues; sharing of data both as a donor and as a recipient; invitations to participate in larger projects; the division of labor and working with people who have complementary skills and personalities; educating graduate and undergraduate students and the desire to give the former a leg up in the job market to encourage the latter to consider PhD study; discussions with my wife about issues she faced as a teacher and an administrator in public education; and efforts to magnify my impact on an area of study by convening conferences, commissioning papers, and seeing them through to publication.

Writing reflective chapters is a labor of love. I have written a number of previous reflective pieces and have found that they help me to understand what I have done, why I have done these things, where I am today, and what I want to do in the future. I regularly encourage my faculty

Table 13.6 Coauthors

Name	*Type*	*Name*	*Type*
Deborah Anderson	G	Jared Levin	U
Orley Ashenfelter	OF	Jean Li	G
Corry Azzi	F	Albert Liu	G
Jean Baderschneider	G	Rebecca Luzadis	G
Burt Barnow	OF	Joyce Main	G
Michael Bognanno	G	Alan Marcus	G
Dominic Brewer	G	Mirinda Martin	G
Sharon Brucker	OF	Michael Matier	IO
Richard Butler	F	Pangiatos Mavros	G
Richard Chaykowski	G	Marquise McGraw	U
John Cheslock	G	George Milkovich	F
Charles Clotfelter	OF	Mordechai Mironi	G
Gary Cohen	G	James Monks	OF
Scott Condie	G	Jesenka Mrdjenovic	IO
Leif Danzinger	F	Susan Murphy	U
Claude Desjardins	OF	Mathew Nagowski	F
Eric Ehrenberg	E	Ronald Oaxaca	U
Randy Ehrenberg	E	Robert Olsen	G
Eric Eide	OF	Richard Patterson	G
Thomas Eisenberg	U	Paul Pieper	OF
Julia Epfantseva	G	Sarah Prenovitz	G
Robert Flanagan	OF	Joseph Price	G
Peter Fontanella	IO	Pamela Rosenberg	IO
Malcom Getz	OF	Daniel Rees	G
Gary Goldberg	G	Michael Rizzo	G
Steven Goldberg	U	Donna Rothstein	G
Gerald Goldstein	OF	Gee San	G
Dan Goldhaber	G	Paul Schumann	G
Jeff Groen	F	Ronald Seeber	F
Kevin Hallock	F	Dan Sherman	G
James Hewlet	G	John Siegfried	OF
Peter Hurst	IO	Chris Smith	U
George Jakubson	F	Robert Smith	F
Todd Jick	G	Eric So	G
Lawrence Kahn	F	Doug Webber	G
Herschel Kasper	F	Kenneth Whelan	G
Andrew Key	U	Rachel Willis	OF
Adam Kezbom	U	J. Douglas Willms	OF
Dan Klaff	U	Liang Zhang	G
Thomas Kochan	F	Harriet Zuckerman	OF

(*continued*)

Table 13.6 (continued)

Name	*Type*	*Name*	*Type*
Dmitry Kotlyarenko	U		

Where, F: Faculty, visiting faculty and postdocs at my own institution; G: Graduate students; U: Undergraduate students; E: Ehrenberg family (wife and son); OF: Faculty and staff at other universities and organizations; IO: Administrators and staff at my own institution

colleagues and my graduate students to think about doing similar pieces during their careers. [32]

Writing this piece was a special pleasure because it provided me the opportunity to think back on all of the coauthors I have worked with who have had such important impacts on my career and life. Many of these coauthors—colleagues from Cornell and around the country, and former graduate and undergraduate students—have become lifelong friends. So add to the reasons that I have enumerated in this chapter for being a coauthor what is perhaps the most important one: the friends you make.

Notes

1. The final interval is seven years long.
2. The publication count does not include working papers that have not yet been published, many of which were coauthored with graduate students. My vita, which includes these, is available at http://faculty.cit.cornell.edu/rge2
3. However, several coauthored papers written with an undergraduate student and other UMass faculty were published in later years.
4. These individuals are listed in Appendix A.
5. Stone (1954).
6. Ehrenberg (1973).
7. Ashenfelter and Ehrenberg (1975).
8. Grossman (1972), Hamermesh Soss (1974).
9. Recently Dan told me that his suicide paper also started as a joke.
10. Azzi and Ronald Ehrenberg (1975).
11. Ehrenberg and Oaxaca (1976).
12. Ehrenberg et al. (1977).
13. Ehrenberg and Smith (1982).

14. The book was Ehrenberg and Jakubson (1988).
15. Clotfelter et al. (1991).
16. Ehrenberg et al. (2010).
17. Ehrenberg and Brewer (1996).
18. Eide et al. (1998) and Brewer et al. (1999).
19. Ehrenberg et al. (2001a, 2001b).
20. Ehrenberg et al. (2000), Ehrenberg and Hurst (1996, 1998).
21. Ehrenberg and Murphy (1993).
22. Monks and Ehrenberg (1999).
23. Ehrenberg et al. (1998).
24. Ehrenberg et al. (1991). My son Eric went on to publish his own paper on K12 education while enrolled at Georgetown Law School (E. Ehrenberg, 1996). My younger son Jason rejected the opportunity to coauthor with me on research while he was a high school student, but the publication bug bit him while he was at Michigan Law School (J. Ehrenberg 1998).
25. Ehrenberg et al. (1988a, 1988b).
26. Ehrenberg et al. (2004).
27. Ehrenberg and Goldberg (1977).
28. But those that did became extraordinarily successful academics including David Bloom (Harvard), Alan Krueger (Princeton), Phil Levin (Wellesley), Peter Capelli (Pennsylvania), and Jan Svejnar (Columbia).
29. Ehrenberg (2005).
30. Crosta and Packman (2005).
31. One notable star student of ours was F. King Alexander, who is now the President of LSU.
32. Ehrenberg (1999, 2005, 2006, 2009).

References

Ashenfelter, O., & Ehrenberg, R. (1975). The demand for labor in the public sector. In D. Hammermesh (Ed.), *Labor in the public and non-profit sectors* (pp. 55–78). Princeton NJ: Princeton University Press.

Azzi, C., & Ehrenberg, R. (1975). Household allocation of time and church attendance. *Journal of Political Economy, 83*(1), 27–56.

Brewer, D., Edie, E., & Ehrenberg, R. (1999). Does it pay to attend an elite private college? Cross-cohort evidence on the effects of college type on earnings. *The Journal of Human Resources, 34*(1), 104–123.

Clotfelter, C., Ehrenberg, R., Getz, M., & Siegfried, J. (1991). *Economic challenges in higher education*. Chicago: University of Chicago Press.
Crosta, P., & Packman, I. (2005). Faculty productivity in supervising doctoral students' dissertations at Cornell University. *Economics of Education Review, 24*(1), 55–65.
Ehrenberg, R. (1973). The demand for state and local government employees. *American Economic Review, 63*(3), 366–379.
Ehrenberg, R. & Oaxaca, R. (1976). Unemployment insurance, duration of unemployment, and subsequent wage gain. *American Economic Review, 66*(5), 756–766.
Ehrenberg, E. (1996). Getting to school: A proposal for a Federal School Choice Transportation Tax Credit. *Journal of Law and Education, 25*(2), 199–218.
Ehrenberg, J. (1998). A call for reform of recent immigration legislation. *Michigan Journal of Law Reform, 32*(1), 195–212.
Ehrenberg, R. (1999). My life and economics. *American Economist, 43*(1), 9–18.
Ehrenberg, R. (2005). Involving undergraduates in research to encourage them to undertake Ph.D. study in economics. *American Economic Association Papers and Proceedings, 95*(2), 194–198.
Ehrenberg, R. (2006). Being a quadruple threat keep things interesting. In G. Bataille & B. Brown (Eds.), *Faculty career paths* (pp. 119–121). Lanham, MD: Rowman & Littlefield.
Ehrenberg, R. (2009). *Last Lecture. Ronald G. Ehrenberg Cornell University*. Retrieved 2 June 2016, from https://courses.cit.cornell.edu/rge2/Last%20Lecture%2009.pdf
Ehrenberg, R., & Brewer, D. (1996). Does it pay to attend an elite private college? *Research in Labor Economics, 15*, 239–272.
Ehrenberg, R., & Goldberg, S. (1977). Officer performance and compensation in local building trades unions. *Industrial and Labor Relations Review, 30*(2), 188–196.
Ehrenberg, R., & Hurst, P. (1996). The 1995 NRC ratings of doctoral programs a hedonic model. *Change: The Magazine of Higher Learning, 28*(3), 46–54.
Ehrenberg, R., & Hurst, P. (1998). The 1995 ratings of doctoral programs: A hedonic model. *Economics of Education Review, 17*(2), 137–148.
Ehrenberg, R., & Jakubson, G. (1988). *Advance Notice Provisions in Plant Closing Legislation*. Kalamazoo, MI: Upjohn Institute for Employment Research.
Ehrenberg, R., Matier, M., & Fontanella, P. (2000). Cornell University Confronts the end of mandatory retirement. In R. Clark & B. Hammonds (Eds.), *To retire or not to retire: Retirement policies and practices in higher education* (pp. 85–102). Philadelphia, PA: University of Pennsylvania Press.
Ehrenberg, R., & Murphy, S. (1993). What price diversity? *Change: The Magazine of Higher Learning, 25*(4), 64–73.

Ehrenberg, R., & Smith, R. (1982). *Modern labor economics.* Glenview, IL: Scott, Foresman.

Ehrenberg, R., Chaykowski, R., & Ehrenberg, R. (1988a). Determinants of the compensation and mobility of school superintendents. *Industrial and Labor Relations Review, 41*(3), 386–401.

Ehrenberg, R., Ehrenberg, R., Chaykowski, R., & Ehrenberg, R. (1988b). Are school superintendents rewarded for performance? In D. Monk & J. Underwood (Eds.), *Micro level school finance: Issues and implications for policy* (pp. 337–364). Cambridge MA: Ballinger Publishing.

Ehrenberg, R., Brewer, D., Gamoran, A., & Willms, J. (2001a). Class size and student achievement. *Psychological Science in the Public Interest, 2*(1), 1–30.

Ehrenberg, R., Brewer, D., Gamoran, A., & Willms, J. (2001b). Does class size matter? *Scientific American, 285*(5), 78–85.

Ehrenberg, R., Ehrenberg, R., Rees, D., & Ehrenberg, E. (1991). School district leave policies, teacher absenteeism, and student achievement. *The Journal of Human Resources, 26*(1), 72–105.

Ehrenberg, R., Ehrenberg, R., Smith, C., & Zhang, L. (2004). Why do school district budget referenda fail? *Educational Evaluation and Policy Analysis, 26*(2), 111–125.

Ehrenberg, R., Hamermesh, D., & Johnson, G. (1977). Policy decisions and research in economics and industrial relations: An exchange of views: Comment. *Industrial and Labor Relations Review, 31*(1), 10–13.

Ehrenberg, R., Pieper, P., & Willis, R. (1998). Do economics departments with lower tenure probabilities pay higher faculty salaries? *Review of Economics and Statistics, 80*(4), 503–512.

Ehrenberg, R., Zuckerman, H., Groen, J., & Brucker, S. (2010). *Educating scholars.* Princeton: Princeton University Press.

Eide, E., Brewer, D., & Ehrenberg, R. (1998). Does it pay to attend an elite private college? Evidence on the effects of undergraduate college quality on graduate school attendance. *Economics of Education Review, 17*(4), 371–376.

Grossman, M. (1972). On the concept of health capital and the demand for health. *Journal of Political Economy, 80*(2), 223–255.

Hamermesh, D. (2015). Age, cohort and co-authorship. *National Bureau of Economic Research Working Paper, No.20398.*

Hamermesh, D., & Soss, N. (1974). An economic theory of suicide. *Journal of Political Economy, 82*(1), 83–98.

Monks, J., & Ehrenberg, R. (1999). U.S. News & World Report's College Rankings: Why they do matter. *Change: The Magazine of Higher Learning, 31*(6), 42–51.

Stone, R. (1954). Linear expenditure systems and demand analysis: An application to the pattern of British demand. *Economic Journal, 64*(255), 511–527.

CHAPTER 14

Two Heads are Better than One, and Three is a Magic Number in Economics

Mary Ellen Benedict

I am deeply honored to be asked to contribute this chapter about research collaboration. I have been very lucky to work with a number of wonderful individuals, sometimes as a neophyte, other times as the mentor, most often as an equal, and in all cases, my experience led to a better result than had I researched alone. Collaboration works for me, not only due to my natural proclivity to work with others but also because of my graduate training at Carnegie Mellon University (CMU).

The "two heads are better than one" proverb is first recorded in John Heywood's *A dialogue conteinyng the nomber in effect of all the prouerbes in the Englishe tongue*, 1546: Some heades haue taken two head is better than one: But ten heads without wit, I wene as good none. http://phrases.org.uk/bulletin_board/59/messages/615.html; "Three is a Magic Number" is the title of a song by Blind Melon, written for the children's show, *Schoolhouse Rock*.

M.E. Benedict (✉)
Bowling Green State University, Bowling Green, OH, USA

M. Szenberg, L.B. Ramrattan (eds.), *Collaborative Research in Economics*, DOI 10.1007/978-3-319-52800-7_14

Let me start by stating that although I am not in the same league as some of those writing for this set of collaboration chapters, I had the incredible luck of meeting and becoming good friends with Michael Szenberg, who requested my chapter. And, luck or fate seemed to put me on a path to work with coauthors who complemented the skills I brought to a project. Collaboration also created a manageable path to professorship in a state university, especially with teaching and service loads that are much greater than those at the premier research institutions. So, my story is about how luck took me down a successful collaboration path.

I began my walk down the collaboration path because of the generosity of two advisors during my doctoral program at the Heinz College at CMU. Ed Montgomery and Kathryn Shaw, already strong researchers early in their careers, not only showed me how to conduct research but also included me in several projects that resulted in publications. The first paper, with Ed Montgomery, was my first time working on an article of publishable quality. We investigated how chief bargainer experience affected the probability and length of teacher strikes; bargainers with little experience tended to be less adept at discovering their opponents' minimum payoffs.[1] I can still remember my delight when a student noticed this paper cited in the labor economics textbook I happened to choose for my class! The next paper, with both Ed and Kathyrn Shaw, examined how individuals trade off pensions for wages and found a large negative tradeoff in a contractual (lifetime) model but only a negligible tradeoff in the spot market model, at the time the general model employed.[2] Kathryn suggested that we use the idea of lifetime pension values to analyze whether pensions affected the income distribution.[3] We discovered that private pensions increased annual income inequality. Estimated lifetime pensions had little effect on the distribution, while social security reduced inequality. These two papers were subsequently cited regularly by those who study pension policy.

My collaboration with Ed and Kathryn helped me to land my current job 23 years ago; it also demonstrated how collaboration should work. I learned how to take and provide respectful constructive criticism; I observed how to solve the problem of different writing styles in a collaborative effort; I discovered that early rejection from a journal editor just means to rethink the problem and the analysis, not to give up, especially when there are others working with you. The old adage, "two heads are better than one" is really true. Not only is there a higher level of critical thinking in collaboration but also there is another person, just as determined as you, to find the right answers.

I was again led down the collaboration path when I began my academic position as a labor economist. At the beginning, it was to work with my previous CMU professors. Later on, I worked with colleagues at my home institution, Bowling Green State University. The collaborative efforts ranged in labor topics from worker dislocation to gender inequality in higher education to income inequality in Estonia; however, it was my collaborative efforts with John Hoag and David McClough that led to some of my favorite research experiences. John was one of my mentors for teaching, and it was his interest in economics education that led to a series of papers culminating in a great deal of intellectual satisfaction. The first paper we worked on investigated how student seating choices in large lectures were tied to class performance. Based on his personal experience, John was convinced that those in the back of the room performed more poorly than those near the front. He thought there might be some self-selection issue associated with the seating choice, but he was not sure what other factors particular to a large lecture mattered (e.g., the ability of the professor to see the student). We worked on all research issues together, with John assigned to writing the front half of the paper and I the back half. Our initial attempts at putting together the project did not fare well. John had a tendency to write with rhetorical questions: "Why do we care about seating choice?Why seating in large lectures? What will this research demonstrate?" I had a tendency to say what I wanted in ten words when five would suffice (still a problem!). Neither of us had a course in survey instrument development, so our first attempt at a survey was far from perfect. Despite the problems, we gathered data over the course of two years and finally ended up with a paper sent to the *Journal of Economics Education*. After what seemed like a decade, we received feedback from the editor and reviewers for a "revise and resubmit." The criticisms were daunting because they made us rework the model and the analysis, but the end result was a paper that we both agreed was ten times better than our original idea.[4] The writing improved, too, and when we sent our final paper back to the *JEE* editor, we were on draft 23, with no rhetorical questions and tightened up verbiage.

John and I worked well together. He was a virtual powerhouse in knowing economic theory and the literature on economics education; I was better with interpreting statistical output and thinking about the policy implications. We also enjoyed working together and subsequently wrote an additional five papers and two book chapters on economics education. The work also led to the two of us meeting and learning from other economists who specialize in economics education, which enhanced our own understanding of student learning in general, and learning economics specifically.

Along the way, we branched into the topic of self-employment and included a third coauthor, David McClough, of Ohio Northern University. For us, three was a magic number. We worked on several papers related to self-employment, including on how self-employment is related to STEM (science, technology, engineering, and mathematics) occupations and the self-employment choice of the educated. From that collaboration, I began a series of work with David, still in progress, related to gender and race inequality for the well educated. The papers often used the remarkably large set of information from the *National Survey of College Graduates*, a National Science Foundation-funded dataset. David, who had received his MA from our program, had grown as a writer and had creative ideas that made the research interesting. He also kept me on track to finish projects with a tenacity that I needed, especially as my service obligations grew. I found that while John and I began as mentors to David, we ended up being equals in research, again using our relative comparative advantages in developing and finishing projects. We are just starting a book chapter on self-employment and its effect on the middle class, thanks to another colleague and friend, Robert Rycroft, and I am excited to work with the two of them again.

David was not the only former student with whom I collaborated. I have been lucky to have several students who had the desire to learn more about research. The work tends to go slower because the students, who are either working toward their MA or undergraduate degrees, need to learn how to conduct a literature review, work a new statistical package, understand advanced statistical models, and write better. Sometimes, the work is published (usually in a lower-tiered journal, but not always). The satisfaction I receive from watching my students grow as independent researchers is enormous. In fact, several of these individuals have gone onto doctoral programs and today are teaching others.

My other collaboration efforts resulted in several projects with the two individuals to whom I am closest. One is my best friend from high school and the other is my husband; both are lawyers with whom I share a common interest in labor and employment law. I worried about working with each of them for different reasons; my friend, Judith, tends to get less enthusiastic as the project wears on, and since I am inclined to procrastinate, there tends to be a lull in the work. My husband, Lou, tends to be a perfectionist to the point that the paper might never get to an editor. I am more cautious about lending criticism because of the closeness of the relationships. In both cases, however, I have had several successful publications, two of which won awards from the journals within which they were published. The most recent papers with Lou have been about higher education unionization. The first paper analyzed the Ohio law that attempted to curtail public unionization in general and faculty unions in particular.[5] The second, recently published in *Academe*, examined faculty workload policy in Ohio. We are currently trying to finish a third paper on the *Yeshiva* decision, a Supreme Court ruling that limits the ability of faculty in private institutions from organizing.

My collaborative efforts have led to working with colleagues, students, friends, and family. I have learned that working with others on research projects has always ended in better work than had I worked alone. I also have had the opportunity to explore a variety of topics that interest me, which works for me, as I get bored with one topic if it lasts too long. I also found that with the right coauthors, one can find immense enjoyment in the research process—discussing the research question, thinking about the model, searching for the right data, writing up the final paper. Although it is common for the process to take an average of 20 drafts, the paper always reads better than it did in draft ten or fifteen. And, sharing the publication satisfaction with those who are important to me is highly gratifying. I only hope that those individuals with whom I have worked, especially my former students, take on the research mentor mantle with their own students and colleagues, because they will find the experience rewarding.

Notes

1. The Impact of Bargainer Experience on Teacher Strikes. 1989. *Industrial and Labor Relations Review* Vol. 42, No. 3 (April), 380–392.
2. "Pension and Wages: A Hedonic Price Theory Approach." 1992. *International Economic Review* Vol. 33, No. 1: 111–128.
3. "The Impact of Pension Benefits on the Distribution of Earned Income." 1995. *Industrial and Labor Relations Review* Vol. 48, No. 4 (July), 740–757.

4. Seating Choice in Large Lectures: Are Students Sitting in the Back of the Room Disadvantaged? 2004. *Journal of Economic Education* Vol. 35, No. 3, 215–227.
5. Ohio SB5 and the Attempt to "Yeshiva" Public University Faculty, *Journal of Collective Bargaining in the Academy*, 2013 Vol. 4.

CHAPTER 15

Why Collaborate in International Finance?

Rachel McCulloch

Many economists, these days perhaps even most, are—like me—inveterate collaborators.[1] But why? What is the appeal? And what is the downside? In the language of economists, what are collaboration's benefits and costs? Here I draw on more than four decades of my own collaborative research, as well as all the good and bad experiences recounted to me over the years by colleagues and students, to consider why we collaborate (or do not), how we collaborate, and even what it means to collaborate.

When I began to think about this subject, it was immediately apparent to me that my fellow economists differ widely in their practices with respect to collaboration. For one thing, some have long-established relationships with a particular research partner, while others might be described as promiscuous collaborators, and still others collaborate rarely or not at all. But I soon realized that even my own collaborative experiences have been

I am indebted to many of the collaborators named in this chapter, as well as several Brandeis colleagues and my daughter, Laura Gehl, for helpful suggestions.

R. McCulloch (✉)
Brandeis University, Waltham, MA, USA

M. Szenberg, L.B. Ramrattan (eds.), *Collaborative Research in Economics*, DOI 10.1007/978-3-319-52800-7_15

quite diverse in their motivation, that is, why I collaborated, or did not, on any particular project. As with my fellow scholars' collaborations, some of the differences reflected individual circumstances and tastes—my own and those of my collaborators—while others were due to characteristics of the research itself.

About half my published work has been jointly authored. My past collaborators now number something in the teens, the exact figure depending on whether I count collaborative experiences or co-authored publications. Of these collaborations, only two persisted over a long period. That they were sustained suggests these long-term collaborations were mutually beneficial in the sense that both my collaborator and I believed the quality and quantity of the work we produced together was greater than it would have been if working on our own—in short, that collaboration enhanced our research productivity. But it seems to me that the same has been true for all my collaborations, including the much larger number that produced only one or two publications, or in a couple of cases, none. That so many of these collaborations did not continue suggests there is indeed a downside—costs of collaboration that can outweigh its favorable productivity effect. Also, my most successful papers in terms of citations and reprinting in collections are ones I wrote on my own. As with reasons to collaborate—sources of benefits—the costs may also differ according to individual circumstances and tastes as well as characteristics of the research.

15.1 How Collaboration Begins

For many economists, the very first collaborative effort is the Ph.D. dissertation. Although the thesis advisor does sometimes become an "official" collaborator, that is, a co-author of at least one resulting publication, more often the advisor remains in the background, with what may be a substantial contribution signaled only in an "Acknowledgements" section of the completed thesis. Yet everyone is aware of the importance in many cases of input from the advisor and perhaps also from other thesis committee members. The advisor frequently suggests the topic, data sources, and potential approaches. The research may receive funding through a grant to the advisor or a fellowship facilitated by the advisor's supporting letter. And perhaps most important, as the work progresses—or fails to progress—the advisor may also nudge the student in a more promising direction or at a later stage help the student transform raw research results into a publishable paper. Given that it is normal for the advisor to make a substantive contribution to the student's work, does this mean the advisor should be listed as a co-author of the paper? The issue is contentious, and practices vary. In fact, the issue of who is a co-author of doctoral research receives a lengthy discussion on a website[2] aimed at Ph.D. students in a range of academic fields.

In economics and many other fields, the thesis work is sometimes only the first step in an ongoing research program carried out jointly by the advisor and the former student. Their respective roles may remain fixed or may evolve over time as the former student becomes a more seasoned participant. But beyond the thesis stage and sometimes even during graduate school, the majority of early-career collaborations are with peers. Early collaboration can begin with friends or colleagues asking, or being asked, for help on a specific project. A labor economist might seek out a colleague with superior econometric skills or access to a relevant dataset; an industrial organization economist might look to a theorist for assistance in modeling strategic behavior. I first teamed up with Chad Bown, who became a long-term collaborator, to produce a paper in an area where the two of us had different but complementary expertise. Alternatively, two economists who are already friends may search actively for a potential area of common interest in which to work together. This was the case in my long-term collaboration with Janet Yellen.

Collaboration can also begin after some of the work has been completed. For example, a reader might suggest a significant change or addition to another's paper. Or perhaps the reader has found a serious flaw in the paper and proposes a correction, or suggests an important generalization or an illuminating context for the results of the paper. In happy circumstances, the reader (who may even be a referee) and the original author(s) collaborate to write one or more superior papers on the subject. My first co-authored publication came about when my thesis advisor, Harry Johnson, read one of my draft chapters and then rewrote the main result in a completely different—and more interesting—way. Handing over the completed new version, Harry asked, "What do you think about a joint note?" It was never clear to me whether this was really a question or only Harry's polite way to announce the chapter's new status. A variation on this theme occurs when a paper is presented at a conference and a listener or discussant is inspired to make a contribution to the subject. In still other cases, colleagues find that each has been working independently on the same question/problem and decide to combine forces. My collaboration with Jose Piñera began when we discovered that we had produced very similar working papers on the effects of the new trade preferences then being extended to developing countries by the USA and other major importers. Sometimes a journal editor is the matchmaker, suggesting collaboration—and shared credit—when two submitted papers are closely related.

I might add here that circumstances are sometimes less than happy. Back in the days when physical working papers were requested and mailed, a young researcher in another country requested one of mine. He then produced his own paper reproducing and extending what I had done. He included a footnote citing my working paper but in no way indicating how much of "his" paper was in fact my work rather than his. Perhaps at that point I could at least have suggested that the paper be joint, but the idea never occurred to me at the time. And after his paper was published in a prominent journal, mine was superfluous and so became unpublishable. But that my paper remained unpublished was also partly my own fault. The previous year I had submitted the paper to the *American Economic Review* and received back what seemed to me a decidedly unenthusiastic response from editor Robert Clower. Clower wrote that he would publish the paper only if I could reduce the length by half. I hated the idea of chopping away so much of my carefully crafted exposition (even decades later I still find it difficult to cut my own work). Stung by Clower's lukewarm response to my magnum opus, I unwisely decided to try to find another outlet. It is possible that a collaborator would have saved me from these rookie errors.

In another unusual case that might be described as unintentional collaboration, the editors of a volume asked me to complete a chapter begun by an author who had been one of my earlier collaborators. Perhaps due to other commitments, he had been unable to finish the work. When the editors sent me the manuscript, I discovered that "his" work had borrowed extensively from the still-unpublished paper I had written on the same subject. So at least it was an easy job for me to complete the chapter. And rather than getting into a discussion with the editors about the details of what had happened, I kept him on as an official co-author of "our" chapter.

When I meet researchers whose work is joint with co-authors at other institutions, often physically distant from their own, I am always curious about the circumstances in which the collaboration was initiated. I have no doubt that physical proximity plays a significant role in facilitating collaboration, though perhaps to a lesser degree in the era of Skype. Even with Skype, time differences can at least complicate communication with a distant colleague. So it is not surprising that collaboration most often begins with a casual conversation between colleagues in the hallway or over coffee. To be sure, researchers with common interests may also meet at professional meetings and commence a collaboration that continues after they return to their separate institutions. And sometimes efforts are made to increase proximity at least temporarily, with the explicit goal of promoting collaboration. Still, all but one of my own collaborations did at least begin with physical proximity. True, Janet Yellen and I did much of the work on our last joint paper after both of us had left Harvard. Likewise, Chad and I managed to complete one paper while we were temporarily in different places in different time zones, and our last joint paper was written entirely after Chad had moved to the World Bank. But were these previously successful research partnerships ultimately sunk by the higher coordination costs imposed by distance?

For me, the one clear exception to the physical proximity rule was a joint project with David Collie at Cardiff University in Wales. As far as I can recall, our paths had never crossed. David wrote to me via email in 2003 that he had read one of my old papers (published 20 years earlier), and he proposed an interesting way to extend its logic to the then-current policy initiative to convert non-tariff trade barriers into equivalent tariffs. Over the next year we exchanged a series of emails, eventually producing a couple of drafts of a joint paper. Alas, in researching the earlier literature, David came across a published paper that had already established our key result. Thus ended our year of email-only collaboration.

15.2 Benefits and Costs of Collaboration

A recent NBER working paper[3] models the decision whether to collaborate as a tradeoff between the benefit of enhanced productive efficiency and two types of costs: coordination costs and allocation of credit for completed work, with emphasis on the latter. The paper analyzes 30 years of data from seven academic departments at MIT, all in the physical sciences. Despite the very different research environment that generated their data, two of the study's findings resonate with my own casual empiricism about collaboration in economics. First, collaboration results in higher quality of publications, where their measure of quality is citations. They also find disproportionate credit attribution. On average, jointly authored papers receive 60 percent more citations than singly authored ones. But other findings contradict my impressions about collaboration in economics. The researchers conclude that collaboration reduces individual productivity. For reasons I discuss below, I think the opposite is more likely to be true, at least in economics. The authors' model assumes a fixed amount of research time to be allocated between individual and collaborative effort, which may be a reasonable approximation for scientists who spend their days in a lab. However, this assumption ensures that time spent in collaboration must come at the cost of individual research. In economics, collaboration often seems to spur researchers to increase total time spent on research. The authors also find no evidence that junior researchers gain from collaboration with someone who is more senior. It is possible that this conclusion reflects the specific nature of collaboration in the physical sciences. In comparison to economics, lab-based research projects typically involve larger groups, specialized equipment, and a more stratified hierarchy, with collaborators ranging from students and post-docs to heads of large research labs. Finally, the authors identify high benefits and low costs associated with cross-departmental collaboration, while my own experience suggests that interdisciplinary efforts are often sunk by high coordination costs due to lack of agreement on the basic paradigms. But their finding may be skewed by the use of publications as an output measure. One of my few efforts at interdisciplinary collaboration, with political scientist Stephen Krasner, bore considerable intellectual fruit but yielded no joint published output. Though we were interested in the same topics—at that point, the political economy of natural resource extraction and associated trade—Steve's main themes were ones I would have relegated to footnote status, and vice versa.

15.3 The Process of Collaboration in Economics

One idealized version of a productivity-enhancing collaboration is two or more people interested in the same question or area, each bringing different expertise and viewpoints, working together until the resulting whole is greater than the possible sum of the parts they could produce individually—benefiting from what an international economist like me would describe as comparative advantage. Without doubt most successful collaboration has at least some tossing of ideas back and forth.

However, other benefits of collaboration may be equally important. To begin with, research can be a very lonely pursuit. Collaborating means there is someone else who shares your passion, one that in most research is highly specialized. And collaboration may also speed up the research process or make it feasible to undertake a larger or more complex project (economies of scale or scope). Also important is that collaboration provides ongoing feedback as the work progresses. While most of our colleagues are focused mainly on their own research, a collaborator is likely to be a (more) willing participant in long discussions as well as a reader of a succession of new drafts and, at least ideally, a careful checker of calculations, tables, and figures. But I have noticed that papers with more than two authors often manage to reach final publication with glaring (at least ex post) errors intact. Do too many cooks spoil the collaborative broth?

Certainly division of labor and monitoring of effort become more complex as the number of collaborators rises. In the natural sciences, projects often involve many researchers, and the contribution of the head of a laboratory may consist largely in dealing with issues of coordination. A significant number of multi-authored papers are later withdrawn; after questions arise, it seems that some of the better-known "co-authors" of these papers have had little contact with their content. While published papers in economics are often subject to many criticisms regarding assumptions, data, methodology, and interpretation, outright fraud of the kind seen in the natural sciences seems to be absent. Perhaps the stakes are not high enough to make fraud an attractive option.

Collaboration can also increase productivity by serving as a commitment device for researchers. We academic economists are obliged to balance our instructional and administrative activities, as well as our responsibilities to family and perhaps community, with our work on research projects. Since lectures must be prepared, classes met, and children picked up from school even when a professor is in the middle of a very exciting discovery, pressure from a research collaborator to move the project forward can be a powerful motivator. Routine academic and family obligations are less likely to preempt the researcher's entire workday when an anxious collaborator is demanding results. For this reason, I believe that collaboration may increase the total time allocated to research, at least for us academic economists. The research-time-increasing effect should be strongest when the collaborator is actually on the spot. Still, I recall one early collaborator who abruptly departed from our work session for a previously scheduled squash game. As he left, he remarked (approximately), "If you don't make time for the really important things in life, they will never happen." That particular collaboration never did produce any publishable results.

At the end of the research process, collaboration can also make the job of turning results into a publishable paper less painful. The joy of research is in the breakthrough discovery of light and truth after wandering through darkness. But after achieving the breakthrough, there remains the tedium of summarizing prior literature, choosing notation, and explaining the model and its implications; for empirical papers, there are also data and econometric techniques as well as notable results, often as figures or tables, to be described. Yet a collaborator can make even this work interesting. I can recall many conversations with co-authors that essentially focused on the right way to market a finding: "If this [our result] is the answer, what is the question?" Often we found we had answered a different question than the one that had originally motivated our efforts. Such discussions with collaborators during the writing period sometimes produced ideas for further joint projects.

Finally, collaboration may facilitate the publication process. Especially for young scholars, collaboration means being able to share the psychological burden of rejection, not to mention the tasks entailed in the multiple revisions that are often necessary steps between "finishing" a paper and achieving the goal of publication. Where a single author might decide to stuff a rejected paper into a bottom drawer (these days only metaphorically) and move on, a co-author may provide the impetus needed to revise the paper and/or submit the work to another journal. And sometimes a co-author's name or contacts can facilitate acceptance by a more prestigious outlet or one with wider circulation.

15.4 Two Long-Term Collaborations

By one measure, the most significant of my collaborative relationships was with Janet Yellen early in our careers. Although our joint research did not produce any path-breaking contributions, it did yield five refereed publications in major journals—solid publications that helped each of us to gain a tenured appointment soon afterward. Our work together began while we were both assistant professors at Harvard and ended after we had both moved on to other places. In a recent conversation Janet suggested that we become collaborators because we were both women at a time when the economics department at Harvard, as at most other universities, had few women. In my view this made it likely that we would become friends but not necessarily collaborators. During those Harvard years I also collaborated with several male colleagues, and Janet likewise collaborated with a male colleague.

Because Janet has recently achieved international prominence in her role as the first woman to chair the Federal Reserve Board, many people have asked me about our early collaboration. Perhaps the most noteworthy thing about our joint research is that the subject was *not* macroeconomic policy—the field in which Janet later emerged as a major figure. Instead, our work was entirely in the area of international trade theory, thus quite close to my own previous and future research but farther from Janet's. But although Janet's doctoral research had dealt with open-economy macroeconomics, international trade was one of her fields in graduate school, and her thesis used a two-sector model similar to the kind in our joint papers. Likewise, while my own thesis was mostly international trade theory, open-economy macro had been an important part of my training, and money and banking was one of my two prelim fields. Thus, open-economy macroeconomics might have been a logical focus of our work together, yet over the years we stuck instead to the "real" (non-monetary) side of international transactions. The reason reflects what might be considered a coordination cost of collaboration. Our intellectual backgrounds in macroeconomics—specifically, Chicago versus Yale—made us incompatible. Any effort to collaborate on a macro topic would likely have been doomed.

While at Harvard Janet also collaborated with another junior faculty member, Jim Adams, producing two joint papers (and eventually refereed publications in major journals) in Jim's area of specialization, industrial organization. One of those, on bundling, has become a classic that I have discussed in my industrial organization course. Janet's published research in her own major area of interest, macroeconomics, started to take off only after she left Harvard, and especially after she began to collaborate with her husband, George Akerlof.

Working with Janet was often great fun. We were friends before we began to collaborate, and I am happy to say that we have remained friends over the subsequent decades—though we still do not agree on macroeconomic matters. Ours was my only collaborative experience that involved actually working together in the same room for hours at a time—a style of collaboration that seems more the exception than the rule in economics. This togetherness did cause a logistical difficulty. Janet tells me it has been nearly four decades since she puffed her last cigarette, but back in the 1970s she had not yet succeeded in her efforts to give up smoking, and smoking had not yet been banned in Harvard offices. As a consequence, we could not work in her office because it was too smoky for me. Likewise, we could not work in my office because I did not want smoke to linger after our session. So we always needed to search for some neutral and preferably well-ventilated workspace. A second problem likely arose from the subject of our research. Janet's commitment to our joint research was, quite naturally, somewhat less than my own. As a result, I was typically the one who was pushing things forward, trying to overcome the competing attractions of lecture preparation (Janet was a legendary teacher, and I believe her expository skill is even more important in her latest position), her research with Jim, and even various non-academic activities. But in most ways, Janet was a wonderful collaborator—knowledgeable in international trade theory, smart, patient, and with a great sense of humor. This last was especially helpful when results were elusive, errors belatedly discovered (I had a cartoon on my wall with the caption, "What is the opposite of Eureka?"), or a manuscript returned with a perfunctory rejection. One referee wrote that our main result was so uninteresting that he would not even assign it as a classroom exercise on a rainy afternoon. Fortunately for us, referees' tastes differ, and on our next try the paper did gain acceptance at an equally prestigious journal.

And when we got to the writing (and rewriting and rewriting) part of the research process, Janet was also outstanding in her ability to organize our results and explain every detail of our approach, a task I dreaded. My part of the job was on the marketing end: to convince readers that our stylized theoretical model actually captured some interesting and important aspect of reality. Alas, my efforts were not highly successful, at least as evidenced by the rather paltry number of citations our articles have gleaned over the years.

My only other long-term collaboration has been with my former Brandeis colleague, Chad Bown, which produced ten joint publications—Chad jokes that this is more than my collaboration with Janet. Our collaborative relationship began soon after Chad arrived as a new assistant professor and wound up soon after he moved to the World Bank, though I nurture the hope that there is still some joint project in our future. In sharp contrast to Janet, who was my peer in academic status during our collaboration, Chad was not only junior in rank but also young enough to be my son. We never discussed this aspect of our relationship and I did not give it much thought at the time, but in retrospect I cannot help wondering whether this was an entirely comfortable situation for Chad.

Our collaboration started when I suggested that we work together on a chapter for a three-volume interdisciplinary treatise on the World Trade Organization (WTO). We chose a subject that interested both of us: trade and environment. While Chad had superior institutional knowledge regarding the WTO, I knew more about the specific issue on which our chapter focused. Chad also stood to benefit from adding a nearly certain publication to his then very slender CV. The project went well, and we continued on to another invited chapter. This time I had been asked to contribute to a festschrift honoring Max Kreinin. After agreeing to write a paper, I learned that the title of the volume was to be *Empirical Methods in International Trade*. Since my credentials as an empirical researcher were close to nonexistent, I would clearly need help in producing an appropriate paper. Chad's own work was heavily empirical. After that, various opportunities arose and we continued to work together, producing eight more papers. Over the same period, I wrote some papers on my own; Chad did likewise and also began work with several other collaborators. By now that number has grown to dozens. His most frequent collaborator is Meredith Crowley, Chad's graduate school classmate at the University of Wisconsin. In one case—it is the one time I have written a paper with more than a single co-author—Chad and I agreed to write a paper with Meredith. As a promised reward for his diligence, Meredith's research assistant at the Chicago Fed became a fourth co-author. He is the only one of my co-authors whom I have never met.

One salient characteristic of my work with Chad is its narrow focus. Over the decades, I have written papers on just about every type of transaction that involves a national boundary, including trade and trade policy, foreign direct investment, international capital movements, exchange rates, immigration, and technology transfer. However, all my papers with Chad are concentrated in a single area: trade policy in the context of the General Agreement on Tariffs and Trade and its successor institution, the WTO. In the course of our work together, I sometimes suggested topics or approaches outside this area, but Chad preferred to remain within what I took to be his comfort zone. I did not mind this, partly because I recognized my own tendency to take on projects that require getting up to speed in completely new areas. My collaboration with Chad thus helped to protect me from spreading myself too thin. Moreover, I interpreted Chad's extreme focus as a wise strategy for a young academic seeking to establish himself as an acknowledged expert in his area. Since Chad was also strategic in publicizing our joint publications, I benefited through resulting readership and citations. Early on, he also urged me to be more active in promoting my own achievements. To this end, he helped me create a personal website. Years later, he organized a conference at Brandeis in honor of my 65th birthday, and he recently spread the word when I received the 2013 Carolyn Shaw Bell Award.

15.5 Short-Term Collaborations

Most of my short-term collaborations have involved a single paper, or in some cases, no paper. (Below I discuss problems that can plague collaborative research.) These collaborations often arose when one or both of us had been invited to contribute a paper for a conference or a volume. Usually the first step was to identify a topic that suited us both. Thus, I collaborated with Dave Richardson, my colleague at the University of Wisconsin, with Robert Owen during a year in which he was a visitor at Wisconsin, and also with several of my Brandeis colleagues, including Peter Petri, Michael Plummer, and Blake LeBaron.

Blake is the colleague I see most often in the course of a typical day at Brandeis, and our conversations range over many topics. We were both graduate students at Chicago and faculty members at Wisconsin, though at different times, then finally met when Blake joined the Brandeis faculty in 1998. At Brandeis, Blake succeeded me as director of our Ph.D. program in international economics and finance, and we still talk often about all the issues that position involves. My collaboration with Blake arose from our frequent discussions about the international monetary system. We had each provided one lecture in a special course our department had organized in the semester following the Asian Financial Crisis. Our paper examined a variety of alternative exchange-rate arrangements and focused in particular on the dollarization that was then in progress in a number of countries. Milton Friedman had quipped that a central bank is a necessary and almost sufficient condition for a financial crisis. For some countries, having their own currency and central bank may be counterproductive. But our favorable view of dollarization may have been overly optimistic. As Argentina has amply demonstrated, dollarization is hardly a panacea.

Peter Petri, my co-author on several papers, is another Brandeis colleague with whom I seem to spend a great deal of time discussing a wide range of topics. By an odd coincidence, I was a member of the thesis committee that approved Peter's long-delayed Ph.D. dissertation while I was still a junior faculty member at Harvard. One notable fact about our collaboration is that Peter is a masterly writer, and he seems much better than I in the marketing aspect of academic writing. Even I become convinced when reading his explanations of why what we have done is so interesting and important. (I once made an investment based on the main argument in one of our papers and promptly lost a significant amount of money.) But Peter and I are incompatible in an important respect. Peter is a great one for the last-minute push. While I do not meet every deadline, I do not have the personality or the stamina to complete work under great time pressure.

My most recent collaborator, and one of the few non-economists, is my sister, Linda Rothschild. Linda is a mathematician who, like me, has recently retired after a long academic career. In 2014 the two of us embarked on our first collaboration: a paper based on our year of shared experiences as students enrolled in the newly popular Massive Online Open Courses (MOOCs). Even before its publication in September 2014, our paper had already achieved a larger readership and a more enthusiastic reception than much of our disciplinary research. Emboldened by the success of our first joint project, we decided to try our luck in a second collaboration. Our work together on the MOOC paper had led in a natural way to a discussion of our various past collaborations and collaborators, examining their motivation and results. We thought it would be interesting to focus on similarities and differences in collaborative research in our two fields. But, alas, our ideas about the extent that we should write explicitly about our own experiences turned out to be incompatible. Our effort collapsed, and I released Linda from her role in creating this paper.

15.6 Collaboration With a Significant Other

These days many women in economics and indeed many other fields collaborate with a significant other. My Chicago classmate, Claudia Goldin, has had many years of fruitful collaboration with Larry Katz. Janet Yellen has written numerous papers with her husband, George Akerlof. And my mathematician sister collaborated for more than two decades with her mathematician husband, Salah Baouendi. Gary Chamberlain, my spouse of nearly four decades, is an econometrician, so people naturally wonder whether we have ever collaborated or even tried to collaborate. The answer is no, though we do often talk about economics at home. So why not collaborate? I reply that I like to go home at night and complain about my collaborator. That is partly an attempt at humor, but there is also some truth in this jest. Even in the most harmonious collaboration, it is refreshing to put work aside for a while at night. And in any long marriage, there are bound to be enough tensions about other issues without adding joint work to the mix. Yet some other couples clearly thrive in this kind of relationship. I am envious of their extra dimension of closeness, yet I do not see this as a model for my own work. On occasion, I do take advantage of my husband's extensive knowledge and attention to detail, especially as an extra reader for papers I write on my own. Gary picks up both the occasional typo and the more worrisome "thinko" that a collaborator might have spotted. And he does it without complaining!

15.7 Collaboration versus Co-authorship

When two or more researchers work together on a research project, whose name(s) should be on the resulting publication? And in what order? The answer varies by discipline. In economics, collaborators are generally assumed to be equal contributors and hence the practice of listing the authors' names in alphabetical order. Indeed, in practice it is often difficult to separate the contributions of the co-authors. However, non-economists frequently assume that the first author is the more important one, which may lead, say, to a journalist directing a question to the first-listed author when in fact that particular aspect of the work is due primarily to the second-listed author.[4] In rare cases where it is possible to say that one author has done "more" in some meaningful sense, the order may be reversed. Hence, Paul Samuelson insisted that Wolfgang Stolper's name appear first in their classic paper. And in an instance relevant to me, Harry Johnson chose to put my name first on the note he drafted based on my thesis chapter.

An important special case is the content of a student's Ph.D. thesis. Although the thesis advisor may be a primary, even maybe the primary, contributor to the ideas in the thesis, the advisor may be reluctant to be listed as a co-author for at least two very different reasons. One is a benevolent impulse on the part of the advisor, reflecting a belief that the young scholar will be better off professionally with at least some singly authored work. Yet the probability of a good outcome in terms of publication and citation may be enhanced by including an established researcher as a co-author. Some students thus actively seek to include an advisor or other senior person as a co-author. A second and less benign motivation is that the quality of the work may be below that for which the advisor wishes to be known. However, with the growing pressure on academic economists at all levels to publish frequently, and in consideration of the many hours spent advising Ph.D. students in their doctoral research, co-publication with thesis students has become more acceptable, even when the research is merely competent rather than outstanding. But is it really appropriate for the thesis advisor to be listed as a co-author of a resulting publication? And where a thesis comprises three essays, is it acceptable for all three to be jointly authored? In the natural sciences, the head of the lab is always included. In economics, this is a less routine matter and can even be a source of controversy within departments. Regardless of the importance of their contributions to their students' finished work, some advisors seem to be listed as a co-author on every paper, while others are never listed.

Other special cases also come to mind, all based on situations described to me by colleagues or former students. Sometimes a collaborator drops out of a project after some of the work has been completed, or at least completed to the satisfaction of all concerned. One collaborator may be eager to implement ideas received from a referee, or to include newly available data, while the other is reluctant to devote more time to the project, or for some reason, such as health, is unable to do so. Does the dropout remain a co-author of the final version of the work? Sometimes a project uses a special proprietary dataset created by others who did not otherwise participate in the research. Is the creator of the data appropriately included as a co-author? One of my colleagues was in this situation due to using, with permission, a proprietary dataset created by another scholar. Perhaps recognizing the questionable appropriateness of requiring his inclusion as a co-author of the paper simply because he had provided the needed data, this scholar offered my colleague various suggestions regarding the research itself. However, because the suggestions were misguided, this merely increased the burden of including him as a co-author. And sometimes one co-author who has otherwise contributed little or nothing to the work has good contacts at a relevant journal or is sufficiently well known to make an editor think twice about a rejection. The case for inclusion may be made by either party. To include this well-connected person as a co-author is certainly questionable, yet the situation is far from unusual.

One last odd case comes from my own experience—co-authorship without collaboration. Labor economist Jonathan Leonard and I both contributed papers to an NBER volume on labor issues arising from international linkages. My paper, which grew out of my earlier work on foreign direct investment in the USA, focused on the motives underlying this then-new trend and its relationship to US trade policy. Jonathan's paper was an empirical analysis of the impact of foreign direct investment on US employment and compensation. For reasons unknown to us, the editors insisted that we merge our two papers into a single chapter. As Jonathan described our non-collaborative final product, we were joined by a staple.

15.8 Possible Downsides of Collaboration

Research collaborations, like all other joint ventures, can lead to unsatisfactory or even unpleasant results. A theoretical analysis may fail to produce the anticipated conclusion. The effects under examination may turn out to be statistically insignificant. Friction between the collaborators may arise if they disagree about whether the remaining scraps are publishable. Another area of disagreement occurs when one collaborator thinks the project is finished and wants to publish and move on, while the other feels that the results are not yet definitive. Tension can arise when a helpful referee points to ways that the result might be extended or generalized or to additional data that might be deployed. Or sometimes one collaborator—or even both—feel that they have done most of the work. And occasionally collaboration never even gets off the ground. This is often because of coordination costs of various kinds. Even so, the would-be collaborators may have gained from better understanding of another way of looking at the issues.

As I mentioned earlier, writing up results is often the least pleasant aspect of research. While a collaborator usually helps with this, the opposite can also happen. A co-author may lose interest in the project and refuse to work on the writing in a timely manner or even to read new drafts. A more common problem is that co-authors disagree about how the paper should be written, for example, how much detail should be included, what references should be cited, and especially which results to emphasize. A thorny issue concerns policy implications of the work. As I looked back over which of my papers were singly authored, I realized that I tended to work on my own mainly when I had a strong point of view to express, one not necessarily shared by otherwise congenial colleagues.

15.9 Some Concluding Thoughts

Formal collaboration is only a small part of the broad range of collegial interactions I have enjoyed as a member of an academic community, whether hallway conversations, seminar discussions, or exchange of new drafts. Newton famously wrote, "If I have seen further it is by standing on the shoulders of giants." I am no Newton, and my colleagues past and present include only a few giants. Still, whatever I have achieved as a student, a scholar, and a teacher of future scholars has been immeasurably enriched by interactions with colleagues. I am especially grateful for the many hours spent with collaborators in pursuit of a common goal, and I hope they agree that the benefits of our collaborations have far exceeded the costs.

Notes

1. In the June 2014 issue of the *American Economic Review,* only five of fourteen articles are singly authored. Two have three co-authors, and three have four authors. Forty years earlier, singly authored articles dominated. In the June 1974 issue of the *American Economic Review*, 13 of 19 articles were singly authored.
2. Ph.D. on Track (www.phdontrack.net).
3. Bikard, Michael, Fiona E. Murray, and Joshua Gans (2013). "Exploring Tradeoffs in the Organization of Scientific Work: Collaboration and Scientific Reward." NBER Working Paper No. 18958.
4. In the natural sciences, the first author is typically the most important one as far as the actual work is concerned, and the last author is often the one in charge of the lab (who may also be the one who procured the funding that paid for the research). The names in the middle are less important. These papers almost always have more than two authors.

CHAPTER 16

My Collaborations in Game Theory

L.G. Telser

This chapter describes three kinds of collaborations. The first is active joint work with one or more associates that results in publications, articles in professional journals and, in one case, a book. The second resembles the relation between a master craftsman, the dissertation supervisor and the apprentice, the PhD student. The third form is a conference on a theme on which the participants, chosen in advance, prepared essays. Preliminary versions of these essays are discussed together in various settings. Final versions were published in one volume as a book or as a special issue of a scholarly journal.

16.1 Collaborations of the First Kind

My six collaborations of the first kind cover a wide range of topics. All but one were relatively brief. The exception is my work with Bob Graves that continued for over a decade. Bob was a professional mathematician specializing in computer science. Our collaboration was harmonious and mutually beneficial.

L.G. Telser (✉)
University of Chicago, Chicago, IL, USA

M. Szenberg, L.B. Ramrattan (eds.), *Collaborative Research in Economics*, DOI 10.1007/978-3-319-52800-7_16

One of my collaborations does not appear as an academic publication. Yet it was very important in my academic research on economic applications of core theory. This collaboration was an economic study of the bankrupt Penn-Central Railroad commissioned by a government agency USRA to A.T. Kearney.

1. Collaboration with William H. Kruskal

1960. William H. Kruskal and Lester G. Telser. Food Prices and the Bureau of Labor Statistics. Journal of Business of the University of Chicago. 23: 258–285 (July). Includes comment by Ewan Clague, Commissioner of Labor Statistics and reply by authors.

First some background. Bill Kruskal was a distinguished professor of statistics at the University of Chicago. I took three courses from him in 1952, one in probability theory and two in mathematical statistics. The assigned text books show the course level. In the first course it was William Feller's Probability, Theory and Its Applications (1950). For the two mathematical statistics courses it was Harald Cramèr's Mathematical Methods of Statistics (1946). Kruskal was a superb teacher. I was an assistant professor in economics at Iowa State College starting in January 1956 before receiving my PhD in economics from the University of Chicago in August 1956. In September 1956 I was inducted into the US Army. I served in a psychological research unit at the Presidio of Monterey, California. I rose to the rank of Specialist 3rd Class. Honorably discharged in June 1958, I returned to the University of Chicago as an assistant professor in the Business School.

Given our backgrounds it may seem surprising that Kruskal and I began a very careful study of the food price component of the Consumer Price Index. This is how the story begins. At that time S&H Green Stamps were a popular form of promotion used by some food retailers. They gave their customers green stamps proportional to the size of their purchases. After accumulating a certain number of these stamps, they could redeem them for various items, often consumer appliances. Chain stores, notably A&P, did not give green stamps. Nor is this all. The A&P did not allow Bureau of Labor Statistics agents into their stores to record prices. Prices in chain stores were generally lower than that in non-chain stores. This may explain why critics of green stamps claimed they caused higher food prices. Retailers, who issued them, as is hardly a surprise, denied this. Indeed some retailers asserted green stamps actually lowered prices. The Bureau of Labor Statistics published two reports on trading stamps as noted in our article, references 31 and 32. The critics appealed to evidence in these reports and other material and claimed it gave empirical support for their views. However, it must be kept in mind that the Consumer Price Index does not measure the price level; it measures the percentage change in the price level. Although chain store prices tend to be lower than non-chain store prices, by itself this says nothing about the percentage changes of prices at the two types of food stores. This controversy led Kruskal as a statistician to wonder about the accuracy of the food price component of the Index. Not only were there formidable statistical problems but there were also longstanding economic questions about these indexes. Here is where I entered the scene. Our goal was to examine in detail the procedure used to obtain price data for the food component of the Consumer Price Index.

Part of the problem of describing the accuracy of the Index arises from ambiguity about its purpose. Changes in the name of the index illustrate this. It began as the Cost of Living Index and morphed into the Consumer Price Index. The food component was called the Food-at-Home Index to distinguish it from prices of restaurant meals.

The importance of price indexes is manifest. We were surprised at the paucity of studies on the accuracy of the Bureau of Labor Statistics price indexes. We read more than 100 articles, reports, manuals and the like. Only one deserves mention as a statistical study of accuracy of the Index. It is an appendix to a study "An Appraisal of the U.S. Bureau of Labor Statistics Cost of Living Index" by a Special Committee of the American Statistical Association published in its Journal in 1943. The Appendix by Dorothy Brady and Solomon Fabricant was published in the JASA in 1944. Our article describes in detail some of their important results. One result we did not mention in our article has special interest. One of the BLS publications claimed that the accuracy of the prices measures had increased as measured by the reduction in the standard deviation of prices among stores in the same city. It turns out that BLS agents could replace a store that dropped out of their sample with another store of their own choice. Brady and Fabricant noted that the distance between stores in the sample decreased with the passage of time. Either the forces of competition or the lack thereof among stores could explain why the standard deviation varies inversely with the distances among them. In any case the stores in the sample are not a random draw from the relevant population. Years later when I told this story at a conference at the University of Florida, Sol Fabricant in the audience confirmed its accuracy.

16.2 Collaboration with Basil S. Yamey

1965. Lester G Telser and B.S. Yamey. Speculation and Margins. Journal of Political Economy. 53:656–7 (December).

Basil Yamey, a faculty member of the London School of Economics, was a visitor at the Business School in the fall of 1963. We had mutual interests in resale price maintenance and in commodity futures markets. On Friday morning, November 22, 1963, President John F. Kennedy was assassinated in Dallas, Texas. The Chicago Board of Trade stopped trading in their futures markets. Trading did not resume until the following Monday. Basil and I went to the market that Monday and spoke to traders who had been on the floor of the exchange that Friday.

The story of what happened on the floor the morning of the assassination is remarkable. All the wire service had news tickers on the floor, AP, UP, Reuters and so on. Traders often walk over to them to see if anything pertinent to commodity prices is happening. We were talking to traders in the wheat pit. Friday morning around 11 AM one of the traders walked over to the AP ticker, came back to the wheat pit and sold 100 or 200 contracts of wheat futures. I do not remember the actual number but it was in that range. A contract is 5000 bushels of wheat. The other traders glanced at him, some bought and the deal was duly recorded. Another trader sauntered over to a ticker, came back and sold a sizeable number of contracts. Like the first trader, he said nothing, just took a short position. Soon several other traders began selling wheat futures. The price rapidly dropped the limit and trading halted. In the Chicago Board of Trade trading stops when prices move up or down a set limit. The following Monday when Basil and I were on the floor, trading was as usual. Prices were back to where they had been before the tragedy.

In the penultimate paragraph of our article we say, "Few would deny that hysterical speculation occurs from time to time with unfortunate effects on price movements and that this may need curbing." (p. 607).

16.3 Collaborations with Robert L. Graves

3.1. 1967. R.L. Graves and L.G. Telser. An Infinite Horizon Discrete Time Quadratic Program as Applied to a Monopoly Problem. Econometrica 35: 234–72. (April).

3.2. 1968. L.G. Telser and R.L. Graves. Continuous and Discrete Time Approaches to a Maximization Problem. Review of Economic Studies. 35: 307–25. (July).
3.3. 1972. Lester G. Telser and Robert L. Graves. Functional Analysis in Mathematical Economics; Optimization over an Infinite Horizon. Chicago: University of Chicago Press.

By 1956 the Business School at the University of Chicago had shrunk to a corporal's guard and was on the verge of disappearing altogether. Allen Wallis took command as Dean. With help from a Ford Foundation grant and by his own outstanding ability, he led a renaissance of the Graduate School of Business. In addition to hiring economists for teaching and research, he brought computer professionals, three mathematicians, to the business school; Robert Ashenhurst, Robert Graves and Alex Orden. The University joined the business school's entry into computer science by hiring Nicholas Metropolis to lead basic research in this field. Metropolis had been director of computing at Los Alamos for the Manhattan Project.

When I joined the faculty of the Business School in 1958, I shared an office with Bob Ashenhurst, who was working closely with Metropolis. I was keenly interested in using computers in economics. Ashenhurst taught me much about computers, their strengths and their weaknesses. Besides a computer Metropolis was building, the University had an early digital computer, Univac I, amazing then but very primitive by present standards. In 1960 Bob Graves delivered a series of lectures on computer programming. Two economists attended these lectures, Milton Friedman and me. This series was my first meeting with Bob Graves.

The next part of my story concerns the Cowles Commission for Research in Economics. It was brought to the University in the late 1930s. It had close relations with the Economics Department. Two of the leading economists at Cowles, Tjalling Koopmans and Jacob Marschack were also professors in the Department. When I entered as a graduate student in the economics department in the fall of 1952 after my first year as an economics graduate student at Harvard in 1951, I was also a research assistant in the Cowles Commission to H.S. Houthakker. We were studying commodity futures markets. This work led to my dissertation topic, futures trading in cotton at the New York Cotton Exchange and in wheat at the Chicago Board of Trade. Later I describe some of my work on futures markets with Harlow Higinbotham.

Econometric models of the economy based on Keynes' General Theory were a major focus of research at Cowles. Models of consumption and investment used difference equations. I had taken an under graduate course on differential equations, a standard tool in mathematics. How to handle difference equations in economic applications became one of my major interests. Difference equations were untouched in standard mathematics courses. Owing to this neglect I was led to seek help from my mathematical colleagues at the Business School. I recall standing one day at a blackboard writing down equations and describing my use of difference equations to Bob Graves and Jerry Gould, another Business School mathematician. Thus began my collaboration with Graves in 1961 on the topics in our first article.

The Cowles Commission had moved from Chicago to Yale at the end of 1954. It changed its name to the Cowles Foundation. I spent 1964–65 as a research fellow at the Foundation. One of my research areas was the theory of the core inspired by the theory of games of von Neumann and Morgenstern. Two notable pioneers in this field, Robert Aumann and Herb Scarf, were at the Cowles Foundation. My second area was applications of difference equations to economics. My office at Cowles was next door to Scarf's. I frequently discussed both of my interests with him. My collaboration with Graves was by mail.

An important result in our research has come to be called rational expectations, a term we did not coin. Our problem was to derive the profit maximizing policy for a monopolist facing a demand equation such that the current quantity demanded depends on the current price and on the past sales of the commodity. The best policy gives the maximum present value of profits over an infinite horizon. Because the policy concerns an infinite sequence of quantities and prices, it poses a problem in the calculus of variations. The best policy must satisfy a Euler equation. Since the current choice depends on past choices and its effects will last for a long time into the future, the best policy depends on this. We showed that the Euler condition necessary for the maximum can be factored into a product of two difference equations whose characteristic roots come in reciprocal pairs with respect to the unit circle in the complex plane. Thus one factor of the Euler equation depends on the past and the other factor depends on the future. Of particular interest is that these factors determine the weights to attach to forecasts of the future as a consequence of the maximum present value. It is intrinsic to the solution.

The policy equation deduced from the Euler equation is determined by the demand relation. Consequently, one can test the validity of the model empirically by estimating the demand equation and deducing the policy equation from the demand equation on the basis of the model. By comparing estimates of the policy equation with the deduced equation the model is amenable to empirical test. I did these tests using estimates of the demand for certain branded commodities of frozen orange juice concentrate, instant coffee and margarine in my (1972, Chap. 7) with very satisfactory results.

Our work on this research first appeared as Cowles Foundation Discussion Paper No. 278. I presented these results in seminars at Cowles and Columbia University. The results in this article, somewhat revised, became the first chapter in our book.

I returned to the University of Chicago in the fall of 1965, having then moved from the Business School to the Economics Department where I have remained. This shift did not affect my collaboration with Bob Graves. We continued our collaboration and met at least weekly for one or two hours in his splendid office as Associate Dean of the Business School.

A common practice at the time was to develop a dynamic theory in terms of differential equations and test it empirically using difference equations in the belief that difference equations approximate differential equations. However, differential equations introduce mathematical assumptions at odds with the economic aspects of the problem. This is a main theme in our Review of Economic Studies paper. For example, if the function representing net revenue at time t depends on a first derivative of the stock of capital, that is, investment, then the optimal policy mandates an instantaneous jump from the given initial stock to the optimal stock. In the discrete time version the move from the given initial stock is never instantaneous. Instead it is a gradual approach to the optimal stock closer and closer but never attaining it.

What lurks behind these results is a reality they try to describe. A derivative of a function gives the slope of a curve. If a continuous curve with a derivative at every point describes a variable moving over time, then its slope is the same before and after the present. This means if you know where you were, then you also know where you will be. This is absurd in real life. A random walk explains formally why it is absurd. A random walk can trace a continuous path over time that nowhere has a slope, a derivative. A random walk says you know where you are, where you were but not where you will be. We show in our paper how to predict the future from the past with as small an error as possible.

If unanticipated events are inevitable, then planning today for tomorrow must reckon on this. The notion that I have in mind an optimal stock today and instantaneously move to it today is absurd because what I think today is best for tomorrow will not be best for tomorrow. Indeed the assumption there is an optimal state is refuted by ignorance of the future. Dynamic programming is one way that tries to handle this problem. It works backward from the future to the present in order to figure out what seems best to do now. However, because the future is indefinitely remote from the present, we must approximate the situation with a never-ending sequence of, say, 5-year plans. Every year requires a new 5 year plan. This unending sequence of plans is the background for our work in Chap. 4.

In 1969–70 I was a Ford Foundation Fellow at Core, Université Catholique du Louvain. Once again the mail was our sole contact. We worked on what became Chaps. 2 and 4 in our book. Chapter 2 studies the demand for many durables as the maximum of the expected present value of utility derived from stocks of durables subject to a wealth constraint. There are also constraints describing the depreciation of the stock of durables. A novel feature is our explanation of time preference. Theorists typically assume present consumption is preferred to future consumption but do not explain why. We do so in Chap. 2. Instead of a discount factor we assume a constant probability of survival. Since survival is uncertain, the life span of a consumer is a random variable. The higher is the probability of survival, the longer the expected life. In terms of the expected present value, the probability of survival replaces the discount factor. To put it plainly, the reason that you prefer current consumption to future consumption is that you might not be around to consume anything in the future. The relevant consumer unit is not an individual but a sequence of descendants, a family tree sure to end sooner or later.

Chapter 4 is the most technical in our book. It considers a very general framework for the problems studied in the three preceding chapters. It does so by finding conditions on the shape of the functions that describe the returns. That more stringent conditions are needed for existence of an optimal policy over an infinite horizon is no surprise. The most useful sufficient condition imposes suitable curvature on these functions so that the model can attain the optimum.

We completed our work when I returned to Chicago in 1970. Our collaboration had continued for more than a decade. Bob rose higher in the administration of the University and became Associate Provost.

16.4 Collaborations with William Best, John Egan and Harlow Higinbotham

For more than 5 years I worked with Best and Egan on various projects as a consultant for A.T. Kearney, a leading management consultant firm. The first project was a study for EPA on the cost and benefits of regulations to abate noise. The most challenging project was a study for USRA, the federally appointed administrator of the bankrupt Penn-Central Railroad (Pennsylvania and New York Central) that hired Kearney to study the economics of their situation. USRA eventually formed Amtrak. This was one of the biggest bankruptcies in US history. By participating in this study I learned many details about running a railroad system. Here is a seemingly simple example. There are single tracks between most cities. To prevent collision between oncoming trains requires signaling systems and sidings so that one of the trains could be shunted on a side track and allow the other to pass. How many sidings? Where to put them? How much advance notice? Railroading poses many combinatorial problems. My experience became an important inspiration for my work on core theory. Eventually, I wrote four books and several articles on economic applications of core theory. Later I describe an article on this topic written together with Bill Sharkey.

My consulting work for A.T. Kearney led to one article published in an academic journal.

1975. The Theory of Supply with Applications to the Ethical Pharmaceutical Industry. Journal of Law and Economics 18:449–78 (October).

Two of my collaborators on this work, Egan and Higinbotham, had been my students. Two, Best and Egan, were consultants at A.T. Kearney. The empirical work in this article in Sections V and VI was for a study by Kearney financed by the Pharmaceutical Manufacturers' Association (PMA). PMA's sponsorship enabled us to get data for the empirical work from IMS of America, a firm that collects detailed data on sales and prices of prescription drugs prescribed by physicians in their private practice and by hospital staffs. Thus some data came from carbons of the physicians' prescriptions. PMA also had data on transaction prices of pharmaceuticals from manufacturers and wholesalers. These data are by 17 therapeutic categories. Only one condition was imposed on us. We could publish summary statistics of our results such as means, variances, correlations, regression equations and the like by these 17 categories, but we could not publish data for individual pharmaceuticals. Otherwise, we could write what we pleased without restrictions or constraints. We could accept or reject comments and criticisms by PMA. The Kearney project gave me a valuable opportunity to study an industry with detailed data rarely accessible to economists.

The first four sections of the article describe in detail a model of an industry on the postulate that industry outputs maximize the maximum net consumer surplus. The model provides a detailed framework using observable variables for our empirical work. It also includes promotional outlays by the manufacturers to measure their effects on prices, quantities and other variables.

Our empirical work divides the pharmaceutical market into two parts: the hospital market and the drug store market. Individual physicians decide for themselves what drugs to prescribe for their patients. It is different in hospitals where the formulary, the list of drugs that can be prescribed by a physician in the hospital, is determined by hospital committees. Although these committees include some physicians who practice in the hospital, we found an interesting difference between the drugs in the formulary and the drugs prescribed by individual physicians in their private practice. Committees were decidedly slower to adopt new drugs and drop old ones than the physicians in their private practice.

Promotional outlays are composed of advertising outlays and the expenses of the detail men who call on individual physicians and hospital physicians. The cost of detailing is a major portion of promotional outlays by pharmaceutical manufacturers. We found that promotional intensity varies inversely with concentration ratios by therapeutic category. The categories with the highest concentrations had the lowest promotional intensities and those with the lowest concentrations had the highest promotional intensities.

5. Collaboration with Harlow N. Higinbotham

1977. Organized Futures Markets: Costs and Benefits. Journal of Political Economy. 85: 969–1000 (October).

During my PhD orals in August 1956, Professor Theodore W. Schultz asked me whether I could explain which commodities are traded on organized futures markets and why similar commodities are not traded in these markets. I had no good answer at the time. I thought about his question for many years. Almost 20 years later many commodities had begun to be traded on organized futures markets. By then interest in answers to Schultz's question became increasingly important to many economists and especially to me.

Harlow was one of my PhD students. His dissertation was on grain futures markets. He became my research assistant on this risky problem. A grant from the National Science Foundation helped pay for his assistance and for the cost of collecting and analyzing the data.

The usual approach to futures markets by economists confines attention to hedging. My approach was different. The basic idea draws on the theory of money. An organized futures market creates a medium of exchange, a futures contract with many of the attributes of money. A futures contract facilitates trade in the commodity in the same way that the use of money in trade has advantages over barter. A transaction in a physical commodity has a myriad of unique features. A standard futures contract as defined by the organized exchange creates a financial instrument that can be traded without the parties to the trade knowing anything about each other apart from the fact that each is a member of the organized market. The seller incurs a liability to the clearing house of the organized market and the buyer acquires an asset from the same organization. Neither need have concern about the integrity of the other in the same sense that a seller who accepts \$10 cash in payment from the buyer need not worry about the buyer's credit rating. The clearing house of the exchange guarantees fulfillment of the terms of a transaction on the exchange. The argument implies that any commodity not made to order can benefit from the introduction of an organized futures market. The latter has a cost. An organized market will appear only for those commodities whose benefits outweigh costs. A typically successful futures market handles an important commodity. One not dominated by a few, relatively large traders. The situation resembles the economic ideal of a competitive market where none can have much effect on prices.

To proceed from this basic premise requires a more elaborate theory with testable implications. This theory forms a large part of the article. We collected data for 51 commodities divided into three groups: actively traded, less actively traded and dormant. In addition to variables measuring the various aspects of the size of the interest in these commodities, we had data on margins and commissions. The results substantially support the theory.

6. Collaboration with William W. Sharkey

1978. William W. Sharkey and Lester G. Telser. Supportable Cost Functions for the Multiproduct Firm. Journal of Economic Theory. 18: 23–37 (June).

I had become interested in economic applications of the theory of the core in the early 1960s. By 1978 I had published two monographs on this topic: first, Competition, Collusion and Game Theory, Chicago: Aldine-Atherton, 1972; second, Economic Theory and the Core, Chicago: University of Chicago Press, 1978. Later I published two more monographs on the core: A Theory of Efficient Cooperation and Competition. Cambridge, U.K.: Cambridge University Press, 1987; The Core Theory in Economics: Problems and Solutions. New York: Routledge, 2007.

Like Harlow Higinbotham, Bill Sharkey was one of my PhD students. His dissertation was "Existence of a Core in a Production Economy with Increasing Returns." My collaboration with Sharkey began after I had completed Economic Theory and the Core. Sharkey's dissertation refined the concept of natural monopoly for a multiproduct firm by using core theory. Technical problems arise when firms must use constant unit prices, not two-part prices. A constant unit price permits customers to buy as much as they want at the given price. A two-part price allows customers to do the same provided they pay a fixed amount at the outset independent of the transaction size, thus a two-part price. The situation using a constant unit price can work only for some commodities. These have cost functions compatible with the assumption of a natural monopoly. In these cases one firm can satisfy demand at a lower cost than two or more firms. These conditions resemble those for a non-empty core in a multiproduct industry.

16.5 Collaborations of the Second and Third Kind

My collaborations began almost at the beginning of my career as a professional economist. They continued for about two decades. Although I was the principal adviser for more than 100 doctoral dissertations, I did not follow a practice more common in the natural sciences, that of writing joint papers with my students on their dissertation research. I was the principal advisor for two of the three doctoral students at the University of Chicago who won the Ford Foundation Doctoral Prize in 1962 and 1963 but wrote no joint article with them. Even the two collaborations I describe here with two of my students, Harlow Higinbotham and Bill Sharkey, were related to but independent of their doctoral research. Two of my Mexican students won prestigious generous prizes from the central bank of Mexico for their doctoral dissertation I had supervised.

My collaborations took the form of supervision of doctoral dissertations. Their research topics often arose from the courses they took from me or from their participation in my workshop. The latter forum was the most active avenue of my collaboration with my graduate students. In short this collaboration which did not result in joint articles was still very important for me.

My collaborations took two other forms starting in 1980. The first was organization of a conference on futures and options markets financed by the Chicago Board of Trade. Eight participants including myself prepared scholarly papers on various topics related to these markets. These papers were presented at various seminars including formal symposia in Washington, D.C. There were lively exchanges among authors, discussants and members of the audience. The final versions were published in a special supplement of the Journal of Business April, 186, Volume 99, Number 2, Part 2.

Monetary economics was one of my major interests going back to 1953 when I was a member of the Money Workshop run by Milton Friedman. The stock market crash of October 1987 abruptly revived my interest. I became a member of a task force that intensively studied Black Monday and its aftermath. Six economists, Robert Barro, Eugene Fama, Daniel Fischel (lawyer), Allan Meltzer, Richard Roll and myself were the members of the task force. We held several meetings and had extensive, often heated, discussions of our results before they were published by Irwin in 1989, Black Monday and the Future of Financial Markets. For the past 20 years my interest in and publications on monetary topics have been one of my major activities.

16.6 Lessons of Collaboration

All my collaborations are voluntary. In some cases there is a division of labor reflecting our specialties, interests or comparative skills such as in exposition. In some cases our work was truly joint on the same topic or problem. Our discussions were always friendly even when critical. No one had the last word on anything. Compromise had to be by agreement. When we finished our joint work, we parted as friends. We remain friends to this day.

CHAPTER 17

Co-authors in History

Stanley Engerman

While reorganizing economics journals in my office, a collection going back about 50 years, there were several striking things to note about significant changes over time. One that has attracted considerable attention, both within and outside the profession, has been the changes in the method of presenting material. At the start, articles were presented mainly in verbal form, with occasional simple algebraic equations, sometimes geometric analysis, and rather straightforward tables of statistical data. Recent years have seen a preponderance of articles that draw heavily on mathematics and/or statistics, generally with multiple regression estimates. Whether, as some claim, this now means that economics as a discipline is now a science or, as others say, it has now been more removed from reality and any practical usefulness is a source of contention and remains debatable. What this suggests will be the nature of economics in the future is not at all clear. This major change, however, is not the subject of interest in this chapter.

S. Engerman (✉)
Department of Economics, University of Rochester, Rochester, NY, USA

M. Szenberg, L.B. Ramrattan (eds.), *Collaborative Research in Economics*, DOI 10.1007/978-3-319-52800-7_17

A second significant change has been in the nature of the authorship of these articles. Prior to the 1950s and 1960s almost all articles (and books) were authored singly, by one person, although the first footnote would contain acknowledgments to some helpful scholars, generally many fewer than we would find in today's articles and books. It is interesting that this now demonstrates a much broader circulation of writings, from early drafts to near-final versions. This aspect characterizes some recent work in other disciplines, such as history, as well as economics. The basic change in economics has been the great increase in the number of books and articles by two or sometimes three or four or even more co-authors. While the number of co-authors has not yet reached the numbers in many scientific papers, which can include a number of co-authors in double figures, and seem to not only include the senior researcher, but also give credit as co-authors to junior researchers, to laboratory assistants, and sundry other contributors.

The cause of the increased amounts of co-authorship in economics has posed a puzzle. There have been two hypotheses suggested in the literature—are the co-authors to be regarded as substitutes or as complements. The initial expectation, based on the importance of the division of labor, would be that co-authorship would include authors with different skills, for example, one based on the presentation of a theoretical argument and the other, an econometrician or empirically based scholar. The alternative argument is based on an economics of scale argument, with the two co-authors being complements, with the same basic skills and provide overlapping contributions. While the former argument, of substitutes, may have much appeal, curiously, at least in economics, co-authors seem to more often have rather similar skills brought to the research and writing, thus seeming to duplicate scholarly input and not following a strict division of labor.

I, myself, have some experience as a co-author of books and articles, and a co-editor of books, as well as being a sole author and editor. As with most who have written both solely and jointly, the published output has varied over time with no apparent logic—it depends on such questions as the nature of the problems, accidents of geography, and the nature of technology. Early on the main basis of exchanging intellectual ideas was direct mail, typed or handwritten matter, or telephone, and then Xerox, fax, computers, Skyping, IPhones, and related technologies, all of which accelerated the process of exchanging ideas and drafts for those co-authors not located at the same institution, as is frequently the case.

Patterns of co-authorship vary, depending on individual tastes and the problem to be studied. Roles are generally not as distinct as one finds in the musical theater, where traditionally one writes the music and the other the lyrics. In some cases there may be differences in which the former is written first and the latter then follows, and vice versa. I have worked as co-author or co-editor with some 50 individuals over a period of a half-century, mostly with economists, and also with a number of historians and a sociologist. While the nature of the collaborations did differ, there are a few general characteristics that I can point to.

The collaborative work on US slavery with Bob Fogel, culminating in the publication of *Time on the Cross,* began when we shared an office in the attic of a building at Johns Hopkins University, me as a TA and he as an instructor in statistics. First-year students were required to make a presentation to a meeting of what was called the Journal Club to discuss a recent journal article since the faculty did not think (correctly) that first-year students could prepare a research paper worth listening to. After some deliberation there was a choice between George Stigler's discussion of Ricardo's 93% labor theory of value and an article by Conrad and Meyer on the profitability of antebellum slavery. I opted for the latter—in retrospect a far, far better choice. The Journal Club had a lively discussion, and Bob and I continued discussions in our office. When Bob went to Rochester, Chicago, and Harvard we explored the possibility of writing an economic history text, which, however, didn't go anywhere. We also did some work on the antebellum iron industry, which led to several published articles.

We were both intrigued by the continued interest in the slavery debates, which until then meant mainly dealing with secondary sources. Our initial grant application was to collect more information from southern archives on slave prices and related materials to provide better estimates of the profitability of slavery. We began to take turns visiting southern archives, as did Bob's students Claudia Goldin and Richard Steckel, and we all found rich bodies of data of interest on aspects of slavery, which led ultimately to studies of fertility, mortality, health, sales of slaves, and numerous other issues providing information for the study of slavery and the southern economy.

My more recent collaborative book, with Kenneth Sokoloff, began from a conversation, this time in my backyard. Ken was a student of Bob's at Harvard, and I had previously spent considerable time talking with him about his thesis work and related research, which continued after he went to UCLA. We were both working with Bob on the project on human heights, while my major research interest continued to be on slavery. Ken's student, Steve Haber, who was at Stanford, organized a conference on the origins of Latin American backwardness and he asked his teacher, Ken, to prepare a paper on how a North American economic historian looked at Latin American backwardness. We discussed this question, including the role of climate and resources in the development of U.S. slavery and the relative decline of Latin American nations. Although there were many differences between North America and Latin America, we realized that we were dealing with similar models and interpretations. After exchanging rough drafts of a few pages, we then decided, with Steve Haber's approval, to write one article for the conference volume which, over several years, expanded into ten papers and one book.

Several of the co-edited books and articles with Bob Gallman and with Lance Davis, as well as an article with Claudia Goldin and several articles with Herb Klein, came about from discussions at meetings of economic historians, such as the Economic History Association, the Cliometrics Society, and the Development of the American Economy group of the National Bureau of Economic Research (NBER). Patrick O'Brien and I became friends when we were both at Oxford at the same time when I was spending a year's leave while he was teaching there. David Eltis was a Ph.D. student of mine in the history department at the University of Rochester. Just about all other collaborations evolved out of friendships, discussions at professional meetings, and scholarly conversations and correspondence.

Perhaps the most important characteristic was that almost all individuals and I had previously been friendly, or at least were acquaintances. And, no doubt luckily, I usually ended up as friendly with all but one or two when we finished as we were when we started. This obviously was a great help to the process. Clearly joint research and writing will lead to numerous debates and disputes that need to be settled in the process of writing, whether about points of presentation or of substance. To satisfactorily resolve these often depended on the logistic of the writing. Some scholars write a series of drafts, each of greater length and complexity, while others prefer to write one draft in consecutive order. Either approach has its advantages, the former may involve one writing the preliminary drafts and the other the making of revisions as they go along, while the latter means continuous discussions about style and substance. In either case, however, certain issues need to be confronted and resolved by one method or another. Usually, with goodwill on both sides, this should be possible with limited acrimony, although in one case an unusual resolution was introduced. When agreement on the wording in the text was not possible, we decided to present one version in the text and to add a footnote that presented the other argument, albeit in a non-combative manner. Periodically, but at first surprisingly rather seldom, some reader will raise a question about an apparent disconnect between the text and the footnote, since they found the conjunction puzzling. This is an extreme case—all others have been more easily solved.

The usual beginning of joint work can explain why most scholars have written with more than just one co-author, since most joint works seem to begin with a specific project in mind. Thus there has been some preliminary discussion and analysis. Sometimes there may be an agreement to work together, and then to try to find something to work on, but this seems less frequent.

What are the advantages and disadvantages of co-authorships? The one major disadvantage can be concern with the allocation of the relative contributions of each co-author, and the determination of how to parcel out credit with the listing of the paper's authorship. This can be done alphabetically, but this can create problems since the ordering of names on the publication can evolve in different ways. Some measured indexes of publications have listed in only the name of the first author given, not separate listings for both. Thus the second listed author is given no credit. In some cases the profession will provide attribution, in the absence of any direct information, to the elder or senior author or the otherwise more distinguished of the co-authors. There is no easy resolution to this problem. It is something that comes with the turf, and the other co-author can only do their best to establish an independent entity without bad-mouthing or antagonizing the other. In a few cases, however, to ensure that any ordering does not lead to invidious ranking, a footnote may be added to the effect that the ordering of names was done by a coin flip or some other random process.

Joint authorship poses some major difficulty for those writing letters of recommendation, where some allocation of relative contributions is needed when attempting to separately evaluate co-authors, and to explain on what basis this was done. Another problem arises if there are disagreements among the co-authors and there is no presentation that can finesse that issue. This separation of authors can be difficult to confront without some professional awkwardness or harassment, and perhaps the way out is to cease joint publication for that paper, with some way to determine who might publish the basic paper.

One major advantage of co-authorship is the division of labor regarding methods of approach. If there is some overlap, with both authors having similar skills, joint work can provide a format for a steady set of conversations exchanging ideas to the benefit of both, in a different manner than if the advice is given at only one time-limited meeting. Even if there is not a division of labor on methodological grounds, it is possible to share many benefits in the project, such as two separate readings of the same material or a division of readings between the co-authors, separate archival trips, and splitting labor and time on statistical analysis.

The recent growth in co-authoring is, no doubt, an indication that, to many, the advantages outweigh the disadvantages. Stanley Engerman, University of Rochester

CHAPTER 18

Collaboration: Making Eclecticism Possible in Economic Law and Politics

Susan Rose-Ackerman

I am essentially a solitary scholar. My most important books have no co-authors. I never collaborated with my thesis advisers or fellow graduate students. I have never run a research "shop" or "lab". I do not supervise large-scale empirical projects with teams of researchers funded by outside grants. Yet, over the years, I have engaged in a good deal of collaborative research.

In preparation for writing this chapter, I went through my resume and picked out my collaborative publications. There are 35 publications, including 8 edited books, and in 2016 I co-authored the second edition of my 1999 book on corruption. From 1997 to the present I have averaged one collaboration per year on a wide range of topics. My first publication in 1970 was a jointly authored article with a colleague at the US Council of Economic Advisers. My current work in comparative administrative law and my recent work on corruption involve co-authors. So why does it seem to me that I remain a solitary scholar in spite of this record?

I think the reason for this sense of independent scholarly practice is that my co-authorship has been very varied and is mostly one-shot. Few people

S. Rose-Ackerman (✉)
Yale Law School and Department of Political Science, New Haven, CT, USA

M. Szenberg, L.B. Ramrattan (eds.), *Collaborative Research in Economics*, DOI 10.1007/978-3-319-52800-7_18

have co-authored with me twice, not because I am hard to work with—I am not—but because my own interests have moved on. I have had many wonderful co-authors, and most of our publications could never have been written by myself acting alone. These collaborators brought specialized knowledge, insights, and time to the projects we worked on together, and our discussions enriched the final results. There is no substitute for a co-author if one seeks a careful reader of drafts.

Well, a spouse who is also an academic *is* a close substitute, and my husband, Bruce Ackerman, and I did work with two other authors on a book on water pollution policy in the Delaware River Estuary published in 1974. The collaboration spanned the birth of our two children—a baby-to-baby book. The end product was a fascinating case study of the political economy of policymaking, but Bruce was clearly the lead author who organized and edited the entire manuscript. I published a single-authored paper on effluent charges in connection with the book, but I decided that if I was ever going to establish myself as an independent scholar it was not a good idea to continue to collaborate with Bruce. He was going to be seen as the first author, not just because his name begins with A. Thus, we moved to the pattern we still follow of reading and discussing each other's work but not co-authoring anything. The result is a fine complementarity of interests and talents.

My subsequent collaborations fall into four categories. The first consists of early papers where my co-authors were more senior colleagues who wanted to work with me because of my specialized knowledge. These were followed, after receiving tenure, by work where I and my co-authors were closer to parity. Second are papers written with students and more junior colleagues where I was now the senior author, benefiting from the skills and knowledge of my collaborators. Third, are edited books organized with the help of other scholars. Finally, my recent work in comparative law and policy also involves mostly more junior scholars in projects that require a level of language ability and detailed country knowledge that would be impossible for me to master on my own.

The first category is small. After 1974 I did not collaborate again until the early 1980s. While still untenured, however, I had two collaborations with more senior Yale economists, J. Michael Montias and Robert Evenson. I was the junior author but one with specialized knowledge that I brought to our research topics. These papers were side projects carried out in parallel to my work on corruption and political economy.

Professor Montias was a specialist on Soviet-style economies, and we wrote a paper on corruption in such systems. Working on the USSR was odd for me as public-policy-oriented economist. Did we really think that Leonid Brezhnev would listen to our claims that the roots of Soviet corruption arose from the nature of the planned economy? In any case, that paper gave me the background later on to think about the shift in corrupt incentives after the fall of the Soviet Union and to contribute to that debate. At the time, it introduced me to the tribe of economists studying the Soviet Union. Because my co-author was out of town, I presented our paper at a conference in honor of the great specialist on the Soviet economy, Abram Bergson, and our article was eventually published in a festschrift for him. This group of scholars was not much interested in corruption per se; rather they were immersed in efforts to guess the size of the Soviet economy. They worried that their estimates were too low because they had poor data on the size of the underground vodka market, which was fueled by corruption.

Robert Evenson was an expert in agricultural economics. Here the connection was my interest in political economy. We studied the allocation of state and federal government funds for agricultural R&D and tried to explain their distribution based on the political incentives of legislators. My dissertation had been a study of the demand for used cars using large data sets covering prices, design features, and repair records. That research was frustrating and unsatisfying, and it put me off statistical work for years. However, I agreed to collaborate because Professor Evenson had the data all prepared, and he also had research assistants to do the actual analysis. I also managed to find data on the occupations of state legislators gathered by the insurance industry. The research proceeded. I am not a statistician but I have a pretty good eye for anomalies. I noticed some in the results, and I was alarmed to discover that two of our data sets measured R&D in man-years and the rest used dollars. Luckily, this could be corrected, but it was a lesson in not taking things for granted. If the results look weird, they probably are. However, this experience further discouraged me from statistical work. I returned to it only after the millennium but only in collaboration with skilled doctoral students.

Beginning in 1982, after receiving tenure at Columbia Law School, I plunged into the study of law, economics, and public policy, and began publishing in law reviews. At the same time, as the culmination of many years of study of the not-for-profit sector, I collaborated with a friend and fellow scholar, Estelle James, on a short book that was part of a series on various aspects of economic research. This was a very productive project that was truly a joint effort. It was a real pleasure to move from being a junior author to a project based on parity and balance. I also wrote an article with Jerry Mashaw of Yale Law School on federalism and regulation that was also a genuine joint effort.

The second phase of my collaborative work began when I returned to Yale in 1987 with a joint appointment between the Law School and the Department of Political Science. I started to supervise doctoral students in both law and political science, a relatively new experience for me. A number of collaborative articles grew out of these relationships. I have never had big, grant-funded projects. Rather, I hired graduate students on an ad hoc basis, worked with them on independent study projects, or identified term papers that might germinate into joint work. I have tried to be generous about joint authorship and to be sure that, if my name is attached, I really did contribute far beyond the usual advice that professors give to students.

In two cases these collaborations with doctoral students were a way to reenter the world of statistical work. A 2005 paper with Jana Kunicová, now at the World Bank, studied the links between corruption and the constitutional structure of government. It showed that presidential systems with proportional representation in the legislature are particularly vulnerable to corruption. Jennifer Tobin, now at Georgetown, is the first author of an article on bilateral investment treaties (BITs) because she is a very talented econometric analyst who was largely responsible for the empirics. Our interest was in the interaction between foreign direct investment and economic growth in low- and middle-income countries. We show that countries with poor institutions cannot bootstrap themselves up through BITs alone; they must also engage in internal reform; just signing treaties is not sufficient.

Other collaborations covered a wide range of topics from federalism, to corruption, to takings law, to executive power, to environmental policy. Sometimes I benefited from a student's skills in formal modeling as in a paper on BITs with Ryan Bubb. Other times it was the student's specialized legal knowledge in such areas as international law (Benjamin Billa) or the oil industry in Angola (Sinéad Hunt). Always, I learned a great deal from working closely on these articles with students and former students.

Third, beginning with my appointment at Columbia Law School, I began to organize conferences. I did so as a way of establishing myself in the field of law and economics and bringing to Columbia scholars I hoped to learn from. The conferences and the subsequent edited volumes were, of course, collaborative efforts in many respects, but the only explicit collaboration was a book on the hostile takeover wave then in progress in the 1980s edited by John Coffee, Louis Lowenstein, and myself, titled *Knights, Raiders, and Targets*. Corporate law is not my field, but I headed the Law School's Center for Law and Economic Studies and helped Jack and Lou put together the program. More important for my own future scholarly development was a conference I organized that, for the first time, brought together professors of administrative law with economists and political scientists studying the modern regulatory state.

More recently, I have also edited a number of volumes, some with co-authors, that reflect my research interests in corruption, government reform, and comparative administrative law. Most of these were preceded by conferences where each chapter was discussed with others who were contributing to the project. I published three co-edited conference volumes on corruption with Donatella della Porta, Tina Søreide, and Paul Carrington, respectively, and two on comparative administrative law both with Peter Lindseth. (The second volume adds Blake Emerson as an editor.) These are all, I believe, volumes that are greater than the sum of their parts. The authors are implicitly in conversation with each other, and as editors we composed introductory essays that develop those connections. In the corruption field, I have repeated that pattern with Paul Lagunes, a former student now on the faculty at Columbia University. We have organized a conference at Yale in 2014 on the topic with an edited volume that appeared in 2015.

The fine example of an edited book that was the product of a deeper collaboration is the project at Collegium Budapest on Honesty and Trust in Post-Socialist Societies. It was the direct outgrowth of my 1999 book *Corruption and Government*, but it went beyond that book's focus on bribery and kickbacks to encompass a range of difficulties facing the post-socialist societies as they transitioned to democracy and the market economy. This collaboration arose when Janos Kornai, a senior Hungarian economist and a fellow of the Collegium, came to believe that the problems of transition in Eastern Europe went beyond macroeconomic reform to encompass problems of honesty and trust in society. He read my 1999 book and contacted me for a conversation at his home in Cambridge, Massachusetts, where he spent half the year teaching at Harvard. Janos had been an early critic of the socialist political-economic system and now saw significant problems with the new regime. We worked together to bring to Budapest a group of scholars both from the region and from Western Europe and the USA with an interest in the creation of legitimate, reform governments. I spent the fall of 2002 working with him at the Collegium, and we organized three workshops there that eventually resulted in two edited books published in 2004 (one with Bo Rothstein as a third editor). This project gave me a chance to continue my interest in comparative law and politics beyond my earlier the work on German and American environmental policy and law. I was able to publish my own book in 2005, *From Elections to Democracy: Building Accountable Government in Hungary and Poland*. Writing that book would not have been feasible without my collaboration with Janos on the broader project.

Finally, my current comparative work deserves special mention. Comparative law is difficult to do on one's own. It is tailor-made for collaborative work. Few scholars have sufficient language facility and country-specific institutional knowledge to range widely on their own. Administrative law, in particular, can be rather insular. Yet, the basic public law problem of combining competence with democratic legitimacy and the protection of rights cuts across borders. Recently, I have been working with a series of co-authors to expand my reach. My first work in comparative public law and policy was a single-authored book on environmental policy in Germany and the USA published in 2005. To write that book, I learned German and lived in Berlin for a year. However, to go further in the comparative direction I needed co-authors, and I have been fortunate to be able to work with several talented colleagues. As the result of a sabbatical at Sciences Po in 2011, I revived my French and began a project on French administrative law. This led to an on-going collaboration with Thomas Perroud, a young French academic specializing in administrative law who has recently been appointed to a professorship at the Sorbonne. In 2011 we went on interviews together, he checked my understanding of French texts, and contributed his own insights. After publishing two articles on administrative law and public policymaking in France, we are discussing follow-up projects. I also collaborated with former students from Argentina and the Philippines on an article on hyper-presidentialism, and with a Brazilian scholar, whose doctoral study was in Italy and France, on judicial review of administrative action in the USA, Canada, France, and Italy. Finally, in 2015 I published a book called *Due Process of Lawmaking: The United States, South Africa, Germany and the European Union* with Stefanie Egidy and James Fowkes, from Germany and South Africa, respectively. While both were students at Yale Law School, we began with the idea of writing a law review article together, but the project burgeoned and took on a book-length life of its own. All these projects arose from conversations with these talented students and scholars that led me to propose collaboration.

How do I actually work with collaborators? It depends on the type of research and the talents of the individual scholars. For statistical papers, my co-author is in charge of the data collection and analysis, and I review and discuss both the empirical strategy ex ante and the results ex post. For papers that require in-depth examination of sources, we share the load. For elite interview studies, I do most of the interviews with my co-author participating whenever language differences could be an issue. For conference organizing, we share the work depending on our relative strengths and time available. For the book on due process of lawmaking, each of us was responsible for our own country chapter, but I read, commented on, and edited the entire manuscript to be sure that the chapters fit together. Often, I will react to a draft by asking a co-author to document or better explain an argument or factual claim. We do multiple drafts—a reflection of the way that I always work. Get something on paper so you have something specific to react to and do not take first efforts too seriously. Reading these early drafts will show you where the holes are in the argument and suggest new directions. There is sometimes a Rashomon-like character to collaboration. I read a draft, see something that does not quite fit, ask my co-author to investigate further, and he or she sometimes returns with an entirely new perspective on the situation we are studying. We iterate, I hope, toward a better understanding of our object of study.

I am very grateful to my co-authors. They have permitted me to expand my reach—both for concrete reasons such as my limited time, econometric training, and language facility, and for intellectual reasons as they challenge and educate me and push my thinking in new directions. It has been fun and will continue to be so.

Collaborative Work in Chronological Order: Susan Rose-Ackerman (With David Ott) "An Analysis of the Revenue Effects of Proposed Substitutes for Tax Exemption of State and Local Bonds," *National Tax Journal* 23:397–406 (December 1970).

(With Bruce A. Ackerman, Dale W. Henderson and James Sawyer, Jr.) *The Uncertain Search for Environmental Quality*, New York: Free Press, 1974. (With Bruce A. Ackerman and Dale W. Henderson) "The Uncertain Search for Environmental Policy: The Costs and Benefits of Pollution Control Along the Delaware River," *University of Pennsylvania Law R.* 121:1225–1309 (1973).

(With J. M. Montias) "Corruption in Soviet-type Economies: Theoretical Considerations." In Steven Rosefielde, ed., *Economic Welfare and the Economics of Soviet Socialism: Essays in Honor of Abram Bergson*, New York: Cambridge University Press, 1981, pp. 53–83.

(With Jerry Mashaw) "Federalism and Regulation," in G. Eads and M. Fix, eds. *The Reagan Regulatory Strategy: An Assessment*, Urban Institute Press, 1984, pp. 111–152.

(With Robert Evenson) "The Political Economy of Agricultural Research and Extension: Grants, Votes and Reapportionment," *American J. of Agricultural Economics* (February 1985) 67:1–14.

(With Estelle James) *The Nonprofit Enterprise in Market Economies*, Chur, Switzerland: Harwood Academic Publishers, 1986.

(With Mark Geistfeld) "The Divergence Between Social and Private Incentives to Sue: A Comment on Shavell, Menell and Kaplow," *Journal of Legal Studies* 16:483–491 (June 1987).

(With John C. Coffee, Jr. and Louis Lowenstein) *Knights, Raiders and Targets: The Impact of the Hostile Takeover*, NY: Oxford University Press, 1988.

(With Nicholas Economides), "Differentiated Public Goods: Privatization and Optimality," in Hiroshi Ohta and Jacques Francois Thiese, eds., *Does Economic Space Matter?*" London: Macmillan, 1993, pp. 111–132.

(With Jonathan Rodden) "Does Federalism Preserve Markets?" *Univ. of Va. Law R.* 83:1521–1572 (1997).

(With Silvia Colazingari) "Corruption in a Paternalistic Democracy: Lessons from Italy for Latin America," *Political Science Quarterly* 113:447–470 (1998).

(With Jacqueline Coolidge) "Kleptocracy and Reform in African Regimes: Theory and Cases," in K.R. Hope and B.C. Chikulo, eds., *Corruption and Development in Africa: Lessons from Country Case Studies*, London: Macmillian Press, 1999.

(With Jim Rossi) "Disentangling Deregulatory Takings," *Virginia L. R.*, 86: 1435–1495 (2000).

(With Kirsten Engel) "Environmental Federalism in the United States: The Risks of Devolution," in Daniel Esty and Damien Geradin, eds., *Regulatory Competition and Economic Integration: Comparative Perspectives*, Oxford: Oxford University Press, 2001, pp. 134–153.

(With Donnatella Della Porta) *Corrupt Exchanges: Empirical Themes in the Politics and Political Economy of Corruption* Baden-Baden: Nomos Verlagsgesellschaft, 2002.

(With Achim Halpaap), "Democratic Environmental Governance and the Aarhus Convention: The Political Economy of Procedural Environmental Rights," in Timothy Swanson and Richard Zerbe, eds., *Research in Law and Economics -- 2001*, Amsterdam: Elsevier, 2002, pp. 27–64.

(With Jeff Bowen), "Partisan Politics and Executive Accountability: Argentina in Comparative Perspective," *Superior Court Economic Review* 10:157–210 (2003).

(With János Kornai) *Building a Trustworthy State in Post-Socialist Societies,* NY: Palgrave, 2004.

(With János Kornai and Bo Rothstein) *Creating Social Trust in Post-Socialist Societies* NY: Palgrave, 2004.

(With Jana Kunicová) "Electoral Rules and Constitutional Structure as Constraints on Corruption," *British Journal of Political Science* 35: 573-606 (2005).

(With Ryan Bubb), "BITs and Bargains: Strategic Aspects of Bilateral and Multilateral Regulation of Foreign Investment," *International Review of Law and Economics* 27: 291-311 (2007).

(With Benjamin Billa), "Treaties and National Security," *NYU Journal of International Law and Politics,* 40:437–496 (Winter 2008).

(With Peter Lindseth) *Comparative Administrative Law* Edward Elgar, Cheltenham UK and Northhampton MA, 2010.

(With Jennifer Tobin), "When BITs Have Some Bite: The Political-Economic Environment for Bilateral Investment Treaties," *Review of International Organizations* 6:1–32 (2011)

(With Diane A. Desierto, & Natalia Volosin), "Hyper-Presidentialism: Separation of Powers without Checks and Balances in Argentina and the Philippines," *Berkeley J. of Inter L.* 29: 101–188 (2011).

(With Tina Søreide) *International Handbook on the Economics of Corruption*, Volume II, Edward Elgar, Cheltenham UK and Northhampton MA, 2011.

(With Sinéad Hunt) "Transparency and Business Advantage: The Impact of International Anti-Corruption Policies on the United States National Interest," *New York University Law School Annual Survey of American Law, 2011* 67: 433–466 (2012).

(With Paul Carrington) *Anti-Corruption Policy: Can International Actors Play a Constructive Role?* Carolina Academic Press, Durham NC, 2013.

(With Rory Truex) "Corruption and Policy Reform," in Bjørn Lomborg, ed. *Global Problems, Smart Solutions: Costs and Benefits*, Cambridge, UK: Cambridge University Press, 2013.

(With Thomas Perroud) "Policymaking and Public Law in France" *Columbia Journal of European Law*,19(2): 225–312 (2013).

(With Thomas Perroud) "Impact Assessment in France: U.S. Models and French Legal Traditions," European Public Law 20(4): 649–680 (November 2014).

(With Eduardo Jordao) "Judicial Review of Executive Policymaking in Advanced Democracies: Beyond Rights Review" *Administrative Law Review* 66(1): 1–72 (March 2014).

(With Stefanie Egidy and James Fowkes) "Due Process of Lawmaking": the United States, South Africa, Germany, and South Africa, Cambridge UK: Cambridge University Press, 2015.

Single-Authored Work Cited: Controlling Environmental Policy: The Limits of Public Law in Germany and the United States, New Haven: Yale University Press, 1995.

Corruption and Government: Causes, Consequences, and Reform, Cambridge: Cambridge University Press, 1999.

From Elections to Democracy: Building Accountable Government in Hungary and Poland, Cambridge and New York: Cambridge University Press, 2005.

CHAPTER 19

Collaboration and the Development of Experimental Economics: A Personal Perspective

Vernon L. Smith

The economics profession has a long tradition of being identified with the sole proprietor model of research, publication, and education. The history of economic thought shows that economics was written by lone contributors from classical to neo-classical economics, and into the mid-twentieth century. Graduate students of mine have read vintage articles and books by individual scholars, as did our predecessors. With a few exceptions I followed that tradition for the first two decades of my career, 1955–1975. The great change came in the years 1975–1985, my first decade at the University of Arizona (U of A). I had followed a student-centered research seminar teaching model at Purdue, from 1963 to 1967, then imported

This entry is a revision and extension of portions of Chap. 13 in my *Discovery a Memoir*, 2008. Also see S. Rassenti, V. Smith and B. Wilson, "Using Experiments to Inform the Privatization/Deregulation Movement in Electricity," *The Cato Journal*, Winter, 21 (3) pp. 515–544, 2002.

V.L. Smith (✉)
Argyros School of Business and Economics and School of Law, Chapman University, Orange, CA, USA

M. Szenberg, L.B. Ramrattan (eds.), *Collaborative Research in Economics*, DOI 10.1007/978-3-319-52800-7_19

that model into Caltech in 1974, but with only a few joint collaborative research exercises. At Caltech, Charlie and I had an undergraduate student, Ross Miller that produced out joint paper for the *Quarterly Journal of Economics*, 1977.

19.1 Students Had a Prominent Role in the Development and Study of Experimental Markets

From the beginning at the U of A I had a number of key undergraduate and graduate students in experimental economics classes who were instrumental in developing and implementing a vision of computerizing the protocols for running subjects in the great range of experiments that we quickly had under way. These students deserve full credit for creating Arizona's methodological revolution in experimental economics. My role was to share my curiosity, discuss designs for experiments, and generally give students wide-ranging freedom to explore. My impression was that they liked it. Most were in economics, but engineering was represented: Arlington Williams and Stephen Rassenti (systems engineering) were graduate students, while Mike Vannoni (mechanical engineering), Vickie Coppinger (Sandler), and Jon Titus were undergraduates in economics. The list was expanded to include undergraduates Jonathan Ketcham and Bruce Roberson, and graduate students, Don Coursey, Dave Porter, and many others in economics who followed the first wave. Without them, their dedication, and incredible smarts—each in his or her own way—nothing very unusual is likely to have come out of Arizona.

The curriculum mechanism for developing this program was to offer an undergraduate and graduate course in experimental economics; at first the two courses had to be combined into one to make a quorum. As in most universities, there was a committee process for getting approval for new courses—a process bound to be compromised or fail when you want to teach any course in a subject that is not recognizable as part of most of the faculty's training when they were in graduate school 25 years earlier. The way to work effectively with this impediment was to use an approved special studies or other inactive course number, and later change its name and description. Every bureaucratic question has a bureaucratic answer. It is good that new course offerings are not slam dunk easy; when experimental economics started the odds that it would fail were high. It turned out to not fail with the students and that was its ultimate success with the profession. I can't imagine it happening in one of our more prestigious universities. You need one that is hungry and backed by an administration that is innovative; for me, Purdue fit that bill, 1955–1967, and U of A, in the transforming years, 1975–1985 and after.

These new courses introduced students to the literature of experimental economics, but I gave them no examinations on their comprehension of the readings. Research is not about memorizing article content, but understanding it well enough to use selectively in your own research development; most of it you probably will not use, and no need to encourage the idea that all results are of equal value.

I did not administer a course examination for the next 25 years; that record has now stretched into 40 years. We used the examination period scheduled at the end of each semester for completing our discussion and presentations. This was probably in violation of a university rule requiring all courses to have a final examination, but neither easily enforced or interpreted. Such rules do not keep chiselers from chiseling, tend to hamper innovation, and are based on a false premise. Education is not about knowing things. It's about discovering and implementing what you can do with what you know. It's about learning to learn, and developing the habit of learning. In place of exams, we each made presentations, and each student was to propose an experimental study. We concentrated heavily on what might be done and then doing it; on learning by doing; on learning new skills and tools, but as part of solving a problem that required one to learn or utilize whatever skills were needed. Just as competition in the economy is a discovery procedure, so is education. Both are search-learning processes.

Several students over these years really got into the exercise and defined projects that required more than a three-credit course investment. I enrolled them in one or two additional special-studies courses to enable them to complete their projects. Some voluntarily learned computer programming as part of their experimental research program.

Arlington Williams was the pioneer. In 1975–1976 Arlie wrote the first electronic version of the continuous double auction (DA is a real-time bid/ask/contacting procedure modeled on the loose rules I had used at Purdue in January 1956). It was tested in the summer of 1976. We ran 12 experiments using designs that were identical to those we had used in earlier oral DA experiments. Arlie wrote up the comparisons showing that, with inexperienced subjects, the oral DA produced equilibrium more rapidly than the new electronic version but that there was no discernible difference for once-experienced subjects.

It seems that the brains of the time learned more rapidly to function in this market task by processing oral input and responding orally than by utilizing visual input followed by typed trading responses. Surely the cost of transacting was higher in the latter than in the former, and illustrates how transactions cost impacts participatory performance. But once those computer-assisted communication channels are practiced and become autonomic, the behavior is the same. By the summer of 1976 Arlie—who was learning by doing—knew a tremendous amount of programming (the Tutor language) for the Plato system. He did what the slovenly would never do; he started over, and rapidly produced a more streamlined piece of software still in use but long under continuous modification.

The new program developed four versions of the bid/ask trading process, allowing us to learn much about the anatomy of the DA rules. This was not the first time for computerized experiments, but it was part of a sustained effort motivated by trading methods in practice … DA, posted offer (PO), sealed bid, and/or offer procedures.

We were doing in the lab what later became known as e-commerce when it emerged on the Internet.

Mike Vannoni was also a front-runner and, at about the same time as Arlie, was into using Plato for sealed-bid-offer, two-sided trading mechanisms. That collaboration led to our American Economic Review (AER) piece in 1982. Vicki Coppinger, Jon Titus, and I ran manual experiments comparing the English, Dutch, Sealed Bid First and Second Price auctions, and Vicki followed up with a Plato version of the sealed-bid auctions. This was the first of several papers that I would write with undergraduates at Arizona. They deserved more than a footnote at the bottom of the title page of the article that resulted from our joint discoveries.

I submitted the Coppinger, Smith, and Titus piece to the *Journal of Political Economy*, where it was accepted subject to the condition that it be drastically shortened. Since I did not want to shorten it for the editor—Sam Peltzman at the time—we sent it to Bob Clower, editor of *Economic Inquiry*, where it appeared in full (1980). That was a good decision: Jon, Vicki, and I won a best-article award from the journal for that paper.

I worked for several months with Jonathan Ketcham to develop a smoothly functioning, rich, multifaceted version of the PO market mechanism, leading to a comparison between DA and PO by Jonathan, Arlie, and me. We published a shortened version of it in the *Review of Economic Studies* (1984).

Mike also developed Plato versions of various public good mechanisms that I had begun studying earlier at Caltech, 1974–1975. The principal study using this software was published in the *American Economic Review* (1980). This was followed up by Don Coursey, who wrote a more comprehensive program for studying private, public, and externality-good decision mechanisms as three different forms of the same underlying software program.

19.2 Rapid but Unanticipated Innovation Soon Followed

When we started to do computer-assisted experiments in economics, 1975–1978, we thought we were making it easier to run the kind of experiments that we had been running for years and to record the observations more easily and accurately. The innovation was introduced in a backward-looking context—natural, because of the great difficulty of resolving forward-looking uncertainties. Within a year or two we found that computerization was changing our experience, and gradually transforming the way we thought about the whole experimental program. The transformation was not planned. That is a fundamental truth about how norms, practices, and institutions emerge, and why they are so far beneath our conscious awareness. What we learned experientially when we became computerized was that we could execute far more complex experiments and process data from much larger message spaces. Soon we were running experiments that we would never have dreamed of doing theretofore. In particular, a central processor could apply optimization, coordination, and scheduling algorithms to the willingness-to-pay and willingness-to-receive messages of decentralized agents with dispersed information.

With Stephen Rassenti—skilled in developing optimization algorithms—we developed a whole new approach to using the lab to test-bed new market designs and person-machine decision interactive systems. The potential was to replace ponderous, inefficient, command-and-control regulatory systems with self-ordering, self-regulating systems within a framework of institutional (property or *propriety* right) rules. Complex markets could be coordinated with support system designs that simplified individual decision operations. Individuals supplied willingness-to-pay and willingness-to-receive judgments based on local knowledge, valuations, and conditions; algorithms, applied to the messages from dispersed human agents, assured that each could do no better for him- or her-self against the constraints expressed by all others and by the physical and security boundaries of the exchange system.

From its 1950s–1960s beginning at Purdue, my thoughts gradually evolved and were influenced by the literature and ideas from many others, including Charles Plott and his co-authors in the late 1970s and into the 1980s. There was a continuous transformation of our thinking as we became more experienced with a great variety of different experimental and institutional contexts. Moreover, the community of scholars participating in that process was growing rapidly. The biggest impact on my thinking came in my joint work with Stephen Rassenti beginning in the 1970s. The airlines were being deregulated, and Stephen was looking for a thesis topic. I pointed out to him that airline "deregulation" concerned only decentralizing the choice of airline operating routes; airplanes still had to land and take off in safety-controlled local air space, and the authorities were not thinking about the runway slot rights. Suppose a market was to be made in these rights. How would you do it? Ask and it shall be given: this led to our first case of a "smart" computer-assisted market and culminated in Stephen's important 1981 thesis "0-1 Allocation Problems: Algorithms and Applications." E-commerce in the lab beginning in 1975 changed the way we thought about market design and test-bedding. It was now possible to combine the information advantages of decentralized decision—for example bidding to supply or to buy—with the coordination advantages of the central processing of messages to achieve more efficient outcomes. The excitement of discovery was exhilarating.

Isaac, Grether, and Plott had been the first in responding to airline deregulation, proposing a complex auction market for runway slots. The slots at each airport would be simultaneously and independently auctioned, followed by an aftermarket where people could re-trade to fill in the missed combinatorial packages. It involved hand-run experiments, but we saw a way of doing it in one primary computer-assisted auction. Moreover, this exercise generalized to the concept of "smart" computer-assisted markets. Some thought the politicians would never buy it, but we could not have cared less because our constituency didn't consist only of politicos. Stephen, I, and a mix of co-authors over the next 20 years—Kevin McCabe, David Porter, Mark Olson, Jim Murphy, Jeff Banks, Bart Wilson, Elizabeth Hoffman, and Brian Binger—would apply these principles to gas pipeline, water, and electrical networks; to scheduling; and to the Federal Communication Commision (FCC) spectrum auctions.

Hence, beginning in the years from 1975 to 1980, test-bedding became an integral part of a much larger program in economic system design, including the developing of the Smart Computer-Assisted Market. The rapid advance in computer and communication technology seemed to me to make this development inevitable.

Every advance always built on the experience of others—there was no need to repeat what turned out after the fact to be earlier shortcomings. Arlie found that out in 1976 and started over, reprogramming his Plato DA software.

New technologies always foster enormous resistance from the status quo alternatives. I had experienced directly the resistance to the computerized trading of securities beginning in the 1960s (See *Discovery*, 2008, pp 201–203), and that resistance would extend to the introduction of derivatives and currency trading—new products traded the old-fashioned way. But after 20–30 years new technologies had started to make inroads, the Internet began—slowly at first—to take over; trading more and more made use of new software innovations. By the 1990s, the world was starting to look more like the one we had been studying in computerized laboratories.

The experimental program at Arizona, particularly its e-commerce version, was operating at full speed by 1980. Based on my earlier work on the Treasury bill auctions and the new experiments on single object auctions with Jon Titus and Vicki Coppinger, I had received an National Science Foundation (NSF) grant to extend the experimental study of auctions. Bruce Roberson had developed the Plato software to do more rigorous computerized experiments for comparing single unit auctions; Jim Cox and Jimmie Walker had joined the Arizona faculty and became part of the NSF project on auction theory and experiment. We lost Jimmie Walker to Indiana University, where he took root in a fertile environment of political economy research with Elinor (Lin) Ostrom.

Mark Isaac had also come to the U of A after completing his Ph.D. at Caltech, and he and I collaborated on several papers dealing with industrial organization and antitrust issues.

19.3 Not All Markets Are Born Equal: The Enigma of Asset Market Bubbles

A really significant new initiative by Arlie and me was our work on asset trading in the early 1980s. At Caltech, Charlie Plott, Ross Miller, and I had done two experiments in which demand had cycled in a regular shifting, repeated "seasonal" pattern of low, high, low, high, and so on, in successive trading periods. In one of these experiments we had six buyers, six sellers, and two "traders." The buyers were assigned unit values, the sellers assigned unit costs, with the traders having the exclusive right to buy in one period and carry over the units for resale in the next period. When demand was low, only the very lowest cost sellers are able to make profitable sales; when demand was high many high cost sellers can sell profitably. The efficiency of this market can be increased by speculative traders who buy in the low price season and resell in the high price season, raising the price in the off-season, lowering the price in the on-season. Speculation worked as predicted by theory: price in both seasons tended toward the same level with traders buying excess units produced above current demand in the low season and reselling them in the high demand season.

The Miller, Plott, and Smith experiments were all done by hand, and Arlie went to work to modify his e-commerce software to allow for the added activity of traders who could buy in any period and sell in another period. The main idea was to replicate and do many more than just two of the original speculation experiments. We did, and new research contributions came out of that exercise.

Independently of this work we had been talking about a research program in which we would study asset market trading. So far, all our work had involved supply and demand markets with per-period flows across successive periods. In effect these were markets for consumer non-durables that could not be re-traded, like hamburgers and haircuts. As I recall it, one day it struck me that Arlie's program introducing speculative traders—who could buy for resale in a supply and demand setting—involved asset purchase and resale. Why not take that new code, add provision for "dividend" realizations from assets units held in a period, and develop a new stand-alone program dedicated to asset trading across time, based on initial assignments of "cash" and "shares" to each subject in an experiment? Arlie disappeared to create the new software and we were soon off and running.

However, our expectations concerning the results from the first asset experiments were not fulfilled by a long shot. We had a lot to learn from our subjects, and nothing to learn from extant theory, about this new environment. Recall that my expectations were not fulfilled in the first supply and demand experiments. Supply and demand theory worked far better than anyone—certainly that I—had expected, and that led to experiments trying to better understand those strong results, and to check its robustness across trading institutions. In the new asset market experiments the data did not converge quickly to the rational expected fundamental dividend holding value of the shares.

Originally the idea had been to begin with a protocol and environment so transparent that we could expect a rational expectations outcome, then—so went our thinking—we would manipulate information and see if we could create bubbles. Those best laid plans got shot down with the very first, "transparent environment experiments." We observed big bubbles—large deviations from fundamental value. (Eventually published in Smith, Vernon L., Gerry L. Suchanek and Arlington W. Williams, 1988. "Bubbles, Crashes and Endogenous Expectations in Experimental Sopt Asset Markets." Econometrica, 56, 1119–1151.) Others could not believe our results—hardly a surprise, neither had we, initially. (As I recall, Collin Camerer, then at Wharton, called our results an "Arizona phenomenon," but subsequently the phenomenon was widely replicated with different subject pools by different, mostly skeptical, experimentalists.)

Charlie Plott did not believe our results. I suggested to Dave Porter that he go to Caltech and conduct one of our asset market experiments, which he did; even better he ran it in Charlie's class. Of course his class yielded pretty much a standard garden variety 15-period asset trading bubble—no surprise event, as by then we were getting used to it. I was yet to run them with corporate middle-level executives and a group of over-the-counter stock traders in Chicago. There was a new wrinkle that Charlie wanted to try: give the subjects a blank table and require them each period to write down what was the next period's fundamental value. Our Plato System software reminded the subjects each period what the new dividend-adjusted value of a share was in the next period, but Charlie thought he would make them write it down! But then, midstream in the experiment, Charlie looked out and notes they are not all of them writing it down. Dave walks to a subject failing to comply, reminds him and is told: "You write it down I am busy trading."

Many experiments and papers later failed to find treatments that squelched these bubble tendencies, with the exception of subject experience: bring the same subjects back a second time, and a third time, and the third time around the trades finally were approximating the decline in true fundamental value. Then, finally, with Mark van Boening and Charissa Wellford we found a simple treatment that defanged bubbles from the start. The new procedure was to pay the dividend at the end of the experiment, based on a single draw from a distribution with mean 15 times larger than had been the mean per-period draw in earlier experiments. Hence, cash dividends were no longer a flow of new money each period into the subjects' trading accounts. We did eight experiments under these conditions and only one yielded a small bubble. In effect, no money flowing in, no bubble. This was further confirmed in a new series of experiments in which we paid half the per-period dividend into their trading account, withholding the rest until paid to them at the end of the experiment; this we surmised should yield bubbles in between the no-dividend and full-dividend per-period payment protocols. It worked: We observed intermediate level bubbles. Hence, bubbles in the lab were driven primarily by the inflow of new cash; stop the inflow and you stop the propensity to bubble. (See our paper "Dividend Timing and Behavior in Laboratory Asset Markets," *Economic Theory*, 16 (3) 2000, pp. 567–583; reprinted in T. Cason and C. Noussair, editors, *Advances in Experimental Economics*. Ney York: Springer, 2000.)

19.4 The Lab as a Test-Bed for Designer Markets

In 1984 The Arizona Corporation Commission (ACC) provided us with an unprecedented opportunity to examine state utility regulation and to consider its alternatives. It was a political accident. The ACC consists of a three-person elected commission. One of the commissioners had died in office; another, with higher political ambitions, had resigned. Arizona's Governor Babbitt appointed two replacement commissioners to sit until the next regular election. One was Marianne Jennings, a professor of business ethics at Arizona State University; the other was Junius Hoffman, professor of law at the University of Arizona. I knew neither of them at the time, but I later heard that both had been astonished to learn what transpires under the heading of "utility regulation." It was a form of the old adage: Once you have seen sausage made, you can't eat it.

Neither of the new Babbitt appointees had any interest in running for the office and continue as commissioners, but they did desire to have some influence on the process beyond their short tenures. Two of our graduate students were working at the ACC: Dave Porter and Glenn Vail. They educated the ACC on the capabilities of experimental methods with the result that the Commission saw an experimental research project as a way of bringing a fresh perspective on regulation into the public domain. They were right, and they were successful in having a long-term impact on utility liberalization, but not seriously in Arizona to this day.

In the 1980s it was almost universally believed that economies of scale, economies of coordination, and "wasteful" duplication of wires in distribution and transmission meant that electricity was inherently a natural monopoly. The same arguments have long been used to justify the US Postal and telephone monopolies.

There were no more than a handful of academic and industry dissenters who saw any merit in deregulating electric generation—one of the latter turned out to be Ted Welp, the innovative president and CEO of Tucson Electric Power (TEP). The traditional unchallenged assumptions of natural monopoly produced a world in which no one had asked, "If you were to deregulate electricity and allow markets to discipline prices, how would you do it, and how might it work?" If you don't ask, you won't think about or investigate possible answers.

A year later, in 1985, we filed our report recommending that the "energy business" be separated from the "wires business." Generators would be sold or financially spun off with separate managements, say into five companies that would bid into a spot market—the Arizona Energy Exchange—to supply power to the network. Local distribution utilities do not have to produce their own energy any more than they need to manufacture the trucks used by their service technicians. Also, we proposed that the Exchange be organized as a two-sided bidding mechanism, with demand-side wholesalers and other buyers empowered to bid any of their interruptible loads into the spot market.

Our experiments would in time show that strategic demand-side bidding easily controlled price spikes in wholesale markets like those in California, the Midwest, the South, and the East Coast. The wires company does not have to provide its customer's energy any more than a car rental company needs to supply you with gasoline—you can buy your own in a separate market. We argued that the rental rate for the wires could or would continue to be regulated, but the utility would be prohibited from having the exclusive legal right to tie the sale of energy to the rental of the wires. Thus any regulations requiring you to buy your energy, as well as rent the wires, from the same local utility would be discarded. In the non-regulated sector of the economy, tie-in sales are illegal, so extending this principle to the utilities was hardly revolutionary. Utility regulation had become an excuse for exempting these companies from antitrust.

To provide some contestability in the wires business, we also proposed that the franchised legal protection of the local wires monopoly be eliminated. Specifically, utility easements on all property would be declared open to entry by alternative cable and pole users, subject only to the usual environmental and safety considerations. If electricity is truly a "natural" monopoly, it doesn't require any "unnatural" legal protection. Right? Not quite: historically, legal help had been supported by the industry just in case the monopoly was not sufficiently "natural." If electricity had ever been a natural monopoly, technological change had undermined it, as it had its sister industry, telecommunications. Our proposed changes would have aligned the organization of the industry with contemporary technology.

Before filing the final report we met with each of the major stakeholders. The utility sector meetings included TEP, where Ted Welp understood our study so well that he chimed in to answer his own management team's objections to our proposals. The other regulated companies were Arizona Public Service, and Salt River Project. We also met with the key people at the Regulated Utilities Consumer Organization (RUCO). This is the watchdog organization created and designed to protect the consumer's interest, and it heartily approved of our study. After the meeting, Mike Block—the overall administrator of our ACC project—and I met with the chairwoman of RUCO. Since she liked our proposal, we asked her if she could publicly support our position after it was announced. She regretted to say that RUCO could not support us publicly. Here was the problem she said: RUCO's budget was up for renewal by the legislative committee; one of the utilities had been exceptionally critical of RUCO's stance lately, and that she was concerned that her budget renewal might be endangered!

Wow, there it was; what is known as the Capture Theory in the economics of regulation. According to this theory the regulated industry necessarily interacts constantly with the regulating organs of government and in time the regulators are captured by the industry. In this case the independent watchdog set up to counteract this had been captured by the industry. RUCO's chairwoman was bearing eloquent witness to this obscure and difficult-to-prove model of the regulatory process. Actually, the two sides are better thought of as capturing each other, since they have a commonality of interest requiring joint attention, with the consumer paying the bill for the costs incurred.

In 1985 the newly constituted commission, with elected replacements for Governor Babbitt's two temporary appointments, rejected our proposal.

19.5 International Reach

The unsympathetic reception of our proposal was not the end of the matter. The study was picked up by many; most prominently the international community, followed by many in the domestic industry, as the liberalization movement picked up steam. Stephen Rassenti and I would eventually serve as research consultants to New Zealand and Australia, to a few companies in this country, and, with various co-authors, conduct many experimental studies of structural issues related to competitiveness in the industry.

When Stephen and I first went to Australia (1993) it was by invitation of Prospect Electricity (later, part of Integral Energy), the second largest distribution company in Australia. This trip was part of the Australian political debate on liberalizing the industry and it was essentially the buy side of the industry—the industrial, commercial, and distribution company buyers of bulk power—that wanted to explore liberalization as a possible means of lowering their energy cost, and who were sponsoring our visit. We listened to their concerns that energy cost in their energy-intensive export industries was crimping their ability to compete internationally. Each state owned its own electricity generating stations and was unfavorably disposed toward the idea of a wholesale power market. We faced many skeptics who believed it was impossible to make a market in electric energy.

The same issues had arisen in New Zealand. I recall speaking at a luncheon in Wellington. Afterwards, a young woman stood up and said that markets would not work; it was an industry that had to be owned by the government; "I know because I am an engineer." I was able to respond to the effect that I was also an engineer; that I once believed the same; I understood what was bothering her; that I was sure I could convince her otherwise from the experiments we had done.

In Australia our approach was to place industry, government, distributors, and other participants attending our workshops into a wholesale market experiment consisting of three radial nodes: a central demand center with limited generating capability and two more remote smaller demand centers with excess generating capacity that could serve the center as well as their local demand. (Conceptually it was the United Kingdom with London served by large power sources to the north and smaller sources to the south.) In our follow-up we could demonstrate that these industry and government participants were quite effective in making an efficient market in power. The questions: Is anything wrong with the experiment? How can we improve it? Implicitly, the burden of proof was on the skeptics to defend their beliefs in the face of this evidence, and we were open to changes if the experiment was flawed. Essentially, we were part of a process that won a series of battles and ultimately the war. The central government had created the National Grid Management Council (NGMC, 1991) that ended up planning and overseeing a wholesale energy market embracing the states, integrated by a national interconnected grid.

Through our Australian contacts we gained approval to conduct laboratory experiments with a prototype for the proposed market. We were consultants on software specifications, and experimental design, but all development and experiments were to be conducted in Australia. This enabled the Aussies to get on-the-ground experience in test cycles of experiment-data feedback-redesign-experiment. The process led to a two-week (7 hours per day) electronic trading experiment using non-industry participants trained in the exchange procedures, and earning significant cash profits based on assigned costs, and demands, using Australian generation and grid parameter characteristics. (We had advised against using industry people—politically biased either for or against—and using subjects who in effect would become trained "professionals" in trading based directly on this experience.) Victoria and New South Wales began separate markets in power in 1996. These and the other Australian coastal states in the southeast joined in the National Electricity Market on December 13, 1998. It was a proud moment: a proof-of-concept lab experiment was merged seamlessly into design experiments, and into the field. The result was a modern late twentieth-century smart computer-assisted market that has been continuously improved and updated in response to ongoing technological change.

19.6 Has Economics Seen an Experimental Turn?

Essentially, my experience in the evolution of experimental economics was strongly influenced by the parallel growth of joint research and authorship after 1975. That experience was further expanded to include engineers, technicians, and management in industry, commerce, and government during the 1980s and 1990s.

We now have a treatment and evaluation of the development of experimental economics by an "outsider," a young historian of economic thought, Adrej Svorencik. In his thesis, *The Experimental Turn in Economics: A History of Experimental Economics* (2015), Svorencik argues that the emergence of a research community in the last half of the 1980s, and committed to the elevation of observation to co-equal status with economic theory, was a central development that accounts for its wider acceptance within economics. Increased collaborative research was an integral part of the development of that community. A second book further explores that development; edited by Andrej Svorencik and Harro Maas, *The Making of Experimental Economics* (2016).

Although this thesis is consistent with my collaborative experience, I would not have been able to see and articulate it in this particular way. Ultimately, only intellectual historians will be able to judge the long-run influence of experimental methodology on how economists think and do economics, and the importance of collaboration in that story.

Index

M. Szenberg, L.B. Ramrattan (eds.), *Collaborative Research in Economics*, DOI 10.1007/978-3-319-52800-7

T

V

Z

The manufacturer's authorised representative in the EU is Springer Nature Customer Service Centre GmbH, Europaplatz 3, 69115 Heidelberg, Germany. If you have any concerns regarding our products, please contact ProductSafety@springernature.com

Printed and bound by CPI Group (UK) Ltd, Croydon, CR0 4YY
30/09/2026
02225216-0015